"This is a brave and engaging book that takes no prisoners. For too long, existential therapy has been recruited in the service of socio-political conformity and evidence-based ortho-doxy. It is not surprising then that many clinicians feel existentialism has failed to live up to its potential for inspiring psychic transformation. In this book, Bazzano has marshalled a formidable array of thinkers, academics and clinicians to provide a significant counter-traditional perspective on existential theory and practice. It offers a fresh and provoca-tive 'take' on radical existential values, making an unmistakable clarion call for therapy whose values are underpinned by creativity rather than compliance, playfulness rather than protocols and meaning rather than medicalisation. It is a book for all thinking therapists. Read, mark, learn and inwardly digest."

Rosemary Rizq. Professor of Psychoanalytic Psychotherapy, University of Roehampton, UK

"With everything that's solid melting into air, therapy has a choice: between peddling yet more conformist ways of adjusting to an unsustainable status quo (the 'data before exist-ence' approach), or daring to ask the deepest existential questions about our humanity and being. With his finger invariably on the pulse, and with therapy-writing set free from its conventional, stultifying moorings, Manu Bazzano has assembled another leading-edge collection that opens up the kind of thinking that we must dare to allow, if we're to make any sense of the current conjuncture. This is a book to work hard at – and a book that anyone caring about our human future must read."

Dr Richard House, Chartered Psychologist and author of Therapy Beyond Modernity *and* In, Against and Beyond Therapy

"An essential and important read for anyone wishing to explore the therapeutic aspects of existentialist philosophy. This collection evades, expands and enfolds traditional Western ideas concerning self and existence and invites into being (or becoming) a new tradition."

Dr Alexander Carter ITO and Academic Director for Philosophy and Interdisciplinary Studies, Institute of Continuing Education, University of Cambridge, UK

"At a time when we are witnessing a move towards reducing our experience of life to linear and well-trodden narratives, this fascinating collection, edited by Manu Bazzano, accompanies us through a familiar philosophical horizon, challenging us to encounter new perspectives."

Jo Hilton, Clinical Fellow, Counselling, Psychotherapy and Applied Social Science, University of Edinburgh, UK

I0130957

Re-Visioning Existential Therapy

Re-Visioning Existential Therapy is a collection of essays from leading practitioners and theorists around the globe which questions some of the key tenets of traditional existential therapy.

The book enlightens, stimulates, and provokes the reader out of complacency. It expands the breadth and scope of the approach, discusses recent developments in psychotherapy and philosophy, and aligns existential therapy to a progressive, radical, and counter-traditional ethos. Through clinical studies, personal reflections, discussions on aspects of theory, and exciting links to art, literature, and contemporary culture, these very diverse and wide-ranging contributions take existential therapy into the fertile wilderness of shared experience. Through renewed links to seminal writers, it captures the subversive spirit, the deep compassion, the unflinching gaze and playfulness that is at the heart of the approach.

The book will share knowledge and enthusiasm for the practice of existential therapy in order to encourage therapists and trainees to partake of the joys and challenges of existential practice.

Manu Bazzano is a psychotherapist/supervisor in private practice and an internationally recognized author, lecturer, and facilitator. He is an associate tutor at Cambridge University. Among his books: *Buddha is Dead* (2006); *Spectre of the Stranger* (2012); *After Mindfulness* (2014); *Therapy and the Counter-tradition* (2016); *Zen and Therapy* (2017); *Re-visioning Person-centred Therapy* (2018); *Nietzsche and Psychotherapy* (2019). He is a regular contributor to several academic journals and magazines.

Also by Manu Bazzano

THE WAY OF AWAKENING (Co-translator)
ZEN POEMS
HAIKU FOR LOVERS
BUDDHA IS DEAD
THE SPEED OF ANGELS
THE PERPETUAL BEGINNER (in Italian)
SPECTRE OF THE STRANGER
AFTER MINDFULNESS (Editor)
THERAPY AND THE COUNTER-TRADITION (Co-editor)
ZEN AND THERAPY: HERETICAL PERSPECTIVES
RE-VISIONING PERSON-CENTRED THERAPY
NIETZSCHE AND PSYCHOTHERAPY

Music albums:

DAEDALO: WALK INSIDE THE PAINTING
NAKED DANCE
SEX, RELIGION AND COSMETICS

Re-Visioning Existential Therapy

Counter-traditional Perspectives

**Edited by
Manu Bazzano**

Routledge
Taylor & Francis Group

LONDON AND NEW YORK

First published 2021
by Routledge
2 Park Square, Milton Park, Abingdon, Oxon OX14 4RN

and by Routledge
52 Vanderbilt Avenue, New York, NY 10017

Routledge is an imprint of the Taylor & Francis Group, an informa business

British Library Cataloguing-in-Publication Data
A catalogue record for this book is available from the British Library

Library of Congress Cataloging-in-Publication Data
A catalog record has been requested for this book

ISBN: 978-0-367-36563-9 (hbk)
ISBN: 978-0-367-36561-5 (pbk)
ISBN: 978-0-429-34711-5 (ebk)

Typeset in Baskerville
by Newgen Publishing UK

Contents

Notes on contributors

Manu Bazzano is a therapist, supervisor, visiting lecturer at several universities and colleges, and an internationally recognized author and facilitator. He has a background in philosophy and rock music and is the author and editor of several books, including *Haiku for Lovers*; *The Speed of Angels*; *Zen Poems*; *Re-visioning Person-centred Therapy*; *Therapy and the Counter-tradition* (co-editor); *Zen and Therapy: Heretical Perspectives* and *Nietzsche and Psychotherapy*. He was editor of *Person-Centered and Experiential Psychotherapies*, and is associate editor for *Self & Society: Journal of Humanistic Psychology*. He studied Eastern contemplative practices since 1980 and in 2004 was ordained in the Soto and Rinzai traditions of Zen Buddhism. www.manubazzano.com.

Ross Crisp is a registered psychologist in Australia with extensive experience as a rehabilitation consultant and psychologist. He has published numerous articles on disability and rehabilitation, in particular on the psychosocial and vocational rehabilitation of persons with spinal cord injuries and traumatic brain injuries. More recently, he has written on the practice of person-centred and experiential psychotherapies in educational and vocational rehabilitation settings, and in relation to trauma and loss. He has also focused on the value of integrating person-centred and experiential psychotherapies with existential philosophies. He is currently a member of the Australian Psychological Society and World Association of Person-Centered and Experiential Psychotherapies.

Yana Gololob is a psychologist and person-centred therapist working with children, young people, and adults in private practice for more than 15 years. She is a PCA trainer with UUAP (Ukrainian Umbrella Association of Psychotherapy) and lives in Dnipro, Ukraine, her city of birth.

Rebecca Greenslade is an existentially trained psychotherapist, supervisor, and writer based in London. She currently works in private practice, with The Psychosis Therapy Project, and as a training and research supervisor at The Minster Centre. She is the Founder and Director of Gaia Therapy Project, a community based psychotherapy service at Hackney City Farm in East London. Her most recent writings consider psychotherapy as philosophical praxis, the therapeutics of social activism, and the articulation of a 21st century feminist psychotherapy. She is a Zen practitioner and student.

Nancy Hakim Dowek is a trained existential psychotherapist practicing in London; she is currently working in private practice and at the *Dilemma* consultancy. She is also working with a number of Cancer support charities (Paul's Cancer Support Centre, Breast Cancer Haven). She completed her doctoral degree (DProf) in Existential Psychotherapy in 2019 at the New School of Psychotherapy and Counselling, where she is currently the foundation course leader and a teacher. She is particularly interested in existential themes relating to experiences which confront us with our life choices and circumstances past, present, and future, and the growth it entails in psychotherapy.

Jeff Harrison is a writer, psychotherapist, and tutor with a PhD in transpersonal psychology. He lives in Liverpool.

Noam Israeli is a consultant counselling psychologist in psychotherapy; family and couples therapist and supervisor, and phenomenological-existential psychotherapist. Noam worked at community mental health teams in Essex and has been a faculty member at Regent's University School of Psychotherapy and Counselling. Upon his return to Israel, he concluded his training in Systemic Therapy and is also a systemic therapist and supervisor. Noam was the head of training at Shinui, an Israeli institute for family and couple's therapy, and was a member of the CPD section of the Israeli Association of Family therapy. Currently, he works in a private practice, in Herzeliya (outside Tel-Aviv), Israel and is a PhD candidate at Philosophy Graduate School, Tel-Aviv University. His research focuses on emotions, inner knowledge, bad faith, and ethics. In his clinical work, Noam focuses on the application of phenomenology with individuals, couples, and families.

Melissa Johnson Carissimo has been developing, researching, and teaching Metaphoric Affect Processing in oncology, psychiatry, palliative care, and, most recently, nephrology, in Genoa's largest public hospitals since 2011. She studied at Amherst College, earned her degree in Literature and Writing from Columbia University, and pursued a career in New York literary publishing and film development before moving to Italy. Today, she divides her time between New York and Genoa, where she is a Professional Counsellor trained in Carl Rogers' Person-Centered Approach. A researcher in the field of medical humanities, she guides individuals, groups, public healthcare clients, and medical staff in the use of metaphor to foster safe self-reflection, empathic listening, and wellbeing in the context of illness.

Tatiana Karyagina is a senior researcher in Psychological Institute of Russian Academy of Education, Laboratory of Counselling Psychology and Psychotherapy (Moscow). She is also a trainer and supervisor in training programmes of the Association for CEP. Her PhD thesis (Moscow State University) was devoted to the evolution of empathy concept in psychology.

She is the author of more than a dozen papers on the theoretical and methodological problems of empathy in psychology and psychotherapy. Her scientific and practical interests are experiential psychotherapy and development of empathy for helping professionals.

Elita Kreislere is an existential therapist, supervisor, and psychologist working in private practice in Riga, Latvia. Elita is a supervisor and existential therapist in the Institute of Humanistic and Existential Psychology (Lithuania) and President of the East European Association for Existential Therapy.

Deborah A. Lee is Senior Lecturer in Sociology at Nottingham Trent University, and a person-centred existentially informed psychotherapist. With interests in sexual violence, psychotherapy training, critiques of psychopathology, and challenging the orthodoxy of case studies particularly via heuristic and autoethnographic research and arts-based, unusual presentations, Deborah has recently written for the *British Journal of Guidance and Counselling*, *Asylum*, *Self & Society*, *Psychotherapy and Politics International*, and the *Journal of Gender-Based Violence*. With Emma Palmer, she is Co-Editor of the new book *#MeToo for Counselling and Psychotherapy* (2020). Deborah is an Associate Editor and Co-Editor for Reviews at *Psychotherapy and Politics International* and a member of the Ethics Committee of the United Kingdom Council for Psychotherapy (UKCP).

Del Loewenthal is Emeritus Professor of Psychotherapy and Counselling and Founder of the Research Centre for Therapeutic Education at the University of Roehampton, UK. He is an existential–analytic psychotherapist (having trained at the Philadelphia Association, London), photographer, and chartered psychologist, with a particular interest in phenomenology. His books include: *Existential Psychotherapy and Counselling after Post-Modernism: The selected works of Del Loewenthal* (2017); *Post-existentialism and the Psychological Therapies: Towards a Therapy without Foundations* (2011); *Phototherapy and Therapeutic Photography in a Digital Age* (2013); with Andrew Samuels, *Relational Psychotherapy, Psychoanalysis and Counselling: Appraisals and reappraisals* (2014); *Critical Psychotherapy, Psychoanalysis and Counselling: Implications for practice* (2015); with Gillian Proctor, *Why Not CBT: Against and For CBT 2nd Edition* (2018); and with Evrinomy Avdi, *Developments in Qualitative Psychotherapy Research* (2019). He is also founding editor of the *European Journal of Psychotherapy and Counselling* (Routledge) and has a private practice in Wimbledon and Brighton.

Nina Lyon is a writer and PhD candidate working on the metaphysics of nonsense at UWE Bristol, UK. She is the author of *Mushroom Season* (2014) and *Uprooted* (2016) and is interested in the intersections of philosophy, cultural history, and the mind.

John Mackessy is a counsellor, supervisor, and advocate who has worked for various charities regarding issues of trauma/abuse, disability, and marginalization. His initial training was integrative and he currently counsels in Higher Education. He teaches and supervises in north London.

Greg Madison, PhD, is an existential psychologist and Focusing-oriented psychotherapist contributing to various activist, academic, and professional communities internationally. For some years Greg has avoided exclusive affiliation with any institution and instead enjoys creative collaborations as an independent person. He has written and co-edited books and articles on Existential Migration, Focusing-oriented therapy, existential therapy, and contemporary topics related to psychology and society. He is a Coordinator for the Focusing Institute and founder of *The London Focusing Institute* (a team of teachers working according to democratic principles).

Mo Mandić is an existential psychotherapist in private practise in London, UK. He teaches, tutors, supervises, and facilitates on the MA Psychotherapy & Counselling programme at Regent's University London's School of Psychotherapy and Psychology. Mo is also Visiting Professor at Union University, Novi Sad, Serbia, where he teaches qualitative approaches to research, ethics in psychotherapy, and existential therapy. Mo's wider interests include the psychotherapist's lived experience of care, more radically hermeneutic approaches to therapy, the central role of moods in therapy, and the therapeutic process of exploring existential disturbances, disruptions, breakdowns, and world-collapses.

Diana Mitchell works as an existential therapist, supervisor, and mediator. She published "Merleau-Ponty, Certain Uncertainty and Existential Psychotherapy" in the *Journal of the Society for Existential Analysis* (1997, 8.2) Her paper, "Is the Concept of Supervision at Odds with Existential Thinking and Therapeutic Practice?" was published in the *Journal of the Society for Existential Analysis* (2002, 13.1). Her chapter, "Responsibility in Existential Supervision" appeared in *Existential Perspectives on Supervision*, edited by Emmy van Deurzen and Sarah Young (2009). She has also written opinion pieces in the Society for Existential Analysis' *Hermeneutic Circular* about the practice of therapy and supervision on a regular basis.

Michael R. Montgomery MA, MSc is a UKCP and MBACP accredited psychotherapist and HCPC registered psychiatric social worker. He has worked in multiple psychosocial environments, both public and private, in the UK, Malaysia, Germany, and currently in the USA. In his writing and clinical practice, he proposes a radical and creative approach to existentialism and contemporary psychoanalytical thinking, prizing the experience of the individual and community over reductive theory or the McDonaldization of psychotherapy. He is exploring new paradigms when working with addiction, consulting with artists and their support teams within the electronic music industry, contributing to a need for healing by bringing together his passion and understanding of the performance of music and his love of psychotherapy. As a long-time daily meditator, he draws creatively from his meditative experience and Eastern philosophy and psychology as part of his therapeutic encounters. He is currently researching the therapist's use of silence as part of a doctoral study.

Virgínia Moreira is a psychotherapist, CNPq researcher in Brazil (PQ-1), Doctor in Clinical Psychology (PUC, São Paulo), and Post-Doctor in Medical Anthropology (Harvard University, USA). She is a former Fulbright Visiting Professor (2003–2004) and Affiliated Faculty (2004–2011) of the Department of Global Health and Social Medicine in the Department of Global Health and Social Medicine of Harvard Medical School, in Boston, USA. She is a Professor of Clinical Humanistic-Phenomenological Psychology and Phenomenological Psychopathology in the Post-Graduation Program of Psychology at Universidade de Fortaleza, in Brazil (www.unifor.br), where she is co-chair of APHETO – Laboratory of Psychopathology and Humanistic Phenomenological Clinic (www.apheto.net). Her researches on individual and group psychotherapy focus on the development of Carl Rogers thought in a phenomenological direction, having Merleau-Ponty's phenomenology as a lens to understand the lived experience. Dr Moreira researches phenomenological methodology in order to understand the lived world of mental illness. She is a member of the World Association of Person Centered and Experiential Psychotherapies. Besides her academic work, she has always had a private practice working as individual and group psychotherapist in Fortaleza, Brazil. She also conducts a clinical group training formation in Humanistic-Phenomenological Psychotherapy. Dr Moreira has published seven books and more than 80 articles about humanistic-phenomenological clinic and phenomenological psychopathology.

Glenn Nicholls is a psychotherapist, supervisor, trainer, executive coach, and organization development consultant. He has a private practice in Cambridge and London and currently leads an integrative supervision training in Central London. Nietzsche has had a profound influence on his personal development as a psychotherapist.

Juliana Pita is a psychologist, Doctor in Psychology (University of Fortaleza – UNIFOR and Université Paris Diderot – Paris 7), with training in Humanistic Phenomenological Psychotherapy. She is a teacher at the University of Fortaleza (UNIFOR) and member of APHETO – Laboratory of Psychopathology and Humanistic Phenomenological Clinic (UNIFOR).

Gabriella Ricciardi Otty is a graduate of the MA course in Psychotherapy and Counselling Psychology at Regents College, a former psychotherapist trainee with the Claremont Project, and bereavement counsellor for Cruse. After a break of six years, she completed her MA dissertation – Where Angels Fear to Tread – in 2017. She is currently developing it into a book, talks, workshops, and a show inspired by her experience as a student, performer, and observer of the art of striptease.

Micah Sadigh is an accomplished composer and a published poet and Professor and Chair of Psychology at Cedar Crest College. He is a graduate of Moravian College and Lehigh University. He was awarded the Diplomate Status in Franklian Psychology and Existential Analysis from the International Viktor

Frankl Institute in 2007. Dr Sadigh is a Fellow of the International College of Psychosomatic Medicine. He was the recipient of the Cedar Crest College Faculty Award for Excellence in Teaching in 2009. He is the author of five books, including an internationally recognized book on the treatment of chronic pain and stress-related disorders. His most recent book, *Existential Journey: Viktor Frankl and Leo Tolstoy on Suffering, Death, and Search for Meaning*, received excellent reviews in European journals. His publications include work on sleep disorders, personality disorders, Applied Psychophysiology, the psychophysiological treatment of pain, and treatment of post-traumatic disorder.

In recent years, he has published several papers on theoretical and philosophical aspects of psychology. He frequently lectures at local, state, national, and international conferences.

Donna Christina Savery is a psychotherapist and group therapist in private practice in Buckinghamshire and Harley Street, London. At Exeter University (1994) she carried out research for her MA, which involved working with schizophrenic patients using drama and myth, an experience that sparked a lifelong interest in psychotherapy and psychoanalysis. Following a career as a theatre director and academic, she retrained in 2010 as an existential therapist, beginning her career at MIND. She is a group work practitioner, having studied at the Institute of Group Analysis, and is currently undergoing training in Daseinsanalysis, an integrated form of psychoanalysis and existentialism. Her clinical work combines different aspects of these trainings and she is never far away from her drama roots in her understanding and approach to working with her patients. Among her publications are: *Echoism: The Silenced Response to Narcissism.* (2018), and *The Challenges of Meaninglessness and Absurdity Addressed Through Myth and Role Play* in: E. Van Deurzen & S. Iacovou (Eds.), *Existential Perspectives in Relationship Therapy* (2013).

Andrew Seed is a psychotherapist and counsellor and currently doing a PHD at the University of Edinburgh. He situates mental ill health primarily in society and explores how psychotherapy can contribute to individual and collective freedom from repression. Having worked in private practice, the NHS, charity sector, and at leading universities, Andrew has observed where the mental health structures support and where they oppress. He has a particular interest in literature and philosophy.

Niklas Serning is a psychotherapist with a background in Buddhism, transpersonal practices and with experience in working in warzones with the United Naations. He worked with OTR Bristol – Bristol's main young people's mental health charity – overseeing a substantial service transformation as their Clinical Director, leading a radical transformation of their ethos from being service led to being user led, so that we went from being a counselling only service to having an array of innovative ways to engage. He is a qualified Vinyasa yoga teacher.

Ondine Smulders is an existential psychotherapist in private practice in London. She also facilitates groups and has an interest in working with meaning, choice, and responsibility. She is the Book Review Editor for the *Journal of Existential Analysis*.

Prior to retraining as a psychotherapist, she enjoyed a varied career spanning more than 25 years, first in investment banking and later as a political/economic analyst at the Economist Newspaper Group. She maintains her business interest through her position as a non-executive director of an energy services company.

Pavlos Zarogiannis lives in Athens, Greece, where he works as a psychotherapist, trainer, and supervisor. He studied Psychology, German Literature and Linguistics in Germany during the 1980s and has been trained in Person Centered Counselling/Psychotherapy and in Focusing.

In 2002 he became a Focusing Certified Coordinator for Greece and he founded – together with Anna Karali – the Hellenic Focusing Center. The following years they created their own training programmes in Person Centered and Focusing-Oriented Counselling/Psychotherapy, in Focusing and in Supervision, which they teach in Athens, in Thessaloniki, and in Cyprus.

He was president of the former Hellenic Person Centred Association from 1998–2003 and he is a founding member of the National Organization for Psychotherapy in Greece (NOPG) and of the new Hellenic Association for Person-Centred and Experiential Approach (HAPCEA). Since 2015 he is also editor of the Greek journal *Εποχή/Epoche – Psychotherapy, Phenomenology, Hermeneutics*.

Introduction

Manu Bazzano

> When someone praised a philosopher … [Diogenes would say]: 'How can he be considered great, since he has been a philosopher for so long and has never *disturbed* anybody?'
>
> (Nietzsche, 1873/1997, p. 193)

> Don't gamble on the future. Act now, without delay.
>
> (De Beauvoir, cited in Blair, 2019, p. 45)

1

There is a certain aura to existentialism. I can tell each time I meet existential trainees for supervision or therapy – especially those coming from abroad. It is true that the aura, as with the non-reproducible work of art, hovers around distant objects, but this is not the whole story. These trainees seem to yearn for a (non) methodology that is more real, more socially progressive and rebellious than what determinist psychoanalysis or socio-politically compliant cognitive-behaviourism would ever allow for. They long for an approach that is more au fait with philosophy, art, and literature. In their longing, they may have stumbled upon a vital aspect of existential thought and practice. They are like someone in love, and while love may be partly made up of our own projected desires, at times it also uncannily perceives a vital and overlooked core in the object.

Typically, these budding therapists have read a book or two by Albert Camus or Simone de Beauvoir and proceeded to imbue the writings with their own surreptitious longings. They found it incredible that somewhere in the world there are actual trainings that draw on exhilarating books whose subjects are freedom, gender equality, social and political justice, books that encourage thinking outside the box. They may have come across the writings of Helene Cixous, Benjamin Fondane, Michel Foucault, or Friedrich Nietzsche and are now eager to see what a psychotherapy practice inspired by these writers may look and feel like. They wish to know, for instance, how one works therapeutically with notions such as *existence before essence*. Sadly, it slowly dawns on them that what they are being taught amounts more to something like *data before existence*. They soon realize that canonical existential quotes and references are used in a thoroughly bland way that fails to utter one dissonant note in the chorus of evidence-based orthodoxy. Sooner or later it dawns on them that they are now seen as an integral component of Conformity Campus.

What they yearned for slowly begins to fade. They may have wanted to pursue their interest in Søren Kierkegaard, Benjamin Fondane, or Lev Shestov, only to realize that these important authors are curiously exiled from the canon. They were keen to understand the link between existential phenomenology and contemporary developments in philosophy, culture, and the arts but found that the key texts they are told to study are unyieldingly tied to a static worldview frozen in time among the pleasant snows of Zollikon and the mystical silence of the Black Forest. Some of them are sincerely baffled by the outlandish and unjustified predominance in their training of the sibylline musings of Martin Heidegger, a writer who at close scrutiny is neither existential nor phenomenological, whose thoughts may have little relevance for therapeutic practice and whose political views are as aberrant, as remote, and as crudely antagonistic to the progressive thinkers they had wanted to study as one can imagine. After the honeymoon, the bitter moon. What happens next is as predictable as it is disheartening. Some decide to leave the training altogether and pursue their existential adventures in other pastures outside academia and the clinic. The majority, carefully considering that they have paid good money, decide to give in: yes, they'll tick those existential boxes, quote the conventional authors, and recycle the tenets of an arbitrary and preposterous existential catechism. They tell themselves they will pursue their original interest after graduation, when they'll finally start to work as therapists.

2

A *re-visioning* of existential therapy may not be possible without undoing its traditional tenets and without an appeal to a counter-traditional, even *counter-existential*, stance. Does this book fulfil the promise of re-visioning stated in the title? I would say it is a valid attempt. If so inclined, discerning readers will find enough material here to ruffle feathers, shake up a foundation or two, and bring some fresh air into what is fast becoming the Existential Therapy Museum. The ETM is a place where past glories are summoned to add a veneer of profundity to an otherwise formulaic practice. It is a place where the writings of radical philosophers who inveighed against conformity and mediocrity are defrosted for consumption in order to embellish a conformist and mediocre practice offering something not all too dissimilar from what all other therapeutic approaches offer: societal *adaptation* and (in worst case scenarios) socio-political *compliance*.

Existential therapy has a reputation for tackling the big questions head-on: freedom, death, embodiment, responsibility, aloneness, relatedness. Some claim that it has a more explicit philosophical component than other orientations. Others stress its thoroughgoing critique of psychopathology and the medical model, offering a reading of mental distress in a person as difficulty in negotiating their way of being in the world. Others still emphasize its humanistic and relational ethos. Like every orientation, existential therapy presents various instances of what Pavlos Zarogiannis (2018, p. 112) calls "linguistic fetishism". It constructs a canon, a litany of givens and a liturgy of tenets. It demarcates its borders, defining (more or less explicitly) orthodoxies and heresies within its ranks.

3

Existential therapy is haunted by the ghosts of long-dead writers whose presence is as real as the taste of this hot coffee burning my lips on this winter morning. So much so that it makes complete sense to speak, after Jacques Derrida (1994), of (existential) *hauntology*, one of the topics examined by Andrew Seed, in chapter 11, a bold, candid, and tender call to arms hosting the subversive spectres of Guy Debord and Antonin Artaud.

Their presence being real may signify, *inter alia*, that existential ghosts are also potential *spectres*: their evanescent figures may belong not to the past but the future. Their vision is as yet *unrealized*. But is not the unrealized (rather than the idle pastime of being or not-being) the true psychotherapeutic and philosophic question? In this sense, Kierkegaard, Nietzsche, and a handful of thinkers are existential spectres. Kierkegaard and Nietzsche may be conventionally depicted as precursors of existentialism, but the fact is, their work does not merely antici-pate it; it *surpasses* it. Take for instance the problem of subjectivity. Despite its gesturing towards the 'other', the 'world', and even despite that Cartesian dead ringer, *Dasein*, existential phenomenology remains, essentially, quite happily mired within the subjectivism of the Cartesian self. This is partly because it did not pay heed to either Kierkegaard or Nietzsche, for these two writers provided ingenious maps out of self-boundedness. Consider the dissemination of the authorial voice in Kierkegaard through his use of various independently existing pseudonyms – a 'post-structuralist' stance avant la lettre, equal in literature only to Fernando Pessoa's. Consider also Nietzsche's notion of the *dividual*, his defence of multiplicity and his psychology of the mask (Bazzano, 2019, pp. 12–43), all of these notions anticipating and even exceeding contemporary conversations about identity.

Clearly, these writers have not been properly read within traditional existential therapy; their incitement to go further and pursue an adventurous path by either leaping (Kierkegaard) or dancing (Nietzsche) has hardly been noticed, let alone applied. But then these two thinkers belong to the counter-tradition while conven-tional existential therapy belongs to the tradition…

Their complex, achingly beautiful and inspiring writings have been by and large reduced to a handful of formulas. It is urgent to begin redressing this problem by reframing their contribution in ways that are more attuned to their spirit and by taking into account the vast Kierkegaardian and Nietzschean scholarship of recent years. What Glenn Nicholls does so well in chapter 3 for Nietzsche is like-wise achieved by Ross Crisp for Kierkegaard in chapter 16; both practitioners presenting an unusual angle on these adventurous thinkers, adding complexity and thought-provoking nuance to the generic and bland praise found in most existential trainings.

4

New strands of thought and practice have emerged since (and out of) Edmund Husserl's classic brand of existential phenomenology. Husserl's own work in later years (prompted by his profound dismay in seeing phenomenology usurped by Heidegger as well as by his desire to move forward, away from the Cartesian transcendentalism of his early work) set the tone for what was to come: among other things, Maurice Merleau-Ponty's phenomenology (discussed in chapter 15) as well as post-phenomenology (discussed by Del Loewenthal in chapter 22).

Merleau-Ponty remains a crucial presence in various other chapters, including Gabriella Ricciardi Otty's (chapter 5), Diana Mitchell's (chapter 6), and Jeff Harrison's (chapter 18).

It is vital to construct links to new currents of thought and practice that have built creatively on classic phenomenology. Differentialism, post-phenomenology, post-structuralism, new materialisms, to name a few, have both questioned and expanded the scope of classical existential phenomenology.

The prefix 'post', especially in postqualitative research, gestures towards the unreliability and even insubstantiality of the subject – researcher, therapist, client, writer – or at the very least it questions the authority of 'I', in many ways an extension of the death of the author proclaimed by Roland Barthes (1967/1987). This is often accompanied by a more experimental and/or direct style and a bold move away from the combined stylistic strictures of academic requirements, case study, routine quotation of the selfsame literature, not to mention increasing forays into facile pop psychology territory which has produced existential therapy texts that are unexciting and repetitive – useful almost exclusively for the recycling of canonical stale knowledge among trainees. The reader will find that some chapters here blend the conventions of psychology writing with the poetic and the epistolary, the heuristic and the confessional, making for a more engaging read. I am thinking of Ondine Smulders' enticing piece on daydreaming (chapter 25), of Deborah A. Lee's direct, heartbreaking account in chapter 26, and of Melissa Johnson Carissimo's foray into poetry in chapter 27.

5

Excessive attention has been given within existential therapy to Heidegger at the expense of more progressive expressions of existential phenomenology. This has arguably resulted in a widespread if understated culture of denial that has defensively ignored Heidegger's nativism, his metaphysical anti-Semitism and his own disavowal of both existentialism and phenomenology. Heidegger's influence is contentious, yet the relevance of Heideggerianism for existential therapy is not openly discussed, let alone questioned. Does Heidegger truly expand on Husserl or does he fall back to Immanuel Kant? Does he provide a cogent alternative to the Cartesian self or is his Dasein a cogito in disguise? In chapter 8, John Mackessy pulls no punches in unveiling Heidegger's gratuitous abstractions and weaving a thoroughgoing and articulate critique of Dasein and even more importantly of the notion of 'the anyone' (*das Man*) that he perceptively sees as shunning the concrete presence of others.

An equally trenchant critique is found in Mackessy and Bazzano's contribution in chapter 1 in relation to intersubjectivity and the current bias on relatedness in existential therapy. In her piece, Rebecca Greenslade (chapter 10) competently unmasks existentialism's prickly relationship with ethics, particularly in relation to feminism, the latter a topic that is only touched upon formally in contemporary existential literature. We are still catching up, both as a profession and within the existential approach, with the formidable challenges posed by feminist thought, gender studies, queer theory, and non-binary stances (e.g. Butler, 2004; Lewis, 2019), especially when they eloquently question natural kinship and the family. Potential for psychical transformation – our own and our clients' – is greatly reduced when we are too invested in bolstering the myth of the happy family, secure attachment, and the chain of delusions and dependences they engender, not to mention the family's 'natural' schooling in conformity, from gender-straitjacketing to racial programming (Lewis, 2019).

An interesting application of this may be found in Juliana Pita and Virgínia Moreira's contribution in chapter 24. Inspired by Merleau-Ponty's notion of a dialectic without synthesis and a view of constant movement in an unfinished world which shuns normatively static dictates of 'mental health', the notion of intersubjectivity takes on a radical meaning, away from the pious platitudes of 'I–Thou' to present instead a view of schizophrenic phenomena that are no longer circumscribed within the sufferer's isolated psychic apparatus but involve and absorb loved ones and family. This is both refreshingly new in current psychopathology as well as reminiscent of R.D. Laing's more 'systemic' readings of schizophrenia which have been quietly confined to oblivion in current discourse.

We are still catching up, and the process of contextualizing existential therapy within a progressive socio-political frame feels unbearably slow at times. In chapter 9, Michael R. Montgomery, inspired by the luminous example of B.R. Ambedkar, extends the meaning of therapeutic work to encompass *Manuski*, a notion of humanity which, in acknowledging our shared fragility, dares to imagine a path without violence.

A necessary break with tradition is needed, Greg Madison says in chapter 12, if we are to break free of the political ideologies that seemingly run the therapy profession and if we are to come anywhere near true innovation.

6

Has existential therapy bypassed (rather than responded to) psychoanalysis? Its dismissal of Sigmund Freud's legacy may be partly seen as an understandable response to a practice that in some cases grew into an arcane practice bound by a language whose convoluted codes were only known to adepts. It was also part of humanistic psychology's broad appeal for greater cultural inclusion. What tends to be forgotten, however, is the hurried rejection of Freud evident in Heidegger's Zollikon seminars. These constitute, for better or worse, an important component of traditional existential therapy's genealogy, and it would be good to pay greater attention to Heidegger's animus against Freud and carefully assess whether there might be similarities with the generalized anti-Semitism with which throughout Europe the 'Jewish art' of psychoanalysis was met (Rose, 2011). In the contemporary landscape, new developments in psychoanalysis may help existential therapy shred some of its more positivist leanings.

A few contributions in this book address this lacuna by creating stimulating links between the two disciplines. In chapter 17, Donna Christina Savery intriguingly explores Wilfred Bion's container-contained model and re-opens the complex discussion on Oedipus (behind whom, lest we forget, is the Sphinx). She develops the specific and overlooked condition of echoism, irreducible to the dominant myth of Narcissus, and highlights some of its uncanny manifestations in couple work.

Innovation often comes from taking on board lessons and insights from other disciplines, within and without the world of psychotherapy and by allowing them, as it were, to fertilize. In chapter 2, Tatiana Karyagina demonstrates how much existential therapy can benefit from greater exposure to the contemporary Russian 'school' of Co-experiencing. She describes the latter as a form of translation from the philosophy of existence into the language of psychology and psychotherapy. It also presents practitioners with engaging alternatives to a phenomenological investigation that is often too subjectivist and self-centred.

7

Why are these offerings 'counter-traditional'? And what is the counter-tradition anyway? Here is some context:

> The official history of Western thought is the history of the Tradition, whose other name is rationalism: the belief that the world is an orderly cosmos, a totality (sometimes called 'Nature') with human reason as an integral part. It has been the dominant mode of thought and it promises to overcome the contingencies of existence and achieve a science (and a technology) that will help us master our destiny. At times the Tradition speaks the language of secular rationalism … loosely inspired by the Enlightenment; at times it speaks the language of religious or spiritual rationalism, from Plato through the Judaeo-Christian orthodoxy.
>
> Alongside the Tradition, there has also been a steady current of thought and practice in western philosophy since the ancient Greeks (beginning with Heraclitus) which continues to remind us of our human limitations and of the ungraspable nature of the world. This is the Counter-Tradition, whose diverse manifestations include humanism, scepticism, fideism, as well as the opening of philosophy to poetry, psychology, and the arts.
>
> (Bazzano & Webb, 2016, p. 2)

Existential phenomenology has had an ambivalent and complicated relationship with the counter-tradition. Some of its exponents (de Beauvoir, Jean-Paul Sartre, and Merleau-Ponty) straddle both worlds; although not avowedly against the tradition, they present rich and provoking counter-traditional values and perspectives that are reflected especially in their progressive emancipatory political stances. Others (Husserl, Heidegger) belong to the tradition. Others still (Nietzsche and Kierkegaard among them, as well as many artists) decidedly belong to the countertradition. What would it mean to bring about a re-vision of existential therapy in counter-traditional terms? What would it take to revive at various levels (e.g. between trainers and trainees, clients and therapists, or in the production of existential literature itself) a more congruent stance that reinstates a therapeutic philosophy and a way of being that refuses to mimic dominant narratives? How can we reaffirm counter-traditional values in existential psychotherapy and counselling? The contributions present here, though widely diverse, are directly or indirectly animated by these questions.

One of the foundations of the philosophical (and religious) tradition is the notion of identity, or rather *ipseity*, i.e., the assumption that what we call 'self' is fundamentally consistent or equal to itself. This is, among other things, a most *sedentary* notion which glorifies belonging and disdains, even condemns, nomadic movement, errancy, and what Nancy Hakim Dowek in chapter 14 calls 'bi-rootedness'.

Reflecting on Laing's struggle to build on Sartre's legacy and unfasten existential practice from the grip of positivism, in chapter 20 Noam Israeli wonders whether our approach has now come full circle, ending up capitulating to a worldview that is at odds with radical existential values, while holding too fast to traditional notions of the self and subjectivity. This position chimes with Mo Mandić's eloquent tribute in chapter 21 to Lev Shestov, a philosopher of existence who alongside a handful of brilliant thinkers, such as Fondane, Jean Wahl, and Rachel Bespaloff, was critical of existential*ism* and of any facile attempt to reduce the complexities of existence into yet another 'ism'. There is a wide gap between the profound acumen and wit of Kierkegaard and the current wisdom-while-u-wait that hides plain banality behind bland appeals to either pragmatism or a 'pluralism' that is eerily close to a notion of choice as consumer choice. It is of course easier (and cheaper) to train technicians than it is to train therapists schooled in the art of living wisely with others, as Del Loewenthal reminds us in chapter 22 in his thoroughgoing critique of traditional existential therapy's unholy alliance with modernism. Even the existential 'educational' training itself can easily default to technique, as evidenced by Elita Kreislere in chapter 28. She presents the rigorous and inspiring methodologies adopted by the Birštonas School of existential therapy, examining for instance how 'bracketing' in mainstream existential therapy tends to abandon rather than attend to our biases and assumptions.

Is counter-traditional existential therapy an art? Is a therapy session, with its delightful moments of seamless connection and awkward slips and stumbles, akin to an improvised dance sequence? – Diana Mitchell asks in chapter 6. A thoroughgoing critique of positivism is at the heart of many chapters, with Pavlos Zarogiannis' performative feat in chapter 4, delivering the meaning of fragmentation in a reading experience that is immersive as it is moving, holding the author's fluency and erudition hidden in order to allow fuller expression – unabashed, unmediated. Balanced, open-minded, and critically alert to the difference between the symbolic, the metaphoric, and the real, Niklas Serning and Nina Lyon's contribution (chapter 23) adds subtlety and daring to a traditional existential frame all too often constricted by a form of rationalism that does not take into account the power of extant and personal myths and mythologies. In similar anti-positivist mode, Yana Gololob (chapter 13) sees therapeutic work as a creative act occurring between client and practitioner and therapy itself as the beginning of the release of creative potential. This stance is all the more powerful against her informative and affecting account of establishing and developing psychotherapy in the face of transgenerational collective trauma experienced by people in Ukraine.

I understand Gololob's contribution to be saying that traumatic experience can at times be a healing force that heralds the dawn of new meanings. The darkest hour, the poet says, comes just before the dawn – a good description, I think, of one core value found within counter-traditional existential therapy.

References

Barthes, R. (1967/1987) *Image, Music, Text.* New York: Fontana.

Bazzano, M. & Webb, J. (2016) 'Introduction' in M. Bazzano & J. Webb (Eds) *Therapy and the Counter-tradition: the Edge of Philosophy.* Abingdon, OX: Routledge, pp 1–5.

Bazzano, M. (2019) *Nietzsche and Psychotherapy.* Abingdon, OX: Routledge.

Blair, E. (2019) 'A Woman's Work', *New York Review of Books*, LXVI, 17, pp 40–47.

Butler J. (2004) *Undoing Gender.* Abingdon, OX: Routledge.

Derrida, J. (1994) *Spectres of Marx.* London: Routledge.

Lewis, S. (2019) *Full Surrogacy Now: Feminism Against Family.* London: Verso.

Nietzsche, F. (1873/1997) *Untimely Meditations*, ed. D. Breazeale, trans. R. J. Hollingdale. Cambridge, MA: Harvard University Press.

Rose, J. (2011) *Proust among the Nations: from Dreyfus to the Middle East.* Chicago, IL: Chicago University Press.

Zarogiannis, P. (2018) 'Person-Centred Approach as Discursivity and Person-centred Therapy as Heterotopic Practice' in M. Bazzano (Ed.) *Re-visioning Person-centred Therapy: Theory and Practice of a Radical Paradigm.* Abingdon, OX: Routledge, pp 110–127.

Part I
The risk of communication

1 Is relatedness a normative ideal?

John Mackessy and Manu Bazzano

To translate is to betray

There is a problem at the heart of existential phenomenology. The very founding call of the tradition – Edmund Husserl's appeal to go 'back to the "things them-selves"' (Husserl, 2001, p.168) – threatens to confound us. This call roused great hope at first. Later, Herbert Marcuse, among others, saw in Martin Heidegger the possibility of 'a new beginning, the first radical attempt to put philosophy on really concrete foundations'. He saw the possibility of a 'philosophy concerned with human existence, the human condition, and not merely with abstract conditions and principles' (Moran, 2000, p.245).

Both phenomenology's vaunting aspirations and its Achilles heel are simultan-eously present here – the yearning for concrete foundations and the assumption of a homogenous human condition upon which a general philosophy of existence may be based. Despite this admirable wish to go beyond abstractions, the very notion of *a* human condition (alongside, for instance, the doctrine of *Dasein*) places abstractions at the heart of the phenomenological project. Just because an idea is conceived in terms of a philosophy of existence does not make it any less abstract than any other thought that has passed through a philosopher's mind.

The call to return to the foundational aspects of experience inspired Heidegger. Despite his rejection of Husserl's transcendental idealism, he went on to resurrect the antique, pre-Kantian convention of *hermeneutics*, a practice which is at heart 'a process of reading … based on a *prior pre-comprehension* or proto-comprehension' (Laplanche, 1996, p.7, emphasis added). Indeed, not only does hermeneutics rely almost entirely on *Auslegung* (interpretation) rather than the enshrined phenom-enological method of description; it is also firmly ensconced within that thor-oughly idealist philosophy which phenomenology had set to demystify in the first place. Heidegger's disinterment of the traditional practice of hermeneutics drew significantly upon Wilhelm Dilthey and Friedrich Schleiermacher, and it was the latter who reminded us of the close connection of interpretation and *translation*. Habitually overlooked within traditional existential therapy, translation is central to hermeneutics; it provides the interpretive *code* or key; there is no hermeneutics without translation. Two important ramifications emerge from this:

(1)   The translator (the hermeneut) is none other than the old unreconstructed Cartesian *cogito*. No matter how inventively cloaked he/she may be (as shepherd of being, Dasein, herald of so-called authenticity, etc.), we are still faced with the same, inescapably self-bound adult human.

(2)   *Tradurre è tradire*, as a proverbial Italian saying has it: *to translate is* (despite our best intentions) *to betray*. It inevitably appropriates and modifies (consciously or not) the clinical content the hermeneut attempts to interpret or describe.

A credible and ingenious way out of this impasse was offered by Maurice Merleau-Ponty (1968, 1942/1983, 1945/1989) through his constant reminder of the possibility of an embodied interpretation of the world, radically different to that of an *abstract* interpreter or *cognitive* 'experiencer'. Regrettably, despite a handful of in-depth studies at the outer reaches of the existential tradition (e.g., Bazzano, 2014; Cayne, 2014; Harrison, 2014; Kennedy, 2014; Moreira, 2014; Synesiou, 2014; Welsh, 2014), plus sporadic intonations of favourite passages from *Phenomenology of Perception* (Merleau-Ponty 1945/1989), Merleau-Ponty's coherent and far-reaching approach hasn't altered traditional existential therapy, particularly in the way it is taught and practised in the U.K. A close look at the studies cited earlier may help us understand why Merleau-Ponty offers real promise to those who feel constrained by the medical model and Cartesian/Kantian dualisms and who wish for a more experiential exploration of the life-world.

Was Heidegger a phenomenologist?

The manner in which Heidegger frames his question of Being casts a long shadow over the existential-phenomenological tradition. Simply put, in Husserl we have a transcendental subject that apprehends a transcendental object. Heidegger's *Dasein* apprehends the disclosure (*aletheia*) of the world and the entities within it: a movement from truth as transcendent knowledge to the truth of transcendental revelation. Heidegger's conceptualization of *aletheia* and the manner in which it relates to 'truth' changed over time, and by the late 1960s, when he wrote *Zur Sache des Denkens* (Heidegger, 2002), we find *aletheia* as disclosure or an opening. This is the opening up to *Dasein* of *presence*, the presence of the world and the entities of the world. If *aletheia* is to be thought of as truth, it is truth *in the ontological context of Dasein's mode of being-in-the-world*. Moreover, the existence of such 'truth' and of *Dasein* itself are unified in the Being behind/within all beings – everything that 'is' shares in Being. Hence, Heidegger's ontology, his theory of Being, is a unifying project with *aletheia*, despite Heidegger's attempts to place it *in the world*, becoming effectively part of an overarching transcendental theory.

One may sensibly ask: 'Why should practicing therapists bother themselves with such abstruse metaphysical reflections any more than pursue the question of how many angels can dance on the head of a pin?' Well, we hold that it is relevant because a Heideggerian perspective, despite its 'worlding', threatens to *disembody and tame experience* in the service of an abstraction called 'Being'. Though it is an entirely philosophical abstraction, 'Being' is held as the fundamental and omnipresent reality, which supposedly grounds and unifies our experience of the world. Why do we label it an abstraction? Because while *beings* and processes are, in a sense, everywhere to be seen, 'Being' proves to be more than a little elusive; it might just be a thought in a philosopher's mind.

It is because of the purported unity of Being and *Dasein* that the latter can allegedly experience things *as they present themselves* to be experienced. It appears to guarantee that a 'phenomenon' can be *something* more than 'merely' a transient phenomenon (because it has Being behind its being, so to speak). The phenomenon, thus, can become disclosed and truly *present* and thereby understandable and interpretable, not just any-old-how, but in a *grounded* and *authentic* way. Thus understood, Heidegger is not, strictly speaking, a phenomenologist, for his interest in any given *phenomenon* (literally 'that which arises' in the process of *becoming*) is only as a preliminary study, as it were, to the disclosure of Being. Our engagement with the world, by this view, becomes authentic when it acknowledges and embraces the nature of Being, of our existential mode of being-in-the-world. With Heidegger, the very language of experience and existence becomes a language of Being. Being-with, Being-towards, etc. and with this, as Derrida observed, comes the imagery of presence and immediacy that Derrida (1978) critiques as *metaphysics of presence.*

Derrida valued much in Heidegger, agreeing with him that philosophy, thinking and, indeed, language were impossible without some form of metaphysics – a going beyond, or transcendence, and a going 'back' towards some ultimate ground or root. However, although Derrida held that we cannot exit metaphysics, his deconstruction constantly sought to show the ultimate contingency and groundlessness of overarching metaphysical systems. In all forms of discourse, he sought that which is privileged or raised above, and what is deployed as a foundation. These tell us a great deal about the founding, and normally unacknowledged, *values* implicit to the discourse.

Even here he was profoundly influenced by Heidegger, with Derrida's 'deconstruction' finding its inspiration in Heidegger's *destruktion*. *Destruktion* was, itself, aimed at earlier ontological thinking. However, what this earlier thought shares with Heidegger's new existential ontology is its desire for wholeness, truth and presence – the unifying wholeness demanded in all metaphysics. Like all holism(s), however, Heidegger's project finds its very wholeness not simply through what it prioritizes and valorizes but in what it excludes in forging this unity. A unity is simply not possible that encompasses all difference. Something is always jettisoned for the sake of coherence and consistency.

Mother's cooking

Heidegger extols a return to Being, a homecoming in which our mode of being and even our language comes closer to the reality of *aletheia* itself. It is not difficult, though, to see the contingency of some of Heidegger's core notions, with some of his values simply elevating his predilections to an unwarranted status. One finds, we believe, a frankly absurd example of this in Heidegger's examination of the relation of language to Being. According to Heidegger, the Ancient Greek and German languages have a closer, more *immediate* relationship to Being than do other, dare we say *degenerate*, languages. Even the German language, however, has become tired and fallen. In *Being and Time*, Heidegger writes that 'the ultimate business of philosophy is to preserve the *force of the most elemental words* in which Dasein expresses itself' (1927/1962, p.262). To deconstruct this is not difficult. Heidegger *preferred* German and Ancient Greek, language, ideas and values. Bravo, but don't try to sell this to us as a fundamental truth about being-in-the-world!

His stance is obviously at odds with the tradition in philosophy, semantics and semiotics initiated by Saussure, in which language is regarded *by its nature* as separate from being. It is the wonder and the creative potential of language that there are *not* 'elemental words'. Words find their meaning, according to Derrida and others, through a dynamic, unstable, unfolding web of associations. No word is elemental, and no meaning should be clung to as if it were, in itself, 'the real thing'.

The notion of elemental language is, at heart, a mystical one and we certainly find it in many traditions. For instance, if we wander a little from European shores, the *Vedic* tradition regards Sanskrit as sacred and the utterance of sacred words, *vac*, are non-different from the divine reality itself. From this we get the chanting of *mantras*, etc. The vibration of the word 'Krishna' *is* Krishna. Heidegger may not go this far but he believes that certain words and certain languages have a more direct connection to Being. They *disclose* the world in a more immediate manner, make it more authentically *present*.

We believe that this is one of the reasons that Heidegger still appeals to many humanistic and existential psychotherapists who have a yearning for 'the sacred', for the ground of Being. Despite his dance of a thousand veils that shroud *aletheia*, Heidegger still tantalizes us with the anticipation of direct contact with Being and, perhaps, with the prospect of 'being fully present in the here and now'. His evident bias towards Ancient Greece and Germany, however, is informative. It affirms how pervasive nationalistic and parochial attitudes can be. *My* language is special, *authentic*; it must be protected from outsiders and degeneration. But there is nothing 'ontological' about this. It is the preference of one man for his mother's cooking.

This 'metaphysics of presence' contains the prospect of an immediate (i.e., unmediated) access to Being or even to the presence of one's own *Dasein*, and is quite at odds with Derrida's *différance* – the idea that meaning is always deferred into the web of meaning and cannot be disclosed in its 'ownmost' being or possibility (Derrida, 1978). The 'system' of meaning, moreover, is also contingent and incomplete: neither in the most exhaustive dictionaries nor in the most revelatory revelations do we uncover uniquely true or original meanings. The world and our own selves, therefore, maintain a dimension of unknowability, strangeness and of emergent possibility.

And herein lies the danger of 'back to the things themselves'. The 'things themselves' *in-themselves* are not available to us, except in fantasy. Phenomena are mediated and become 'themselves' in relation to other 'things' in the context of a 'world' of experience. Perhaps, then, a phenomenologist might better ground understanding not through direct access to phenomena, but rather, through the system of signification itself, the 'life-world'. Here the focus is not upon individual phenomena but upon the meaning system in which phenomena emerge. This, however, may simply bump the problem down the road – to find the true meaning in the system itself and, perhaps, in the human capacity to systematize. This, for example, is how the influential structuralist Claude Levi-Strauss approaches the meaning of diverse myths in his seminal study *Myth and Meaning* (1978/2005) and this is, of course, typical of 'structuralism'.

Relatedness as normative ideal

'World view' and 'worlding' – with the attendant structures of meaning – are matters to which Spinelli (2014), among others, has paid much attention, articulating a structuralist perspective that has become influential within existential psychotherapy. There is the acknowledgement in Spinelli that we are talking to some extent about multiple worlds or frameworks of meaning. We do not all entirely share the same experiential world, and phenomena do not always disclose themselves in the same way to all of us. Psychotherapy involves, as best we can, endeavouring to understand the world of another. However, the idea of 'world' and Spinelli's 'worlding' may be somewhat problematic. His approach, even where it appears to engage with multiplicity, relies on assumptions that posit a holistic, inter-connected *system* of consciousness, rather than a more fragmentary and contingent set of processes.

This, of course, brings us back to Heidegger. The assumption is that we are all *Dasein* and that on some fundamental existential level we have a shared world of experience. By the nature of our being, we share the existential givens of death, freedom, facticity, throwness and choice *in the same manner*. These existential givens, therefore, form the ground for our mode of being-in-the-world. We can understand, therefore, why Spinelli (2016) writes of 'being-in-the-world [as] a unitary phenomenon' (p.316). Moreover, it is a short step from this 'existential union' to regarding Dasein as an ontological union in which, Spinelli goes on to write, 'there is no divide between subject and object, nor between internal and external' (ibid, p.316). For Heidegger, he writes, the 'I' itself 'expresses the wholeness of being' (p.317) and must be read 'as a general term rather than … that which designates a specific and singular entity or agent' (ibid).

This also appears to be consistent with Spinelli's belief in the 'indivisible grounding of relatedness' (2014, p.47). However, thinking of 'relationship' in these terms entails a relationship, as it were, of primary *identity* rather than the relationship/interaction of disparate entities or processes. I can relate to you because you are another 'self', 'another like me'. Perhaps there may be superficial signs of difference, but there is a deeper identity between us. The stance of another Heideggerian populariser, Hans-Georg Gadamer, is unsurprisingly very similar, replicating what we believe to be a fundamental error common to both relatedness and hermeneutics: namely, the omission of the *inherent asymmetry* present in any relationship alongside the fundamental otherness of the other (Bazzano, 2012). The difference the other presents us with is a tangible breach in the linear process of the self and our genuine aspiration to engage with the other's difference amounts to an *interruption* of the self.

The undisputed merit of Spinelli's own version of inter-relatedness – or the 'Grand Theory [of] … universal relatedness' (Spinelli, 2016, p.310) – consists in having revitalized as well as articulated in captivating and profound ways (by skilfully weaving together Heidegger, Gadamer and constructionist theory) what is effectively, in the hands of many a practitioner and many a training course, the terminally inert, platitudinous and tautological notion of the *centrality of the therapeutic relationship in therapy*.

Unholy trinity

For Spinelli (2014), *worlding* is where non-systematized, 'raw' experience can disrupt the system and indeed lead to its overthrow and replacement with a more adequate worldview. Here's the rub, however. Spinelli takes his unitarian thesis even further when he writes that 'even if the worldview cannot entirely correspond to worlding, it can attempt an increasingly adequate correspondence' (ibid, p.63). It can, in other words, approach 'truth'. That is a comforting idea, but there is no actual way in experience to validate this assertion – it is simply a transcendental assumption. It is also worth noting that the concepts of 'world' and 'worlding' are inherently unitary or holistic, in that they name a supposedly coherent whole, a thing that can be thought of as 'one'. Interestingly, too, Spinelli depicts the 'worlding' phase of his hermeneutic circle as a transitional and 'meaningless' state as one moves towards a new 'worldview'. It is meaningless in that one's experience of being is:

> unfixed in the necessary fixedness of structure that meaning requires. [...] [T]hat which is meaningful is experienced cognitively, emotionally and 'feelingly', as an overall 'mood' expressive of a stance taken towards currently lived existence. It is only when a 'mood stance' is experienced through the reflective structuring of the worldview that it can be said to be meaningful.
> (Spinelli, 2014, p.62)

So, without a thoroughly structured, consistent, fixed worldview, by this account, there can be no 'meaning'. This, in our view, is simply a fetishization of system, of unifying structure. The structure guarantees meaning and unity. But we have a little problem – the existing structure of an open, *developing* and creative system, such as language, is *not* complete, fixed or whole (even if we imagine it as such). Such a lived-system can only ever be partial/multiple, as it is always prone to mutation, change, destabilization and ambiguity. Foreign bodies continually threaten its integrity and it is riven with difference, anomaly and paradox.

Spinelli seems to say that through worlding new elements can always be incorporated and/or a new structure created. Otherwise we'd be plunged into the meaninglessness of perpetual worlding. This for us, though, is 'the emperor's new clothes', as the 'meaninglessness' is already here; it is everywhere. The virus is alive in 'the system', spawning the types of mutations and anomalies that defy family-resemblance and homecomings. Spinelli may be aware of the paradoxical relationship between worlding and worldview but he seems to ally himself with the forces of 'meaning' and structure. He frequently wears the old-fashioned and somewhat conservative garb of a structuralist at a time when the contingency of structures is well established and the need to subvert them most pointed.

To move on to how Spinelli's 'structuralism' informs his important formulation of human inter-relatedness, he approvingly cites Valle and King, writing: 'From an existential perspective, human existence reveals the total, indissoluble unity or interrelationship of the individual and his or her world' (in Spinelli, 2014, p.81). Tellingly, unity and interrelationship are conflated here, and this conflation does not operate solely at the intrapersonal level, but at the interpersonal too, as we saw earlier in Spinelli's discussion of how the 'I' expresses the 'wholeness of being'.

As outlined earlier, we hold there to be a sort of unholy trinity in Spinelli – inter-subjectivity = inter-relationality = unity. This is a structuralist and thereby essentially 'conservative' approach to meaning. In other words, it resists plurality and difference.

Unity underlies difference. Priority is given to unity and frames the very nature of relationality. Difference is merely apparent, an epiphenomenon. As Derrida observed in 'White Mythology', a chapter in his *Margins of Philosophy* (Derrida, 1984), transcendental thinking has just this tendency to assume a narrative implicitly affirming unity and wholeness. To this end 'discontinuities' are seen as part of the overall 'structure' of the whole and thus may be misnamed as 'contraries' (Bazzano, 2017a, p.122). From here, it is a short step from such holistic inter-relatedness to an underlying mystical union of opposites. This is, then, at heart a form of theology, rather than phenomenology, existential or otherwise.

If we think about this, though, from a Derridean perspective, it is difference, and *différance*, not just systematic 'unity' that makes meaning possible. It is the 'non-identity' of factors within a presupposed 'system' that allows differentiation of meanings to occur at all. Thus, the operation of language or of any meaning system is dependent upon difference. The system itself, however, does not guarantee or provide a unity or a grounding of meaning. It *simply allows meaning to work* with a modicum of intelligibility. There is no return here to fundamental meanings and no homecoming to 'truth'. As Ole Wæver has observed in his critique of the hermeneutics of Heidegger and Gadamer, 'All meaning systems are open-ended systems of signs referring to signs referring to signs. No concept can therefore have an ultimate, unequivocal meaning' (1996, p.171). We omit here, of course, *formally* closed, model-systems such as may be theoretically deployed in physics, mathematics and computer programming, as these are not lived systems of meaning.

Therefore, if difference is overcome or undermined, meaning itself becomes impossible. This is only a problem if we are seeking a non-equivocal truth, a return to Being, and if our desire is 'to be true to being' (Spinelli, 2014, p.48).

Despite apparent theoretical differences, Spinelli's notion of inter-relatedness also echoes, albeit indirectly, the influential concept of *intersubjectivity* within psychoanalysis, broadly defined by Jessica Benjamin as the 'interpenetration of minds, conscious and unconscious' (Benjamin, 2018, p.1). At this point, a brief investigation of psychoanalytic intersubjectivity may help shed some light on the notion of relatedness in traditional existential therapy.

Negation and the risk of communication

Benjamin's starting point is G. W. F. Hegel's *Anerkennung* (acknowledgment/recognition, usually rendered as recognition), developed in *Phenomenology of Spirit* (1807/1977) and thoroughly absent in traditional existential therapy – shockingly so, considering how central it is in most accounts of the relational and political dimensions within French existentialism, Critical Theory and beyond. It was central, for instance, to Merleau-Ponty's own formulation of being-in-the-world as being-in-the-*social*-world, a felicitous formula largely ignored in traditional existential therapy. Yet it is in Hegel's early writings that one finds the source for a sound philosophy of encounter which inspired Merleau-Ponty's (1968) definition of dialogue as the art of taking the risk of communicating.

Unlike the *a-historical, symmetrical* perspectives of traditional existential narratives of relatedness, Benjamin's intersubjectivity has the merit of adopting an *asymmetric* and *historico-dialectical* view of the therapeutic encounter. Both perspectives, however, rely on the twin assumptions that recognition is achievable (be brought to consciousness) and that it is the very condition (a 'given' in existential terms) under which acceptance and self-understanding takes place. Complementarity in the meeting of self and other is more or less explicitly taken for granted. Both views neglect the ever-present possibility of disruption and negation. While acknowledging the vital role of negation in human interaction (e.g. Sartrean 'conflict', rhetorically upheld yet seldom applied in traditional existential therapy's accounts) both perspectives hold as true that destruction can be averted and that we can survive at a more 'authentic' level. Judith Butler's incisive critique of psychoanalytic intersubjectivity might be effectively applied to existential relatedness, particularly when she asks:

> My question is whether intersubjective space, in its 'authentic' mode, is really ever free of destruction. And if it is free of destruction, utterly, is it also beyond the psyche in a way that is no longer of use to psychoanalysis.
>
> (Butler, 2004, p.145)

The implication is anathema to existential accounts of relatedness which indulge in sentimental renderings of Buber's 'I–Thou', as if it were a natural and intrinsic (authentic) form of connection, that we can settle into when we decide not to be beastly to one another. However, from a less complacent viewpoint, we might see that this form of relationship is *accidental* rather than a necessary given (Bazzano,

2012, 2013). The therapeutic dyad is 'an achievement, not a presupposition' (Butler, 2004, p.146).

Importantly, a normative (*prescriptive*) notion of the dyadic encounter frequently and complacently presumes the 'availability' of a symmetrical therapeutic relationship. Ironically, this benign 'meeting', by its very presupposition of I–Thou relatedness, can end up disavowing the all-too-real presence of history – of destruction, negation, cruelty and exploitation as much as of kinship and love – and in so doing be of little use for psychical transformation. Well-intentioned notions of intersubjectivity and quasi-theological notions of universal relatedness are, moreover, understandably popular in a neoliberal age which demands tacit compliance and the bending of therapeutic work to genteel psychological adjustment and change.

The city and the city

Let us try to move this examination of relationality into the therapeutic space. Given the uncritical, unreserved acceptance of universal relatedness and intersubjectivity in contemporary therapy culture alongside the high-flown talk of I–Thou and deep relationality, what type of relationships are we actually able to offer to our clients? Do we offer unconditional positive regard or authenticity? Even where this is an aspiration, the fact is that any relationship we may offer to a client is everywhere contingent, conditional and framed by difference and the dynamics of power. Many approaches to therapy seek to acknowledge and engage with these asymmetries, but frequently assume that behind them lies a deeper unity of human connection. Is this thoroughly the case?

John, for instance, is aware that his frequently impoverished and disenfranchised clients in many ways do not occupy the same world as he and that there are limits in how far they can understand one another. One student who grew up on the very same streets as he told him of the gang culture she had been born into. Her Islington and John's were two very different spaces. In this brief encounter, John was reminded of China Miéville's brilliant novel *The City and The City* (Miéville, 2011) in which two distinct cities occupy 'the same' physical space. It has become second nature for citizens of one city to 'unsee' the other, and this is also required of them by the laws put in place to keep the cities distinct. There are cues and clues to what you shouldn't see. You might not understand it anyway, as it's not of your world. So, interestingly, Miéville's book describes the system and laws that both unite and separate these worlds.

As John's client described growing up in Islington she might as well have been describing Mogadishu, so unfamiliar and unseen was this place. She managed, he believes, to translate some of this experience for him, but he was left with the strong sense that his understanding was at best partial and most certainly that of an outsider. A friendly confidante, maybe, but a stranger nonetheless.

Several years ago, Manu experienced something similar as a trainee therapist. He was working with 'Sabur', a man in his early thirties who was going through a crisis: his father had died two months before and the Imam of his local mosque had failed to provide the spiritual support he and his large family had expected. He felt let down, angry and sad, and for the first time in his life had serious doubts about his beliefs. He also felt embarrassed and somehow at fault for coming to counselling and seeking help outside religion. Manu was perplexed and a little uncomfortable. In spite of his travels and his diverse cultural interests, he had never engaged in close conversation with a Muslim person before. Sabur expressed frustration at the demands put on him by his relations; he felt guilty for not being 'morally upright' and 'doing what was required' of him at a time of crisis. He talked of a growing desire to be alone, to start another life by himself, of leaving his wife and relations, and of abandoning his religion. Listening attentively and engaging with him in the best way he could, Manu started to read his client's crisis in terms of his western frame: autonomy from the family womb and individuation. He felt they were making progress. Until on the tenth session Sabur said how counselling had been helpful in realizing how truly important family and religion were to him. The momentary lapse had made him appreciate them more; it had helped him see how loved and supported he was by both. This had come up in a family meeting where they had managed to reconnect and talk and pray together. Although naturally pleased for him, Manu also felt sorely humbled by his obvious inability to suspend his own worldview.

Identity-thinking

By far the most important connection between worlds and worldviews is the unifying notion of 'the human'. It is the ethos and accepted rhetoric of humanism, with such notions as 'inalienable human rights', that pervades psychotherapeutic approaches to dialogue. Only the most complacent of thinkers, though, could believe that a dialogue of symmetrical power and autonomy exists as much more than an aspiration or delusion. Show us an inalienable human right, and we'll show you myriad instances of its alienation. Being human *guarantees* you nothing at all, and certainly not that your therapist, having walked a mile in your moccasins, can inhabit your frame of reference. Relatedness and dialogue, even at its best, is not the symmetry of 'I–Thou'. It is always surrounded by and imbued with asymmetries and dynamics of various stripes – asymmetries of power being not the least of them.

It is, perhaps, comforting to us as therapists (and human beings) to believe that we offer a real I–Thou relationship to our clients and to ignore the contingencies. We say this not to decry contact or relationship, but because it seems to us that complacent and sentimentalized notions of relationship do not serve either our clients or their therapy very well.

Many years ago, John worked for a charity that supported clients, some of whom took complaints to the BACP, UKCP and elsewhere. In terms of the relational dimensions of complaints, John felt there were broadly two different types – those where complaints were against therapists experienced as cold, unavailable and withholding (frequently psychodynamic/psychoanalytic) and those where therapists offered 'too much' relationship or promised more than they could give (frequently these were humanistic/existential). Very many of John's clients did not wish to take forward a complaint but mainly wished to make sense of what had happened to them in the therapeutic relationship and to gain some acknowledgement of this. Often too, they felt that there had been no ill-intention or cynical grooming involved. He remembers one client who mentioned quite simply how their therapist had said to them – 'I will always be there for you'. This instance, though insidious, is clearly not the most egregious therapeutic conduct and it was certainly indicative of much of the self-deception that permeated many of these therapeutic relationships.

We believe that it would be helpful to try to rebalance our conceptual framework to try to address the overemphasis on a grand unity of being and upon intersubjective primary identity. We might benefit, in other words, from a form of enquiry that encourages a more rigorous, unsentimental engagement with difference.

We find interesting models for this in the writings of Theodor Adorno and others associated with the Critical Theory of the Frankfurt School and also in later post-structuralist thinking. Within the existential tradition, we also have Jean-Paul Sartre and Emmanuel Levinas, among others, who also endeavoured to explore more deeply issues of identity and difference and who have arguably been overlooked within traditional existential therapy.

In his *Negative Dialectics*, Adorno (1966/1981) critiques identity-thinking and also explores a critical philosophy which seeks to avoid conceptual homogenization. Non-identity-thinking involves a willingness to think against the concept. For Adorno, identity is a conceptual creation, which operates, in part, through ignoring and excluding differences. While such manoeuvres are conceptually necessary, for the creation of any concept, they frequently involve overgeneralization and the creation of conceptually unified but spurious concepts and 'entities'. Some of this, of course, is fairly benign; for instance, the concept of tree creates a unity by ignoring certain differences between various trees (differences deemed as minor and non-essential). Whether, though, a unified concept such as *Dasein* is as useful or benign is more questionable. Adorno's request is that we not put our conceptualizations on a sure footing, but be willing to constantly interrogate and revise them. This might be called an *immanent* critique that engages with the paradoxes, aporia and lacunae in our conceptual frame, but does not seek to 'solve' these via unifying transcendental formulations.

Exiting the house of Being

Can we ever break free of *the cult of relationship* (Bazzano, 2017b) that has taken hold of contemporary psychotherapy discourse? A way out may involve embracing 'fallenness from being' or exile and actively accepting the difficult realization that there will be no final homecoming. In its origin and indeed in its very etymology, the philosophy of <u>ex</u>istence embraced the modern ontological condition of <u>ex</u>ile. The very word existentialism, beginning with the prefix *ex* ('out' or 'out of') aligns it with *existence exile, exodus, exit, exteriority*; these words 'bear a meaning that is not negative' (Blanchot, 1993, p.127), a meaning that challenges the sedentary predilection of the philosophical tradition for home, identity and self-sameness.

Counter-traditional accounts within the philosophy of existence (e.g. Levinas, 2001) endeavoured at times to describe existence in the absence of a subject – a quasi-subject, in any case, whose nature has no ultimate foundation but is, rather, groundless. These counter-traditional strands within existential phenomenology – at times present within the same author alongside the 'tradition' (most visibly in Merleau-Ponty) – dared to meet the philosophical tradition head-on to challenge its false hopes, and endeavoured to engage with displacement, absence and other-ness – those fallen, forgotten and abject conditions.

This 'fall' may, however, itself be something to celebrate, because it is not simply destructive or unsettling but clears the way for the future. Likewise, a lack of firm ontological 'foundations' (those that Marcuse so admired in Heidegger) may leave us freer to roam and to explore a less pre-defined 'interpersonal' space. We may need, however, to leave the so-called house of Being and become recep-tive to exteriority and the unknown, for it is through the unknown that most likely we'll find the new.

References

Adorno, T. (1966/1981) *Negative Dialectics*. London: Continuum.

Bazzano, M. (2012) *Spectre of the Stranger: towards a Phenomenology of Hospitality*. Eastbourne: Sussex Academic Press.

Bazzano, M. (2013) 'Togetherness: Intersubjectivity Revisited', *Person-Centered & Experiential Psychotherapies*, DOI:10.1080/14779757.2013.852613

Bazzano, M. (2014) 'The Poetry of the World: a Tribute to the Phenomenology of Merleau-Ponty', *Self and Society*, 41, 3, pp 7–12.

Bazzano, M. (2017a) *Zen and Therapy: Heretical Perspectives*. Abingdon, OX: Routledge.

Bazzano, M. (2017b) 'Grace and Danger', *Existential Analysis*, 29, 1, pp 16–27.

Benjamin, J. (2018). *Beyond Doer and Done to: Recognition theory, intersubjectivity and the third*. Abingdon, OX: Routledge.

Blanchot, M. (1993) *The Infinite Conversation*. Minneapolis, MN: University of Minnesota Press.

Butler, J. (2004) *Undoing Gender*. Abingdon, OX: Routledge.

Cayne, J. (2014) 'Disorientation and Wild Delusion: on Merleau-Ponty's The Visible and the Invisible', *Self and Society*, 41, 3, pp 46–48.

Derrida, J. (1978) *Writing and Difference*. Trans. A. Bass. London and New York: Routledge.

Derrida, J. (1984) *Margins of Philosophy*. Chicago, IL: Chicago University Press.

Harrison, J. (2014) 'Two-way Street: the Textures of Living in Merleau-Ponty', *Self and Society*, 41, 3, pp 28–32.

Hegel, G. W. F. (1807/1977) *Phenomenology of Spirit*. Trans. A. V. Miller. Oxford, OX: Oxford University Press.

Heidegger, M. (1927/1962) *Being and Time*. London: SCM Press.

Heidegger, M. (2002) *On Time and Being*. Chicago, IL: University of Chicago Press.

Husserl, E. (2001[1900/1901]) *Logical Investigations*. Ed. Dermot Moran. 2nd ed. 2 vols. London: Routledge.

Kennedy, D. (2014) 'Perception as the Upsurge of the World', *Self and Society*, 41, 3, pp 33–38.

Laplanche, J. (1996) 'Psychoanalysis as Anti-hermeneutics', *Radical Philosophy*, 79, September/October, pp 7–12.

Levinas, E. (2001) *Existence and Existents*. Pittsburgh, PA: Duquesne University Press.

Levi-Strauss, C. (1978/2005) *Myth and Meaning*. London: Routledge.

Merleau-Ponty, M. (1968) *The Visible and The Invisible*. Evanston, IL: Northwestern University Press.

Merleau-Ponty, M. (1942/1983) *The Structure of Behaviour*. Pittsburgh, PA: Duquesne University Press.

Merleau-Ponty, M. (1945/1989) *Phenomenology of Perception*. London: Routledge.

Miéville, C. (2011) *The City and The City*. London: Pan Macmillan.

Moreira, V. (2014) 'Merleau-Ponty and the Experience of Anxiety in Humanistic/ Phenomenological Therapy', *Self and Society*, 41, 3, pp 39–47.

Moran, D. (2000) *Introduction to Phenomenology*. London: Routledge.

Spinelli, E. (2014) *Practising Existential Therapy*. London: Sage.

Spinelli, E. (2016) 'Relatedness: Contextualizing Being and Doing in Existential Therapy', *Existential Analysis*, 27, 2, pp 303–329.

Synesiou, N. (2014) 'Boundary and Ambiguity: Merleau-Ponty and the Space of Psychotherapy', *Self and Society*, 41, 3, pp 13–19.

Wæver, O. (1996) 'The Rise and Fall of the Inter-paradigm Debate'. In S. Smith et al. (eds), *International Theory: Positivism and Beyond*. Cambridge: Cambridge University Press.

Welsh, T. (2014) 'Idealism Revisited: Merleau-Ponty and the Space of Psychotherapy', *Self and Society*, 41, 3, pp 20–27'.

2 Existential aspects of experiencing

Tatiana Karyagina

Introduction

Humanistic and existential psychotherapies look at human nature in different ways. There is, however, significant commonality of vision in therapeutic goals and values and in their adherence to the phenomenological method. The holistic vision of a person in both approaches determines the basic value of meaning, the authenticity of being in a person their main task – the exploration of how a person lives his life. The concept that best expresses these goals and values in humanistic psychotherapy is *experiencing*. Interestingly, the creator of the most elaborated theory of experiencing, Eugene Gendlin, saw experiencing as complementary to existentialism. In Gendlin's theory, as with contemporary experiential schools, experiencing presents a certain duality. Experiencing is meaningful and value-oriented, but at the same time it has the character of spontaneous, self-contained process, a flow that is closed within the human monad, and thus is set counter to life, the world and the Other. The roots of this way of understanding experiencing can be traced in Cartesian dualism and beyond. As a result, a person can only be a witness of his experiencing, trying to express it. In *Co-experiencing Psychotherapy* (CEP), an experiential approach based on cultural activity psychological theory (Vygotsky, 1931; Leontiev, 1977), experiencing is an *activity*, with the person as subject and author of this activity. This allows us to consider experiencing as a multi-level process, its interpersonal origination and dialogical character, to phenomenologically typologize the experiencing in connection with various types of life necessities, and to explore its existential dimensions.

How can we set the question of the existential aspects of experiencing?

Vanhooren (2018) sets it in two ways. First, there are so-called existential givens – death, loneliness, meaninglessness, etc. – which highlight the topics of human life problems that do not have a "practical" solution and, therefore, do not fit into the mainstream of solution-oriented approaches. Being with existence is a serious challenge for therapists who are good at working with micro-tasks, markers, protocols, etc. But even person-centred practitioners emphasize the importance of infusing existential topics within their intrinsically optimistic humanism. In my opinion, such combination looks "external", superficial: existential topics seem to arise from the client himself, but at the same time, attending to them, the therapist seems to go beyond his method, speaking, as it were, a foreign language. Vanhooren (ibid) also offers a different way and talks about the existential roots of experiential approaches. From this point of view, the focusing method proposed by Gendlin is a way of direct access to being as *Dasein* (being-in-the-world).

In this chapter I will dwell in more details on this position of relatedness between *existentialism* and *experientialism*; I will then try to demonstrate how such relatedness is realized in the experiential approach of CEP.

Experiencing as translation from the language of existential philosophy into the language of psychology and psychotherapy

Gendlin, founder of experiential psychotherapy, was a philosopher by training. Existentialism served as a starting point in his reflections on the psychotherapeutic practice and the therapeutic meaning of the concept of experiencing. He wrote:

> Existential psychotherapy holds that one makes and changes oneself in pre-
> sent living. One's past and "internal machinery" do not fully determine
> living... Persons are existence not definitions. Solutions are ... in living radic-
> ally open to choices... existentialism seems negative; it tells how one cannot
> define humans, cannot hold them static, cannot reduce them to mathematical
> necessity, but doesn't say how to make positive sense and life use of these
> negatives. The positive use rests on direct access to one's living process which
> is beyond words and ultimate definitions.
>
> (Gendlin, 1973, pp. 317–18)

He went on to say:

> Experiential philosophy... begins *where the existentialist philosophers left off*, namely
> with the problem of just how symbols (thoughts, speech, other symbols) are
> related to, or based on, concrete experiencing...The existentialist philosophers
> and theorists emphasize that thought and action can be "authentic" or not,
> that is to say can follow from, or be based on concrete experiencing, or not.
> But they do not say how one recognizes when something is authentic and
> when it is not. Yet just this is their central principle.
>
> (Gendlin, 1973, p. 320 emphasis added)

Thus, Gendlin directly connects existential thought with experiential theory and method.

The concept of experience in philosophy, psychology and psychotherapy has a long history. The etymology of the English word "experience" goes back to the Latin *experiri* – to test, try, learn by practical trial. Experience is empirical know-ledge; it is given to us directly as the content of our consciousness. The subject of classical associative psychology was the inner life of the soul, which develops as the sum of experiences connected by the laws of associations.

Both the German *Erlebnis*, and the Russian *perezhivanie*[1], have as their root the word "life". Erlebnis is sometimes translated as "lived experience".

In this tradition:

• life is given to me in my acts of experiencing (Dilthey, 1910/2004);
• experiences are the intentional acts of consciousness (Husserl, 1913/1999).

Experience is holistic, and this holism represents the interconnectedness, meaningfulness and integrity of mental life (Dilthey, 1910/2004):

• experiencing is a life event *per se* (Dilthey, 1910/2004);
• experience is a unit of analysis of the psychical, in which, as in a molecule, unlike in an atom, all the properties of the whole (i.e. the proprieties of the psychical as such) are manifested (Vygotsky 1933/1984).

Dilthey put forward two key ideas about experiencing, which can be traced in any experiential method. First, it is what I call *the triad of experiencing*: experience is (a) experienced; (b) expressed, including being symbolized; and (c) understood. Second, a true understanding of experiencing is possible only in dialogue. The other person understands your experiencing through a certain kind of co-experiencing (*Nacherlebnis*) – putting oneself in another person's shoes, empathy, etc. (Dilthey, 1910/2004).

We can see how such an understanding of experiencing vividly embodies the new trends in the humanities: holistic integrity of the psyche, its intentionality and intersubjectivity. It expresses an important shift in understanding of the subject of psychology – *from the inner life of anima to the animated life*, as Vasilyuk's pun has it (Vasilyuk, 2016, personal communication). For academic psychology, which divides a person into traits and functions, this is still a difficult task. However, such a vision is distinctive of psychotherapy, dealing with a "privateness of the human condition" (Brodsky, 1987). In all these directions of thought – Dilthey's descriptive psychology, phenomenology, existentialism – the overcoming of Cartesian dualism, of the separation of internal and external, subject and object was made through thesis: not a person and the world opposing him, but a person living in the world and experiencing his own unique life.

In existential philosophy, no special attention was paid to the category of experiencing. It was almost replaced – possibly bypassed – by the category of Dasein. It could be said, in fact, that *through the notion of experiencing, Gendlin's theory, "translated" the philosophical concept of Dasein into the language of psychology and psychotherapy*.

The process of experiencing, according to Gendlin, is pre-reflective, pre-conceptual, holistic, multifaceted, but at the same time internally differentiable. This is all the felt datum that we discover by turning our attention inward. Gendlin writes:

> Suppose, for example, that you are walking home at night, and you sense a group of men following you. You don't merely perceive them. You don't

merely hear them there, in the space behind you. Your body-sense instantly includes also your hope that perhaps they aren't following you. It includes your alarm and many past experiences — too many to separate out — and surely also the need to do something, be it walk faster, change your course, escape into a house, get ready to fight, run, shout.

(Gendlin, 2003)

This process is bodily felt and potentially contains the complexity of our living being. For Gendlin (1973), this bodily sense of the intricacy of our situations is the felt sense.

We can express, symbolize this felt sense, but symbolization does not mean replacing the experiencing with a concept or image. It is itself a "form" of experiencing. In psychotherapy, the client refers directly to the felt sense, allowing words, images, deeds to grow out of it.

Such a development of experiencing from within, due to the discovery and entrance into force of the nuances implicitly contained in it, Gendlin calls "carrying forward" (Gendlin, 1973, p. 325). The substantiation of this self-development ability of experiencing is the basis of his therapeutic method, the foundation on which experiential psychotherapy rests. The therapist's task is to initiate and support the process of experiencing. The practice of focusing helps the client perceive, symbolize and comprehend her felt sense.

Thus, in experiential psychotherapy experiencing presents the following characteristics:

- it is *a meaningful integrity*; experiencing as a category actually overcomes the division of affect and intellect;
- it is *involuntary* – it cannot be rescinded;
- it is directly given to us, and therefore subjectively always true, with the client held as the authority on her own experiencing;
- it is productive.

Experiencing as a process

Process, *stream* or *flow* are the main words for positioning experiencing according to Gendlin. What does such categorization provide us with? First of all, it emphasizes the opposition of dynamics to statics: process and movement are more important than outcome and content.

What can our actions be in relation to our own or another's process? We can join in, follow or even surrender; we can slow down or accelerate. When we talk about the process, it is not so important what started it, but rather the fact that it is happening, what the possible obstacles to the flow may be, why it has slowed down or got stuck. The therapist's principles of working with process correspond to these characteristics.

Broadly put, existentialism is even more committed to the language of process, and rejects structural concepts that in psychotherapy relate to the notion of the self.

A significant topic for existentialism is positing the problem of freedom, defined as a *choice* among countless possibilities that the person could make. Human beings create and comprehend their essence throughout their lives and are responsible for every action they perform. Thus, existentialism thinks of a person as a *project* creating itself.

What is the *direction* of the process or flow? The person-centred approach (PCA) answers: if nothing interferes with the process, then it moves in the right direction due to the organismic actualizing tendency. That is why the process can be trusted. It is at this point that the PCA is most actively criticized by existential therapists for its excessive optimism and naivety. Gendlin did not speak directly about the actualizing tendency, but for him values, guiding the experiencing, are implicitly presented in the experiencing itself.

> Experiencing is purposive, valuative, focal. Experiencing has direction. Just some and no other further steps will "carry forward." Anything else is an abrupt change or stasis … For example, if the room is overheated, a person's bodily experienced sensation of being "hot" is also an implying of something further, some way of acting or talking to make it cooler. When a person is "hot," it may not yet be clear whether to open the window or go outside, whether to turn the air-conditioning on or to fan oneself, but the implying of something cooling is there, and is not separate from being hot. To be cooler is not a value separately added onto some neutral experience of temperature.
>
> (Gendlin, 1973, p. 326)

Thus, the criterion of authenticity of an action is its ability to develop experiencing.

Such a deep rooted "rightness" of experiencing in combination with its involuntary character is perceived as the source of its healing power in psychotherapy from its very beginnings – recall the instruction of the free association method. Both this procedure and focusing create the conditions for the greatest manifestation of this free force. The "inner critic" or Super-Ego must be switched off for its unfolding. Gendlin meant the same when he wrote:

> Concepts and values come from experience in the first place, but people have been taught many abstractions which do not emerge from their experiencing. … Such general principles can help, but only if one uses them to seek a step that emerges experientially. Such a step is recognizable by a felt expansion and release.
>
> (Gendlin, 1973, p. 327)

For Gendlin, openness to experiencing is both the pre-condition and the desired outcome of psychotherapy. The key thesis is bodily-felt character of felt sense and felt shift. Despite its deep elaboration by Gendlin, this is actively debated; the necessity of bodily sensibility and ultimate trust in the body is doubted. The main criticism comes from some focusing practitioners such as Campbell Purton (2016).

Our own experience also shows how easily the focusing process turns into, as one of my colleagues put it, "listening to the left heel". Of course, this is largely a matter of skills. However, the transformation of felt sense into an inner object, as Purton writes, theoretically reduces the therapeutic process to inner goings-on (Purton, 2016). Note that, in fact, this is elimination of that very unity of the human and the world given to us in experiencing, which makes up the main heuristic potential of this category.

In an attempt to clarify this further, we can say that experiencing easily turns into self-contained reality, and the experiencing person turns into the witness of experiencing, not its subject. It is not for nothing that Barbara Brodley, a representative of the "orthodox" branch of the client-centered approach, compared the focusing procedure with the client watching a video about her life and retelling it to the therapist (Brodley, 1990).

Purton writes:

> The difficulty is essentially that 'experiencing' is not a thing or process; we experience things, processes, situations, and also our own responses, but we don't experience experiences or experiencing ... If we ask a traveler about his experiences in Burma, we expect to hear about what he did, what happened to him, how he responded, and not about any 'inner goings-on'.
>
> (Purton, 2016, p. 63)

Rather than paying attention inward, Purton emphasizes deep reflection of the life situation as a whole and finding the best way for a person's articulation of responding to the situation.

We can see some dialectical tension between the two meanings of the category of experiencing here: "experience" and "Erlebnis", i.e. directly given inner process as opposed to lived experiencing. This dialectic manifest itself in the embeddedness of focusing procedures in a classic relational client-centered setting, in the consideration of both purposeful and spontaneous focusing as productivity condition for any psychotherapy. The predominant use of one category and not two is in my opinion, not only a tribute to translation traditions, but reflects essential commonality of two meanings, which, nevertheless, needs to be revealed and substantiated.

How can one categorically substantiate a vision of experiencing as lived, capable of leading us out of "inner goings-on" while retaining all that characteristics of experiencing as described by Gendlin? To this purpose, I turn to the category of experiencing as an *activity* as it is elaborated in the experiential approach of Co-experiencing psychotherapy (Vasilyuk, 1991, 2015; Vasilyuk et al, 2019).

Experiencing as activity

The category of activity was elaborated in Soviet psychology from the 1930s. Acting as a meta-theory, cultural-historical-activity psychology (CHAT), as it is commonly called, gave life to applied theories and studies of cognition, learning, neuropsychology, etc. (e.g. Luria, 1971). Its beginning is associated with the works of Lev S. Vygotsky (Leontiev, 1979/1987). The theory of activity was developed in the writings of his student and junior colleague Alexei N. Leontiev. Drawing on Marxist philosophy, Leontiev set the task of theoretical overcoming both Cartesian dualism and a behaviouristic understanding of man as a passive imprint of environmental influences. For Marx (1845/1969), activity is a human way of relating to the world. It is a process through which a person creatively transforms nature, including his own nature, thereby making himself an active subject (Marx, 1845/1969). Thus, life itself – lived relationships of the subject and the world – manifests as activity.

In CHAT, activity is a molar, not a unit added to life (Leontiev, 1977). Activity is multi-leveled as well as multi-motivated. It is prompted by motives and consists of actions aimed at specific goals for the realization of the motive. It is fundamentally and from the very beginning social. In the joint activity between child and adult, only higher mental functions are formed. They are mediated, according to Vygotsky (1931), by symbolic cultural means. The structure of this joint activity is assimilated, interiorized. As a result, consciousness as internal mental activity appears.

The process character of the psyche is certainly recognized by the activity theory, but to look at the mental life or at the person as a process is not enough. Using the category of activity, we emphasize its opposition to *reactivity*. Reactivity is connected with adaptation, but activity – with transformation.

Fyodor Vasilyuk, creator of CEP, was the last postgraduate student of Alexei Leontiev. He admitted that he was always interested in how people overcome difficult situations in their lives. What do they do with themselves, what processes do they rely on in their experiencing? How can they survive the grief and continue to live on, finding new meanings, and not just live out their lives after the loss? The idea that experiencing is a productive activity, soul's *work*, was elaborated in his book *The Psychology of Experiencing* (Vasilyuk, 1991).

Experiencing is, in his theory, the activity employed in resolving critical situations. A critical situation is a situation of impossibility of realizing life's necessities, one that is accompanied by loss of meaning. The outcome of experiencing is creation of meaning. Thus understood, existential givens can be defined as extreme critical situations. The person is the subject, or, more precisely, the author of the experiencing (Karyagina & Vasilyuk, 2018).

Given the etymological proximity of the Russian word for *experiencing* with *living*, the priority of its psychological meaning as lived experiencing is natural. However, the duality inherent to experiencing is reflected in the theory of CEP in a particular way. Vasilyuk used two concepts – "experiencing-work" (activity) and "immediate experiencing" (sometimes in his articles they are written as "*E*xperiencing" and "*e*xperiencing").

Each concept gains its meaning from different contexts, through different comparisons and oppositions. Experiencing as an activity is contrasted to object-oriented activities. With its special outcome, – meaning, it is opposed to those activities where product is a concrete object, material or ideal (knowledge, image, etc.). At the same time, any of these object-oriented activities can carry out the work of experiencing (reading books, writing pictures or poems, purposeful recollection and imagination, etc.).

The immediate experiencing is conceptualized through the category of consciousness and contrasted with its other modes – apprehension, reflection and the unconscious (Vasilyuk, 2015; Vasilyuk et al, 2019). Its qualities such as involuntary character, ability to capture a person, irrevocable subjective truth, "thirst" to be expressed all come to the forefront – this is equivalent to Gendlin's "experiencing".

Vasilyuk described the differences between Gendlin and himself in the following way:

> Gendlin believes that immediate experiencing is the primary psychological substance: it is an original, self-determined and existing-for-itself reality. In the course of its self-realization it produces several side effects, though very important for the life of the subject. Among them there is the function of meaning processing, and that is the function of experiencing-work. We adhere to the opposite point of view: in the relations between these two processes, it is experiencing-work that is the primary substance, and immediate experiencing, with all its phenomenological colorfulness, has only apparent self-determination. It is only one of the organs, means and levels of experiencing-work.
>
> (Vasilyuk, 2005, pp. 37–38)

How is such theoretical distinction realized in therapeutic practice? CEP's phenomenological methods are based on the specifics of consciousness modes. The therapist's empathy facilitates and promotes the client's immediate experiencing, clarification – a client's processes of apprehension, maieutics – and his processes of reflection (Vasilyuk, 2015; Vasilyuk et al, 2019).

Experiencing as an activity is more related to the tactics and strategies of therapeutic work. It is embodied in a number of categories and typologies: lived world, vital necessities, types of critical situations in which vital necessities are blocked, types of experiencing, and types of lived worlds (Vasilyuk, 2015; Vasilyuk et al, 2019).

The subject of therapeutic work in CEP is experiencing, taking place in the person's lived world. The lived world can't be attributed to one of the poles of the opposition "subjective–objective", it is a "subjective objectivity" and "objective subjectivity". Phenomenologically, the lived world is considered as the entire spatio-temporal volume of reality embracing a person – with things, other people and living beings inhabiting it, organized as a whole by a specific person's relations to them. The typology of lived worlds is constructed with respect to vital necessities and conditions in which activities to realize them are unfolding (for example, the difficulty and/or complexity of the lived world).

Table 2.1 summarizes several typologies.

One and the same life situation, for example an illness, can gain different qualities and be experienced in different ways in different lived worlds. In the case of the impossibility of resolving a particular critical situation by its type

Table 2.1

Life necessity	Ontological field	Normal conditions	Type of activity	Type of critical situation	Type of experiencing
Here-and-now satisfaction	"Vitality"	Directly given life-benefits	Life of the organism	Stress	Infantile, directed by the principle of pleasure; example – simple defensive mechanisms
Actualization of motive	A particular life relation	Difficulty	Action	Frustration	Realistic, directed by the principle of reality; example – coping mechanisms, planning, etc.
Internal consonance	The internal world	Complexity	Consciousness	Conflict	Value, directed by the principle of value; moral choice
Actualization of life-intent	Life as a whole	Difficulty and complexity	Will	Crisis	Creative, directed by the principle of creativity; example – re-creating life narrative, etc.

of experiencing (for example, frustration by the means of realistic experiencing), the problem can be more productively solved when moving to a "higher" level of experiencing (you can resolve frustration by the means of value or creative experiencing). For example, you should not cling stubbornly onto realistic experiencing when the goal can't be reached. Maybe it's time to switch to other ways of experiencing – to explore values which determine the goal, life narrative and so on.

More precisely, it is not just the type of experiencing that can or should be changed – the lived world is changing.

Experiencing may be mediated by a transition of a person's life-world from one state to another. Such a transition in itself, and not merely the content-and-meaning-oriented processing of a critical situation, changes its status (e.g. what seemed to be a crisis turns out to be only stress) and engages additional resources in the work of experiencing. This conclusion is very important for developing concepts regarding the tactics of co-experiencing psychotherapy: efforts may frequently be aimed not so much at working through the actual critical situation in which a patient has found himself as at helping him to attain the new dimension of a "higher" life-world, where the situation will be resolved by the forces of that world" (Vasilyuk, 2015, p. 17).

I would like to illustrate these ideas by focusing on the subject of hope in relation to the existentiality of experiencing.

Hope and despair

Hope dies last, we say. I guess this is because it is born first. In the first weeks of life, infants find the impossibility to satisfy their needs immediately, as it was habitual for them in the prenatal period (here-and-now satisfaction in pure form). Gradually, via good enough interactions, infants understand that their needs will be met, the pain will pass, and that they just have to wait. The chaotic, all-absorbing sense of catastrophe accompanying the baby's dissatisfaction is replaced by a simpler frustration. Frustration already has boundaries, primarily temporary ones, and can be tolerated. This may be the way in which hope surfaces in the life of a human being, and it could be defined as a partial subjective actualization of the missing good, and the possibility of filling the gap between now and then. We can then perhaps formulate the following assumption: patience and hope create the psychological time of the individual, which can be filled with the activity of experiencing the critical situation.

What does despair mean? In despair, there is no hope to satisfy my need. Usually we cope with frustration realistically. The slogan of realistic experiencing is "Do not give up!" You should wait, or set intermediate goals, or look for ways around the problem, etc.

In situations of despair and hopelessness, there are of course a lot of nuances, but I would like to look at them from the perspective of time. Hope creates psychological time. When hope dies, there is no longer a landmark; the future disappears; the person's psychological time disappears. Despair is this timelessness. Can a person live outside and/or beyond of time? How is this possible?

One of the sources giving us an understanding of life at the top of despair are the diaries of the residents of besieged Leningrad during World War Two[2].

Many residents of the city kept diaries. A diary is not just a fastening of the moment. It is the creation of psychological time. Interestingly, the authorities urged Leningrad residents to keep diaries. We cannot say what was their intention – whether ideological or intuitively therapeutic – but the fact is, there are a lot of diaries which have been preserved and are being actively studied, especially in recent years (e.g. Peri, 2017).

In the diaries we see several strategies at work for restoring and maintaining psychological time in a situation of extreme despair and hopelessness.

One of the strategies is connected with the principles of realistic experiencing – the maintenance of a "little time" and "little life". Most of the people who wrote the diaries did not really hope to survive. They just waited for their turn to die, but in their diaries we see painstaking attention to each day with its terrible routine of finding food, ways to warm up, deaths and funerals of loved ones. They are saying: "I'm writing, I'm alive, I still have my life. Every hour, every day is important". In a certain sense, they have not given up.

Other strategies seem to reflect a departure from realistic experiencing. This is a way of creating value, of creative experiencing, and the combination of the two. In the words of a teenage girl: *Diary, keep my story*. "Little time", "little life" goes into a big life, into History. The hope that the diaries will be read by the descendants after the author's death was mentioned by many. Their task was to convey their thoughts about their past, feelings and ideas about their present. They didn't mention their future, but dreamt about the future of their partners or children evacuated from Leningrad. Surprisingly, many people in such terrible conditions wrote about the beauty of nature, music, favourite books, etc. The authors viewed their life as a meaningful whole, as a message to the world, they turned to face the world, went outside themselves, beyond their own limits. They created and recreated their life narratives. Hope is revived, therefore, with regard to their life-plan and life-intent. They made out their life as a story inscribed in the history of the country and its people; to convey the message that "My life and death are not in vain". This step beyond oneself, this departure from the egocentric position, this turning to others are the main features here.

We associate a special strategy with a value experiencing. Phenomenologically, it creates a very special time. When hope is dead, I live as if there is no more time at all. I am, in a sense, invulnerable: because I gave up hope, I am as if I was dead, and you cannot die twice. If you have no hope, you are absolutely free, and life suddenly becomes easy. You are face to face with eternity – with the ultimate last values: God, Love, Truth, Beauty, the Good. Reality does not matter – there are only higher values. All you can do is make a choice and follow it.

There are many such examples in the history of besieged Leningrad. The most well-known is the story about people working in the storage of unique seeds collected by the geneticist Vavilov all over the world. They were dying of hunger, but still kept their collection to the last gram.

Value exists beyond time and beyond individual existence. Because of this, the power of value is such that it can give strength in despairing situations. A sense of value focuses the mind and one's whole life. In acute forms of experiencing Me is no longer Me, I become just a conduit of value.

Conclusion

We live in post-postmodern times, in times of fluid identity, and it seems to me that one of the main challenges is a genuine return of the person to a sense of agency. We should thank Roland Barthes and his followers for a better understanding of the powerful, impersonal processes that in some way own us. But equally we should find strength and the wherewithal to regain authorship of our life and of experiencing – both with a capital and with a small letter. The author is alive.

Notes

1 In Russian "perezhivanie" – a noun from the verb "perezhivat" – going through the life or life events: "to live" + prefix "pere-", which usually means "over, over again" implying overcoming some obstacles.
2 I am very grateful to Elena Sheryagina, my colleague, one of the first students of Fyodor Vasilyuk, for bringing these materials to the discussion.

References

Brodley, B.T. (1990). Client-centered and experiential: two different therapies. In G. Lietaer, J. Rombauts and R. Balen (Eds), *Client-centered and experiential psychotherapy in the nineties* (pp.87–108). Leuven: Leuven University Press.

Brodsky, J. (1987). Nobel lecture. From: www.nobelprize.org/prizes/literature/1987/brodsky/lecture/

Dilthey, W. (1910/2004). *Postroenie istoricheskogo mira v naukakh o dukhe [The Formation of the Historical World in the Human Sciences]*. Moscow: Tri kvadrata.

Gendlin, E.T. (1973). Experiential psychotherapy. In R. Corsini (Ed.), *Current psychotherapies* (pp.317–352). Itasca, IL: Peacock. From www.focusing.org/gendlin/docs/gol_2029.html

Gendlin, E.T. (2003). Beyond postmodernism: from concepts through experiencing. In Roger Frie (Ed.), *Understanding experience: psychotherapy and postmodernism* (pp.100–115). London and New York: Routledge. From www.focusing.org/gendlin/docs/gol_2164.html

Husserl, E. (1913/1999). *Idei k chistoi fenomenologii i fenomenologicheskoi filosofii [Ideas Pertaining to a Pure Phenomenology and to a Phenomenological Philosophy]*. Vol. 1. Moscow: DIK.

Karyagina, T., & Vasilyuk F. (2018). Dialectics of person and experiencing. In M. Bazzano (Ed.), *Re-visioning person-centred therapy. Theory and practice of a radical paradigm* (pp.79–92). London and New York: Routledge.

Leontiev, A. (1977). *Activity and Consciousness*. Marxists Internet Archive. From: www.marxists.org/archive/leontev/works/activity-consciousness.pdf

Leontiev, A. (1979/1987). On Vygotsky's creative development. In *Vygotsky's Collected Works Vol.3. Problems of the Theory and History of Psychology (Preface). Springer Science & Business Media*. Marxists Internet Archive. From: www.marxists.org/archive/leontev/works/1979/vygotsky.htm

Luria, A.R. (1971). Metaprinciples in Luria's neuropsychology. Marxists Internet Archive. From: www.marxists.org/archive/luria/works/1971/metaprinciples.pdf

Marx, K. (1845/1969). *Theses on Feuerbach*. Marxists Internet Archive. From: www.marxists.org/archive/marx/works/1845/theses/theses.pdf

Peri, A. (2017). *The war within: diaries from the siege of Leningrad*. Cambridge, MA: Harvard University Press.

Purton, C. (2016). Focusing-oriented therapy. In P. Sanders (Ed.), *The tribes of the person-centred nation* (pp.47–70). Monmouth: PCCS books.

Vanhooren, S. (2018). Experiential-existential psychotherapy: deepening existence, engaging with life. In M. Bazzano (Ed.), *Re-visioning person-centred therapy. Theory and practice of a radical paradigm* (pp.151–160). London and New York: Routledge.

Vasilyuk, F. (1991). *The psychology of experiencing*. New York and London: Harvester Wheatsheaf.

Vasilyuk, F. (2005). *Perezhivanie i molitva [Experiencing and Prayer]*. Moscow: Smysl.

Vasilyuk, F. (2015). Coexperiencing psychotherapy as a psychotechnical system, *Journal of Russian & East European Psychology*, 52:1, 1–58.

Vasilyuk, F., Cornelius-White, J., & Shankov, F. (2019). Co-experiencing psychotherapy explained in a dialogue, *Person-Centered & Experiential Psychotherapies*, 18–2, 166–179.

Vygotsky, L.S. (1931). *The History of the Development of the Higher Mental Functions.* Marxists Internet Archive. From: www.marxists.org/archive/vygotsky/works/1931/higher-mental-functions.htm

Vygotsky, L.S. (1933/1984). Krizis semi let [Crisis at age of 7]. In *Collected works, vol.4.* pp.376–385. Moscow: Pedagogika.

3 Learn to forget

A Nietzschean revaluation of forgetting in psychotherapy

Glenn Nicholls

There are hundred ways to listen to your conscience… But that you feel something to be right may have its cause in you never having thought much about yourself and having blindly accepted what has been labelled *right* since your childhood.

(Nietzsche, 1882/2001, p. 188)

But in the smallest and greatest happiness there is always one thing that makes it happiness: the power of forgetting.

(Nietzsche, 1874/2005, p. 62)

One is best punished for one's virtues.

(Nietzsche, 1886/1979, p. 82)

'You don't know my name! How's that even possible?' Asks the nameless man sat opposite me.

'I don't know, I can't remember ever knowing it.'

He looks bewildered. 'You must have, we've been working together for eighteen months.'

'I've got your contact details with your initials, but no name.'

'I don't know what to say.'

'How do you feel?' I ask.

'Shocked.'

'Anything else?'

'Like what? What do you expect?' He pauses for breath. 'I feel okay … I'm a bit angry, confused, I guess. What do you feel? You've obviously known about it.'

'I feel excited,' I've thought about this conversation many times, I knew that not knowing his name over such a long period was significant.

'Excited? How? I mean, what's there to be excited about?'

'I knew forgetting your name had to be important, we all forget names now and then, but not for this long. It always seemed less important than what we were doing; mentioning it earlier would have been a distraction.'

'Hang on, how can it be important? And why are you excited?'

'Well, I feel pulled in two different directions. On the one hand I thought I should know your name, and on the other I could see through the "shoulds," the "rights," the "wrongs"; they have no basis in anything beyond a misguided sense of duty.'

'But knowing my name – that's more than duty, surely? I mean you could've found out, asked me early on. You didn't need to let me know after all this time.'

'You'd prefer dishonesty?'

'No, but it doesn't feel right, it feels dismissive.'

'I can see that, it certainly wasn't my intention. I went with it because I didn't want to undermine the process.'

'Okay, you've said before that the process is the most important thing here, as a therapist I get that. But you see why I feel dismissed?'

'Yes, oh god, of course; it's consistent with how you feel in relationships, your divorce, your childhood. It's at odds with the norms of intimacy, and now your therapist forgets your name.'

'Sure, but I think this is more about you, than me.'

'Yes it *is* about me, and it *is* also about you, and it's about us. We agreed to be honest with each other, not to censor or dismiss any thought or feeling. It's honesty that led us to this point. I'm excited and curious about what this means for both of us.'

'Okay, fair point, but I don't see what's intimate about forgetting my name.'

'Okay, so think about children playing together in a park. When they go back to their mum, mum asks, "Who was that you were playing with?" Most children just look blank and say "I don't know".' He smiles his recognition, I continue, 'It's not important to them, their play is often intimate or solitary, immersive, focused, they don't think to ask names – it's just not important.'

'Yeah, I've seen that with my two; they never cared about kids' names. But you and I are not children.'

'True, but children care – not about names – they care about the serious business of play. They're immersed in make-believe, their reality, their creativity; this is what they care about.'

'Yes,' he nods slowly.

'Everything else is superfluous, in fact it's an obstacle. Social etiquette, "oughts" and "shoulds", "I can't say this", "I mustn't say that"; forgetting can break us free from all that; we *need* to forget. Creativity *is* necessarily subversive, it's chaotic – forgetting facilitates becoming creative.'

'Okay so that's you and me playing together as children; more you than me I think,' he smiles, then adds, 'So what about you?'

'It's also about you.'

'Tell me what it has to do with you first, then we can talk about me.'

'Well, they're all linked…'

He interjects, 'I knew you'd say that.'

'So, you know I'm interested in the work of Nietzsche, right?'

'Yes, I've read it in your blog.'

'Okay … perhaps his central idea was the *Revaluation of all values*, without going too much into it, it is as it sounds. It means revaluating norms, étiquette, what's considered valuable in psychotherapy, even you and I. It's also a revaluation of duty, responsibility and ultimately reality. I think there are greater values than remembering names, and I think *this* is what freed me to forget.'

'So what did you think when you first realised you'd forgotten my name?'

'The first time I realised I thought about it for a while, and then let it go; I was struck that it just didn't seem important. However, I couldn't forget that I'd forgotten, remembering names was a part of my old set of values, and so inevitably it kept coming up in my thoughts. It seemed significant; this is what excites me.'

'Okay that's interesting. So what is the value of forgetting?'

'Well, Nietzsche has this idea of *The Three Metamorphoses*; Camel, Lion and Child. Basically the camel is a beast of burden, of duty; its purpose is to bare a heavy load – it is obedient.'

'Yeah that's me, I'm the Camel.'

'Ah, I can see that…' he cuts in before I can continue.

'We can come back to me as Camel. What about the Lion?'

'The Lion is king; it tears everything up; values, beliefs, rules, everything; it can be scary becoming a Lion.'

'Powerful though!'

'Yes in a way, but not as powerful as Child. Only Child has the power to create. Child is characterised by forgetfulness, innocence and affirmation of life.'

'So forgetting is a value?'

'Yes, it's a value in its own right. And it's necessary for creating new values.'

'You said even you and I are subject to revaluation; so forgetting me implies I have no value?'

I smile, thinking how to answer.

He continues, 'You do know this is my therapy, I think I'm quite important to this process, no?'

'Well, you're not unimportant, nor am I, there's just something more valuable than you and I. And that's the process, what is happening here.'

'That makes sense, although, if I'm Camel I won't create anything.'

'You seem to be doing a fair job of tearing things up,' I offer.

'Maybe I'm also Lion; I'm questioning pretty much everything right now.'

'Say more,' I urge him.

'I don't believe in God any longer. I don't recognise myself. I don't speak much to my parents, to my ex, it's even a strain with my children. You know there's a lot I wish I could forget, but you can't control what to forget.'

'True. Although since I don't value remembering names, it doesn't surprise me that I forgot yours. Actually it delights me, I wish I could forget my own name,' this thought takes me by surprise; I want to stay with it.

The man sitting opposite laughs and says, 'I like the idea of forgetting myself, what a relief! But what does that actually mean; to "forget yourself"?'

'When I thought about finding out your name I just felt heavy; I feel it now just saying it. And then, when it dawned on me to just tell you I didn't know it – I felt light, weightless; I realised there's no conflict. The lightness *was* me forgetting myself, and yet I felt *more* myself. Does that make any sense?'

'Maybe, you were uninhibited and you didn't fear my reaction,' says the man with no name.

He adds, 'So you apply Nietzsche to your work.'

'No, I don't think Nietzsche can be applied. It's more like applying Nietzsche to yourself, no actually it's more like being gripped by the throat, you can't get away. It's as though he's speaking directly to you, you're on your own; you don't even have him for company. I've read Nietzsche on and off for about thirty years and it's still fresh, alive, even now. He is the ultimate dead therapist. He said "If you gaze long into the abyss, the abyss gazes back into you," that's the best description of what happens when you apply yourself to reading Nietzsche,' I interrupt myself, 'Sorry I'm getting carried away.'

He grins back at me, 'No, that's okay; I asked; besides you are showing me your excitement.'

'So let's talk about you,' I prompt him.

'Well I think a lot of what we've covered speaks directly to me.'

I wait for him to continue.

'Hmm, I've never liked my name, besides life it was the first thing my parents gave me, one of the few things, besides indoctrination.'

'What don't you like about your name?'

'It's funny you asking me how I feel about my name and yet you don't even know it!'

'Would you like to introduce yourself?'

He is silent for a moment and then a puzzled look comes over him, 'It's odd I've never liked my name, and now that you ask, I don't mind using it, but then I don't really feel as though it's me.'

'Ah yes … Go on.'

'It's like I feel free from it, I don't really identify with it, and yet it's mine…' He pauses as though willing something more to surface.

'Keep going,' I urge him.

'Umm, I've always felt like I belonged to *it*, it wasn't *my* name. It was *never* my name, though I was expected to grow into it I guess, or rather, I felt like I had to somehow do justice to it.'

'I'd ask you what your name is – I'd like to know – and at the same time it doesn't sound like it's that important – no not important … you sound … ambivalent. It's as though it has nothing to do with you.'

'Yes that's it,' he looks deep in thought.

We look at one another without speaking; I let him have time to process his thoughts, although I don't know if that's what he's doing.

After a while he looks at me and grins, 'I don't know whether to tell you my name.'

'Wow, that would be strange, you not telling me your name.'

'Well it's not that important, I mean not telling you wouldn't be like an act of rebellion.'

'How so?'

'It's funny, not telling you would in a way balance you not knowing my name.'

'Yes I see that, can you go back to "doing it justice,"' I ask.

'The church, my family; naming was really important, in the church your name directs your path in life,' he looks heavy in the silence.

Then, in a deep voice he says, 'I'm not going to tell you my name.'

'Yes,' I shoot back a hushed reply, I completely agree, although I'm not sure what this means.

'It's funny how the more we talk about it, the less of an issue it is. It's still weird though, isn't it? Knowing someone so well and not knowing their name.'

'I'm curious how, between us, we've both kept your name out. I mean it's almost certain you communicated it in some way, at the beginning, but since then neither of us have brought it up; you haven't talked about its significance, and I hadn't said I didn't know it.'

'You brought it up today,' he smiles.

'I'm glad I did. Let's discuss it more next week; we're out of time.'

'You know it's odd, it feels more balanced now; you know lots about me and my life, and I know very little about you, and yet I know your name, and you don't know mine.'

Forgetting

> This has caused me the greatest trouble and still does always cause me the greatest trouble: to realise that *what things are called* is unspeakably more important than what they are.
>
> (Nietzsche, 1882/2001, p. 69)

Forgetting his name was a therapeutic intervention. If it seems odd to think of forgetting as an intervention it is perhaps because psychoanalytic ideas around forgetting have passed into the mainstream of talking therapies. Psychoanalysis sees forgetting as unconscious defence or attack (they can be the same thing); for example, if you don't really like someone you might forget their name, even though you want to remember it. This way of thinking frames forgetting as a countertransference; an analyst's dislike of their patient is a response to something unlikeable about the patient.

A more conventional view of forgetting is to see it as a failure of memory; the therapist needs to train their memory better. Or forgetting is a mistake which brings up questions of competency. Both assume that therapists should remember. Perhaps underlying this assumption are our broader beliefs about forgetting. Forgetting is generally seen as a weakening of the mind; the memory begins to fail as we get older. People fear dementia more than anything else about getting old. With dementia you're still alive and yet *you* are gone; locked-in somewhere unable to relate to the world as yourself. There is a lot of fear about becoming forgetful. Part of this fear is a fear of the unknown.

What I have just described is what I think Nietzsche would term 'passive forgetting'. Nietzsche is more interested in *active forgetting*; described as an 'ability', to 'possess power', it is 'essential to action', and 'essential to the life of everything'

(Nietzsche, 1874/2005, p. 62). I think I actively forgot my client's name making it a therapeutic intervention. Before I describe active forgetting, I want to pick up on the possible rupture it led to. He seemed shocked that I didn't know his name, and as is often the case with shock, he was apparently able to continue the session 'normally'. I took his shock, initial response and the difference in our perspectives to indicate the likelihood of rupture.

Rupture

It was apparent that there was some sort of rupture and how we now progressed in the session would determine its outcome. I had anticipated his shock as I could see that not knowing his name cut across social norms. My intervention highlighted a clear difference between us. If our difference were too great then the rupture might well be irreparable.

If I had asked him 'Do you usually feel forgotten?', or 'Does this remind you of anything?', it would have been a deflection away from what was happening in the room. The client could then have gone back to previous experiences of being forgotten or abandoned, and likely got lost in the drama and emotionality of his story. I wanted to stay with what was happening between us. Going back would have framed what was happening now through the lens of previous experience.

His questions were an attempt to make sense, and as we began looking at the rupture it became apparent that my forgetting was not a mistake or a lack of competence. We agreed it was odd, outside the norm; his comment 'it doesn't feel right' reflects this, it also hints at it being morally questionable. I will pick up on the moral question later.

We valued forgetting very differently; this indicated that the rupture was evaluative. He wanted to know how I had evaluated forgetting as beneficial to our work. At this point our differences might have been enough to have ruptured our working alliance. To work together he had to have trust in my approach, this would be difficult if he couldn't see value in it. Talking our differences through became reparative in itself; we did not necessarily need to agree, although we did need a common understanding. My goal was not for him to similarly value forgetting, rather I saw the rupture, if it was a rupture, as an opportunity for him to question his own values, be curious about mine and to wonder what it is we are doing together.

Revaluation of all values

> There are no moral phenomena at all, but only a moral interpretation of phenomena.
>
> (Nietzsche, 1886/1979, p. 78)

Nietzsche's far reaching project was the 'revaluation of all values'. Many aspects of his work come under this incomplete project. It is impossible to give more than a superficial account of it here. However, the process of creating new values is itself an expression of value; forgetting is a key value for creativity and creating values. I perceive my client to be at a point in his life where his old values no longer work for him, and so our work is partly about taking stock of this and how he might go about creating new values for himself. It's worth pointing out that Nietzsche was something of an elitist; he thought few people are capable of creating values, as it is no easy under-taking.

On the genealogy of morality

Nietzsche argues that all values have a history, a genealogy, and so to evaluate a value you have to understand its history. Nietzsche points out that it is not possible to say what forgetting *is* exactly: 'Only that which has no history is definable' (1886/1979, p. 53). He traces the value of forgetting back to a basic form of the creditor/debtor relationship. It was essential, particularly before money was invented, that each party entering into a contract remember what goods or services they had promised the other party, and vice versa.

Nietzsche thought it significant that the German word for guilt, *schuld*, has the same root as the German word for debt. Guilt in this context would be the result of going back on your word, failure to pay your debt, or of remaining in debt to the other. Nietzsche describes 'guilt' (sometimes translated as 'ought') as the 'central moral concept' (Nietzsche, 1887/1998, p. 39) and says that it emerges from the 'very material concept "debt"' (Ibid). To act on one's promises, to make good, is to be responsible; Nietzsche sees here the beginnings of morality. Guilt says, 'I do not really want to be what I think I ought to be'; guilt then becomes a moral compass.

'One burns something in so that it remains in one's memory: only that which does not cease *to give pain* remains in one's memory' (Nietzsche, 1887/1998, p. 37).

The most obvious example is the promise 'We must never forget' associated with The Holocaust. This promise is intended to ensure such atrocities never happen again; this is the debt we owe and the promise *we* do not keep. The fear of what we are capable of is underscored by the thought that *we could* forget something so appalling. Guilt is the personal price of the unpaid debt; *feeling* guilty lets us off the hook. Guilt is the guilty pleasure of moral men and women.

It is worth noting that in the previous quote 'to burn something in' sounds traumatic, suggesting that promising is a form of self mutilation. He goes on to say:

> [the] entirety of asceticism belongs here: a few ideas are to be made indelible, omnipresent, unforgettable, "fixed", for the sake of hypnotizing the entire nervous and intellectual system with these "fixed ideas" – and the ascetic procedures and forms of life are means for taking these ideas out of competition with all other ideas in order to make them "unforgettable".
>
> (Nietzsche, 1887/1998, p. 38)

Omnipresent suggests an all-seeing-god; indelible ideas put us under continual surveillance. Perhaps, unlike a belief in god, not believing in guilt is no protection from it; how often do people say 'I know I shouldn't feel guilty, but…'. In describing fixed ideas as unforgettable, Nietzsche gives us the key to breaking free: forgetting.

Nietzsche describes forgetfulness as:

> a door keeper as it were, an upholder of psychic order, of rest, of etiquette: from which one can immediately anticipate the degree to which there could be no happiness, no cheerfulness, no hope, no pride, no real *present*, without forgetfulness.
>
> (Nietzsche, 1887/1998, p. 35)

To be able to actively forget would benefit all manner and creed of mental health practitioners. How then does one actively forget?

Active forgetting

Active forgetting requires making promises in accord with your own values, and having sufficient will to make and keep the promise. Making and failing to keep a promise would mean feeling guilty and a sense of further indebtedness. For Nietzsche it is only those who have the strength to determine their own values that have the power to promise since they have the will to keep a promise. They are not shaped by oughts or by guilt; Nietzsche named this person the 'sovereign individual' (Nietzsche, 1887/1998, p. 36). The sovereign individual is someone 'resembling only himself … free again from the morality of custom … and is *permitted to promise*' (Ibid). The sovereign individual decides for herself what is most valuable; her values are not determined by external mores and moralities. He is fit, *permitted* to make promises, since he has the will and power to make, keep and break them if he chooses. For a sovereign individual breaking a promise would be an act of will, not a failure, although it would almost certainly attract moral critique. However the sovereign individual is impervious to guilt-inducing sickness; what Nietzsche calls 'moralic acid' (Nietzsche, 1895/1990, p. 128).

The therapeutic relationship

The relationship between client and psychotherapist is that of creditor/debtor, and for that reason morals, owing and indebtedness are implicit. A contract is entered into and a fee is promised by the client in exchange for services promised by the psychotherapist. The service provider (the psychotherapist) is indebted to the client; any contract is likely to be equivocal since it is not possible to say where the work will go or what the client will get in return. Much is assumed by both parties of the other, and of themselves, and since both people sit within their own respective cultural milieu they likely have differing unspoken expectations. He had assumed I ought to know his name; even though we never contracted for this. Nietzsche describes this dynamic as: 'He who does not know how to put his will into things at least puts a *meaning* into them: that is, he believes there is a will in them already' (Nietzsche, 1889/1990, p. 34).

One way to read this quote in relation to my client is to see *his* meaning as necessarily discounting any expression of will that contradicts it. It is not that he is unable to will, rather he lacks the 'know how', indeed Nietzsche suggests that his meaning *is* his will, and so for the client meaning dictates will. To him our contract implies the moral imperative for me to know his name. Any moral 'high-ground' he then assumes masks his lack of know-how, whilst also giving him a feeling of moral compensation.

He would not have known that I have long since devalued remembering names. Over the time I spent thinking about not knowing his name – having first remembered that I'd forgotten it – I noticed no guilt. I had no moral imperative to remember; I no longer suffered from it being 'burnt in'. Through a revaluation of values, I see it as neither 'right' nor 'wrong'; it is more or less useful.

When he said 'It doesn't feel right' in response to me asking if he'd prefer I be dishonest, I took his comment to be a moral critique; it may have been an attempt to fault me, or perhaps his way of showing me how he was feeling. In any event, it highlighted how pernicious guilt and moralising can be. For Nietzsche, striving to be human is inextricably linked with our predilection for cruelty:

'We modern humans – he writes – are the heirs of millennia of conscience-vivisection and cruelty to the animal-self' (Nietzsche, 1887/1998, p. 65). Nietzsche would see the introjection, 'I must remember my client's name', as an act of cruelty to myself; to my unconscious animal-self. The paradox is that by cultivating forgetfulness, I also become free to remember. As I pointed out to my client, knowing and remembering his name is extraneous to how I work. Forgetting his name *is* part of the work. Guilt tells us how we ought to be, it can even seduce us into thinking this is who we are. Without guilt it is possible to forget yourself. Nietzsche puts it another way: 'What we do in dreams we also do when we are awake: we invent and fabricate the person with whom we associate – and immediately forget we have done so' (Nietzsche, 1886/1979, p. 83).

For Nietzsche the self is an invention. In my client's mind we are therefore both fabrications of an invention. Nietzsche draws our attention to the similarities between dream and waking life: who we think we are requires forgetting the self-deception at the heart of self-creation. My client believed that I am someone who values knowing his name, and that he is someone who knows who he is; he had, as it were, dreamt us both up. His last statement speaks of equality between us; he is saying (I think) that we are differently equal and equally different. This indicated that our working alliance was now sufficiently restored for us to continue.

Child's play

Writing about the metamorphosis from the Lion to the Child, Nietzsche says:

> The child is innocence and forgetfulness, a new beginning, a sport, a self-propelling wheel, a first motion, a sacred Yes. Yes, a sacred Yes is needed, my brothers, for the sport of creation: the spirit now wills *its own* will, the spirit sundered from the world now wins *its own* world.
>
> (Nietzsche, 1883/1969, pp. 54–55)

Nietzsche's style in Zarathustra is particularly poetic, 'biblical' in tone and can be off-putting to some, and yet he never presents the child in a romantic way. He saw the human animal as cruel; we know children can be cruel, and the innocence Nietzsche has in mind does not preclude cruelty. He refers to the child when he says: 'I know of no other way of dealing with great tasks than that of play' (Nietzsche, 1908/1992, p. 37). It is the play of the metamorphosed Child, and not of the adult *trying* to play; trying is not metamorphosis. Active forgetting is the adult's attempt to regain a child-like forgetfulness. The adult has to work to forget themselves; a child does not need to; this is the innocence of the child. Nietzsche's 'innocence of becoming' (Nietzsche, 1889/1990, p. 65) is the adult's innocence in becoming who he is; he forgets himself to become himself. Becoming is guilty of nothing; there is no *being* standing behind, above or beyond, or anywhere – there can be no guilty *being*. Child's play is serious business; it is in play that we first learn to be serious: 'Mature manhood: that means to rediscover the seriousness one had as a child at play' (Nietzsche, 1886/1979, p. 76).

Seriousness belongs in play; taking it out of play (and vice versa) *is* taking seriousness out of context. The psychoanalyst Donald Winnicott agrees with Nietzsche in his estimation of play; he describes psychotherapy as 'The overlap of the two play areas, that of the patient, and that of the therapist. If the therapist cannot play, then he is not suitable for the work' (Winnicott, 1971/1986, p. 63). For Winnicott the object of play is discovery of the self, whereas for Nietzsche play and forgetting, and the *play of forgetting* are both ends *and* means. For Nietzsche they are expressions of self-overcoming, of will and affirmation of life.

Conclusion

I have contrasted Nietzsche's active forgetting with the gravity of a more orthodox psychotherapeutic interpretation of forgetting. It was apparent that forgetting my client's name challenged his assumptions and what we considered therapeutic about my approach. This led to a rupture in our therapeutic alliance.

Taking Nietzsche's creditor/debtor relationship as a template for the therapeutic relationship, I reframe our conflict as primarily moral rather than qualitative. This shift freed us from the perceived debt I owed him and so resolved the conflict. With active forgetting, guilt and self consciousness start to lose their grip; we then became curious as to what was happening. Our curiosity engendered spontaneity and play.

Explaining play rarely enhances it; it's more likely to shut it down. Forgetting ourselves takes us into a liminal space where we are freed from taking ourselves seriously. This is when psychotherapy is at its best; it keeps open the question of what and who we are, and what we are up to.

References

Nietzsche, F. (1883/1969) *Thus Spoke Zarathustra: A Book for All and None*, trans. R. J. Hollingdale. London: Penguin.

Nietzsche, F. (1886/1979) *Beyond Good and Evil: Prelude to a Philosophy of the Future*, trans. R. J. Hollingdale. London: Penguin.

Nietzsche, F. (1889/1990 & 1895/1990) *Twilight of the Idols/The Anti-Christ*, trans. R. J. Hollingdale. London: Penguin.

Nietzsche, F. (1908/1992) *Ecce Homo: How One Becomes What One is*, trans. R. J. Hollingdale. London: Penguin.

Nietzsche, F. (1887/1998) *On the Genealogy of Morality*, trans. M. Clark and A. Swenson. Indiana: Hackett Publishing Company, Inc.

Nietzsche, F. (1882/2001) *The Gay Science. With a Prelude of Rhymes and an Appendix of Songs*, trans. J. Nauckhoff. Cambridge: Cambridge University Press.

Nietzsche, F. (1874/2005) *Untimely Meditations*, trans. R. J. Hollingdale. Cambridge: Cambridge University Press.

Winnicott, D. (1971/1986) *Playing and Reality*, London: Penguin.

4   fragments of (an) existential discourse

Pavlos Zarogiannis

1

… existential therapy, as every therapy, cultivates its own discourse, language, narrative, speech (Van Deurzen et al, 2019) … with its own grammar and syntax … its own metaphoric and rhetoric … a discourse that claims to be close to life … that wants to be the speech, the language of life … but … is there such a thing as an existential discourse? … most importantly, can it be … should it be one? … and if yes, how would it look … sound like? … and what … would be the relation of such a speech to life? … to ordinary, plain life … can an existential speech suppress the gap between the actual, everyday life and the narration of it (let's say in therapy)? … life is gift, not guilt, not shame … life lives … language speaks … and writes … life materializes … language dematerializes and essentializes … life and language … different events … different orders … different frequencies … do they cross? … where do they cross? … is the body the place where they cross? … is therapy another place, wherein they cross again? … but… does life need therapy? … does existence need therapy? … can life, or being, or existence be sick? … or, maybe … is language sick? … may the language of today be sick? … what is a sick language? … don't we always speak a sick language? … a language that gives us the illusion that … we know what we say … that we say what we mean … that we live a coherent … meaningful life … while what we actually have – our life – is but an intricate knot … no beginnings … no ends … only parts, fragments … and so … this porous text … what I write here … what I can write … my words are nothing but fragile fragments … fragments of life … a life? … one life? … my life? …

2

… my life … "but isn't it true that an author can write only about himself" (Kundera, 2000, p. 215)? … well … that's a bit questionable … arguable … and relative … and … my life? … my history? … my self? … you think my life is the same as that … that what I write about my life … and myself … as that what I write about myself … honestly? … now, that can be an error … a huge error … but also a soothing error … of course … (I shouldn't begin this way … speak too soon … must go back to the introduction … start again) … all these words … existential … therapy … discourse … language … I … life … guilt … death … shame … me … being … suffering … meaning … end … myself … wow! … what a vocabulary! … words of an unspeakable weight … where are they coming from? … who? … what? … I? … no … not I …

… "what matter who's speaking, someone said, what matter who's speaking?" (Beckett, 1974, p. 16) … yes … yes … it matters … really … it matters … I find myself drowning … embedded up to my mouth in words … in a mound of words … vanished almost … lost … closed in … locked up … in a prison of words … of sentences … in the prison of language … I struggle … I fight … trying to find … to open … a way through letters, through words … trying to open a path … I hurt the words … I tear letters and words apart … I must … I must pass through this invisible veil of language … ah! … this veil of language … between us … this net … this web … sticky web … sticks on me … on my skin … my mind … my soul … lost in it … lost without it … without this invisible web … sometimes nurturing … soothing almost … calming … hypnotizing … another times upsetting … disturbing … frustrating … seducing … like the Sirens' song … hearing myself talking … talking in a foreign language … strange feeling … should I apologize for my mistakes? … should I let them be corrected? … but … how much of me would be then authentically here? … how much of my life can fit in a foreign language? … in any language? … born in Greece … studied in Germany … writing in bad English … how much of me is actually here? … with or without mistakes …

… words don't come easily … as they should … birds … sometimes I imagine the words like birds … yes … words should be like migratory birds … words should fly … should go away and come back … disappear and appear … be free like birds … neither locked behind bars nor in cages … words should fly … following the winds … the times … neither down to earth nor up in heaven … they should be … light … without gravity … like feathers … should follow the seasons … be ethereal … like whispers … like waves … in constant move … changing always … infinitely moving … language, an oceanic tapestry … an event of life … but … still … a grille … language … a "language mesh" (Celan, 1972, p. 50) …

… but don't worry dear … sometime in the future we'll wake up and … "[t]housands of words will suddenly be deleted, the ones that were used to name things, faces, acts and feelings, to put the world in order, make the heart beat and the sex grow moist" (Ernaux, 2017, p. 10) …

… but I still wonder … who? … what? … I? … no … not I … what is the proper way to speak? … active or passive voice? … passive better … but how? … haven't I learned that passive … isn't acting always a responding? … doesn't touching mean … presuppose to be touched? … if things … if things are revealed … appear … happen to me (Malebranche, 1997; Merleau-Ponty, 2001) … if the world … you … others … God … if everything appears to me … then … I'm not the cause … I am my responding … the how and the what of me responding … then I am the answer I give to the mystery of the world … and that's heavy, dear … very, very heavy … because then … even my slightest breath is an answer? … a response? … a responsibility? … then I am always responsible for the world order

… and that's an unbearable thing to know … to live with … although … sometimes? … always? … "in the vertigo of immanence" (Agamben, 1999, p. 226) I am the cause … "an immanent cause" (ibid, p. 226) … agent and patient in one … constituting and manifesting myself … as … "the vertigo of immanence is that it describes the infinite movement of the self-constitution and self-manifestation of Being" (ibid, p. 235) (!) … could … should then all verbs be reflexive? …

… but did you … did you notice what just happened? … I wanted to talk about language … and words … but my words … my thoughts and feelings … carried me away … I have to keep that in mind … it happens sometimes … I find myself carried away … so I go back … and ask again … what is the proper way to speak phenomenologically … existentially … experientially … in the active or in the passive voice? …

… and you? … can you follow me? … sad that you don't see me … sad that you don't hear me … you only read my voice … you read my words … I write them while you are reading them … one letter after the other … one word after the other … one sentence … another one … another one … a whole paragraph … this text …

… and while I'm writing I'm trying to imagine you … and you may try to imagine me … and it's sad … no, it's not sad … not sad at all that you don't see me … actually I am as you imagine me … exactly this … or that … all this or that … mold me as you wish … and I will still be me … I will be this … or that … don't bother any more trying to guess me … I will give you a hint … try to imagine my words as my skin … my skin reveals me and hides me … the fault-lines in my skin … my wrinkles … are the ruptures … the gaps of my life … follow them as you read the words … my words … they reveal me and hide me … they breathe … live … die … hold me … protect me … they are me … a part of me … so take my words and shape me … shape my feet … my hands … my back … my neck … my head … my belly … my words are my skin … they stretch … they bend … they shrink … see me as you would see my skin … as you would see me through my skin … now … you can even touch me … feel me … understand me … you come close … not too much … careful … otherwise you will overrun me … absorb me … soak me … occupy me … we must keep a distance … we must remain strangers … something like close strangers … related strangers … because we always are … aren't we? … now … I should stop talking now … I should close my eyes … and try to imagine you … try to imagine how you look … sit … read … better pause for a while and give me and you … give us … the possibility to breathe … to think … to feel … to sense …

…

… "other people's memories gave us a place in the world" (Ernaux, 2017, p. 27) … now, I would really like to hear you … talking … talking back to me … hear you share something … something from yourself … one of your ideas … you could give me some advice … a hint … you could suggest how to continue … I wouldn't be alone with my thoughts … my feelings … my words … I need you … you could stop me … yes … but … since I've started … words are coming … it's so very difficult to stop this … this "stream of words" (Beckett, 2012b, p. 524) …

of my words? … really? … my words? … since when my words are my words? … since when language is my language? … since when your words are your words? … do I own language? … do I own words? … does someone own language … body … life? … "all we have is our history, and it does not belong to us" (Ortega Y Gasset, in Ernaux, 2017, p. 5) … what an illusion to think you own … something … someone … what a comforting illusion … my words are your words too … your words are mine too … they have always been … words make us related strangers … and yet I write them … and you read them … and I read what I write thinking of you … desiring you … longing for you … oh … if … if I … "If I were like you. If you were like me" (Celan, 1972) … then no words would be needed … you could think my thoughts … feel my feelings … I could think your thoughts … feel your feelings … (you think you got me now … I am not talking about something symbiotic) … but can we bear to live without words? … what would we have without them? some? ten? seven? three? "two mouthsfull of silence?" (ibid).

… right! … now… how would it be if I could stop being me for a while? … stop being myself … not me …, not I … and be you … stop seeing things from mywhere and have a view from yourwhere … if I could be the air … a cloud … a tree … the world … an animal … a book … music … the light … my father … my mother … my lover … nothing … everything … every one … have a view from everywhere … not just my view, my first person view … that keeps me trapped in my self-righteousness … in the limits of my myness …

… "[w]hen the child was a child, It was the time for these questions: why am I me, and why not you?" (Handke, 1986) … but how … how could that be possible? … to be you while still be my body? … can I be not body? … can I borrow yours? … can you borrow mine? … would that help? … would that decrease loneliness? … would that sublate alienation? … who knows? … you see? … talking about talking … talking about language … words … me … you … I slipped and landed on the body … how could it be otherwise … since language … talking … writing … is bodily … a bodily event … not the other way around … body is not a language event … as some would say … do say … language is a bodily event … because language needs a body … a body does not need language necessarily … body is already language … a language … its own language … body … bodies create languages if they feel they need to …

… did I start talking about the body? … oh, God … I must … be careful now … very careful … not to land into a metaphysics of bodyness … into an ontology of the body … even though … would that be terrible? … maybe not … if an ontology of body is the same as an actuality … of body … but who cares really anyway? … since *a* body is always *the* body … *this* body (Agamben, 1999, p. 224) … since body is always situated … historicized … always (many other) bodies … since my body interacts … interconnects … intertwines … with other bodies all the times … in every now … my body interacts and communicates with your body … just right now … at this very moment … we are irreversibly entangled … tiny little body atoms in the universe … regardless of the distancing between us … "why am I here, and why not there?" (Handke, 1986) …

… imagine … body … as some other 'things' … like atmosphere … life … death … is not … body happens … manifests … materializes … actualizes itself by creating space and time constantly in the process of its becoming … (wow!) … that's it … it lives … body happens … only now … in the presence … a kind of timeless present … but it carries the past in it … on it … reveals it, but doesn't live it … it anticipates the future … predicts it … but it exists only now … timeless present … (what a phrase again!) … there is a clock on the opposite wall … that used to show time … but now since a couple of days ago it is broken, because of an earthquake … it fell down and broke … time stopped … clock hands don't move anymore … they show only one time … that time … if I only could seize time and … if only could time stand still … for a while! … if not forever … no, that would be too greedy … if a minute could last some hours … timeless present … then in the grammar of my existence there could be some space "to have a break, to rest: to cease and go with time, to be in the flow of time, to tarry with, to dwell on moments of time" (Stephenson & Papadopoulos 2006, p. 32).

… drifted away again … sorry … you must be of good will … otherwise you'll get irritated … confused … even upset … "I do appreciate your goodness I know what an effort it costs you" (Beckett, 2012b, p. 224) … appreciate your patience … your understanding … need a second or two … now …

… oh, yes … talking about the body … about the time … and space … of the body again … and again … body? … what body? … my body … my? … really? … how do I become body? … when? … how? … "it is only by slow degrees that from these formless, anonymous bodies their own bodies emerge" (Duras, 1961, p. 8) … when and how did my body emerge? … when and how does my body emerge every day? … through pain? … through you? … does the sense of my body reflect the way it is perceived by others? …

… the body … a field of forces … of energies … matter … but … although the body is thrown in language … although "[l]anguage has been granted too much power" (Barad, 2003, p. 801) … and although "it seems that … lately every 'thing' – even materiality – is turned into a matter of language or some other form of cultural representation" (ibid, p. 801) … language can never fully explain … describe the materiality of the body … the bodyness of the body … "the nature we are ourselves" (Böhme, 2017, p. 307) … body precedes always … body is matter … and map too … you can read my body and have a sense of my history … of my life … (my) body is (my) life … almost all my life experiences … sufferings … traumata are written in and on my body … cells … organs … every living body has wrinkles … wounds … injuries … stitches … there is a scar … visible or invisible … on and in my body for every yes and every no I have said in my life … my body is … has become the map of my life … on my face you can see my shame … on my head resides anxiety … in my heart is stress … on my back fear … anger dwells in my throat … on my skin guilt … sadness on my chest … my eyes express a persistent question … a continuing question … is it true? … that "my only contribution to the whirlpool of the world is my steady breath?" (Anghelaki-Rooke, 2011) …

… body is powerful … because of its materiality … fragile and vulnerable too … body lives … can be sick … feel pain … existence cannot be sick … Dasein cannot be sick ... Dasein "is never hungry" (Levinas, 1979, p. 134) ... or thirsty ... or ... Dasein doesn't breathe (Irigaray, 1999) ... being cannot be sick ... although ... I can be sick from ... I can suffer ... from my own being (Holzey-Kunz, 2014) ... on the contrary ... body can be sick ... have fever ... disease ... and ... so ... my body ... hurts ... feels pain ... back pain ... weak ... I am weak ... what weight do I carry? ... what obstacle holds me back? ... what force pulls me down? ... the past? ... maybe ... it is nostalgia (Cassin, 2016) ... this unbearable seducing and captivating feeling of nostalgia ... this pain, this suffering (*algos*) caused by the impossible and unsatisfied ... unfulfilled ... desire ... of coming back (*nostos*) ... as in Andrei Tarkovski's (1983) film *Nostalgia?* ... it is nostalgia ... and memory ... this powerful archivist/librarian ... who very thoroughly curates the remnants of the past ... is the color of memory black-and-white ... as in Alfonso Cuarón's (2018) *Roma?* ...

... uninvited a memory comes and goes ... unintentionally ... as the wind ... soft ... cool ... moderate ... other times strong ... hot ... harsh ... so strong ... so hot ... so harsh ... it burns your skin ... my skin ... deeply ... it almost kills you ... kills me ... have such dangerous ... painful memories ... and you? ...

... "and finally the lark had a solution. She decided to bury her father in the back of her own head. And this was the beginning of memory. Because before this no one could remember a thing" (Anderson, 2010) ... has the body memory? ... memory? ... when does my memory begin? ... does my memory begin with a death? ... no, not death ... loss ... a loss of a part of myself ... when I was three ... and when I was five ... six ... ten ... "when the child was a child, it awoke once in a strange bed" (Handke, 1986) ... seventeen ... twenty seven ... and ... and ... not a loss, losses ... not a part ... parts of myself ... each time I was losing a part of myself ... my memory was getting bigger ... larger ... older ... losing me is remembering me ... grieving ... suffering ... being in pain ... does pain constitute memory? ... does pain have memory? ... does memory have pain? ... "like you, I have memory. I know what it is to forget ... Why deny the obvious necessity for memory?" (Duras, 1961, p. 23) ...

... pain ... pains ... pain eliminates ... eradicates ... everything ... almost everything ... thoughts ... language ... feelings ... senses ... self ... world ... who am I when I am in pain? ... where am I then? ... I am in my body ... I am my body ... only (my) body ... absolutely ... entirely ... completely ... become body ... body suffering ... this immediacy of my body-in-pain ... the presence of pain ... the presence of my body ... pain is (only) now ... pain is experienced by my body now ... here ... pain is absolute presence ... absolute actuality of the body ... pain that has been ... is not actual pain ... is not real pain (any more) ... and pain that will be ... is not real pain yet ... the memory of pain or the anticipation of pain ... the had-been-pain and the will-be-pain ... are not ...

... and now this! ... in pain ... the ontic and the ontological cross ... collide ... run into each other ... become one ... my concrete, immediate pain encounters my ontological background ... or ... my ontological background encounters my concrete, immediate pain ... the same applies ... to ... the body ... body is ontic ... and ontological ... at the same time ... body ... my body ... every body ... it knows no difference … accepts no difference … bears no difference … between the ontic and the ontological … does not need no concepts to live … (… must better be cautious now … my language style can easily become rigid … wooden … I really do not need to be so dramatic …) … body is singular … always … but body is plural too … always … body is never alone … (as I said before …) … body is bodies … body is life …

… now … my dear … write about life … not about being … not about essence … try to describe life … as if life were an object, (a) something that could be described … as if it were narratable (Cavarero, 2000) … and if yes … by whom? … no … no … there is a big difference between life … and the storytelling of that life … and this is something that should not … be forgotten … one should not ever confuse life … and the storytelling of that life … it would be dangerous … sometimes … although one feels often the desire … to tell their life … disclose it … close it in (nice) words … in metaphors … in allegories … because … telling is remembering … struggling against forgetting … an attempt to keep the past … and justify the future … or justify the past … understand … find meaning … afterwards always … retrospectively … to give an account of oneself (Butler, 2005) … although … although …

… "to know nothing about [myself] is to live? … to know [myself] badly is to think?" (Pessoa, 2002, p. 153) … i.e., there is a difference … between knowing (myself) and thinking and living my life … if so … what is … knowing … thinking … living … anyway? … do I live when I do not know myself? … when I do not bother with my insignificances? … when I am not myself … when I forget me … forget … that I am … when I forget … my Dasein … my existence … I live when I just live … let life be … allow life to happen … in me … in everyone … in everything … there … is the center of gravity of my life … in this letting go … in this releasement (Heidegger, 2010, p. 70) … this carefreeness (Levinas, 1979, p 134) … this openness to the possible … to the contingent … to the many "roads of life" (Dinesen, 1992, p. 229) …

> … a man, who lived by a pond, was awakened one night by a great noise. He went out into the night and headed to the pond, but in the darkness, running up and down, back and forth, guided only by the noise, he stumbled and fell repeatedly. At last, he found a leak in the dike, from which water and fish were escaping. He set to work plugging the leak and only when he had finished went back to bed. The next morning, looking out of the window, he saw with surprise that his footprints had traced the figure of a stork on the ground.
>
> (Cavarero, 2000, p. 1)

… and what shall I see … what shall other people see … when the design of my life is complete? … life experienced and life lived … what figure will have traced my footprints on the ground? … oh! … it is better to not know it … much better … otherwise I would bang my feet and fall … trying to walk rightly in order to draw the perfect design … which means … I would not really live then …

... live ... life ... life is the antidote ... the medicine to language ... or ... at least ... to too much languaging ... life is action ... touch ... acting ... touching ... life finds me ... as everything else ... love ... happiness ... sorrow ... the air ... beauty ... sickness ... the blue sky ... rain ... nothingness ... helplessness ... God ... doubt ... my body ... world ... a thought ... you ... oh, life ... "God knows how I adore life" (Gibbons & Man, 2002) ... if I could only write an ode to life ... not an ontology of life ... no ... (ontology ... what a pretentious word) ... always leading to mistakes ... to errors ... to dead ends ... an ode-elegy to life that would be proper to life ... what a fallacy actually to believe that life can be measured ... researched ... objectified ... reified ... without consequences ...

... oh, if I could only write about life ... my life ... this is my most favorite life ... the only one I have ... and (my) life happens now ... as I write ... as you read ... as I read ... my life happens writing ... and reading ... (my) life happens every day ... in every breath I take ... every minute ... in every move ... do I live an authentic life? ... do I act ... ethically? ... do I make ... the right choices? ... haven't authenticity ... uniqueness ... singularity ... become advertising brands? ... an imperative accessory? ... (my) life is more than that ... more than ... authentic moments ... and ... ethically right thoughts ... and actions ... more than ... right choices ... my life is my body ... my life is moves ... gestures ... affirmations ... negations ... errors ... mistakes ... sorrows ... regrets ... stumbling ... falling ... getting up ... stumbling ... falling ... getting up ... working ... breathing ...

... and you ... what about your life? ... what about the happy days of your life ... and the unhappy ones ... have you ever found yourself in happiness? ... in sadness? ... in guilt? ... in pain? ... trapped? ... free? ... in laugh? ... in careless calmness? ... "[t]o live is to play ... simply play or enjoyment of life. It is carefreeness with regard to existence" (Levinas, 1979, p. 134) ... so ... (do) laugh ... enjoy ... remember ... forget ... live ... despite ... because ... since ... due to ... against ... ~~despite~~ ... although ... precisely ... whereas ... even if ... albeit ... due to ... by virtue of ... for the sake of ...

... life is a gift ... has been said ... neither obligation ... nor duty ... debt ... contract ... promise ... even though sometimes it feels like ... even though sometimes it feels as if it were ... even though sometimes at some places it is not a mere gift ... but a burden ... "You were born. And so you're free" (Anderson, 1982) ... born ... "out ... into this world ... this world" (Beckett, 2012b, p. 556) ... trying to find the place and the time where (my) life crosses with (my) being ... so ... when I was a child I often wished ... I could be like a feather ... wished I could fly ... live ... in these ever changing ... ever moving clouds ... escape the earthy living ... live in ether like ... never mind ... oh, I love clouds ... clouds are the best metaphor for my life ... for life ... maybe even better than waves ... love the shape of clouds ... their color ... texture ... taste ... "the sky, heart-grey, must be near" (Celan, 1972) ...

... well ... "to be born" (Irigaray, 2017) ... and free ... free to enjoy my natality ... my aliveness ... but ... how ... how can I actually honor life? ... do I honor life while I live? ... the very fact of writing this, this text, is because of life ... not because of existence ... not because of being ... of Dasein ... but because of life

… because I owe to life … life … ontology cannot live … the ontic lives … when ontology lives it becomes ontic … ontology is not living … life needs no ontology … is not anthropocentric … and not implicitly hierarchical … life happens … all the time … do I need a thread through life? … instructions? … no … it can't be an ontology of life … that would be an ideo-onto-logy again … yes … life precedes … exceeds everything … because everything is an event of life … everything reveals life … everything is a revelation of life … of the living process … even language … art … literature … science … nature … culture … theory …. being … existence … Dasein … existentialism … existential psychotherapy … me … you … us …

… life … "the totality of those functions which resist death" (Bichat, 1809, p. 1) … life is immanence … "absolute immanence" (Agamben, 1999, p. 220ff) … first life … then everything else … you should not think now that I suffer … from self-deception … that I pretend to know what language … body … life is … who? … me? … no! not I … not I … I only know that everything is always more … more than that … that can be said about it … but … talking about … let's say … life … it gives me some times the soothing illusion … that I do know … and it is ok … I need this illusion … like a game …a hide-and-seek-game with me … with you … with death … with God …

… coming to the end … I realize … I talked about so many things … language … body … memory … pain … life … all these things that seem (to be) very existential … but do I have anything to say about love? … really? … seriously? … not a paragraph? … not even a sentence? … a small phrase? … I could … I would … I even should … but now it is too late … is it ever late for love? … to love? … "and the moments that I enjoy … a place of love and mystery … I'll be there anytime" (Gibbons & Man, 2002) … to love … to live … "love is real enough; … but it has one arch-enemy – and that is life" (Anouilh, 1951, p. 10) … that's not true … at least not true all the time … since … a very small difference … between 'live' and 'love' … it is only one letter … so that … these two words … can easily replace … enlighten … inform … reflect … mirror … complete … cross … imply … form … transform each other … in an endless spiral … live/love is what makes a human … being … and what makes every being … human … one should write therefore a life's discourse as once "a lover's discourse" (Barthes, 1979) has been written …

… well … then … why is there existential therapy anyway? … for what? … what exactly does existential therapy cure? … existence? … Being? … is existence … is being … treatable? … curable? … do they need therapy? … and what about life? … "life that does not consist only in its confrontation with death?" (Agamben, 1999, p. 238) … does life need therapy? … is life to be cured? … from what? … or is life itself a disease? … an error? … is there a sickness into life? … for life? … can someone get sick from life? … from too much life? … oh, yes … sometimes … some do not suffer from "anorexia of existence" (Anghelaki-Rooke, 2011) … but from bulimia of life … yes … right … so … "existential therapy does not cure being … existence … life" (Van Deurzen et al, 2019, pp. 2–3) … but what? … me? … me that I'm … exist … live … and suffer from my being … from the fact that

I exist and live? … yes … but … has existential therapy … existential philosophy … existentialism …

> Fortunately, it is not the existence of humans but existentialism as a doctrine that represents one of the lowest points in the abandonment by philosophy of the world as it is known to science and experienced by living creatures. But, of course, there is no way to abandon existentialism …
>
> (Latour, 2005, p. 7)

… ever thought about its ideology? … its constitutive conditions? … its very own pre-ontological inclusion? … its conditions of emergence … "of appearance and regularity? … its conditions of possibility?" (Foucault, 1981, p. 67) … what does existential therapy exclude in order to be? … what is the invisible … unseen site of existential therapy as phenomenon? …

3

… no … no … not philosophy … not all these big fat philosophical names … this physical … metaphysical … modern … postmodern … pre- and post- whatever philosophy … not philosophy … no … not philosophy … if there should be a foundation of psychology/psychotherapy outside of psychology/psychotherapy … and it should be … then … this very foundation is art and especially literature … that's it … literature is the true foundation … for existential psychology/therapy … for every psychology/therapy … or do you actually think literature is too weak? … too unsteady? … too subjective? … too fictional? … in order to count for reality? … and for the ontic facts of psychology? … or the heaviness of the ontological facts of existential psychology? … really? … do you really believe that is literature? … well … maybe … may be … but it may be too that literature is more … more … than an endless source for examples … mottos … or pieces of evidence for the ontological truths of existentialism … maybe literature is more … than a decorative ornament for scientific texts … because literature has an inexhaustible power … it actualizes itself in different times … in different forms … literature has already taken so many different forms … that it cannot be recognized as literature any more … mythology … theology … philosophy … sociology … anthropology … psychoanalysis … psychology … psychotherapy … all these discourses are but facets … unfoldings of literature … in the process of its own becoming … unfoldings … facets … rhizomes … actualized possibilities … explications of the intricate multiplicity of literature … whatever name is just another metaphor or metonymy … you think you can escape literature by being scientific? … by being objective? … strong? … not fictional? … by seeking evidence? … really? … well … science is literature too … a special kind of literature … literature has become in the western world many things … science is just one among them … science is transformed literature … just like psychology … and therapy … so … still … and again … if you … if I … if we … must talk … write … speak … think … about life … the most proper way to do it … is not psychology … not science … it is literature …

References

Agamben, G. (1999) *Potentialities: Collected Essays in Philosophy*. Stanford, California: Stanford University Press.

Anderson, L. (1982) 'Born, never asked' from the album *Big science*. Warner records.

Anderson, L. (2010) 'The beginning of memory' from the album *Homeland*. NonesuchRecords Inc.

Anghelaki-Rooke, K. (2011) *The Anorexia of Existence*. www.pwf.cz/archivy/texts/cafe-central/katerina-anghelaki-rooke-the-anorexia-of-existence_8608.html

Anouilh, J. (1951) *Ardele*. London: Methuen and Co. Ltd.

Barad, K. (2003) Posthumanist Performativity: Toward an Understanding of How Matter Comes to Matter. In: *Signs: Journal of Women in Culture and Society*, 28 (3), 801–31.

Barthes, R. (1979) *A Lover's Discourse*. London: Penguin Books.

Beckett, S. (1974) *Texts for Nothing*. London: Calder & Boyars.

Beckett, S. (2012a) *Happy Days*. In: *The Complete Dramatic Works*. London: Faber & Faber, ebook edition.

Beckett, S. (2012b) Not I. In: *The Complete Dramatic Works*. London: Faber & Faber, ebook edition.

Bichat, X. (1809) *Physiological Researches upon Life and Death*. Philadelphia: Smith and Maxwell.

Böhme, G. (2017). *The Aesthetics of Atmospheres* (edited by J. P. Thibaud). London and New York: Routledge, ebook edition.

Butler, J. (2005) *Giving an Account of Oneself*. New York: Fordham University Press.

Cassin, B. (2016) *Nostalgia: When Are We Ever at Home?* New York: Fordham University Press.

Cavarero, A. (2000) *Relating Narratives. Storytelling and Selfhood*. London and New York: Routledge.

Celan, P. (1972) *Paul Celan: Selected Poems*. Middlesex, England: Penguin Books.

Dinesen, I. (1992) *Out of Afrika*. New York: Random House, Inc.

Duras, M. (1961) *Hiroshima mon amour*. New York: Glove Press.

Ernaux, A. (2017) *The Years*. New York: Seven Stories Press, ebook edition.

Foucault, M. (1981) The order of discourse. In: Young R. (ed.) *Untying the Text. A Post-Structuralsit Reader*. Boston, London, Henley: Routledge and Kegan Paul, 51–78.

Gibbons, B. & Man, R. (2002) 'Mysteries' from the album *Out of season*. Go! Beat Records.

Handke, P. (1986) *Song of Childhood* www.babelmatrix.org/works/de/Handke%2C_Peter1942/Lied_Vom_Kindsein/en/42791-Song_of_Childhood

Heidegger, M. (2010) *Country Path Conversations*. Bloomington and Indianapolis: Indiana University Press.

Holzey-Kunz, A. (2014) *Daseinsanalysis*. London: Free Association Books.

Irigaray, L. (1999) *The Forgetting of Air in Martin Heidegger*. London: The Athlone Press.

Irigaray, L. (2017) *To Be Born: Genesis of a New Human Being*. Basingstoke: Palgrave Macmillan.

Kundera, M. (2000) *The Unbearable Lightness of Being*. London: Faber & Faber.

Latour, B. (2005) What is given in experience? www.bruno-latour.fr/sites/default/files/93-STENGERS-GB.pdf

Levinas, E. (1979) *Totality and Infinity*. The Hague: Martinus Nijhoff Publishers and Duquesne University Press.

Malebranche, N. (1997) *The Search after Truth*. Cambridge: Cambridge University Press.

Merleau-Ponty, M (2001) *The Incarnate Subject. Malebranche, Biran, and Bergson on the Union of Body and Soul*. Amherst, New York: Humanity Books.

Nostalgia (1983) directed by A. Tarkovski. Film.

Pessoa, F. (2002) *The Book of Disquiet*. London: Penguin Classics.

Roma (2018) directed by Alfonso Cuarón. Film.

Stephenson, N. & Papadopoulos, D. (2006) *Analysing Everyday Experience Social Research and Political Change*. Hampshire: Palgrave.

Van Deurzen, E., Craig, E., Längle, A. (2019) (eds) *The Wiley World Handbook of Existential Therapy*. New Jersey: John Wiley & Sons Ltd.

5 Where angels fear to tread

A lived experience of striptease

Gabriella Ricciardi Otty

Introduction

A woman in a twin set steps on the anonymous stage of a burlesque club. Her eyes are glued to the floor; the costume she was supposed to wear for her act has been lost in transport and, now, an air of despair hangs from her shoulders like a cape. And yet, as the bars of a deep, thumping blues spread across the hall, a startling piece of alchemy begins to unfold. With each note the woman's subdued walk morphs into a slow, self-assured stride. Long, muscular limbs snap into action as if responding to a drill: feet pointing, legs stretching, hips rising and falling, shoulders rolling back. For a split second she stands with her back to the audience, head in profile, hands on hips, jaw jutting out. A blonde curl quivers before her blue eyes softening the gaze she trails over the audience.

She is lodged in my memory at the centre of that stage, mistress of her world – a precious segment of time and space that erases everything that comes before or after; that she fills with consummate skill, physical stamina, and the unbridled sexual energy of her body. She is no more than a fantasy reflected in my eyes, but she leaves my body gasping for something I can't yet name – a different kind of air to the one I breathe every day – less pure, less proper, less strained and rarefied by intellectual and political dilemmas.

It's the late 1990s and, on a rainy night, I curl up on the sofa to watch *Liberty Heights*, a coming of age comedy that has received great critical acclaim. Having settled down to follow the story of a Jewish boy growing up in post-war, newly de-segregated Baltimore, the last thing I expect is to be plunged headlong into a movie where scenes from the boy's life are interspersed with long, sultry sequences of burlesque striptease acts.

After the initial surprise I am mesmerised, enthralled, electrified by the playfulness, the audacity, the sheer sexiness of the main act. And yet there is a part of me that feels almost bereft as I long not just to be able to do what the woman does, but to know what it might feel like to *be* her – to be so in control, so seemingly comfortable in one's skin, so able to harness and modulate one's sexual energy to tease and seduce another person or an audience. It is an emotion of such intensity, such urgency, I have to acknowledge it and, most importantly, act upon it.

Weeks later, having endured a bewildering mixture of curiosity, excitement and anxiety on my way to the dance studio, I attend my first class of striptease. A year later I make my debut on the London burlesque scene as Ms Liberty Heights, my stage name a homage to the film that has acted as a catalyst for one of the most enriching and transformative experiences of my life.

The body that points out and the body that speaks

Maurice Merleau-Ponty (1962) states:

> It has always been observed that speech or gesture transfigures the body, but no more was said on the subject than they develop and disclose another power, that of thought or soul. The fact was overlooked that, in order to express it, the body must in the last analysis become the thought or intention that it signifies for us. It is the body which points out and which speaks.
>
> (p. 225)

This chapter is an account of a very personal experience of this statement; of how my body spoke or, rather, asked stubborn questions, at a crucial juncture in my life; of how, over the course of twenty years, it has pointed the way and taken me on an unplanned adventure – my lived, embodied experience as a student, performer and observer of the art of striptease. It evokes something of the essence of this experience – the deeply intimate encounter with my body that continually transforms my relationship with it, with the world and others. It tells the story of a quest – to understand the place and significance of this encounter in my life; to explore, articulate and conceptualise it through the prism of existential philosophy. Above all, it is a personal and intimate portrayal of female embodiment, which I offer in the hope that the carnal specificity of my experience may be a testament to the need for an increased focus on the body and sexuality – the therapist's as well as the client's – if psychotherapy is to remain alive and relevant as a tool to explore and understand human existence.

What would it feel like to be her, to be so in control, so seemingly comfortable in one's skin?

The words travelled from my guts to my brain like a swirling mass of yearning, breaking through the last barrier of judgement and drowning the elation that had originally filled me. This was not my reality. Or, rather, it was a reality I only ever experienced on a sporadic basis. My body was rarely my temple. More often than not, it felt like a war zone – a battlefield where belligerent inner forces would try to wipe each other out. For as long as I could remember, the obsessive concern with the states and moods of my body had been a feature of my life. As a child I was aware of them long before I discovered other aspects of myself. It was through my body, through varied and often bewildering physical manifestations, that I felt, expressed, and somehow processed the unformed thoughts and unspoken emotions that filled my childhood existence. As I grew up, new and equally bewildering bodily metamorphoses punctuated my transition into puberty. And as an adult – the adult that now sat transfixed on the sofa – it was in my body that I felt the touch, the scratch, the caress and the blow of each emotion that coloured my life vicissitudes.

My body occupied me relentlessly, it had the power to oppress me and, for many years, I perceived it as the force that hampered my realisation and held me back from my projects. And yet, even as child, as I saw my bodily manifestations pathologised as 'psychosomatic behaviour', I sensed the danger of a label that while consistently failing to grasp, let alone resolve, the most problematic aspects of my body, flatly denied the vibrancy and vitality of others.

Merleau-Ponty asserts that 'It is through my body that I understand other people, just as it is through my body that I perceive things' (Merleau-Ponty, 1962, p. 216). He also states: 'I am all that I see, I am an intersubjective field, not despite my body and my historical situation, but, on the contrary, by being this body and this situation, and through them, all the rest' (Merleau-Ponty, 1962, p. 525).

When I first discovered Merleau-Ponty's notion of embodied consciousness I felt I had found the antidote to an approach – traditional psychotherapy – that remained fundamentally committed to a theoretical and philosophical – rather than embodied – understanding of human experience; an approach which, I felt, turned psychotherapists into oddly disembodied creatures who, just like angels – immaterial beings and dwellers of the heavens – remained intrinsically engaged in a lofty pursuit largely unconnected with the bodily vicissitudes of human existence. There was something profound in the notion of a consciousness that was in and of this world, constantly moving towards it in response to a call; that expressed intentionality through its capacity for action – a dynamic *I can* as opposed to the static *I think* of the Cartesian cogito – a consciousness that was ready to touch the world, to dirty its hands, in order to grasp and mould it even as the world grasped and moulded it in turn. There was something satisfying in the notion of a sexed, situated, historical and acculturated body (Merleau-Ponty, 1962), if it meant that angels would be forced into the place where they feared to tread, forced to touch the coarse texture of human life and delve into the crevices of human fears, needs and desires.

And, yet, since the night when my consciousness was aroused by the 'call' of striptease – by the possibility of a different way of experiencing and expressing sexuality – and every time I have subsequently explored the different facets of my encounter with this art, my situatedness has oppressed and confused me.

What would it feel like to be able to harness and modulate one's sexual energy to tease and seduce another person or an audience?

The question haunted me. It filled me with a restless energy. It gave way to misgivings that refused to be quelled. My curiosity exposed a troublesome fact of my life. It forced me to take stock of a decision, or rather an omission – a decision to not do or express something – that was both personal and collective, that defined me as a certain kind of woman and sealed my place in the socio-economic group I belonged to. I wasn't wondering about a restrained, between-the-lines sexuality, the kind of sexuality that comes as an ancillary attribute of middle-class, educated femininity. What aroused and unsettled me was something brazen and explicit, an unashamed display of sexuality; it was a statement of intention – I will tease and seduce you – that pitted me against a myriad personal and cultural beliefs about the person I should be and the kind of sexuality I might be able to express. It opened my eyes to the acts of mortification, self-denial and repudiation that continued to turn so many women, across so many generations, into ghosts rather than sexual beings; bodies moulded from the outside rather than created from the inside; acts that condemned to invisibility – sometimes to nothingness – the most vital, vibrant and carnal core of female beings.

The mutinous body

Twenty years ago, even as my body swelled with elation and curiosity, its message remained tenuous and confused, my bodily perception overwhelmed by pressures and terrors that were as powerful and real as the dark longings that stirred inside me. Years later, these feelings come back to haunt me when, as I tackle an irksome literary review for my dissertation on the topic of striptease, I come across *Throwing like a Girl* by Iris Marion Young (2005).

In this unsettling essay, first published in 1980, Young (2005) draws on Merleau-Ponty's (1962) *Phenomenology of Perception* to paint a picture of feminine bodily existence as '*ambiguous transcendence*', '*inhibited intentionality*' and '*discontinuous unity with its surroundings*' (Young, 2005, p. 35, emphasis in the original). The source of these modalities lies in 'a woman's experience of her body as a *thing* at the same time that she experiences it as a capacity' (Young, 2005, p. 35), a split that Young sees as the product of 'the particular *situation* of women as conditioned by their sexist oppression in contemporary society' (Young, 2005, p. 42,). Thus, her conclusion hits me, 'by repressing or withholding its own motile energy' [intentionality] 'feminine bodily existence frequently projects an "I can" and an "I cannot" with respect to the very same end' (Young, 2005, p. 37).

This portrayal of female subjectivity builds a lump of sadness in my throat. I see the female body forged by the demands, injustices and inequalities of patriarchal culture; I recognise my own body – the war zone, the battlefield, the source of impenetrable ailments, so often misunderstood and pathologised. But I also detect the split subjectivity of a modern woman forced to deal with a new set of archetypes. I may no longer need to be a 'virgin', but I am, or should be, a feminist – an image which comes in many guises and carries its own set of intellectual, emotional, sexual dilemmas, and a different – but not less insidious – kind of shame.

Abandoning myself to the pleasure of unveiling my body exposes me. I feel that words and actions that question the norms imposed on modern women carry a price – I may not become a 'whore', but perhaps something worse: a renegade,

complicit with a system that seeks to objectify and control me. I sense the predicament of an angel caught at the crossroad between goodness and transgression,
prudence and recklessness, propriety and impropriety. I realise the angel is me
and I am dismayed to find so much tension, so much ambivalence entrenched
inside me despite my belief, and the abundant bodily evidence which supports
it, that my encounter with striptease, far from diminishing me, has enriched and
transformed me.

Throwing Like a Girl is clearly the product of the anti-objectification militancy
that cemented feminist discourse between the mid-1970s and the 1980s, but the
rest of Young's work, as well as her emphasis on the need for a phenomenological
approach, is, in fact, the result of her own search for a model that might rescue
the *lived*, carnal body of feminine experience from the invisibility to which both
Western thought and gendered feminist discourse have confined it.

My heart lifts. Young sees her approach as honouring the meaning of 'situation' or 'situatedness' of existential theory, that is, the 'produce of *facticity* and
freedom' (Young, 2005, p. 16), a notion that Toril Moi (2001) in her essay *What is a
Woman?* expands by stating that 'to claim that the body is a situation is to acknowledge that the meaning of a woman's body is bound up with the way she uses her
freedom' (Moi, 2001, p. 65).

The tension and ambivalence I sense inside me express the implications of
this fact. In the *Happy Stripper*, Jackie Wilson (2008) articulates for me the significance of this statement in relation to my body. Burlesque, she argues, is firmly at
the centre of what 'is and has been the most vibrant, ambivalent, and provoca-
tively divisive debate in feminist discourse – the female body, its representation and
pleasure' (Wilson, 2008, p. 11). Burlesque, she believes, acts as the point of intersection that binds together 'kicking and screaming' with dissonant views of this
movement 'in the dangerously pleasurable "low" "Nude Woman"' (Wilson, 2008,
p. 11). I am the 'low' 'Nude 'Woman'. I am the mutinous, exuberant body that
gasps for a different kind of air; I am the woman who uses her freedom to push
through social, cultural and intellectual dilemmas, discarding age, physical shape
and class, to alter the situation and meaning of her body; to unveil something that
might feel closer to the truth.

The fragility of mind–body integration

'Integration is never absolute and always fails', Merleau-Ponty states (Merleau-
Ponty, 1983, in Toadvine, 2016, p. 9), which, in turn, makes the dualism of mind
and body not just a 'simple fact' but 'founded in principle – all integration presupposing the normal functioning of subordinated formations, which always demand
their own due' (Merleau-Ponty, 1983, in Toadvine, 2016, p. 9).

This discovery moves me more deeply than I can ever express, left, as I am,
suspended between a sense of relief and one of startled loss. The sense of inad-
equacy and inauthenticity that has pursued me throughout this quest – for
succumbing to doubt, ambivalence and fear – is dispelled by the newly found
awareness of the *fragility* of the synthesis that my mind and body must continually

attempt at the moment of perception. My restless body is the lower, subordinated formation clamouring at the gates of my intellect and I become acutely aware of the extent to which, in the process of reflecting on my experience, often through the prism of other authors' views, I have entirely lost touch with the lived embodied encounter at its core.

At the same time, a spell has been broken. The belief I have held so far in the primacy of my bodily perception has been countered by the *reality* of perceptual consciousness, that is, by the paradox of an embodied consciousness that forgets its debt to lower formations in the creation of meaning and the plight of a body that finds itself becoming redundant even as it moves towards the world and others (Merleau-Ponty, 1962; Leder, 1990).

As I absorb this truth, my search for my body intensifies. It is almost as though my newly found awareness of a 'glitch' in my capacity for bodily perception has sharpened my resolve to give my body new opportunities to re-enter this process and, myself, the chance to truly listen to its communications, however tenuous and confused they may be. And this is when I grasp, almost with a sense of averted catastrophe, that striptease may have provided me with just that opportunity – to give back its voice to my body, so that it may sing its beautiful and unique song, however unsettling it might be.

Teasestrip

As the hot, heavy bars of a blues surge around me, I listen for my body's sounds: the slow intake of breath that lets the music in, the murmurs and whispers that carry instructions to my limbs: feet pointing, legs stretching, hips rising and falling, shoulders rolling back. As the music moves inside me, I feel the pounding beat in my gut, like a thick, throbbing magma of lust. I feel the heat against the walls of my body, as though a hand were caressing them from the inside. The thick, aching chords of a saxophone leave trails of longings inside me; I am this longing and this longing is me. I let it shape the rhythmic rotations of my hips, I let it ripple through my hair, I let my hands drape it over my body, smoothing its rough texture into the silky softness of my dress.

There is method in striptease. In this method one discerns the purpose and guiding principles of this art, that is, to take normally an audience – the 'other' – but, in fact, oneself first, on a gradual journey of discovery and eventually revelation. The 'tease' element of striptease – the dancing, the gaze, the wink, the smile – is designed to engage, maintain and increase the other's conscious attention to one's body (thus, a more accurate term would be 'teasestrip'). Furthermore, each time I 'present' a part of my body to my audience – which I do by directing my own gaze to it – I am also directing the other's gaze to the particular part I intend to reveal. In this respect, at a practical level, the 'tease' is a way of binding my own and the other's consciousness to my body; at a deeper level, though, it is a way of fully inhabiting the ambiguity of my body (Merleau-Ponty, 1962), the essence of my condition as a transcendence rooted in immanence and, thus, always suspended in the tension between nature and culture, specificity and generality, visibility and invisibility (Merleau-Ponty, 1962). And, yet, it is also a way to resolve or, at the very least, *suspend*, this ambiguity, even if only for a few moments, by performing something akin to the 'fundamental philosophical act' – 'the return to the lived world beneath the objective world' (Merleau-Ponty, 1962, p. 57) – which, alone, can reinstate bodily perception and bodily expression to its fullest and richest form. As I remove each item of clothing, I am symbolically, but also quite literally, teasing out something that is intrinsic to my body from under layers of familial, social and cultural sedimentations – the primordial erotic power of my body.

As I return to my body, I relish the joy of self-discovery and self-celebration. In this body I do not fear the gaze of the other, I invite it, I actively seek it as a vital component of an intimate process of self-exploration. Furthermore, in so far as self-exploration constitutes a form of narcissism, I rewrite the gaze as the fundamental element of what Merleau-Ponty (1968) describes as 'the … most profound sense of … narcissism' – a proposition that is as terrifying as it is intoxicating: 'to be seen from the outside, to exist within it, to emigrate into it, to be seduced, captivated … so that the seer and the visible reciprocate one another and we no longer know which sees and which is seen' (Merleau-Ponty, 1968, p. 139). At its most erotic, striptease becomes for me a life-enhancing, bodily experience of the intertwining – the *chiasm* (Merleau-Ponty, 1968, p. 130) – that merges me into the world and others.

Finally, in so far as striptease allows me to perform a 'fundamental philosophical act' (Merleau-Ponty, 1962, p. 57), it alters my deportment – the way I relate and, quite literally, move towards the world and others. In a striptease act there can be no shame, uncertainty or ambivalence. My walk, sensuous and deliberate, my very stillness as I pose to let myself be admired, provide a vivid counterpoint to the strained female embodiment painted by Young (2005). In my walk, the tension between 'I can' and 'I cannot' that inhibits feminine intentionality (Young, 2005, p. 36) is resolved in a definitive, unapologetic 'I can' (Merleau-Ponty, 1962, pp. 137, 148).

Inhabiting the body of love

It is 'not so much whether human life does or does not rest on sexuality', Merleau-Ponty (1962) observes, 'as to what it is to be understood by sexuality' (Merleau-Ponty, 1962, p. 158). When I return to my body my sexuality surprises me as a form of original intentionality – an exquisite moment of self-consciousness which reveals my embodied presence to the world and, above all, to myself (Merleau-Ponty, 1962). In this body, longing and loss transmute into lust. In this body I find the language to pose 'the mute and permanent question' (Merleau-Ponty, 1962, p. 156) that discloses my attitude towards being with others.

'*The mute and permanent question*', that lingers '*like an atmosphere*', that '*spreads forth like an odour or like a sound*' (Merleau-Ponty, 1962, p. 168, my emphasis). Merleau-Ponty's words brush against my skin soft and fluid like silk, their texture a testament to the richness of a language that seeks to evoke, rather than define and seal meaning; a language expansive enough to accommodate the pleasures and pangs of ambiguity.

I have asked the mute and permanent question many times: as a child, curled in my mother's arms, seeking and receiving her warm embraces; I have asked it and felt a response in the tip of my mother's fingernails on my skin, as she traces 'curlicues' – round interlacing shapes – over my bare back. I listen to the answers as they reach me from the folds of my memory – a soothing mixture of sounds, glances and smells that softens my body. *What's it like to make love?* I ask her one day. 'It's like when I draw curlicues on your back', she replies, 'something that gives you pleasure'. A question answered, a simple embodied connection established for me when I am young and inquisitive but unaware of the significance of my mother's words; my mother's gift to me, so that unlike her, who has had to overcome the restrictions and judgements of a lifetime, I will not spend the rest of my own life trying to work out that connection for myself; or trying to extricate my capacity for sexual pleasure from shame or the prerequisite of love.

I sense this question as I hold my daughters in my arms at the edge of the sea, all of us lost in separate and yet intertwined reveries; in my fingers that trace the shape of their tiny limbs, in my lips that meet their foreheads in small continuous kisses while their bodies become heavier against mine and I know that images and dreams will form in their minds as they drift away from me. I hear the sound of the waves, I let the pungent smell of salt bring back memories from the depths of my body and, as I too drift into sleep, my eyes linger on a shape in a bikini that moves gracefully away from me towards a shimmering blue sea in my past. Then like now, on this beach with my daughters in my arms, the warmth of my mother's body hangs inside me and in the air around me.

I feel the atmosphere in an image that lingers in my mind: my striptease teacher Anna with her back to the audience, a hand gracefully lifted to her side, the other trailing up her spine snapping open her corset one hook at a time. I am struck by just how slowly she seems to move, how unhurried her hand seems to be as it works its way up her spine, how Anna seems to relish and expand the stillness of each pose she strikes. 'The things have us … it is not we who have the things' (Merleau-Ponty, 1968, p. 194). I feel a summons, a call emanating from Anna's body that brings me back to my own body. Her seemingly unhurried movements, her capacity for stillness express an embodied presence of such intensity that it requires – demands – an equal response from the audience. Anna is teasing our senses and in the process she is teasing a carnal, primordial core out of our dis-embodied – absent – selves. She makes us sit up, so that we may feel the depth, weight and texture of our own bodies, so that we may fully inhabit, just as she is doing on stage, the space in which we exist. Eros – the creation of a sexual atmosphere – Anna's offering to her audience and my beautiful discovery on this momentous night; there is no point in unveiling my body unless I too can offer this gift.

X-rated. The strip: the flow and gift of pleasure

I let the scent of my memories transport me to another stage.

I am standing at the centre of a warm light, my back is slightly arched and the pinch in my spine gives a carnal consistency to this moment. I have removed the top half of my dress and I am turning away from the audience to remove the rest. My hips sway, caressed and guided by my hands; it is called a step turn and I lengthen and expand the rotation of my hips dancing over the beat. My pleasure flows from me to the audience and comes back to me in their intensified gaze. I lift the hem of my dress imperceptibly to brush the bare skin of my legs and tease them with a glimpse of fuchsia lace, then I turn my head slightly to meet their gaze.

This is my gift to my audience – the swaying of my hips, the peak of fuchsia lace under the hem of my dress – a visual feast, a fantasy that emanates from a carnal being's capacity for lust and pleasure. Eros – beauty and pleasure that stem from and are continually enriched in my connection with the other and their connection with me.

As I turn, the air moves slowly with me and I find myself standing in another room, another city, another scented time of my life.

I have just moved to the window and closed my 'act' by letting my body ease into a pose. The damp, quivering stillness of this moment steadies my breath; behind me, my husband is sitting in semi-darkness and he, too, is savouring the stillness of this moment. The pose is meant for him to take me in and, with me, the rough, stark elegance of the city's skyline. I meet my eyes through the glass and through my eyes I see the lights that twinkle in the distance. I stand inside the frame of the window, my naked body silhouetted against the velvety blue sky. I am a fantasy, a dream, but my body trembles at the sight of such beauty. My husband's gaze caresses my skin; New York whispers and pulls me into her.

Conclusion

As I retrace the rugged perimeter of my encounter with striptease, the question I find myself pondering (not dissimilarly from the question that is often asked of phenomenology) is not so much what *I* have done with striptease, but what striptease has done with *me*.

In this respect, this chapter also tells the story of a startling realisation: perhaps my quest for understanding has not so much yielded profound philosophical insights into an embodied experience, as a true (or truer) bodily understanding of philosophical tenets – a carnal route to the alluring but elusive notion of embodied consciousness. At the end of this route, I have found this notion stripped bare – stripped of the romantic belief in the primacy of my bodily perception that underpinned it and, yet, infinitely more tangible because it has the weight and substance of my body.

In so far as striptease has allowed a return to my body, it has also showed me the difficulty of holding on to it, and, ultimately, the impossibility of ever fully inhabiting the ontological and epistemological position proposed by Merleau-Ponty (1962) or to fully accomplish the fundamental philosophical act (Merleau-Ponty, 1962). And yet, even as it has forced me to reckon with the imperfect, incomplete nature of bodily perception, it has alerted me to the dangers of dismissing it, because it would mean condemning almost certainly the most vital and vibrant part of my body – of any body – to invisibility. It would mean depriving it of the opportunity to unveil its own truth, however perspectival and incomplete that truth may be, while simultaneously denying it the endless possibilities of expression that might be available to it. It would mean – a prospect that makes me pause both as an individual and especially as a psychotherapist – stripping that body of its autonomy, its experience of dignity, and the person who inhabits it, of her capacity to interpret herself.

The more I unveil my body, the more I realise how difficult it is to tease it out of its concealment; and so, guarding, as Merleau-Ponty (1983) reminds us, against the fragility of the integration between mind and body, is akin to an act of discipline; something that requires patience, commitment and curiosity on a daily basis, moment by moment. It is ultimately, or at least it was for me, a choice I had to make between living in solitude as a dweller of the heavens, or venture into the place where angels fear to tread to dig inside – and play with – the maddening and beautiful ambiguity of my body.

References

Leder, D. (1990) *The absent body*. Chicago and London: The University of Chicago Press.

Merleau-Ponty, M. (1962) *Phenomenology of perception*. Trans. Smith, C., London: Routledge.

Merleau-Ponty, M. (1968) *The visible and the invisible (Followed by Working notes)*. Trans. Lingis, A., Evanston: Northwestern University Press.

Merleau-Ponty, M. (1983) *The structure of behavior*. Trans. Fisher, A., Pittsburgh: Duquesne University Press.

Moi, T. (2001) *What is a woman? And other essays*. New York: Oxford University Press.

Toadvine, T. (2016) "Maurice Merleau-Ponty", in E. N. Zalta (ed.) *The Stanford Encyclopedia of Philosophy* Available at: https://plato.stanford.edu/archives/win2016/entries/merleau-ponty/ (Accessed: 10 October 2017, then copied to Books, p. 9 of 28)

Wilson, J. (2008) *The happy stripper – pleasures and politics of the new burlesque*. London and New York: I.B. Tauris.

Young, I. M. (2005) *On female body experience: "Throwing like a girl" and other essays*. Oxford: Oxford University Press.

6 Existential therapy
Relational creative engagement in action

Diana Mitchell

Introduction

> It is through my body that I understand other people, just as it is through my body that I perceive 'things'. The meaning of a gesture thus 'understood' is not behind it; it is intermingled with the structure of the world outlined by the gesture, and which I take up on my own account.
>
> (Merleau-Ponty, 1962, p. 186)

In this chapter I will chart my process via my experience as a dancer to my therapy training days and beyond. I will show where I am now with my understanding of what existential therapy has become for me. I can't now think about therapy without thinking about how influential my training as a ballet dancer has been.

I see re-visioning existential therapy as a never-ending process. Where I am now is partly in response to my age and this culture of certainty and accountability that we now find ourselves in. Existential therapy has been accused of being too abstract; I hope to show through my account how it is rooted instead in every day experience.

I had lived many lives in different countries by the time I started training to work as an existential therapist – professional ballet dancer, West End wardrobe mistress, cleaning lady, photographic assistant, catering supervisor, waitress, shop-girl, receptionist and photo-shoot coordinator for Dorling Kindersley.

Uncertainty has at times been an adventure into the unknown, unexplored opportunities in my world and in myself. This seems to exist alongside my need for security, certainty and the sense of having some degree of control in my everyday life.

As a child I remember waking up every morning and thinking, 'I wonder what will happen today?' I hoped to be surprised by the unexpected. This was an expression of my optimism, the sense of being lucky to find myself in a safe and secure family set-up.

Embarking on therapy training at the age of 44 was a big step into the unknown. I was not at all sure if I would be suitable as a professional therapist. I decided to have a go knowing that I would gain from the experience regardless of the outcome. Those six years played an important part in challenging my assumptions and refreshing my understanding of myself in relation to others and to the situations I found and placed myself in.

My subsequent loss of hearing has highlighted something that I already knew as a therapist: we all share and recognise fear, anxiety, grief, loss, confusion, panic, distress, anger, frustration, pride, joy, excitement, doubt, shame and many more moods and emotional states that are all expressed through the body (Mitchell, 2018b).

The talking therapy must also always be about a connection that is experienced through and with our bodies and our whole way of being in the moment.

Ballet training and therapy training

From my existential perspective the term 'training' is so wrong in the context of existential therapy – a practice that is all about the unique, never to be fully understood relationship that emerges between the client and the therapist, a relationship that will never be repeated with another client, where the therapist taps into his or her sense of the other person in a personal way that also reveals who the therapist is to the client. Both client and therapist are often caught-up in that relationship and ideally both gain from the relationship.

As an ex ballet dancer, I know that training was crucial in order to master the technique required. But therapy in practice is completely different because there is no technique involved. For Alexander Badkhen (2019, p. 76), 'it is important to remember that the instrument in psychotherapy is not the approach nor the technique, but the psychotherapist himself'. Of course, there are skills that can come with a deeper understanding and a more heightened self-awareness of how we are and respond in different relationships, but neither client nor therapist can ever fully grasp or articulate what happens between them.

With ballet training the saying 'practice makes perfect' makes sense from a technical point of view, but that is only part of it. It is only when the dancer expresses his or her unique personal qualities in a natural way that she can connect to and with the audience as a human being. This is when the dancing becomes meaningful and at times moving. It's all about connection. Even if we replace the term practice and say 'experience makes perfect' in the practice of therapy, this is not necessarily so because we all select from and digest our experiences differently.

I see therapy as a creative process, creative because the therapist taps into his or her whole way of being in order to connect with the client. There can be no clear plan or strategy and yet there is a form of discipline; the therapist has a clear role in the relationship. Self-discipline makes sure that the therapist remembers his or her function within the relationship. It is only when the therapist steps away from worrying what the guidelines dictate that a spontaneous duet can emerge.

No dancing by numbers

My hunch is that there is far too much attention given to the negative and poten-tially problematic in psychotherapy training. The life experience and natural qualities that trainee therapists already have before their training begins is often overlooked. Even worse, therapy trainees bit by bit stop expressing what they are really thinking and who they are. I have witnessed that by the end of training, therapists talk and write to the tune of assessment guidelines.

Ballet training tends to focus on the dancer's weaknesses and yet it has now come to light that the best teachers and choreographers don't work that way. They understand that to get the most and the best from dancers means to hand that responsibility of being critical over to the dancer while the teacher is there to encourage and not to shy away from appreciating the dancer's unique qualities. I have never known a dancer who was not his or her own harshest critic. In fact, it is often easier to find fault with ourselves and to be self-critical than to admit our strengths and I think this applies to therapy training as well.

The person who influenced me most as a therapist, supervisor and tutor was Maria Fay, a very special Hungarian ballerina, teacher and writer who was able and willing to tune into every dancer in the room as a unique human being and to help the dancers, no matter how inexperienced or experienced, to build on their strengths. Her aim was to enhance our confidence and self-esteem, not to reduce it or take it away. Her confidence and belief in us helped us all in our never-ending struggle with our weaknesses. Humour also played an important part inside and outside of her classes. She was the only ballet teacher who never counted along to the steps and moves. We were encouraged to listen, move and relate to the music. This was seen as an almost holy relationship … no dancing by numbers on her watch! She hated the term training and preferred the term teaching. She certainly managed to take the training out of teaching.

We all got to know each other by having lunch together every day between our morning and afternoon class. In her book, *Mind over Body* (Fay, 1997) she stressed how important the relationship is between dancer and teacher, regardless of their age and experience: 'knowing more about them and their ways of seeing problems will build up friendship, mutual understanding and trust' (p. 98). She was also the person who introduced me to existentialism in one of our many discussions about literature and philosophy. This happened almost thirty years before I embarked on my therapy training.

The power of the group vs. trusting myself

It was not surprising that as a trainee therapist I discovered very early on that my tendency to trust my clients and myself did not necessarily fit with being an inex-perienced therapist. This was particularly true in supervision where there seemed to be an unspoken belief that trainee therapists could not be trusted. This was a culture shock for me: we had to be monitored carefully in case we damaged our clients in some way. As trainees, we would often pick up this mind-set so we would be eager to show our supervisors and tutors how self-aware and how openly self-critical we were.

The supervisors I gained the most from seemed to convey trust and without exception they interrupted the least. It was almost as if the 'supervision' had been taken out of supervision. The relationship was between two adult therapists with different styles and points of view, both prone to make mistakes and both hopefully gaining and learning from each other via the relationship.

And yet I also tried hard to fit in and comply and behave as I thought an inexperienced therapist was expected to behave. These feelings went hand in hand with self-doubt and a constant worry that I was not acceptable therapist material because I never experienced those 'Ah ha' moments that more experienced therapists wrote and spoke about.

For some strange reason we were led to believe that our clients would want to know what our orientation was at the beginning of their first session, so I thought I'd have a go when I started with my first placement client. I think I must have picked this idea up from my fellow trainee therapists who to me seemed more 'in the know' than I was. In fact, I remember telling the course director that I needed to find a way of being 'less like myself'. I can still see the puzzled look on his face!

My little speech with a new client went something like this:

ME There are different schools of therapy, my way of working is existential phenomenological.

CLIENT Ugh? (looking puzzled)

ME Ok, let me tell you a bit about how it goes. I am not an expert who can tell you what to do or give you advice on what you should do, unlike some other therapists, I won't make interpretations on your behalf. That's for you to do, not me.

CLIENT (looking disappointed) Oh? But I've come to see you for help, otherwise I might as well talk to a friend … so what do you do?

ME (heartbeat quickening) The idea is that you will help yourself, I can't do anything for you … mmh, this is your space (cringe) but that does not mean that I'll just sit here like a nodding dog (cliché alert) and not say anything.

CLIENT (looking irritated) I hope not! My last therapist hardly said anything, and that was a total waste of my time!

ME (feeling flushed and quickly looking at the clock) Shall we start now and see how it goes?

While this rather fraught exchange was taking place, there was a little voice telling me that I should not have dropped this exchange so abruptly. My supervisor or someone in the group was bound to want to know if I had explored my client's need for help, or what it was like to have a silent therapist or how my client was now feeling about our relationship so far. My thinking was that at this stage I'd rather not know what my client was thinking before I had a chance to show that I was made of the right stuff … whatever that was.

Needless to say, this was the last time I volunteered this information. If my client asked me how I worked or what to expect then I'd say that the best way to find out was for us to get cracking and have our session. It's far better to have a shared real experience than to predict an ideal experience in theory. I bought into this because I assumed it was the correct thing to do. Little did I know that this was a trap I was responsible for setting for myself. How on earth could I possibly know or predict how I would be or not be and how these sessions would evolve? This was also a very valuable lesson in how important it is to be open to other views while also honouring our own gut feeling and values.

Supervision as assessment

My greatest confusion came when I discovered that the concept of supervision was not an existentially-friendly concept for me (Mitchell, 1997). I can now see that I gave some of the supervisors too much power by initially assuming that a more experienced therapist who had reached the status of supervisor knew what was best for my client. As an inexperienced trainee therapist I had naively assumed that existential supervision would be influenced by, and fall into line with, the ethos and existential thinking that was encouraged and facilitated on the course – a course that encouraged everyone to express his or her unique response to philo-sophical texts, to the tutors and to fellow students without worrying about being hampered by the idea that there was a right or wrong response.

Assessing is part of how we try to understand each other. This is something we all do; our clients assess us and we assess them; we judge and form understandings and opinions. This is the one area where we as therapists try to 'un-know' our knee jerk assessments long enough to hear and try to understand what our client is trying to tell us from their point of view. But it won't be long before our own views come bouncing back again. This will happen to experienced and inexperienced therapists alike. As a supervisor, I have often jumped to 'knee jerk' conclusions about someone in my group before I had got the more complex picture that comes from getting to know the person a bit better. Even though the 'picture' is never complete or finished, an understanding that happens too quickly can seem prematurely final.

I have always made it clear that my assessment is simply my personal take of the qualities that I have noticed in each therapist in our group because that is what I have experienced. I have had no experience of the therapist with his or her client, just as I have no first-hand experience of my client in his or her relationships.

Maybe existential supervision could be seen as a 'master class' between two therapists in the art of self-supervising.

General assumptions about existential therapy

My earlier example of how I tried to explain to my client how I as an existential phenomenological therapist worked was also an example of how difficult it was to defend ourselves as existential therapists when we were being accused of not 'doing' anything, or not having a theory. The verdict seemed to be something like 'with those existential therapists anything goes'!

What was that all about? No wonder existential therapy had a reputation for being airy-fairy by some. In other circles we were seen as highly intellectual and taken to quoting Heidegger, Kierkegaard or Nietzsche to our clients. Some dismissed our acceptance of death and anxiety as too grim. Meanwhile, some existential therapists were referring to the relationships that they had with their clients as being 'real', more real than therapists from different orientations. I think this came about in the early 1990s in response to the psychodynamic therapists who worked with transference and countertransference. Try as I may, I find it hard to imagine what an unreal relationship might be. How is it possible not to be real?

Another puzzling statement was that existential therapists were really 'real' because there was no theory in the background that was followed or 'applied' in order to practice therapy or to understand clients with.

But meanwhile on the ground there were still traces of psychodynamic thinking; existential therapists were rigorously keeping to the 50-minute hour, subtly (or not so subtly) conveying to clients that asking the therapist personal questions was not the 'done thing'. Therapists made sure that there were no personal photos in view in their therapy rooms while the pictures on the walls were often bland and safe. The theory seemed to say that the therapist must not have too many personal clues on show … in order to keep self-disclosure to the bare minimum.

At the beginning of this chapter I quoted Merleau-Ponty because it was such a clear example of my own experience during my days as a trainee existential therapist. Here is an example of me being inspired by philosophical thought; thinking that resonated with my views in a learned way.

For instance, my view or thoughts on small talk that I will get to in a moment, is expressed in my practice with certain clients, or I could say that my practice and attitude expressed this view at times. This view comes from my own experience, so it makes sense to me.

To present myself as a 'blank screen' with my clients would never work for me. The corresponding theory is not my view or part of my belief system. Many therapists use this theory because it also makes sense to them in a personal way, while some might apply a theory that is outside of their own lived experience. I see those relationships as being just as real as mine are to me.

I do believe that generalisation is the enemy of the existential approach and yet most existential therapists seem to agree that we share a lot simply by being human beings who find themselves in the world. Our lives are going to end, we don't know when or how, but we know it silently and uncomfortably. This knowledge, combined with uncertainty, is highly uncomfortable so we set about controlling what we can and creating certainty, order and purpose in our lives. We live our lives 'as if' we are in control but the hovering and all-knowing anxiety is never far away, reminding us that we are not in control as much as we like to think we are.

We are all compelled to respond – this is at the heart of every relationship and situation we find ourselves in. There is always a context and there are always others. While all of this is going on, we are often spontaneously and sometimes thoughtfully creating meaning in our lives. Meaning is not 'out there'. It is already a unique part of who we are and how we make sense of our past, present and future.

My experience so far tells me that the relationship is crucial – a relationship where the therapist tunes into the client's 'way of being' and emotions, in much the same way as a dancer's relationship to the music expresses the dancer's unique personality.

My experience of therapy was and is quite similar to an improvised dance sequence where there might be blissful moments of a smooth and seamless connection but these can be followed by awkward uncoordinated slips and stumbles. Therapy is a chaotic mysterious process cloaked in uncertainty more than clarity and like life. It is full of ups and downs and unfinished business – always unfinished business.

Small talk and self-disclosure

As therapists we are taught not to indulge in or collude with our client's small talk. Self-disclosure is very carefully handled when spoken about by therapists but I bet that if I was a fly on the wall in many therapy sessions, I would experience humour and spontaneous throw away remarks about weather, TV, films, favourite food. I hope that's not wishful thinking on my part. By colluding I don't simply mean 'allowing it to happen', but actively engaging in small talk banter with clients. I noticed that for some clients their way into what was really bothering them was sometimes via small talk or humour: talking about themselves in a light-hearted, everyday kind of way. I decided that it was not for me to let them know that this was not proper client speak. I reminded myself that it was my job to find a way into their world, rather than for me to show them the way into the therapy world. There was no right or wrong way to be a client/person and the last thing I wanted was clients who could show me that they had graduated from client school!

This 'idle' talk is, in my experience, never a waste of time. It is at times like a creative process where I start doodling and then notice that something is taking shape. It is as if the client also experiences the spontaneity that releases me from trying to behave like a therapist. So-called small talk is no less significant than other forms of self-expression. I try not to jump to conclusions by assuming to know what is significant because I can't possibly know. Some clients discover what really matters to them when they hear themselves speak. What happens between us throughout our sessions might be therapeutic for my client at some point or maybe not at all. 'Small talk' can also act as a form of self-disclosure; it can become a more natural, spontaneous way for client and therapist to get to know each other. In my experience this kind of easy talking, that might feel to be unconnected and outside the remit of what therapy should be, can play an important part in paving the way for the areas that are more difficult to share and talk about. I believe that a therapist who accepts and respects the client's way of expressing him/herself will by default encourage the client to open up. Therapy is basically a creative happening and creativity happens when there is openness and spontaneity.

Ditching linear thinking

We therapists write case studies showing how we have guided and helped our clients to 'work through' and understand what is troubling them, how they become more aware of their possibilities and choices and therefore less stuck.

Where did we get this idea that 'working through' implied that if something had been understood and 'processed' it would be put to rest forever more? Don't we know from our own experience that there is a lot of truth in the fact that we actually 'don't learn from our mistakes'? We are not creatures who can logically work through and draw lines under our 'issues' and then 'move on' with our newfound understanding firmly in place. We can at times revert back to a form of non-understanding. This can often be the cause of great frustration for therapists who can't believe that what seems to have been achieved may suddenly not be significant any more. We are complex, multi-dimensional creatures where every line that is drawn seems to belong to the context and emotional moment it was drawn in, but loses the same meaning in new situations and in time.

It is wishful linear thinking to assume that this newfound freedom would happen once our clients understood their issues and were aware of their options and choices. But we are not dealing with logic. Sure, logic is there and so is the will to act and create change, but we are also propelled along by our contradictory changing emotions, which I believe call the shots more than our considered logical 'common sense' thinking.

I remember hearing the wonderful German choreographer Pina Bausch (1940–2009) saying once (I paraphrase), 'Repetition is not repetition, the same action makes you feel something completely different by the end'. I believe this is also true for therapy when clients seem to be endlessly going around in circles repeating the same thing. My response can never be the same as I listen to my client's familiar story. I have done this myself on occasions but there was always a need attached to it. For me it is never a waste of time; some experiences need to run their course but this repetition might also indicate that the client does not quite feel heard or believed or something completely different.

This requires patience and a tolerance of uncertainty by the therapist who might experience the client as being stuck just because there doesn't seem to be any visible change happening. Feeling stuck is useful for client and therapist because it can sometimes reveal an expectation of what 'should' be happening. Being stuck is somewhere, not nowhere.

Conclusion

The way we treat each other is the treatment (Laing, 1989).

Many existential therapists are fearful of not being taken seriously and that existential therapy will die and vanish unless we step back under the medical model umbrella that has become the norm. Therapists are now required to record how their clients respond to the therapy treatment and in turn clients are also sucked into this system where they grade and track their symptoms and progress.

However, there is a big difference in complying with a system that runs counter to my own beliefs and buying into it by believing that it is helpful for me as a therapist and my clients (Mitchell, 2018a). Don't we already know from our own life experience that we are not objects that can be fixed? How is it possible to believe in a simplistic linear process from an existential perspective? As in life, our progress and process is unpredictable, chaotic and mysterious. Change will always happen, but therapists can rarely make or even facilitate change or a new understanding within a certain time limit if it is the wrong time.

Existential therapy is a creative process that relies on uncertainty in order to allow the unexpected to happen; two human beings, who already share so much on one level but who respond to 'what is' in a uniquely different way. Mutual trust and respect are the foundations of the relationship. As a therapist I try to be mindful as well as open minded, a trusting and a respectful follower in my client's process during therapy and in their lives. I believe that the client will feel and sense this attitude if it is natural and not artificially 'applied'. It must come from who the therapist is in relation to his or her client and not be a system that is unconnected to the world outside the therapy room. Merleau-Ponty (1964) expresses this so well: 'For us the body is much more than an instrument or a means; it is our expression in the world, the visible form of our intentions' (p. 5).

References

Badkhen, A. (2019) *In the Presence of Another – A Lyrical Exploration of Psychotherapy*. Trans. Anna Badkhen. USA Middletown, DE: Uniterra Foundations.

Fay, M. (1997) *Mind over Body*. London: A & C Black.

Laing, R.D. (1989) *Did you used to be R.D. Laing?* Tougas and Shandel Documentary, Third Mind Productions.

Merleau-Ponty, M. (1962) *Phenomenology of Perception*. Trans. Colin Smith. Routledge and Kegan Paul Ltd.

Merleau-Ponty, M. (1964) *The Primacy of Perception*. Ed. James M. Edie Northwestern University Press, USA.

Mitchell, D. (1997) Merleau-Ponty, Certain Uncertainty and Existential Psychotherapy, *Existential Analysis* 8.2.

Mitchell, D. (2018a) Un-measurable Lives, *Hermeneutic Circular*, April.

Mitchell. D. (2018b) Researching Therapies or Therapies as Research?, *Hermeneutic Circular*, October.

Part II

Compliance and emancipation

7 Psychotherapy in an age of stupidity

Manu Bazzano

Introduction

> Stupidity always triumphs … it is always on the side of the victor.
>
> (Derrida, 2011, p. 183)

Our age is the age of stupidity. Sometimes described as neoliberalism, it breeds many ills, stupidity being, arguably, the most prominent. Other contenders include disengagement, indifference, and alienation. Stupidity is not lack of education; it is not the opposite of cleverness; being too clever by half is a sure sign of stupidity. It is a systemic condition brought about by an invasive corporate technostructure which undermines freedom of thought and short-circuits spaces of learning. Like other practices, psychotherapy now increasingly operates within the confines of the corporate technostructure.

Jacques Derrida's pessimistic assessment quoted at the start of this chapter is all the more poignant for having been uttered one year before his death in 2004. It rings true today in a geopolitical landscape which favours rogues and treacherous clowns as heads of state, and is beleaguered by the global rise of right-wing populism and misinformation. It rings truer than ever in a psychic landscape marred by misogyny, racism, homophobia, hatred of difference, and xenophobia and at a time when we witness concerted attacks on the humanities and on psychotherapy in particular, an insidious attempt to turn this deeply transformative art and science into a banal exercise in mental hygiene at the service of the status quo.

Is it possible to adopt alongside this pessimism of the intellect a small dose of optimism of the will? Is there a way out of stupidity? These are some of the questions pursued in this chapter. To begin, it may be useful to look at one definition of stupidity by Friedrich Nietzsche.

Existential individuation

In an uncharacteristic praise of Socrates, Nietzsche discusses stupidity in section 328 of *Gay Science*. The real obstacle to human flourishing is not selfishness, the bête noire of all pious narratives, but stupidity:

> The ancient philosophers taught that the main source of misfortune was something very different [than selfishness]. Beginning with Socrates, these thinkers never wearied of preaching: 'Your thoughtlessness and stupidity, the way you live according to the rule, your submission to your neighbour's opinion is the reason why you so rarely achieve happiness; we thinkers, as thinkers, are the happiest of all'. ... This sermon ... deprived stupidity of its good conscience; these philosophers *harmed* stupidity.
>
> (Nietzsche, 1882/1974, p. 258)

Stupidity reflects our compulsion to follow the herd. It represents our inability to question (or momentarily suspend) the introjected rules of our particular tribe, herd, and nation. It is, I would add, our inability to go through a process of *existential individuation*. The latter is my designation for a difficult movement witnessed in my clinical work, a movement towards self-direction and authorship, often resulting in the expansion of one's self-construct and greater alignment with the organismic domain of experience. One key aspect of this process is acceptance of essential solitude, what Derrida calls "the absolute *solitude* of the *existent* in its *existence*" (2005, p. 110). Another aspect is developing greater sensitivity towards (and readiness to learn from) the unknown and the unconscious, as it is often through exploration of these enigmatic and uncertain terrain that new vistas might open. Signposts in the directions of human flourishing (*eudaimonia*) also emerge from those passions or *daimon(s)* whose intrinsic intelligence is often neglected by an increasingly fearful psychotherapy culture in favour of legalistic obeisance to the rules of social and mental hygiene.

I speak of *existential* individuation to differentiate it from the notion of individuation popularized by Jung (1928) who, for reasons examined elsewhere (Bazzano, 2017, 2019a), chose to frame it in terms of intrapsychic integration, thus in my view failing to appreciate the realities of separation, fragmentation, and difference. Despite his own rather pallid version, Jung at least acknowledged individuation. Contemporary psychotherapy promptly consigned it to oblivion in favour of *integration*. Interestingly, the latter is a fairly dependable replica of the coercive pressure lived in the public sphere by migrants and refugees routinely required to integrate into cultures which are said to host them. It is also a replica of the covert or overt demands imposed by our societies of control (Deleuze, 1992) on anyone who dares to challenge the status quo. *No dominant political discourse ever asks people to individuate. It invariably expects us to integrate within the existing order.* This is (sort of) understandable; it's in the very nature of the Powers to behave in this way. What is astonishing is how gladly psychotherapy culture follows suit. The effect is disastrous: it prevents real psycho-therapeutic exploration from happening; it short-circuits the transitional space, that vital "intermediate area of experiencing to which inner reality and external life both contribute" (Winnicott, 1971, p. 3). By supinely accepting the dictates of a pervasive neoliberal ideology, psychotherapy effectively *poisons* the transitional space by establishing "a relationship ... of compliance" (Winnicott, 1971, p. 87) with reality. Our connection to reality is distorted: "[T]he world and its details [are] recognized … only as something to be fitted in with our demanding adaptation. Compliance carries with it a sense of futility for the individual and is associated with the idea that nothing matters" (ibid).

Institutional power demands compliance: we become subjects through our subjugation to the existing order. We become a self or a subject "through our primary submission to power" (Butler, 1997, p. 2). My identity is one with *interpellation*: in Althusser's famous example, a policeman calls a passerby and the latter responds identifying herself as the one who is called (Althusser, 1970).

Compliance and emancipation

Psychotherapy's desertion of (existential) individuation is parallel to desertion of the fundamental psychological and political value of *emancipation* (from *emancipare* – to be sent out, i.e. to be freed from external control) in favour of avowed obeisance to customs, conventions, and traditions – what Hegel, in a discussion of Spirit in chapter 6 of his *Phenomenology* (Hegel, 1807/1977), called *Sittlichkeit*. As a result, therapy across all theoretical orientations now works as a rule in the service of compliance rather than emancipation. Lingos and methodologies vary; what does not vary is overall genuflection to normative adaptation, to the rules of a stultifying project whose drive is to control the perceived chaos of human experience.

Hegel's *custom* is an apt term here, given that in the age of stupidity the ethical order is wholly indistinguishable from rules of behaviour internalized through acculturation. The term used by the philosopher Bernard Stiegler (2013) for this rife state of affairs is *disindividuation*, defined as "a deficient relation to potentiality, a failure of individuation" (p. 62). A telling example of how the obliteration of the transformative notion of existential individuation has occurred within traditional existential therapy is through the literalization and dilution of the writings of two pre-existential thinkers and archenemies of ethics-as-custom: Kierkegaard and Nietzsche. In *Fear and Trembling*, Kierkegaard (1843/2005) presents us with the most confrontational example of individuation: God's horrifying call to Abraham to kill his beloved son, to give up what he cherished the most – to go against morality and humanity, foreswear all sensible customs and humane decrees in the name of an allegedly divine and patently cruel logic.

Kierkegaard's teleological suspension of the ethical is far from gratuitous. It is educational as well as *metaphorical* (Bazzano, 2017), i.e., conveying the persistence of the aesthete's sublated sensibility in a sophisticated spoof of Hegelian dialectics that journeys from *aesthetics* through *ethics* to *religion*. Crucially for our investigation, he also conveys in the most tragic form the dangers attendant to the *essential solitude* of becoming oneself. Sadly, contemporary psychotherapy culture (including traditional existential therapy) understands solitude negatively, as something to be conquered through relatedness, possibly in the attempt to build a manic defense against solitude. Whatever the case, I believe the loss is enormous. A culture that does not value solitude prevents us from growing out of stupidity; it does not allow us to accept the pain that comes, as Melanie Klein (1975) maintained, with the loss of imaginary omnipotence. It prevents us from appreciating the difficult loneliness of the woman in Adrienne Rich's poem *Song* who passes through towns and villages that she might have lived and died in. Nor can we notice the solitary beauty and splendour of the rowboat in a winter landscape that knows itself to be separate from winter light and the iced lake – a boat that knows itself to be wood, with a talent for burning (Rich, 2013).

A *literal* reading of Kierkegaard – this most exciting, superb, and maddeningly ambiguous religious poet – misses his barbed incitement to a dangerous and meaningful life modelled after the radical example of Christ. To classify his plea as a "dangerous folly" in the name of an ostensibly didactic appeal to morality, as an influential voice in traditional existential therapy has done (Spinelli, 2017) implicitly endorses the regrettable development we are witnessing at present, namely existential therapy's turn from a potentially emancipatory methodology into a project of social and political compliance.

Heteronomy and dividuation

Suppressed from current discourse, existential individuation is still merely the necessary first step, the catalyst for an enquiry that takes us away from a narcissistic search for authenticity towards greater recognition of the primarily multiple, non-atomistic nature of the self – what Nietzsche (1878/1984) calls *dividual* or "dividuum" (p. 54). Existential individuation is not individualism, for it recognizes that we are but a *coalition of affects*, while individualism anachronistically defends an atomistic view of the human subject. In Spinoza (1677/1996), autonomy is parallel to increased *receptivity*; power corresponds to the power to be affected. This is true for both facets, as it were, of the bodymind continuum: as the mind's power to think is linked to its "receptivity to external ideas" [so] the body's power to act is intimately linked to our body's "sensitivity to other bodies" (Hardt, 2007, p. x). Greater autonomy is grounded in, and constituted by, *heteronomy*, i.e., the concrete influence of others.

Alienation and inauthenticity

A similar operation to the substitution of individuation with integration has taken place in contemporary psychotherapy with the replacement of *alienation* with *inauthenticity*. The difference between the two could not be greater. The notion of alienation is receptive to the socio-political context in which the therapeutic encounter necessarily occurs. It is a dialectical, historical notion (Goldmann, 1977; Lukács, 1968), presupposing estrangement from one's own self and from others. It first emerged "in a certain historical condition, with the generalization of market production [and with] … reification" (Goldmann, 1977, p 33). Reification is the turning of a living human being into a thing (*res*), for the purposes of creating profit for the ruling class. Alienation is the product of the colonization of the everyday at the hands of late capitalism.

Inauthenticity, the product, for Lucien Goldmann, of Heidegger's misappropriation of Lukács's notion of alienation, is abstractly ontological; it is a-historical, non-dialectical, and, in the ways in which it has been popularized in existential/humanistic therapy, entirely imputable to the individual. Society, history, and politics vanish into thin air. It is now the person's task to confront and surpass her alienation through cultivating empathic attunement and striving in the wild-goose chase for authenticity.

Alienation is still a fruitful notion in an era of accelerated exploitation of human and natural resources, an era which has morphed into something worse than capitalism and neoliberalism, with the creation of a new class, the *vectoralist* class (Wark, 2019), the 1% of the population that owns the *vector* or information infrastructure. Mackenzie Wark explains:

> The dominant ruling class of our time no longer maintains its rule through the ownership of the means of production as capitalists do. Nor through the ownership of land as landlords do. The dominant ruling class of our time owns and controls information.
>
> (2019, p. 5)

As for the remaining 99%, we produce information which then gets sold, arranged, and organized. No matter how innovative or radical our ideas may be, we only have to post our scribbling online or write a book for an academic publisher to realize that we're now ensconced within a technostructure that will eat up and regurgitate us alongside our 'product' before we can say 'authentic'. We'll be promptly itemized within an information market driven by a cluster of stereotypical and bigoted algorithms. Whatever one chooses to call this sad state of affairs – capitalism is as good a word as any – one of the things it breeds, alongside alienation and disengagement, is stupidity.

The technostructure has grown in size and complexity since Galbraith (1967/2007) first coined the term fifty years ago. The once rather abstracted network of managers who controlled the economy both within and beyond individual corporate groups has in recent years flaunted its dark heart. We live now in the age of *surveillance capitalism*, "a new type of commerce that reimagines us through the lens of its own distinctive power" (Zuboff, 2019, p. 352). Under its auspices, social life is achieving new levels of degradation (Taplin, 2018; Vaidhyanathan, 2018), bringing Marcusian repressive desublimation to new heights by "turning libidinous impulses into marketable products" (Seymour, 2019, p. 162).

Atrophy of the noetic

In a world where the Enlightenment's dream of universality is finally achieved, tragically, by the market; in a world where ontology is effectively, in Mark Fisher's words, business ontology (Fisher, 2009), the other thing that happens is *atrophy of the noetic*, i.e., a shrinking of the ability to produce creative thoughts and to imagine the new – for instance the ability to fathom a different economic system other than capitalism.

The ability to think freely and creatively has a long and venerable history, the momentous event of the Enlightenment – *Aufklärung* in German, the clearing of clouds – being one case in point, a mode of thinking and seeing the world that may bring about, in the words of Kant (1991), *Mündigkeit* (maturity), i.e., one's "inability to use one's own judgement without the guidance of another" (p. 54), the ability to think without an external locus of evaluation (Rogers, 1951) and without juvenile handing over of one's freedoms and responsibilities to political leaders (de Beauvoir, 1948/1976).

Reason, properly understood, is at the very centre of this project of maturation. For Adorno and Horkheimer (1944/1997), reason has degenerated into *rationalization*, a socially accepted form of stupidity. But rationalization is not reason; it is *irrational*. This compulsion to conform, this lack of autonomous thought, has become widespread with the acceleration of capitalism into vectoralism and with systemic disindividuation.

For Stiegler (2013, p. 27) "rationalization … destroys reason as desire" because it is in effect a process of vulgarization that shuts down potential space for imaginative and independent thought. Our societies of control create a *pervasive* condition in which "drive-based tendencies are systematically exploited while its sublimatory tendencies are systematically short-circuited in such a way that pathos has essentially become poisonous" (Stiegler, 2013, ibid). Because it is pervasive, no one within a "consumerist industrial system" (ibid) escapes it. A similar critique of rationalization is found in Husserl, who wrote the following lines with Hitler, already chancellor for two years, and when a plebiscite would grant him the title of Führer and the support of 92% of the German population:

> The exclusiveness with which the total worldview of modern man in the second half of the nineteen century let itself be determined by the positive sciences and blinded by the 'prosperity' they produced mean an indifferent turning-away from the questions which are decisive for a genuine humanity. *More sciences of facts produce a humanity of facts.*
>
> (Husserl, 1954/1970, pp 5–6, emphasis added)

Anamnesis

Surprisingly, I found in Plato (a thinker I'd spent years opposing) the most helpful insights in trying to make sense of the current situation: his notions of *anamnesis* and *hypomnesis*.

Anamnesis means recollection or remembering, a process intimately linked to psyché, to the imagination, where autonomous and creative thinking can emerge. For Plato (2009), anamnesis constitutes the very origin of philosophical knowledge/wisdom. He lamented that the original process of memorizing and conceptualizing through the dynamic spoken word had degenerated into *hypomnesis*, i.e. the use of other – indirect, automatic – means of memorization. For him the culprit at the time was writing: by the time a living thought (born of conversation) is written down, we are distanced from the dynamic flow of ideas. *Philo-sophia*, a term coined by Plato, is love of wisdom. But love of wisdom is not wisdom itself; the love in question is for something at a slight remove, something we try to reclaim.

Anamnesis is the potential antidote for this gap: the recreation of the imaginative space of memory, a space that fosters autonomy out of which flourishing may emerge. Derrida helped us understand, however, that autonomy has always to do with *heteronomy*. The two do not *oppose*, as Plato thought. They *compose*. The tangible presence of others, alive or dead, human or nonhumans, is within us. Their ambivalent message is implanted in us (Laplanche, 1996). Sigmund Freud's famous dictum *where it was, there I shall be*, may be rendered as *where it was, there others shall be*.

In the beginning was exteriority

Hypomnesis – memory through technical means –does *not* signal a fall or the loss of the imaginary virgin terrain of human interiority. Exteriority was there from the start, implanting indelible and fertile messages, creating the very space of psyche. Time was out of joint since the beginning of time. What hypomnesis does signal, however, is the short-circuiting of the potential space that may assist the emergence of existential individuation. The struggle against the technologization and commodification of human experience is genuinely valid; yet it would be naive to discount the originally *pharmacological* constitution of spirit itself (Stiegler, 2013).

Something similar may have happened with the Buddha's teachings: like anamnesis, *smṛti*, the Sanskrit word commonly translated as mindfulness, also means memory. This was not meant as the worship of a decontextualized cognitive faculty that is popular today through corporate mindfulness, but as mindfulness *of impermanence*: alertness to our own mortality, the transient nature of life and our own insubstantiality (Bazzano, 2010, 2013, 2014, 2019b). This form of contemplation and practice is fertile ground in the process of existential individuation. Without this context, mindfulness is another manifestation of stupidity, in this case applied to the Buddha's teachings – a vulgarization of the complex mythic, religious, spiritual, ethical, and psychological richness of the Dharma.

Communalization

Moving out of stupidity means recreating the anamnesic circuit, but this doesn't have to mean rejection of technology and regressive defense of the human inner life. Creation of technology and reaction to it are part of the very same thing – what Derrida (1981) called pharmacology. Pharmakon is both poison and remedy. What is needed is a pharmacology of the spirit (Stiegler, 2013), and here counter-traditional existential therapy might help.

Rebuilding the anamnesic circuit means to some extent recreating on a transindividual/cultural scale the equivalent of Winnicott's transitional space, a space where independent thinking can be fostered through experimentation and playful, committed adherence to development and maturity. This is a space where the writer-artist's authorship, the art of creating one's own life (de Beauvoir, 1948/1976), can come into being – a space where existential individuation can materialize. In the cultural sphere this was potentially fostered by what Husserl (1962) called *communalization*, an environment created by a community of peers nurtured by conversations/encounters, fostered by an educational system whose task is to store up and transmit tertiary retentions (an archive of texts, oral teachings, libraries) plus numerous other means of documenting and granting access to material that aids reflection and recollection.

How alive are these networks today? How effective? Most of these forms of tertiary retentions have been "monopolized by the culture industries" (Stiegler, 2015, p. 211) with a lethal effect on communalization itself: "[It] produced an asymmetry between producers [who complied] with the criteria of these financial backers … and … the mass of consumers who no longer from publics in a public space and public time, but audiences for publicity" (ibid).

The result was *de-communalization*, which Stiegler describes as "dissociation of symbolic milieus and … *disindividuation*" (ibid, emphasis added). We may still use the word 'existential' when describing our approach to therapy. Do we refer to a form of communalization that was rife in the heyday of existential phenomenology and has now expired, leaving us with a carapace of empty signifiers?

Tribal enclaves

I've often wondered whether the apocalyptic narratives arguably predominant in current progressive discourse emerge not solely as a response to the undeniable urgency of climate change and the global shift to the right, but also because the closing down of the transitional space in the culture leaves us with nowhere to turn. The three major movements of the last two decades or so – *Anti-globalization*, *Occupy*, and *Extinction Rebellion* – are driven by a spirit of self-preservation against the greed of institutional and financial power. The generous excesses, utopian reformulations ('power to the imagination!'), and anarchist ethics that were a feature of the insurgencies of the 1960s and 1970s are simply absent, perhaps unthinkable. We now seem happy with asking modestly for a slightly fairer, more humane world, or at least for the chance for us and our children to go on surviving, *please*. Imagination is not entirely dead: it can easily envision the death of the planet but is nevertheless incapable of ever imagining the end of capitalism.

Nor can we fathom the end of our insularity and parochial belonging to nation-states and/or compartmentalized identities, including theoretical identities within the world of psychotherapy. The best we can muster, within our little tribal enclaves (if and when we grasp that our struggle is common to the struggle of other groups), is to speak of solidarity. I am reminded of Rosa Luxemburg (1995), for whom to think of solidarity as if two equally disenfranchised groups were 'external' to each other is buying wholesale the 'divide and rule' ideology of the Powers. Hardt and Negri (2019) mention the analogous examples of Iris Young and Keeanga-Yamahtta Taylor. Young (1981) urges male socialists to leave behind empty talk of solidarity with feminism and appreciate feminist fight against patriarchy as part of the very same social and political struggle: anti-capitalism and feminism are, in this sense, "mutually constitutive" (p. 90). And in her book *From #BlackLivesMatter to Black Liberation*, Taylor (2016) makes a similar case, urging us to understand anti-racism and anti-capitalism as one and the same struggle. "In fact – she writes – the American working class is female, immigrant, Black, white, Latino/a and more. Immigrant issues, gender issues and antiracisms *are* working-class issues" (p. 216).

All of this is relevant to existential therapy, not only because it is crucial to inscribe the latter within a progressive political project, but also because current fragmentation into insular tribes is one of the consequences of the short-circuiting of the potential space that psychotherapy might help re-open.

Shepherds of stupidity

Psychotherapists can be instrumental in rebuilding an anamnesic circuit, alongside those of us involved in facilitating and delivering psychotherapy trainings in universities and colleges. The great difficulty is that the therapeutic space has been commodified and turned into a repository where clients go in order to convalesce before re-occupying their reserved seats in the traffic jam. As for universities and colleges, they are now by and large corporate businesses whose priorities only indirectly contain true learning. Therapists and trainers/academics alike are currently required to be *shepherds of stupidity*. We are obliged to be the *rationalisers*: in many cases our designated task is transmitting to clients and trainees a peculiar condition and institutionally endorsed pathology: OMD, *obsessive measurement disorder* – a term coined by Andrew Natsios (2010), once administrator of the US Agency for International Development (USAID). This is a condition also known as the *McNamara* or *quantitative fallacy*, named after Robert McNamara, the US secretary of defense from 1961 to 1968. It involves making a decision based solely on quantitative observations (or metrics) and ignoring others. The reason given is often that these other observations cannot be proven. I hear this sort of complaint regularly by trainees who have been told that neither empathy, nor the unconscious exist because they can't be measured (Bazzano, 2020). Yankelovich (1972) summarized the stages of this major pitfall:

> The first step is to measure whatever can be easily measured. This is OK as far as it goes. The second step is to disregard that which can't be easily measured or to give it an arbitrary quantitative value. This is artificial and misleading. The third step is to presume that what can't be measured easily really isn't important. This is blindness. The fourth step is to say that what can't be easily measured really doesn't exist. This is suicide.

What can be done? Help comes from a variety of sources. One of these is Nietzsche's use of the mask – understood not as concealment but artistry. For centuries, philosophers had to wear "the mask of the contemplative priest, for their vocation was suspect" (Bazzano, 2019a, p. 57), and at times did so in order "not to be burned at the stake" (ibid, p. 96). They did so intelligently, some of them succeeding in transmitting the subversive teachings of untimely and radical philosophies. Like Nietzsche's free spirits, we too may need to wear the mask of the academic and the therapist in order to *sub-vert* (turn from below) what these particular professions have become and to redirect their energies away from reactive forces and in favour of active forces. This brings us to another definition of stupidity: what makes a particular entity stupid is when it is being ruled by *reactive* rather than *active* forces (Deleuze, 1962/2006; Bazzano, 2019a).

A reactive force is a natural force that has turned against itself and is unable to reach the deep end of where it can go. It is dominated by calculability and self-preservation. To turn a profession, an activity, or a craft from reactive to active is a difficult task. An active, life-affirming force that does not denigrate life and can trust its own momentum is an extraordinary thing. Almost nothing within the tradition supports it, because the tradition is built on foundations made up of reactive forces.

The other useful inspiration comes from the Situationists: it is the practice of *detournement* (Debord, 1994) which consists in learning, absorbing a particular frame, discipline, or form of communication within the tradition and subsequently bend it in favour of emancipation. An example of this is already found in the writings of Karl Marx: a traditional, learned analysis of economy is put to use for the subversion of the status quo. A more recent case is that of the activist group *Pussy Riot*, which made headlines when five of its members staged a Situationist-type performance inside Moscow's Cathedral of Christ the Saviour in 2012. They have gone on to make incisive videos against the Trump presidency, the police state, and in solidarity of Eric Garner who died after an NYPD officer put him in a headlock in July 2014. Sophisticated, media-savvy, and well-produced, these videos are exemplary of Situationist *detournement*: turning expressions of a system of exploitation against itself.

Acting out

We might be able to gradually move out of stupidity by *acting out* (Voela & Rothschild, 2018). In order to do that, it would be helpful to stop genuflecting at the altar of that shadow of God, Heidegger's 'Being', and boldly embrace an *ontology of actuality*, a key notion in the writings of the Frankfurt School (Dews, 1986). This is closely linked, in my understanding, to two fecund notions which applied together would propel existential therapy out of its theological closet. The first one is Whitehead's *process philosophy*, a "philosophy of the organism [where] the subject emerges *from* the world" (Whitehead, 1978, p. 88, emphasis added). The second notion is *expressionism*: a thoroughgoing critique of *intentionality* in favour of *expression* and *expressionism in psychotherapy*. Strangely unquestioned in existential trainings and writings, intentionality substantiates the internal properties of experience and leaves current existential theory stuck within the boundaries of the Cartesian subject. Expression is its necessary antidote, the basis for a different notion of subjectivation as *heterology* or logic of the other. My 'identity' – its 'imprint' – is clarified through *expression*, through action (the domain of history, ethics, of finite, embodied existence) with others, through the way it affects others and I am affected by them. It cannot be mere assertion of subjectivity (and on its basis, the establishing of a 'consensus'). Emancipation then becomes political subjectivation, i.e. the formation of an identity that is not a self but a concrete, conflictual (and loving) relation of self to another.

Acting out – a phrase condescendingly used in everyday language for reprimanding unruly behaviour and bad habits in a client – means engaging in actions which by their very nature long for a response, summoning a relational domain – not as given, but as object of desire whose realization is forever uncertain.

Acting is not reacting. It calls upon active forces; it expresses a desire for the lost communalization that was dear to Husserl and that is vital to a *living* practice, as opposed to that treasured museum exhibit called 'existential therapy'. This call to action is far from the metaphysical wish, rife within traditional existential therapy, to salvage an imaginary 'Being' from an equally imaginary 'fall from Being'. Being or not-being – this is no longer the question; the question is the *unrealized*. Equally, this call to action does not ache for libidinal liberation either, nor does it presuppose the reality of a beach beneath the street – however alluring these reveries may be. This call is pragmatic, expressed within the pharmalogical domain: it is both poison *and* remedy (Bazzano, 2019a), pp. 127–142) but no less urgent or utopian in its ambition: it demands the (re)creation of a transitional and transindividual space.

For Gilbert Simondon, the chief philosophical error is to believe that the individual comes *before* individuation (Combes, 2013): individuation is a process out of which the individual emerges. The deed comes before the doer, and the doer recognizes her imprint in the deed.

Similarly for Nietzsche (1882/1974), the very notion of the self comes out of our chronic belief in causality, the idea that there is an 'I' (cause) behind a deed (effect): "an intellect that could see cause and effect as a continuum – he writes – would repudiate the concept of cause and effect and deny all conditionality" (p. 173).

We step out of stupidity by doing something stupid. This is how I read, incidentally, the activism of groups such as Extinction Rebellion: as a set of stupid actions that are useful in getting things moving, awkward actions that get it wrong until they get it right; actions that "enacts the desire for a relational holding" (Voela & Rothschild, 2018, p. 60). Acting is an act of faith: by acting we conjure up a transitional space implicitly conceived as capable of containing our actions through an adequate degree of attention, care, and desire – all necessary attributes of therapy. The latter creates an environment where the client may act out, is allowed to repeatedly fail and fail even better, and through her words and actions begin to sketch a kernel of her individuating process.

Conversely, there is a specific name for an environment that cannot tolerate stupid actions, experimentation, and least of all creative uncertainty. In his essay *Communicating and not-communicating*, Winnicott calls it *fascism* (1963, pp 179–192).

References

Adorno, T. W. & Horkheimer, W. (1944/1997) *Dialectic of Enlightenment*. London: Verso.

Althusser, L. (1970) *Lenin and Philosophy and Other Essays*. London: Verso.

Bazzano, M. (2010) Mindfulness in Context, *Therapy Today*, April, pp. 33–36.

Bazzano, M. (2013) In Praise of Stress Induction: Mindfulness Revisited, *European Journal of Psychotherapy & Counselling*, 15:2, 174–185, DOI: 10.1080/13642537.2013.793474.

Bazzano, M. (2014) (Ed) *After Mindfulness: New Perspectives on Psychology and Meditation*. New York, NY: Palgrave Macmillan.

Bazzano, M. (2017) Grace and Danger, *Existential Analysis*, 29:1, 16–27.

Bazzano, M. (2019a) *Nietzsche and Psychotherapy*. Abingdon, OX: Routledge.

Bazzano, M. (2019b) Meditation and the Post-secular Condition, Psychotherapy and Politics International, https://doi.org/10.1002/ppi.1490.

Bazzano, M. (2020) The Skin is Faster than the Word, *Existential Analysis*, 31:1, 53–64.

Butler, J. (1997) *Undoing Gender*. Abingdon, OX: Routledge.

Combes, M. (2013) *Gilbert Simondon and the Philosophy of the Transindividual*. Boston, MA: M.I.T.

de Beauvoir, S. (1948/1976) *The Ethics of Ambiguity*. New York, NY: Kensington Publishing.

Debord, G. (1994) *The Society of the Spectacle*. New York, NY: Zone Books.

Deleuze, G. (1962/2006) *Nietzsche and Philosophy*, trans. by Hugh Tomlinson. London: Continuum.

Deleuze, G. (1992) Postscript on the Societies of Control https://cidadeinseguranca.files.wordpress.com/2012/02/deleuze_control.pdf Retrieved 10 Oct .19

Derrida, J. (1981) *Dissemination*, trans. by Barbara Johnson. Chicago, IL: University of Chicago Press.

Derrida, J. (2005) *Writing and Difference*. London: Routledge.

Derrida, J. (2011) *The Beast and the Sovereign, Volume I (The Seminars of Jacques Derrida)*. Chicago, IL: Chicago University Press.

Dews, P. (1986) Adorno, Post-Structuralism and the Critique of Identity, *New Left Review* I, 157, 28–44.

Fisher, M. (2009) *Capitalist Realism: Is there no Alternative?* London: O Books.

Galbraith, J. K. (1967/2007) *The New Industrial State*. Princeton, NJ: Princeton University Press.

Goldmann, L. (1977) *Lukács and Heidegger: towards a New Philosophy*. London: Routledge.

Hardt, M. (2007) 'Foreword: What Affects are Good for' in Clough, P. T. & Halley, J. (eds.) *The Affective Turn*. Durham and London: Duke University Press.

Hardt, M. & Negri, A. (2019) Empire, Twenty Years On, *New Left Review*, November/December, 67–92.

Hegel, G. W. F. (1807/1977) *Phenomenology of Spirit*, trans. by A. V. Miller. Oxford: Oxford University Press.

Husserl, E. (1954/1970) *The Crisis of European Sciences and Transcendental Phenomenology*, trans. by David Carr. Evanston, IL: Northwestern University Press.

Husserl, E. (1962) *Husserl's Origin of Geometry, with an Introduction by Jacques Derrida*. Lincoln, NE: University of Nebraska Press.

Jung, C. G. (1928) 'The Relation between the Ego and the Unconscious' in Read, H., Fordham, M., Adler, G. & McGuire, W. (eds.) *Collected Works*, 20 vols, trans. R. F. C. Hull. London: Routledge.

Kant, I. (1991) *Political Writings*. Cambridge, MA: Cambridge University Press.

Kierkegaard, S. (1847/2005) *Fear and Trembling*. London: Penguin.

Klein, M. (1975) *Love, Guilt and Reparation and Other Works*. New York: Free Press.

Laplanche, J. (1996) Psychoanalysis as Anti-Hermeneutics, *Radical Philosophy*, 79 September/October, 7–12.

Lukács, G. (1968) *History and Class Consciousness*. Boston, MA: MIT Press.

Luxemburg R. (1995) *The Mass Strike*. London: Bookmarks.

Natsios, A. (2010) 'The Clash of the Counter-bureaucracy and Development', Center for Global Development, retrieved 20 Nov. 19.

Nietzsche, F. (1878/1984) *Human, all too Human: A Book for Free Spirits*, trans. J. R. Hollingdale. Cambridge: Cambridge University Press.

Nietzsche, F. (1882/1974) *The Gay Science. With a Prelude in Rhymes and an Appendix of Songs*, trans. W. Kaufmann. New York: Random House.

Plato (2009) *Phaedo*. Oxford, NY: Oxford University Press.

Rich, A. (2013) 'Song', Southern Cross Review, https://southerncrossreview.org/41/rich.htm retrieved 26 Dec. 19.

Rogers, C. (1951) *Client-centered Therapy*. London: Constable.

Seymour, R. (2019) *The Twittering Machine*. London: Indigo.

Spinelli, E. (2017) Kierkegaard's Dangerous Folly, *Existential Analysis*, 28.2, 288–300.

Spinoza, B. (1677/1996) *Ethics*, trans. E. Curley. London: Penguin.

Stiegler, B. (2013) *What Makes Life Worth Living: on Pharmacology*, trans. Daniel Ross. Cambridge: Polity.

Stiegler, B. (2015) *States of Shock: Stupidity and Knowledge in the 21st Century*, trans. Daniel Ross. Malden, MA: Polity.

Taplin, J. (2018) *Move Fast and Break Things*. London: Pan Macmillan.

Taylor, K.-Y. (2016) *From #BlackLivesMatter to Black Liberation*. Chicago, IL: Haymarket.

Vaidhyanathan, S. (2018) *Antisocial Media: how Facebook Disconnects Us and Undermines Democracy*. Oxford: Oxford University Press.

Voela, A. & Rothschild, L. (2018) Creative Failure: Stiegler, Psychoanalysis and the Promise of a Life Worth Living, *New Formations*, 95, London: Lawrence & Wishart, pp. 54–69.

Wark, M. (2019) *Capital is Dead: is this Something Worse?* London and New York: Verso.

Whitehead, A. N. (1978) *Process and Reality*. New York: The Free Press.

Winnicott, D. W. (1963) *The Maturational Process and the Facilitating Environment*. New York: International Universities Press.

Winnicott, D. W. (1971) *Playing and Reality*. London: Routledge.

Yankelovich, D. (1972) *Corporate Priorities: A Continuing Study of the New Demands on Business*. Stamford, CT: D. Yankelovich Inc.

Young, I. (1981) 'Beyond the Unhappy Marriage: A Critique of the Dual Systems Theory', in L. Sargent (Ed.), *Women and Revolution: A Discussion of the Unhappy Marriage of Marxism and Feminism*. Boston, MA: South End Press, pp. 43–69.

Zuboff, S. (2019) *The Age of Surveillance Capitalism: the Fight for a Human Future at the New Frontier*. New York: Hachette.

8   Authenticity and difference

Heidegger's ontological problem

John Mackessy

Introduction

> If Dasein discovers the world in its own way and brings it close, if it discloses to itself its own authentic Being, then this discovery of the "world" and this disclosure of Dasein are always accomplished as a clearing-away of concealments and obscurities, as a breaking up of the disguises with which Dasein bars its own way.
>
> (Heidegger, 1962, p.167)

Martin Heidegger is, perhaps, the epitome of a profound and committed thinker. He took life seriously and urged his readers to do so. Not that he demanded of us joyless lives of self-abnegation. No, but to live one's life with a sense of responsibility and purpose, to own one's life and to engage with life *authentically* – this might lead us to what he called a 'sober joy', an existence not lost in the intoxications of worldly trends and trivia (Guignon, 1983, p.135).

In an age of inane reality TV, noxious populist politics and ecologically devastating disposable fashion, surely this perspective can only be a good thing.

Many years ago, I taught English in London to adults from overseas. By far the most challenging students, for me, were the Japanese young adults. It was a task to coax a monosyllable from them. Inequitably, I regarded them as pathologically shy and longed for them to express themselves with greater 'authenticity'.

My preconceptions briskly bit the dust when we experimented with role play. What a transition – they chewed the furniture like the most wanton thespians. These classes brimmed, if we employ Heideggerian terminology, with the key signs of inauthenticity: there was much *idle talk* and trivial prattle, more than a little transient and uncommitted *curiosity* and an abundance of *ambiguity*. One could try to portray this as a serious and authentic endeavour by pointing to the students' underlying commitment to their project of learning. This, however, might be akin to claiming that a man, fond of beer, lives in engaged commitment to the local community pub. The students, I believe, simply enjoyed the opportunity to step out of a role they had felt to be required of them and to play.

I came to believe that Oscar Wilde had expressed a significant insight when he wrote that 'Man is least himself when he talks in his own person. Give him a mask, and he will tell you the truth' (1968, p. 389). Wilde was famous for the flamboyant *bon mot* but perhaps less associated with great depth of thought. So, it is easy to regard this as a throw-away line. One might say, too, that I never got to know these students as I only ever saw them playing roles rather than 'being themselves'. But I did see *how* they played – the energy and wit or sullenness of their play. I saw what they *projected* into the world. I got to know these students, I believe, really quite well.

It is interesting that play opens up opportunities for ambiguity and for an improvised and unplanned immersion in the world, often joyful and exuberant. In play things can change meanings, genders, spawn multiple narratives and confound existing narratives and identities.

Being and authenticity

In Heidegger's *Being and Time*, we enter very different terrain. We encounter not the play of meanings but rather a clearing away of concealments towards the disclosure of truth, *aletheia*.

We also encounter authentic *Dasein*, 'the entity whose kind of Being is anticipation itself' (Heidegger, 1962, p.307), clear-sightedly and resolutely living to build its biography. Indeed, Heidegger goes so far as to say that 'resoluteness is authentically and wholly what it can be, only as *anticipatory resoluteness*' (ibid, p.356). One chooses and commits to make a life, or life-project, and thereby projects *oneself* into that future.

Guignon (1993) writes:

> Achieving the narrative continuity of authentic existence is what first makes possible personal identity understood as the "constancy of the self" – its "steadiness" and "steadfastness" – stretched out across a life span. According to Heidegger, it is by taking a stand on one's life as a whole that one satisfies Pindar's counsel to "become what you are".
>
> (p.230)

Playfulness, on the other hand, runs the risk of *inconsistency* and of not being who/ what we take ourselves to be. Or, perhaps, it may give us some distance from the tyranny of an overpowering narrative of self and an escape from 'identity'. As Jean-Paul Sartre somewhat gnomically comments, 'I am not what I am' (1992, p.264) – I am, in my possibility, also always something other/more.

To me, Guignon's depiction of narrative consistency stands as an excellent account of second-rate genre fiction. There our craving for certainty and sense-making is satisfied in two dimensional characters, well-constructed plots and we may even find a comforting sense of resolution or of wholeness. Such narratives resist complexity, ambiguity and, ultimately, real possibility. Sometimes, of course, they are stories we like to hear.

I do not mean to reject entirely Heidegger's promotion of a thoughtful and responsible life, but as depicted, it looks like the life of … a traditional philosopher. The considered life that ponders the problem of Being is the worthwhile, authentic life. I can justly be accused of oversimplifying Heidegger's view. For instance, he points out that inauthentic or 'fallen' existence is not to be judged as *lesser* than authenticity (1962, p.68). We all, necessarily, live much of the time in the dispersed they-life of fallenness. However, one has only to consider his language and how the concept of 'authenticity' has been deployed to know such a defence to be disingenuous. No one has ever been praised or valued for his or her inauthenticity, fallenness or worldliness:

> Dasein has, [...] fallen away from itself as an authentic potentiality for Being its Self, and has fallen into the "world". "Fallenness" into the "world" means an absorption into the Being-with-one-another, insofar as the latter is guided by idle talk, curiosity and ambiguity.
>
> (Heidegger, 1962, p.220)

Poor us! How are we to wake up, get serious and truly seize our lives?

Heidegger's depiction of human agency and authenticity is neither naive nor unsophisticated. He does not espouse a facile Rousseau-inspired model of individualism. His model of authenticity, or *Eigentlichkeit*, purports to be embedded in the world, including the social world, with its limits and traditions as well as its creativity and freedom. *Eigentlichkeit* involves not only being-for-oneself but being-with-others, *Mitsein*, as part of its necessary structure. We are born into a shared world of meanings and purposes. However, authenticity involves us individually taking a stand over who we are and how we live. Ostensibly, this sounds laudable, empowering and liberating.

Heidegger, moreover, emphasizes that *Dasein* is not a fixed thing – as an entity it is temporal and inherently related to our inalienable capacity for choice and becoming. We find a real tension here, however, in that for the entity *Dasein* to be regarded as living authentically, Heidegger demands that it become stabilized through a clear-sighted and resolute commitment to and anticipation of one's life project. This is what gives us authentic constancy of self. So, though his philosophy is permeated with the language of process and choice, his frequent deployment of a stabilized conception of self begins to suggest a particular type of something rather than a complex, unpredictable and evolving process.

Again, although frequently Heidegger is at pains to avoid reifying the notion of an underlying or fundamental self, he does hold a commitment to what he calls *eigentliche Selbst* (own or authentic Self). And one can see how authenticity lends itself to being read/misread as related to an underlying real self. Such tensions between thingness and process are ever-present in Heidegger. It has been said that post *Being and Time* he addressed such concerns, as when he redefined *aletheia* as disclosure, rather than as disclosure of truth. To me, though, this is not convincing, as his commitment to a fundamental underlying ontology remains firm.

Heidegger's notion of authenticity as becoming what you are is further simplified and confused within the Humanistic tradition; for instance, in romantically individualized views, as when Maslow writes that, 'A musician must make music, an artist must paint, a poet must write, if he is to be ultimately happy. What a man can be, he must be. This need we call self-actualization' (1943, p.384). Notably, Maslow has little to say on the self-actualization of an 'average', not particularly creative person. A tax assessor must assess taxes! A van driver must drive vans!, might conceivably become a new humanistic *motto*.

Or, perhaps, these ordinary folk have just *failed* to meet their authentic potential. Imagine the existential guilt they must feel for not making the grade and being the utmost that some philosopher or psychologist thinks they could/should be. Or, worse, perhaps they are so forgetful of Being and lost in they-being that they are not even really conscious of the banal lives they lead. Let me own the tone of disdain here – I sincerely believe this to be a reasonable reading of the underlying values of Heidegger's *Eigentlichkeit*. Ascribing authenticity or fallenness involves, at its core, just such a parochial value judgement. If we are to make such judgements, though, let us own them rather than affect the view that the fallen life is not lesser.

Of death and taxes

Humanistic psychology is, of course, committed to the human as a distinct and irreducible category, for want of a better word, and notions of the human frame its core values. Heidegger interestingly avoids such terminology, instead utilizing the term *Dasein*. It has been argued, convincingly, that he does so to bracket the assumptions and values that accompany 'human'. Moreover, if little green men on some adjacent planet live lives of awareness and choice, then they too would be *Dasein*.

Heidegger's project is a phenomenological and hermeneutic one and *Dasein* appears to offer a clearer space to begin such an enquiry. *Dasein* moves us away from that *species* term and circumvents psychologistic and scientific assumptions about human nature. He observes in his *Letter on Humanism* that 'The human body is essentially something other than an animal organism' (1978, p.204).

Yet, one might argue that employing this new *philosophical* conception ultimately de-physicalizes the human subject and devalues and evades forms of discourse other than the philosophical. No one, it seems, can get at fundamental ontological truth quite like a philosopher in introspection.

Why, indeed, would one wish to bother with deterministic and reductionist perspectives? Therein, many of the insights of psychology, biology and neurology appear to run counter to Heidegger's fundamental commitments around freedom and choice. One might, of course, try to extend the notion of facticity to include biology as a factor affecting our choices, but this is clearly an encroachment of the sciences into the ontological realm of freedom which Heidegger would have rejected.

Although there was clearly much value in Heidegger's critique of scientism, his approach has at least one significant flaw – by devaluing other disciplines it tends to close in upon itself and become philosophical to a solipsistic extent. However, one might argue, that *if* all Being is fundamentally unified in some manner, then one *Dasein*'s philosophical reflection on its own mode of Being may uncover something universal. This is Heidegger's position, but, to my mind at least, it appears to be a phenomenological article of faith, rather than an existential given, or any sort of fact at all. Is *Dasein* really so fundamentally homogenous and unified, or is this simply a philosopher's projection of his own commitment regarding the nature of Being?

Such questions as, 'Are non-neurotypical persons *Dasein*?' or 'Does testosterone influence the prevalence of violence in *Dasein*?' are utterly anomalous, and indicate uncomfortable and very un-Heideggerian interfaces of enquiry. Given *Dasein*'s inalienable capacity for choice, how might one even approach such questions as whether there is a minimum level of intelligence or a particular way of experiencing the world which are prerequisites for being *Dasein*? A significantly brain-damaged person may not be *Dasein*; a boy or girl with profound learning-disabilities may not be *Dasein*. This is not mere pedantic quibbling, but indicates that *Dasein* is not only a de-physicalized concept but a de-humanized one. Precisely who or what is *Dasein*, if anything, other than an abstract philosophical concept?

Heidegger's phenomenological enquiry into Being may be regarded as comprising two dimensions – firstly, it is Heidegger's analysis of that which is 'uncovered' in *his* experience as *Dasein*. Secondly, and beyond this, it turns his investigation of *Dasein* into a philosophical analysis of the supposedly *necessary* and *universal* structure of experience and of Being for all others who are *Dasein*.

In this respect, Heidegger claims to uncover certain existential givens about how it is to be *Dasein*. These are phenomena which, he holds, are there *in fundamentally the same manner for all of us* and which are inescapable for any *Dasein*. Hence they unify *the conception* of *Dasein*'s Being and the very nature of *Dasein*'s being-in-the-world.

For instance, we have facticity and thrownness (one does not choose or control the circumstances in which one comes into being etc.). Then there is the unavoidability of freedom and choice (within certain limits and circumstances we cannot but choose and thereby create ourselves and our lives) and, also, as temporal beings, there is the fact of one's death to come (our mortality and what Heidegger calls our being-towards-death).

So, of death and taxes, death is a necessity but taxes are optional. Taxes are contingent 'ontic' matters but not 'ontologically' inherent to the very structure of Being. If we follow Heidegger's analysis, then we also have to regard such things as biological sex as ontic rather than ontological. One's sex happens to be a fact about one and might have been otherwise, but it is not *integral* to one's experience or one's Being as *Dasein*. As *Dasein*, men and women fundamentally share the same experiential world. They just happen to be men and women … (evidently).

It is these existential givens that unify and hold the whole edifice of Heidegger's systematic philosophy of existence together. They also entirely determine his conception of what it is to live in authenticity. We will die and we have freedom whether we like these facts or not. Interpret away, my friend, the grave awaits you. To own one's life is to face these basic facts with courage, clear-sightedness and integrity.

I can look only briefly at the existential givens of mortality and choice and how they might relate to authenticity.

Dasein's temporality and mortality are at the very core of authenticity for Heidegger: '[W]hen one has an understanding of being-towards-death – towards death as one's *ownmost possibility* – one's potentiality for being becomes authentic and wholly transparent' (1962, p.307).

Heideggerians have observed that he is neither encouraging a morbid fascination with death nor a morbid way of being, but rather indicating that it is through not evading the existential fact of one's mortality that one can begin to live fully and honestly.

Critics of Heidegger, notably Levinas (1987) and, within the world of psychotherapy, Bazzano (2017), have indicated concerns regarding his ontological analysis of death. Both have observed that being-towards-death cannot be an existential given, as death is not a phenomenon that can be directly experienced, nor does death have a fundamental meaning to be 'anticipated' and faced in advance. Our own mortality is *directly* knowable to us, neither as fact, nor event, nor even as the horizon of facts and events.

Bazzano examines the narcissistic insolence at the heart of regarding death as something one can stare at and face down (2017, pp.35–38). It is hubris to think one can anticipate death or its meaning. This 'being-towards' has but a fantastical object. Whatever one may believe, death may turn another face – to terrorize us, sweep our knowing away or to come to us as a gift. Death is not there to be domesticated and its anxieties cannot be cauterized in advance.

Bazzano also observes how Heidegger seeks to ground even *nothingness* in terms of Being.

One might think of this, I suggest, as analogous to defining the feminine or female psycho-sexual development in terms of the 'lack' of the phallus. 'Being' is Heidegger's 'phallus', his primary signifier. Thereby, the inconceivable and even 'the possibility of our impossibility' (our mortality) become part of an *ontological* system of signification and are rendered 'knowable'. Being is placed as the fundamental truth, even of non-being or nothingness. You can have any flavour you want as long as it's ontological.

Grounding authenticity in terms of ontology and death is to give it no ground at all, unless one is willing to reify the meaning of death and to assume that one's contingent notions of death indicate a transcendent ontological truth.

We are also what we are not

To move on to how choice relates to authenticity, it is certainly one of the shibboleths of both Heidegger's philosophy and later existentialism that we are free, within certain constraints, to make our own choices and that authenticity involves owning these choices. Heidegger did not, however, hold a crudely individualistic view of human freedom or how this frames our choices.

Sartre's view of authenticity, or his refinement of it in his notion of 'good faith', differs from Heidegger. He offers, however, a generally illuminative set of examples in *Being & Nothingness*. Exploring one of these will, I believe, help us to understand some reductive narrative assumptions that operate when we begin to consider contingent human choices from the perspective of a normative concept of authenticity or good/bad faith. Many would argue that authenticity is not a normative concept. Sartre's examples, as I hope to show, fundamentally give the lie to this.

Reworking Heidegger's ideas, Sartre says that we can disown our relationship to choice in two ways, both of which are instances of bad faith. Firstly, we can disown the extent of our freedom by presenting ourselves as objects in the world, determined by various historical or situational forces. 'I had no choice' might be the refrain here. Or secondly, we can deny our facticity by presenting ourselves as completely free to create ourselves, unaffected by historical influences or situational factors. Our sanctimonious contemporary dictum, 'you can be whatever you want to be, if only you try' would be an example of this.

Interestingly, and this takes us, I believe, beyond the limitations of Heidegger's fundamental ontology, Sartre sees 'sincerity' itself as bad faith. Speaking with the voice of sincerity involves us in taking ourselves 'to be what we are', delimiting or defining ourselves in some manner. In so doing, we represent ourselves as objects, as some particular type of thing in the world. For Sartre this is a partial and self-deceptive understanding, for we are also *what we are not*. Because of our freedom there is more to us than how we or others may wish to see or represent ourselves.

Despite this anti-essentialist insight, Sartre's discussion of 'patterns of bad faith' offers a famous example relating to how a woman responds to the advances of a man (Sartre, 1992, p.96ff). Sartre represents the woman as choosing to ignore certain features of the situation, such that 'she does not wish to read in the phrases he addresses to her anything other than their explicit meaning'. If he says to her, 'I find you so attractive!' she disarms this phrase of its sexual background' (ibid, p.96). Sartre goes on to comment that her selective reading of this situation springs from the fact that:

> she does not quite know what she wants. She is profoundly aware of the desire which she inspires, but the desire cruel and naked would horrify her. Yet she could find no charm in a respect that would only be respect.
>
> (ibid, p.97)

He explains that she wants to be desired in her wholeness and freedom but also as a body, an object, and cannot reconcile the two desires. Her bad faith lies in disowning either her facticity (her thingness as a body, etc.) or her transcendence (her freedom and choice). Interestingly, one could argue that 'good faith' here would involve the woman in acknowledging her ambivalence and the ambiguity of her situation.

Sartre then suggests that the man takes her hand, writing:

> We know what happens next; the young woman leaves her hand there, but she does not notice that she is leaving it [...] the hand rests inert between the warm hands of her companion – neither consenting nor resisting – a thing.
>
> (ibid, p.97)

Sartre holds that the woman uses her freedom to disavow her freedom. Thereby she *chooses* to maintain her position of bad faith and disowns the incongruous nature of her choices, and of her desires. She maintains a desirable illusion by keeping her facticity and her transcendence separated.

Although, Sartre claims, it is clear what this man's intentions are (no ambiguity there, apparently), to me Sartre's account itself is redolent of bad faith by ignoring, among other things, the possibility of the woman being able to *transcend* through her choice to act or not to act. Her choice to 'ignore' aspects of this man's behaviour may be in good faith in that she may be refusing either to regard herself *unambiguously* as an object or as self-determining in this situation.

However, in this phenomenological exploration Sartre seems to have entered this woman's experience, determined its meaning, foreclosed her ability to choose and judged her to be in bad faith. One might argue that Sartre, man of his time and culture, has failed to bracket certain phallocentric assumptions.

Sartre's reading of this situation is fascinating, and he is, *of course*, guilty of exactly what he imputes to his fantasy woman – he pays attention, selectively, to the features which fit the narrative that he wishes to develop and holds at bay or excludes possibilities that threaten this narrative. Thus, the reading of this woman's bad faith is a game played by his rules with a range of meanings constrained by his master-narrative. There is something that Sartre disowns in this account.

As with many a narrative, it is interesting what Sartre chooses to exclude. We have very little context to the encounter between this man and this woman. They are, apparently, an autonomous male and an autonomous female, free to make what choices they wish in relation to one another. Whatever Sartre may say of facticity, the facticity of these persons' existences is notable in its absence. So, interestingly, this is exclusively a formalized or idealized account of this woman's choices, stripped of context.

Is there anything, however, about these two persons or around them that might configure their engagement? Would it make a difference, for instance, if the woman were the man's boss, or if she were his secretary? What of the environment? Is there anything about being this woman or this man in this particular environment that might be pertinent? All of these form parts of the facticity of this situation and, as Sartre and Heidegger have taught us, it is bad faith to ignore facticity.

Interestingly, the two other examples of patterns of bad faith given by Sartre in the same text involve the overly subservient behaviour of a waiter and the disowned sexuality of a homosexual man. Again they are notably decontextualized/ desubjectivized and all three examples possess unexamined power dynamics.

None of Sartre's examples involves the powerful presence and perhaps sometimes contriving sexuality of an eminent and influential French philosopher. Let's imagine this philosopher with a particular woman – let's call her Wanda K – who didn't wish to enter his bed but may have wished to continue to appear in his plays. She may also, possibly, have chosen not to engage directly with his advances. A little context can go a long way in aiding our understanding of what otherwise remains a formal and idealized structure of engagement.

Let us remember, too, that for Sartre and Heidegger context and facticity does not *ever* mean that we do not have choice. No matter how oppressive the facticity, or how overpowering the power dynamics, there is always, by their views, choice. If this view holds a quantum of truth, it also opens up some very uncomfortable issues to explore. It would be interesting to get the views of Sartre and Heidegger on recent debates regarding coerced consent, Mr Weinstein *et al.*

'The Anyone' and concrete others

To defend Sartre for a moment, he does attempt to address issues of oppression. His existentialism, he states, is 'a humanism'. He believes that when one makes a choice, one also, in a sense, chooses for the whole of humanity. Therefore choices made in good faith consider fellow humans and seek to preclude oppression and exploitation. Well, this sounds lovely, but is it not simply a fantastical device?

For instance, I act in good faith and take my fellow humankind into account by supporting Mao and his Little Red Book. My neighbour does likewise but with a predilection for the Liberal Democrats, regarding me as one of the benighted oppressors of humanity. We end up where some Marxists have used the term 'false consciousness' to describe the alienated consciousness of those proletarians who do not perceive the reality of their class interests. So, we're back in the domain of master-narratives and essentialized conceptions of truth. Sartre's socialization of choice has left us – in the absence of God-like omniscience – with a device which in practice is little more than a *boo* or *hurrah* for various choices and value systems. Alternatively, we might hold a less socialized, more self-referential model of authenticity, such as Heidegger's being true to one's own vision. Without some sort of developed ethics or axiology, though, such resoluteness may apply as validly to Pol Pot as to Mahatma Gandhi. As Heidegger sententiously remarks in *Being and Time*, 'Only in a resolution is resoluteness sure of itself' (1962, p.345).

For all my criticism of Sartre, he did try to explore being-with-others more extensively than does Heidegger with *Mitsein*. Tellingly, *Mitsein*, or 'being-with', is one of the *a priori features* of *Dasein*'s mode of being in the world. Such being-with-others is a *necessary* part of *Dasein*'s ontological structure. *Dasein*'s world and *Dasein*'s relation to the world in its projects are inconceivable without *Mitsein*. To be, to have a world, is inherently to have a world with others. Others have even formed one's language, itself the very 'house of Being' (Heidegger, 1978, p.193).

Our relation to others, in Heidegger, is one of solicitude, which sounds benign, but fundamentally refers to our concern with others in relation to our projects. Even Heidegger's call of conscience is something that brings one *away* from the they-self and back to one's own Being. He writes that when this call is heard 'the "*they*" collapses' (1962, p.317). In fact, Heidegger does not develop a phenomenology of *Mitsein* or of solicitude very far at all. There are allusions, as in Sartre, to not treating others as mere objects in the world, but neither Heidegger nor Sartre convincingly develops ethics or axiology. Within the existential/phenomenological tradition the place of ethics has, of course, been regarded as a more central concern by Simone de Beauvoir, Levinas and others.

Heidegger's focus and certainly his emphasis in his conception of authenticity *was not on an ethics of being-with-others* but on a mode of living that could be *Dasein's own* and not simply absorbed into *das Man* (variously translated as 'the They' 'the Anyone' 'the Others' etc.). Other people and society are depicted as 'levelling down [...] all the possibilities of Being' of individual *Dasein* (Heidegger, 1962, p.165).

Heidegger's way of writing about *das Man*, I feel, can be quite chilling. For instance:

> Dasein, as everyday Being-with-another, stands in *subjection* to Others. It itself *is* not; its Being has been taken away by the Others. Dasein's everyday possibilities of Being are for the Others to dispose of as they please. These Others, moreover, are not definite Others. On the contrary, any Other can represent them. What is decisive is just that inconspicuous domination by Others.
>
> (1962, p.164)

So, these Others, crucially, are conceived neither as actual groups nor real individuated others – hence the suggestion that *das Man* might be better translated as *the Anyone*. I suggest that this conception of alterity fails even to try to represent the range of possibilities of real relationships with others, nor can it address any situational ethics that might emerge in such real encounters. Rather, *das Man* comes across as a formal, idealized construct related to the structure of *Dasein's* being-in-the-world and *Dasein's* relationship with an *idealized* notion of otherness. The Other, as part of such a construct, becomes merely a hypostasized appendage to *Dasein*. *Dasein* is the ground on which otherness is based. This is virtually the antithesis of Lévinas's description of 'ipseity', the embodied sense of individual identity which arises when otherness impresses itself upon us – whereupon, one needs to react, as a subject, to deal with a world that is not merely an extension of oneself (cf. 1981, pp.xvii–xviii).

Heidegger, with his insistence upon the quality of mine-ness of authentic *Dasein*, is, however, interested in *Dasein's* heritage – with *my* own history, *my* own people and even the destiny of *my* people. As Polt explains, 'Authenticity does not involve jettisoning one's own tradition – which is impossible – but clear-sightedly and resolutely pursuing a possibility that is opened up by this tradition' (1999, p.63).

We can see here, I believe, a *homogenizing and deeply conservative strand* in Heidegger's philosophy. Perhaps, I might paraphrase the previous quote thus: 'The Others threaten to take over my very Being. So, I must honour that which is truly mine and the tradition from which it springs'. A precept for the Brexit generation, perhaps; for those who are sure of who they are, where they have come from, the ground of their Being and the danger that the imagined Others pose.

Difference, ambiguity and tradition

In our current times, with issues of identity and difference critiqued and lived out in different ways, we have interesting perspectives from which to examine some of the core commitments of Heidegger's philosophy of Being, or indeed any philosophy that utilizes ontology to ground a normative framework of understanding.

I am not arguing that we reject tradition or owning one's own life, but simply that we look at the implications of Heidegger's grounding assumptions. In his notion of authenticity and his commitment to the unfolding of an authentic Self, Heidegger excludes at least two crucial and interrelated dimensions of human existence – *ambiguity* and the possibility of radical *alterity*.

Ambiguity he excludes in his commitment to disclosedness (*aletheia*) and to an authentic or fundamentally true mode of Being. The alleged clear-sightedness of *Dasein*'s project, and its 'anticipatory resoluteness' (Heidegger, 1962, p.356), is in itself the antithesis of an ambiguity that allows for *other* possibilities.

Secondly, he excludes radical alterity, the fact that this Other, his or her life, death and choices may elude one's framework of understanding. One needs, I believe, to entertain the possibility that the Other may not be *essentially like me*, and that their experience may not be like mine or even structured like mine.

For instance, with his synaesthesia, the great Russian painter, Kandinsky, developed an influential colour theory through his ability to 'see sounds' and 'hear colours'. In this regard, it is not at all clear how *Dasein*'s experiential world is 'unified' by Heidegger, considering the diversity of humankind, including those who are non-neurotypical. There must, therefore, exist at least the possibility that another's existential condition be quite different to one's own. The unity of experience and of *our* mode of being-in-the world is, by that view, simply a complacently assumed universal.

Early in *Being and Time* Heidegger asserts that we are able to ask the question of Being because we have some fore-knowledge of what it is we are asking. If language is the house of Being, for example, and we are born into that house, it cannot be truly unknown to us. We live it and live through it every day. It is there too in our cultures and traditions.

This may assuage our fears of being lost in the world and portrays us as inherently connected in our very Being to others who inhabit our world. It does not, however, engage with true difference or the instability of systems of meaning. If we already have a pre-understanding of the question of Being and of who we are in our *ownmost* potential, we diminish the possibilities that may emerge through 'not knowing' or by encountering something new and radically different to what we expect.

Closing thoughts

The notion of authenticity, as it is framed by Heidegger, is related to a steadfastness of vision and constancy of self which result in the unfolding of authentic Selfhood. To my mind, a stabilization of *process* may certainly be helpful, for instance, for a client who has experienced trauma or incapacitating anxiety, as might a sense of personal and interpersonal security. However, I do not see what positing a stabilized authentic self or authentic mode of being adds to this; other than a commitment in advance to something to which one needs to conform in forging a narratively-consistent biography.

An immersion in life, without over-reliance on a cognized self-concept or a life-project-concept, is a less 'philosophical' approach to living. However, without the need to abandon reflection, it may give more sway to the affective and embodied dimensions of our existences, including an engagement with ambiguity.

This touches on another concern I have regarding Heidegger. His system is rather more *dogmatic* than *experiential* as regards the nature of being-in-the-world. His project is simply too exclusively philosophical, abstract and formal. One might expect of a phenomenology a nuanced and intimate account of direct experience. However, Heidegger's commitment to a fundamental ontology means that everything is viewed through a unifying conception of Being. More often than not he is actually engaged in abstruse musings on the meaning of Being. The concept of *Dasein* and its relation to *Mitsein* is a case in point, as is his treatment of the Others, which turns alterity into little more than a vapid philosophical concept. Even Heidegger's existential givens, such as being-towards-death and freedom are actually either decontextualized abstractions or *a priori* philosophical constructs. In each case, he systematically excludes the contingencies of actual lived experience; how we might actually face the meaning of our deaths; or, how far as beings who are also animals, with psyches and biologies, we actually do make free choices.

Heideggerian authenticity supposedly moves towards the truth (*aletheia*) of Being, clearing-away concealments and obscurities. Alongside this, an authentic understanding of being-towards-death purportedly makes our potential for Being 'wholly transparent' (1962, p.307). *What, though, is such living-in-truth other than a crypto-religious dogma?* One might believe it, and soothe oneself with its narrative coherence, or one might try to engage with the unknown and difference such that they not be so neatly packaged but continue to challenge and defy us.

To conclude, I must say that I do not see what, other than false comfort, we might gain as human beings or as therapists from notions of authenticity or even the more nuanced notions of good and bad faith. Despite Heidegger's protestation that the fallen life is not less than those moments of authenticity, authenticity *is* employed as a normative concept, knowingly or not.

There is, moreover, a profound danger in embracing these conceptions in psychotherapy. They have the potential to turn complexity, difference and ambiguity into something that can be conveniently and piously defused, even where we claim not to do so. As with Sartre and his imaginary woman, it is likely that we act out an agenda or a particular type of fore-knowledge when we attempt to strip things down to judgements of authenticity or good/bad faith. We tacitly claim a knowledge of the other's experience or indeed a transparent insight into ourselves that is simply not available to us in our profound contingency and diversity.

As a practitioner and a supervisor, I have certainly seen this lead to the most complacent of practice, resting upon bland and entitled assumptions of a shared, homogenous 'human condition'.

I want to be clear that I am not asserting that there cannot be a profound and meaningful connection between our clients and ourselves. It is simply that such a connection cannot be honoured through conceptions such as authenticity that rely on a fundamental homogenization or unity of Being.

The Other, the one whom we may *actually* encounter, may not wish to play by our rules or even to condone our games. At least, I hope not, for to return to Mr Wilde, 'Consistency is the last refuge of the unimaginative' (1968, p.18).

References

Bazzano, M. (2017) *Zen and Therapy: Heretical Perspectives*. Abingdon, OX: Routledge.

Guignon, C.B. (1983) *Heidegger and the Problem of Knowledge*. Indiana: Hackett.

Guignon, C.B. (1993) 'Authenticity, Moral Values, and Psychotherapy', in Guignon, C.B. (Ed), *The Cambridge Companion to Heidegger*. Cambridge University Press.

Heiddeger, M. (1962) *Being and Time*. London: SCM Press.

Heiddeger, M. (1978) *Basic Writings*. London: Routledge and Kegan Paul.

Levinas, E. (1987) *Time and the Other*. Pittsburgh: Duquesne University Press.

Levinas, E. (1981) *Otherwise than being, or, Beyond essence*. The Hague: Nijhoff.

Maslow, A.H. (1943) 'A Theory of Human Motivation'. *Psychological Review*, 50(4), 370–396. http://dx.doi.org/10.1037/h0054346.

Polt, R. (1999) *Heidegger – an Introduction*. New York: Cornell University Press.

Sartre, J.P. (1992) *Being and Nothingness*. New York: Washington Square Press.

Wilde, O. (1968) *The Artist as Critic: Critical Writings of Oscar Wilde*, Ellman, R. (Ed). New York: Random House.

9 Radical existentialism is *manuski*

Existentially influenced psychoanalytic psychotherapy

Michael R. Montgomery

Introduction

As someone who identifies as a contemporary psychoanalytic psychotherapist influenced by existential-phenomenological approaches to therapy, I am most grateful to be included in this volume. In addition, perhaps giving voice to a minority within a minority has helped me consolidate my thinking and experience both personally and professionally. It is also a moment for me to publicly nail my colours to the mast. I am now living, practising and researching psychotherapy in a fourth country, with a rich multitude of cultures, so my perspective is very much an international one.

Rollo May (1961, p.19) argued that existentialism is a term that demarcates an attitude rather than a special school or group, 'it is not a system of therapy but an attitude toward therapy, not a set of new techniques but a deep concern with an understanding and structure of the human being and his experience that must underlie all techniques'.

For many 'existentialists', the very idea of endeavouring to combine psycho-analytic thinking and existential-phenomenological thinking is an oxymoron. My partner laughs at me on many occasions, but two extreme examples come to mind. Once, while on a trip to Disneyland, there was a sequence in one of the show-case events where visitors were given the opportunity to make a wish. My partner looked at me and said 'you wished for world peace, didn't you?' I could not decide which offended me more: my own transparency or their mockery.

The other occasion was when I was asked what my greatest fear was. The resulting belly laugh affronted me. Was 'totalitarianism' so outlandish an answer? I grew up in Northern Ireland during the violent time known as 'The Troubles'. Perhaps living through an armed conflict makes the naïve wish for peace, and in my case, a morbid fear of extremism. In this chapter I hope to touch on what I believe is a road toward peace via connection and an antidote to totalitarianism – even, dare I be so bold as to say, therapeutic theoretical conflict and dogma.

I will begin by unpacking what philosophy and the term existential-phenomenological means for my practice and research.

Philosophy as Mandelbrot set

Philosophy can be daunting. The sheer amount of words written, the many complex ideas expressed, challenged and deconstructed: the sheer weight of what I don't know or understand can be disheartening. One can be forgiven for thinking that there was a pure unbroken lineage of truth in European philosophers from Kierkegaard to Sartre. Perhaps in part this is why Foucault referred to him as the last prophet (Wade, 2019).

When given further exploration, the flow of ideas is not so linear. Pick any well documented philosopher and over time, they will be seen to have shifted their views from some of their most seminal writings. Often their work is translated, but which is the definitive version? Whose, if any, is the definitive interpretation? I have experienced the deep exploration of philosophy and its ways, rather like the visual representation of the Mandelbrot set. One can choose any aspect of the most intricate pattern and go into it seemingly indefinitely, returning eventually to the original and distinctive fractal pattern. An old Buddhist teacher said to me once: 'there is as much dharma as there is human confusion'. As the original psychology, is philosophy the 'endless trip' matching humans at their level of confusion?

Before we rush to dust off the old tie-dyes and go a bit woo, it must be noted that philosophy, when it hardens, can become another dogmatic excuse for tyranny. The seduction of painful uncertainty, replaced by concrete ideas, offers a certain direction for the fragile human story. Take the case of Nietzsche. (Mis) interpretation of him became a predicate for racial supremacy and unmitigated nihilistic violence. Heidegger (1962), whose *Being and Time* seems to be the theoretical antidote to some of the horrors of the last century, paradoxically and painfully for readers, joined one of the main parties that would commit them. Would Sartre and Simone de Beauvoir's alleged sexual exploits (Seymour-Jones, 2009) have been overlooked and their reputations survived had they lived through the #MeToo era? I still shudder when recalling infamous killer Ian Brady referring to his heinous torture and murder of children as an 'existential exercise'.

With a degree of intellectual fatigue, irreconcilable visceral concerns and disappointments, I have tried unsuccessfully to wrestle psychotherapy away from this endless Mandelbrot set but I simply cannot. Like or not, conscious or otherwise, philosophical beliefs underpin how we choose to live our life and practice therapy. People live their life with foundational belief systems that impact their behaviour:

> *pay now, play later*: 'eternalists' e.g. suicide bombers, puritanical religious people
> *play now, there is no later*: 'nihilists' e.g. climate-change deniers, the Trump administration's policies
> *people are essentially good*: 'humanists' e.g. Rogerians, hippies
> *people are essentially bad*: 'theistic religions' e.g. Westboro Baptist Church, Kleinians

For me one of the most important philosophical underpinnings is how we choose to treat others. It was through the study of existential thinker and psychiatrist R.D. Laing (1927–1989) that I learnt the most basic idea of 'treatment'. In the clinical sense, it is ultimately how we choose to *treat* someone we encounter in distress and need. Am I, the all-knowing therapist doing something to you, or are we doing something collaboratively together? Are *your* views of *your* world less valid than some deep insight that we pretend that I hold? Or am I simply the facilitator of your journey, to your own answers, core, true-self or authentic-self, and ultimate interconnectedness?

There are challenges required on the whole structure of western educa-tion and its inherent capacity to exclude contributions from other cultures and viewpoints. As someone who has studied Eastern philosophy, I found it astonishing that it was never given a mention in psychotherapy courses. With even a tertiary understanding of Buddhism one can connect easily with Heidegger's seemingly more esoteric concepts, and their potentially hidden sources (May, 1996).

Are some of these dead white men and women simply canonised because they fit the dominant hierarchical narrative, or have they still something valid to con-tribute to the practice of psychotherapy?

Buffet philosophy

In the Society for Existential Analysis (SEA, 2019), an international member organisation to which I belong, there is a simple, yet in my humble opinion, powerful aim: 'to provide a forum for the expression of views and the exchange of ideas amongst those interested in the analysis of existence from philosophical and psychological perspectives.' Boom! This clear aim provides a conduit to a space that can hold wildly different views and ideas yet manage to stay in com-munity with one another – we exist. The Society could be demarcated by the more seriously philosophically minded: those who could spend a year debating the efficacy of free-will compared to the others who I would describe as buffet philosophers. They believe philosophers have placed their ideas in a public place and practitioners can serve themselves. I have another name for items that most people in the Society consume.

Existential soup

In conversation, when I use the term existential to refer to an influence on my life and work, it is an abbreviation for existential-phenomenological concepts. It is an example of how easy it is to use and misuse the word. Returning to May (1961), we see that he cautioned about the dubious term existentialism. The regrettably inter-changeable use of existentialist and existential is highlighted in significant detail by Webber (2018). With this in mind, it is easily possible to deep-dive once again into the Mandelbrot set. Although I have given considerable thought and study to these challenges and debates, I leave them by settling on the terms existential and phenomenological for my soup:

Existential – Thinkers who are concerned with the meanings of lived experience. When termed 'existential thinkers', it allows for the inclusion of 'existentialist deniers' such as Heidegger and Albert Camus and an abundance of literature and art concerned with living in the face of mortality, freedom, aloneness and meaninglessness.

Phenomenology – A truer term that might define itself would be hermeneutic phenomenology (Bracken and Thomas, 2005). In other words, a concern with what it means to be, the examination of experience in the lived world. How the world makes sense to the individual through their experience and the meaning that they attribute to that. 'Symptoms' can have meaning, not something simply to be eradicated without consideration. Although I view this phenomenology to be both client-centred and humanistic, it delineates specifically from 'humanistic existentialism' with the view that people are neither essentially good nor bad. As Laing (1987, p.206) so eloquently phrased it: 'Phenomenology is an attempt to release our minds from the bland, uncritical attachment to any set of miserable meanings – right or wrong, true or false'.

I am aware that, in an effort to define these terms, I may seem reductive and simplistic. Nuance is central to my work and central to my thinking. Whilst attempting to try and apply them to practice, I think the nuance will become apparent.

My own experience of these philosophers and their application to psychotherapy and how they were presented in the UK therapy circles left a lot to be desired. Heidegger and Sartre were taught without as much as a footnote to the fact that Heidegger was an unapologetic Nazi and Sartre continued to support global communism, long after the horrors of the Russian, Chinese and Vietnamese genocides were accepted facts.

There are many teachers and adherents who present Heidegger's (1962) *Being and Time* as if it were a holy book, each line speaking a profound, yet indecipherable, truth that can somewhat shift upon each reading. What is regrettable in the existential school of thought, Lomas (1999) argues, is the degree to which it is preoccupied with obscure philosophical argument.

The danger of course with a soup is if one is not careful, anything or everything could get thrown in. When stirred, some of the ideas and concepts can seem muddled, confused and contradictory. The non-Cartesian or Cartesian foundations fudged in favour of a sickly mono or critical fracture. Despite these complexities, there remains a beauty, excitement and contemporary relevancy, even necessity, in the reappraisal of their core ideas. As Cooper (1990, p.vii) so powerfully states 'existentialism is worth revisiting at intervals for the help it may offer with themes of contemporary interest'.

To free some of the gold of existential thinking from the dross, I think it needs re-visioning to embrace its critics before returning to its application in therapy and human encounter.

Radical existentialism

In her book *At the Existential Café*, Bakewell (2016) nostalgically locates existentialism in a historic time and a space, positing that it has never seemed as raw and dangerous as it did back then. I disagree profoundly, and if the sales of her book are anything to go by (excuse the pun) then existentialism retains an interest for the wider public and certainly holds a relevancy. The term 'existential crises' gets trotted out on a daily basis, to describe everything from the woes of football teams to the consequences of political decision-making. The usage may be precarious but the term remains very much in the public parlance.

Existentialism's implied narcissism is called out by Loewenthal (2011) in his prizing of existential notions of experience and meaning over any theoretically driven model of therapy. He argues for the consideration of post-modern thinkers in his concept of post-existentialism. I recently re-read a chunk of Michel Foucault (1926–1984), having felt increasingly alienated from some of the rhetoric of the more politically active and their interpretation of Foucault, which I did not fully recognise.

Foucault was a thinker who, when I first read him, offered an insight and path into how I could work to empower oppressed groups, as opposed to a blueprint for nihilistic terror (Dustin and Montgomery, 2010). His critique of phenomenology is vital. However, I think both are necessary. The reality of structural systemic inequalities is getting drowned out by the politically weaponised use of rhetoric. In many parts of America, the experience for a black man being stopped by the police, compared to that for a white man, will be objectively different. Recently the phenomenon of white Americans calling the police for what Thurston (2019) called 'living while black' has been documented by citizens' cellphones for the world to witness.

Recognising the need for an evolution of existential thinking, I proposed the term radical existentialism (Montgomery, 2017). After a few years of percolation, I reflected on whether 'radical' was simply lazily being attached to anything and everything to make it more edgy, and therefore toyed with the idea of calling it contemporary existentialism. It may be simply semantics, but after some more reading I retained radical existentialism as the term that best captures the rational and intuitive reconstruction of existential ideas and concepts.

The initial liberation offered by existential thinkers can soon run into an opposing force for sedimentation. As Lomas (1999, p.48) argues: 'The flight from the ordinary is very pervasive. It appears that if we eschew the religious dogma we fall into the hands of science, and if we escape from science, we become dazzled by the intricacies of philosophical debate.'

The jargon of Heidegger, Theodor Adorno (2003) argues, fails to reveal the lack of freedom inherent in the capitalist context in which it was written. The lack of freedom inherent in every socialist society to date is maybe for discussion at another time.

'A concept is a brick', Massumi (2003, p.xii) proposed; 'it can be used to build a courthouse of reason. Or it can be thrown through the window.' I am getting older, I haven't time to denote the nuances of a badly translated German sentence. The world is facing untold challenges. I would propose that existential thinking has always been radical and astonishing in its spirit and its heart. When applied to the realm of psychotherapy, its application is both accessible and practical.

I will offer just a handful of concept-bricks that support a delineating of my practice and how it is directly influenced by existential-phenomenological thinking.

In practice

Having worked and researched in Malaysia, Germany, the UK and the USA, I can confirm that the term psychoanalytic (or influenced) psychotherapist is a very broad and conflicted one. The basic cornerstones of psychoanalytic thinking, hardened rules and the inherent patriarchy have been rejected by many in favour of a relational focus or like some existential practitioners, a licence for freestyle. There are, however, core psychoanalytic concepts that remain important to my practice:

- Interpretation (making suggestions about how I understand what the client is presenting).
- Free-association-light (suggesting that saying whatever comes to mind might be a good thing at times).
- History does matter. People are not their past, but nor is the present completely free from it.
- Exploring the transference-counter-transference in the here-and-now (the dynamics of the therapeutic relationship) can yield significant insights into how the client is living interpersonally.
- The unconscious (the concept that we are not always fully aware of everything that is influencing our thoughts and behaviours).

Through the influence of existential-phenomenological thinking these concepts garner a more radical presentation:

- The client's well-being takes priority before any theory or approach.
- The therapeutic relationship is collaborative.
- The clients' lived experience, understanding and experience are more important than any label.
- Any interpretation is hermeneutic and not reductive.
- All interpretation is provisional, something proposed and not imposed.
- The centrality of not locating suffering uniquely within the individual (she isn't depressed, she is unemployed; he isn't aggressive, he is asking for help in the only way he knows how).
- People cannot be reduced to mechanical scientific principles.

Objectification and nuance

For anyone still retaining the capacity to think for themselves-with-others, these can be disheartening times. I won't go into the truth and fact-fractal fracas but rather I want to touch on nuance. History leaves little room for nuance in terms of winners and losers. Moral clarity seems apparent, the American Civil War, the defeat of Nazism, the Civil Rights Movement. There is an apparent polarisation in the USA and UK, summarised in two words: 'Brexit' and 'Trump'. History has yet to be written on these seismic and still-unfolding events, but within them there is surely moral clarity; separating children from families, profiling on the grounds of gender or race, the freedom for one to love a consenting other.

There is a worrying objectification in these battles. With the objectification of the Other comes the enviable shadow of 'less than' (Smith, 2012). Parasitic language creeps quickly in, and with it fear followed swiftly by hate.

Psychotherapists have not been free from these tensions. Politics, it seems, has become a pole with which to prod one other. I maintain that it is possible to remain publicly non-partisan whilst being morally clear. It is a personal view that psychotherapists sacrifice a more public, personal persona in favour of radical openness. We need thinkers and we need people unplugged from the attacks from partisan news media that can scream moral clarity when it is called for, free from petty party and often personality allegiances.

The over-medicalisation and excessive labelling of human suffering is simply wrong. Mourning, sadness, anxiety, paranoia even, all have purpose in their healthy amounts – the spectrum of human-being. With a quickness to label we objectify and potentially imply 'less than human'. The 'worried-well', the 'unwell', the 'mad', the 'crazy' ones, all have a story to tell. A brutal psychoanalytic supervisor once accused me of being 'a storyteller'. It was meant in a disparaging way. Too much storytelling and not enough complex psychoanalytic jargon to describe the patient they frequently referred to as a 'pervert'. I knew at that point that I had arrived as a psychotherapist, I certainly *did* want to give voice to the dispossessed, to tell their stories from underneath the weight of frequent stigma, social exclusion and diagnosis. It was the influence of existential-phenomenological thinking that allowed me to see the individual, locate them in societal structures, and to keep what was useful of psychoanalytic theory when it served to liberate them.

Annihilation of caste

Many years ago, I had the chance to share a room in a spiritual community with a man newly arrived from Poona. He was a medical doctor but had come to England to pursue ordination as a Buddhist. It was a chaotic cultural combustion. He read Tagore with fervour to me and I played the Beatles at full volume to him. He was passionate about many things but none so much as the reverence that he paid to Dr Ambedkar (1891–1956) or Babasaheb (respected father) as he affectionately referred to him. My dear friend and family were originally from the Untouchable caste; or, as they prefer to be called, the Dalit people.

The Dalit are a collection of Depressed Class ethnic groups excluded from the four-fold Varna system of Hinduism. There are an estimated more than 160 million people in Indian tainted by their birth into a caste system that views them as impure, less than human, expendable. The daily abuses against these people remain legion but seemingly globally overlooked. Murder, rape and violence are a daily occurrence to those who are seen as 'less than' by the mere fact of the family they were born into.

The unavoidable caste by birth was something I also experienced in Belfast. When a friend of mine opened a Buddhist Centre in Belfast, the paramilitaries asked her, unjokingly and with some menace, if she was a Protestant Buddhist or Catholic Buddhist. As a local, despite her shaved head, vow of celibacy and brightly coloured robes, it mattered very much which caste she originated from. So was the depth of division, hatred and fear of the Other. I have dark memories of being asked to verify my religion of birth and facing the 50–50 chances of getting a hiding for the wrong answer. What areas you freely went, what colours you wore and with whom you associated were dictated by religious caste, whether believer or not.

Bhimrao Ramji Ambedkar (2016) was an Untouchable; as such he was excluded from temples, not allowed to draw water from public tanks or wells, denied access to school and had restricted movement in public places. His father had been in the army and as such benefited from some formal education. This he shared with his son who eventually passed the entrance exam to university and continued his education in London. After a successful career as a lawyer, teacher and politician, holding some significant governmental roles, he was central in developing the Indian Constitution.

He campaigned against the social discrimination levied toward the Dalit community. It may surprise many that Mahatma Gandhi (1869–1948) proclaimed that the Caste system was the natural order of society and to destroy it would lead to chaos (Roy, 2016). My roommate was incensed that I had a well-thumbed copy of Gandhi's biography – I had to remove it from our room. He argued that Gandhi offered Dalits a pity-charity narrative and actively resisted their chance for autonomy and self-determination. This was solidified, through a now-historic hunger strike against Ambedkar's proposed amendment of the first constitution, which sought separate elections for the Depressed Classes. Ambedkar conceded the exclusion of the amendment for the real fear of Gandhi's death causing retaliatory violence against his people.

History matters. My friend's story, the plight of the Dalit people today, and indeed the incredible contribution of Ambedkar all seem suspiciously overlooked in the West. I find the push toward a collective consciousness at the experience of individual (not to be confused with individualistic) liberation troubling. My fear or experience of totalitarianism is triggered. Totalitarianism begins with an idea. It reeks of Orwell's (1949) Ingsoc party line and a distortion of everything great about individual liberty (I repeat not individualistic). In the immortal words of Gil Scott-Heron (1970), 'The revolution will not be televised.' The first revolution takes place in the mind, brothers and sisters – yes and the mind is in the world, if you really must! That change cannot be seen externally prior to the point of action. We see Rosa Parks on the bus but not the moment she decided she was worthy enough to not give up her seat. The concept of interiority is foundational to psychoanalytic thinking and by contrast comes under significant attack from the pioneers of existential thought. In brief, 'interiority cannot be conceptually taken for granted or intellectually glossed over' (Brooke, 2013, p.4).

Manuski

I am told by people who knew him that Dr. Ambedkar often used the (Marathi) word *manuski*. He translated and conceptualised it as humanity, compassionate action and mutual respect between the members of the society. I mythologise that it was his own connection with *manuski* that saw the most urgent need for Dalits to be freed from an oppressive systemic system.

If I were to translate *manuski* simply as meaning humanity, then the title of this chapter could be virtually 'existentialism is a humanism'. Given that the concept of humanity isn't always seen as a positive one, I have elevated or deepened its meaning to represent a connection in our shared fragility, beyond gender, sexuality, religion, lack of religion, ideology, causes or caste – to allow, even if only for a second, a space where an alternative path from violence may be found. A connection that cannot be televised but can be expressed, meaning a shift in one's deepest perception of the Other that corresponds with the deepest connection with oneself; between therapist and client, a relatedness, a being-with, a becoming; a revolution.

I was truly inspired by Ambedkar, his vision, and his actions, his people (the many ex-Untouchables that I eventually had the honour and privilege of meeting). As a Dalit, he contentiously said, 'I was born a Hindu, but I will not die a Hindu.' Ambedkar attempted to annihilate the social inequalities inherent in caste Hinduism by offering mass conversions from that system to Buddhism (Sangharakshita, 2016). But the first step had to take place in the individual who had a revolution of spirit, who saw the internalised truth of *manuski*, which resulted in them turning up to the rally. However, it remains a daily struggle. The Dalit people, whether having converted to Buddhism or remained within Hinduism, remain continual targets for objectification and hate. For those who have converted, it must remain a daily practice to connect with *manuski* and to hold their course.

Explaining her actions, Rosa Parks (Marsh, 2006, p. 21) said 'I had been pushed as far as I could stand to be pushed and decided I would have to know once and for all what rights I had as a human being and a citizen.' The critics of interiority may argue it was the actions of the bus driver that finally pushed her into action but unless one jettisons the concept of free-will, she, we, still choose how to respond. Martin Luther King (2005) who rose to fame due to his involvement in the bus boycotts states the influence of existentialism on his thinking.

I like to think Ambedkar experienced *manuski* when he studied and travelled abroad, finding his worth in an alternative environment and structure. It was upon his return to India that he refused to be treated as less than.

Having lived through an armed conflict for the first 25 years of my life, and trying to work out what happened ever since, I often reflected on what would happen if you locked the main protagonists in a room knowing they would all die by the stroke of midnight. Would they, could they, really remain hardened and inflexible, maintaining the mutual animosity to the final hour? Or is it possible that they would experience *manuski*, the variable of shared fate helping connect them beyond ideology? Would the same thought experiment change how we practised therapy if it were client and therapist facing certain doom at the end of the therapeutic hour? After all, there is no guarantee of the client's return.

The reality is we are all facing death and the end of the session. Not at midnight but rather, for most of us, at an unknown time. I found inspiration in the Japanese concept of *'ichi-go ichi-e'*, roughly translated as 'one time, one meeting'. Interpreted crudely by me: as you only ever have one chance at a meeting, make it count. Even if it's the same person you are meeting, treat that occasion like it could be the last. I believe that this high ideal is so applicable to how we live our lives, but more pointedly how we view the therapeutic encounter. Not all encounters are long term. That brief encounter could be what shapes the person's impression of psychotherapy and how they frame their troubled lives. Can we find *manuski* in that one meeting?

Radical existentialism is *manuski*

Radical existentialism interprets that freedom is *awareness* of *our* existence, and in it 'existence precedes essence' (Sartre, 2003), not just as we are burdened to be free (many of our brothers and sisters are not – slaves to circumstance; slaves to debt; actual slaves) but rather that, in and of ourselves, everyone is worthy and has value by our very existence – *manuski*. For the truly aware, existential-phenomenologically informed psychotherapy *manuski* is as an ideal at least and as such is surely non-negotiable. Without it we are left with caste, endless hierarchy and a missed opportunity for relatedness and depth.

I hope, in the course of this personal exposure to my thinking, life and practice I have offered some understanding of how existential-phenomenological thinking, as I understand it, impacts my world. Perhaps you can find some inspiration from it.

The title of the chapter posits that radical existentialism is *manuski*. I believe when the radical existential concepts are applied to how one treats the individual we encounter, then there is an opportunity for a mutual uncovering of a shared being and becoming beyond the limits of reductive terminology or philosophy, ideology or self-held beliefs: an experiential moment that is both expansive and potentially healing for individuals, communities, society and yes, Walt – the world.

References

Adorno, T. (2003). *The Jargon of Authenticity*. London: Routledge.
Ambedkar, B.R. (2016). *The Annihilation of Caste. The Annotated Critical Edition*. London: Verso.
Bakewell, S. (2016). *The Existential Café*. London: Chatto & Windus.

Bracken, P. and Thomas , P. (2005). *Post Psychiatry: Mental Health in a Postmodern World*. Oxford: Oxford University Press.

Brooke, R. (2013). Notes on the phenomenology of interiority and the foundations of psychology. *International Journal of Jungian Studies*, 5(1), pp.3–18.

Cooper, D. (1990). *Existentialism: A Reconstruction*. Oxford: Blackwell.

Dustin, D. and Montgomery, M.R. (2010). The use of social theory in reflecting on anti-oppressive practice with final year BSc social work students, *Social Work Education*, 29(4), pp.386–401.

Heidegger, M. (1962). *Being and Time*. London: Blackwell Publishing.

King, M.L. (2005). *The Papers of Martin Luther Kind, Jr. Volume V*. Berkeley: University of California Press.

Laing, R.D. (1987). The use of phenomenology is psychotherapy. In Zeig, J.K. (Ed.), *The Evolution of Psychotherapy*. New York: Brunner.

Loewenthal, D. (2011). *Post-Existentialism and the Psychological Therapies*. London: Karnac.

Lomas, P. (1999). *Doing Good? Psychotherapy Out of its Depth*. Oxford: Oxford University Press.

Massumi, B. (2003). Translator's foreword. In Deleuze, G. and Guattari, F. (Eds), *A Thousand Plateaus*. London: Continuum.

Marsh, C. (2006). *The Beloved Community: How Faith Shapes Social Justice from the Civil Rights to Today*. New York: Basic Books.

May, R. (1961). *Existential Psychology*. New York: Random House.

May, R. (1996). *Heidegger's Hidden Sources*. London: Routledge.

Montgomery, M.R. (2017). Radical existentialism – the outsider. *Journal of Existential Analysis*, 28(1), pp.4–19.

Orwell, G. (1949). *Nineteen Eighty-Four*. London: Secker & Warburg.

Roy, A. (2016). The doctor and the saint. In Ambedkar, B.R. (Ed.), *The Annihilation of Caste*. The Annotated Critical Edition. London: Verso.

Sartre, J.-P. (2003). *Being and Nothingness*. London: Routledge.

Sangharakshita. (2016). *Dr Ambedkar and the Revival of Buddhism I*. Cambridge: Windhorse Publications.

Scott-Heron, G. (1970). *The Revolution Will Not Be Televised. On Pieces of a Man*. New York: Flying Dutchman Records.

SEA. (2019). The Society for Existential Analysis. Retrieved from: https://existentialanalysis. org.uk

Seymour-Jones, C. (2009). *Dangerous Liaison*. New York: The Overlook Press.

Smith, D.L. (2012). *Less Than Human*. London: Griffin.

Thurston, B. (2019, April). *How to Deconstruct Racism, One Headline at a Time* [Video file]. Retrieved from: www.ted.com/talks/baratunde_thurston_how_to_deconstruct_racism_one_headline_at_a_time

Wade, S. (2019). *Foucault in California*. Berkeley: Hey Day Books.

Webber, J. (2018). *Rethinking Existentialism*. Oxford: Oxford University Press.

10 The other of a feminist praxis of empathy

Rebecca Greenslade

> If the subject is ambiguous, difficult to locate and properly name, then to whom shall we ascribe this life?
>
> (Butler, 2012, p. 4)

Ethics and existential Eurocentrism

On the final day of my two-year advanced training in existential psychotherapy we were taught 'ethics'. Our tutor posed an 'ethical' dilemma to my training group: 'What would you do if one of your clients left you a large sum of money in their will?' We scoured our handouts of the BACP and UKCP ethical frameworks for our answers, wrestling with this hypothetical account of moral conflict. Existentialism teaches us that we are burdened with the freedom of choice, not only in relation to moral conflict, but with choosing the values that inform how we engage with our lives. Perhaps the burden was so much that day – our final day – that we were allowed a moment's respite as we holidayed together in collective bad faith, seeking our answers within institutionalized perspectives, in contrast to possibly engaging with an enquiry into what an ethics of care for an existential psychotherapy practice might be. Together, we took a position of standing outside of knowledge; through examining our capacities for reason, we withdrew ourselves from the ethical dilemma itself. We took the very position that Hegel criticized Kant's moral philosophy for, in that 'it does not account for fundamental aspects of the situation: the societies, traditions, relationships and commitments in which we are embedded and that precede our existence as autonomous subjects' (Rasheed, 2019, p. 56).

Existentialism has a prickly relationship to ethics. Perhaps I could account for the absence of ethical enquiry in my training as symptomatic of the moral subjectivism that existentialism is often accused of; since our primary concern as existential psychotherapists is with the lived experience of our clients, does this not allow us to abandon ethical enquiry within the domain of individual preference? Who am I, the therapist, to judge whether one client's morality is better than another? And what of our loyalty to phenomenology? A primary concern with ontology and the description of experiences as they appear to us is very different to ethical concerns with how to be in the world, what Crowe (2004) describes as the 'chasm between "is" and "ought" ', as propounded by David Hume. Western phenomenology is concerned more with methodology than with method.

I have no doubt that gender bias, deeply and painfully embedded in my training, had its part to play. Over two years, I was taught solely by white men and every required reading text they asked my training group to read was written by a white, European male. The singular lens of a white male Eurocentric perspective will inevitably impact how ethical enquiry is approached and engaged with, unless it is met with a level of accountability and criticality which Foucault considered so necessary to ethical enquiry – a notion which Butler develops further: 'Ethical reflection – she writes – is bound in the operation of critique' (2005, p. 8). She continues: "Critique finds that it cannot go forward without a consideration of how the deliberating subject comes into being and how a deliberating subject might actually live or appropriate a set of norms' (ibid, p. 8).

Critiquing her mentor's (developmental psychologist Lawrence Kohlberg) claims that men have moral maturity over women, ethicist Carol Gilligan (1982) explored the ways in which men and women are situated antithetically in society. This situatedness can impact how men and women approach ethics differently, an insight that should not surprise existential psychotherapists, since this phenomenological understanding of the self as situated formed much of de Beauvoir's analysis in *The Second Sex* (1949/2011). Yet even de Beauvoir did not make our reading lists; it was not until I left the academy that I began to discover her feminist ethics, leading me to re-consider my own existential psychotherapy practice through the lens of a feminist ethics of care.

In her chapter *At the Intersection: Existentialism, Critical Philosophies of Race and Feminism*, Kathryn T. Gines (2018) calls on existential scholars to be critical of the dominant representations of existentialism as European in origin and the ways in which 'this myopic representation of existentialism is perpetuated in anthologies from the 1950s to 2008' (p. 88), a call which much surely extends to those forming our existential psychotherapy curriculums and editing existential publications. Gines demands us to expand our community of inquiry – her own work focuses upon the intersections and influences between critical philosophies of race and feminist philosophies engaging with issues of race with thinkers including Lewis Gordon, Franz Fanon, Lorraine Hansberry, Richard Wright and Simone de Beauvoir. In his introduction to the blistering anthology, *Existence is Black*, Gordon (1997) reminds us that we can consider *existentialism* as a fundamentally European historical phenomenon and confine ourselves to the history of European literature that carries that name, or alternatively, we can consider *philosophy of existence* as a philosophical inquiry 'premised upon concerns of freedom, anguish, responsibility, embodied agency, sociality and liberation' which 'is marked by a centering of what is often known as the "situation" of questioning or inquiry itself' (p. 3), a perspective that both precedes and exceeds the current community of inquiry that Gines critiques. Diversity must be reflected in our curriculums, faculties and therapeutic spaces.

I recently attended the grandiosely titled *World Congress in Existential Psychotherapy*. Despite an international audience and being in Buenos Aires, not one of the presentations I attended moved beyond a white, male Eurocentric perspective. Yet, if existential psychotherapy is to have a credible future, and if we are to take the project of Re-visioning Existential Psychotherapy seriously, the starting point must surely begin with an ethical critique of the predominately white, Eurocentric positions we have internalized from our training and which continue to dominate our discourses. We need to converse with a broad range of perspectives and begin a critique of our thinking and practices, diversifying the range of thinkers we include both within our community of inquiry and the methods that inform them.

Dissent and re-politicization

My suggestion that perhaps an ongoing ethical inquiry should have begun on the first day of our training, and not the last, was met with an exasperation that I had become accustomed to as a dissenting existential psychotherapy trainee. Such exasperation had confused me throughout because what drew me into existential psychotherapy in the first place was its dissenting voice. The social phenomenology of R.D. Laing – which critiqued conventional psychiatric treatments, generating an intellectual and cultural polemic that reached far beyond the psychiatric community of its time – drew me into the world of therapy and continues to accompany me as I sit with my clients. I did not learn at that time the influence of, and our indebtedness to, second wave feminism's voice of dissent within anti-psychiatry, and of the movement's collective commitment towards the de-pathologization of human experience. The etymological root of the word 'existence' comes from the Latin existere, translating as 'to stand forth', or 'to take a stand'. I entered into my existential psychotherapy training with a desire for revolution. I wanted to take a stand against the standardized and sanitized individualism that constitutes much therapeutic practice today, with its focus upon risk more than ethics and outcomes over values. But, cocooned from politics and the socio-cultural issues of our time, our naive existential spirits never soared beyond the walls of a classroom or the therapy rooms we shared with our training clients. It always confused me that I was never asked to give an account of myself beyond the therapeutic mask I learned to wear, of my socialization beyond the individual and familial domains that psychotherapy so often reduces us to. My social world and political views had no place in personal process reports and case studies. As *Le Monde*, the Parisian newspaper that circulated existential ideas in the 1940s, has detailed, existentialism much like faith cannot be explained; it can only be lived (Crowe, 2004). We needed to move beyond aspects of academic existentialism into an exploration of the conditions of our ethical codes as they are constituted by that which precedes and exceeds us. When posed with the ethical dilemma that completed our existential training, the only way to approach it, as Rainer Maria Rilke reminds us, is to live our way to the answer. This embodied answer, to paraphrase the American writer Grace Paley, is to begin from what we know and move into what we don't know (Bach and Hall, 2013, p. 176). Doing this, Butler tells us (2005), is to form an ethical enquiry. What this requires of us is 'to risk ourselves precisely at moments of unknowingness, when what forms us diverges from what lies before us, when our willingness to become undone in relation to others constitutes our chance of becoming human' (p. 136).

This sense of irresolution, of an inherent value in darkness or lack of closure seemed to find resonance through my first encounters with clients, often looking for answers in the 'service' they thought I was providing. The very idea of our space as shared, one that fostered not answers but more questions – embracing the non-verbal where language itself was often deficient – seemed anathema to the expectations I encountered, and therein lay its value. If Maya Angelou (1984) has allowed us to understand the agony of carrying untold stories within ourselves, then Butler might very well nod to a related burden of an agency that always demands answers, closure, light with no shadow. Between them is a world of partial disclosures, thoughts fleetingly held – in short the temporal nature of our changing, incomplete and always relational selves. Our agony resides in the polarities of absolute light, absolute darkness and the inability to live fully those messy interstices of time that are, like ourselves, entropic, finite and never fully told.

Like most therapies, existential psychotherapy is keen on universalisms. Considering its emphasis on subjective lived experience, I have always been bemused by oxymoronic existential formulations captured in emotional wheels and cycles of authenticity. There were plenty of these at the fore-mentioned *World Congress in Existential Psychotherapy*. The theme of the Congress was 'Anxiety', an area of great expertise for us existential psychotherapists. How can we not be experts when we have had continental philosophical perspectives on anxiety drilled into us for the durations of our training? Quotations from Kierkegaard, Paul Tillich, Heidegger and Viktor Frankl pepper many existential therapist's websites, and informed a plethora of *PowerPoint* presentations at the Congress. Anxiety, the speakers universally declared, is an opportunity to find deeper meaning in, and thus live fuller, lives. Take it, plunge into it with us – your therapists – and your authentic selves will emerge the other side of a good dose of existential therapy. In doing so, we risk both the essentialism of notions of authentic selfhood and empty platitudes of universalism. I am not arguing against universality per se, but agree with Butler when she warns us against a form of universality that 'fails to be responsive to cultural particularity and fails to undergo a reformulation of itself in response to the social and cultural conditions it includes within its scope of applicability' (2005, p. 6). The subject cannot understand itself in separation from its social and historical conditions, although the pursuit of authenticity is in danger of doing just that.

Butler, following Hegel, points towards a different formation of self, one that finds value in the partial, the irrecoverable, a certain negative capacity that understands loss as inherent in recognition. This takes in the ontological necessity of moving outside ourselves as a means of self-realization, one that forms a cornerstone of Hegel's *Phenomenology*, which Butler draws upon extensively in *Subjects of Desire* (2012). I began to understand that by going back to these situated substrates – some of which existentialism has drawn upon – I could shape an ethical pragmatism for a renewed feminist psychotherapy, through Butler's partial reconstruction of Hegel out of the shackles of his 20th century interlocutors. Our inherent relatedness, of the fissures that exist between the peril of absolute freedom – one that Sartre has famously warned against – and absolute bondage, is where I began to locate the potential value of therapeutic enquiry.

It was through my paper *Existential Psychotherapy and the Therapeutics of Activism* (2018) that I found my way to the political philosophies of Sartre, de Beauvoir and Fanon – omitted from my training curricula – all leading me to question the apolitical nature adopted by existential psychotherapy institutions for the past thirty years. This practice has, in my view, orientated itself more within an anthropocentrism that places emphasis on the individual, for example Kierkegaard's concern with personal conversion in contrast to political upheaval, and Nietzsche's concern with individual formation in contrast to societal transformation – neither addressing issues of social responsibility and ethics. This is in stark contrast to the existential analyses of oppression offered to us by Sartre (whose philosophy developed from a concern with individual ontology towards a socio-political philosophy of liberation), Fanon and de Beauvoir. It led me to conclude that – at least in my own work – existential psychotherapy must be, first and foremost, a social practice where existential psychotherapists actively take into account and engage with the social structures and conditions that generate such distress. The freedom we are burdened with is dependent upon actively working towards the freedom of others. Not to do so is to become complicit with the oppression itself (Greenslade, 2018).

In *Capitalist Realism* (2009), Mark Fisher confronted the absence of an alternative political ontology that can oppose neo-liberal capitalism. He emphatically correlates the regulatory function of capitalist ideology with 'mental health', writing, 'the current ruling ontology denies any possibility of a social causation of mental illness. The chemico-biologization of mental illness is of course strictly commensurate with its de-politicization' (Fisher, 2009, p. 37). For R.D. Laing, insanity is a rational adjustment to living in an insane world (Agel, 1971). How then should existential therapists respond to societal norms that are complicit in the common experience of anxiety and depression? After all, the catchy subtitle of *The Radical Therapist* (Agel, 1971) – the most influential text upon my own practice – is 'therapy means change not adjustment'. An existential psychotherapeutic ethics of care should involve the re-politicization of 'mental illness' that we saw beginning with second-wave feminism with the reformulation of personal problems as social ones. The therapeutic professions are indebted to second-wave feminism's critique of the patriarchal constitution of psychoanalysis and of the psychiatric profession's ever-increasing stronghold on conceptions and treatments of 'mental illness'. Feminism did not consider the problem to be better off treated with individual psychotherapy but with social change. Social critique and conjecture are necessary to both individual and social transformations. Carol Hanisch (1970) has been attributed with providing the feminist movement with one of its core political ideas: the personal is political. It still is. Hanisch challenged psychotherapy's assumption that a personal solution, or cure, could be found for woman's difficulties. This, at best, was simply a process of adaptation to a sexist society. In contrast to seeking a personal solution within individual psychotherapy, radical feminists chose to bring the minutiae of gendered suffering into the public consciousness, making the personal political. How is it that memories disappear?

In his conversation with writer and filmmaker Michael Ventura, Jungian analyst James Hillman said that therapy's big mistake is introspection. Try telling that to your students who, deeply ensconced in their 'personal process', have committed to both the emotional and financial expense of years of personal therapy. It reminds me of a time during a month-long solitary meditation retreat, one of the guiding teachers told me: you know, you'd probably have been better off giving your spare room to a Syrian refugee than coming here.

Social theorizing and recognition

I am meeting Mary for the first time. She began to tell me about herself. Now fifty, she received a diagnosis of clinical depression and chronic anxiety aged nineteen. She tentatively begins to describe the emotional and psychological abuse she has experienced from her mother since she was a child. "For some reason", she says, "my mother has never been able to love me". During the past twenty-eight years Mary has seen a number of therapists, both short and long term through the NHS and charity sector. I ask about her many experiences of therapy and she becomes tearful. "Not very good", she replies. I ask if she could tell me more about this and she says that she has never had a therapist who allowed an exploration of her experiences in the way she has wanted. Mary looks at me with uncertainty. "I want to understand things from a feminist perspective", she says. "I wanted to be able to talk about how my mother internalized the misogyny she experienced and what it was like being a first generation Black woman in the UK whose husband left her with two young children. I think it's all socially related". Her eyes fill. "I just want to understand why my mother has never been able to love me". I am deeply affected. Feminist psychotherapists are committed to self-disclosure as a means to openly acknowledge the constructions of power within the therapeutic relationship. I tell her that my own practice is influenced by feminist perspectives. I tell her that, in my view, if we do not think and practice socially, therapy is lacking. I am sorry for her experience that kept her firmly in the place of intro-spection, in contrast to social theorizing. She is weeping now. And as we continue to talk together, I understand that through the relief of my own disclosure, I have also been recognized. Butler explains, 'the "I" has no story of it is own that is not also the story of a relation – or set of relations – to a set of norms' (2005, p. 8). Through Mary being refused the possibility of locating her 'I' within the social conditions she emerged from and responded to, are we not othering her and per-petuating the isolation that has pervaded her life? As Hegel wrote, 'self conscious-ness exists in and for itself when, and by the fact that, it so exists for another; that is it exists only in being acknowledged' (1807/1977, p. 111).

Heather's first sexual experience resulted in a ripped vagina. Mid-way through the sex, which although painful seemed caring and attentive, her partner covered her mouth with one hand and pushed her down with the other, instructed her not to move or speak and began thrusting his penis with such force and aggression that it tore her. Confused – after all she told herself she had consented and had wanted to lose her virginity to this man – she told no-one until the wound became infected and had to see a doctor. Now too late for stitches she suffered months of pain, infections and anti-biotic treatment in silence. Eight years on, she had only had sex a few times, each time a drunken one night stand, each time barely memorable, her now fully developed woman's body yet to experience orgasm. In our sessions together we neither ignored nor focused on that traumatic event, but explored the ambiguities of consent and how this is reflected in different media, such as the portrayal of heterosexual sex in films and the latent misogyny of porn. We reflected upon the way women historically have been treated in her culture and family, the possible abuse of a sibling by an older cousin that was never more than a brief hushed conversation between her mother and her aunt behind a closed door. We talked about not just her experience but the daily biographies of violence that women experience that objectify and violate the female body. Our discussions gave her confidence in opening up to friends, to express through poetry her anger about discovering that many of her friends endured similar early sexual experiences. For the first time she brought her rage to the stage, speaking her words and touching others with her experiences. We theorized together about the experience of womanhood and she took this theorizing into the world. Hegel told us that to retrieve itself fully, the self-conscious subject must also work to change the external world, for contemplation is by itself insufficient. As we reflected on our time together, we agreed that to have restricted our 'work' to internal narratives alone would have been limiting and collusive with the silencing of female voices. Such silencing has a long history – almost 3000 years – beginning with Homer's loyal wife, Penelope, who was banished to her quarters by her son Telemachus, when she asked a performing bard to change the song he sang to her suitors (Beard, 2017, p. 3). Butler tells us:

> [W]hen the "I" seeks to give an account of itself, an account that must include the conditions of its own emergence, it must as a matter of necessity become a social theorist … not only does ethics find itself embroiled in the task of social theory, but social theory, if it is to yield non-violent results, must find a living place for this.
>
> (2005, p. 8)

It is an ethical imperative that therapy be a locus for social theorizing, perhaps akin to what Hillman is suggesting when he asked, 'could analysis have new fantasies of itself, so that the consulting room is a cell in which revolution is prepared?' (Hillman and Ventura, 1992, p. 38). He continues:

> [T]herapy might imagine itself investigating immediate social causes, even while keeping its vocabulary of abuse and victimization – that we are abused

and victimized less by our personal lives of the past and by a present system … Then the consulting room becomes a cell of revolution, because we would be also talking about, "What is actually abusing me right now?" And that would be a great venture, for therapy to talk that way.

(ibid, pp. 38–9)

Through writing, I no longer remain an 'interior subject, closed upon myself, solipsistic, posing questions of myself alone' (Butler, 2005, p. 32). I participate in a dyadic encounter between myself and the reader. Implicit in my writing is the acknowledgement that it will always be incomplete, partial, never reaching totality, never fully understanding myself. Yet in the act of recognizing other as 'I', I account for an agency which is process, porous, a shadowy subject – preceding and superseding. It is an understanding or mode of being, as Hegel has pointed out, that finds truth through temporal returns from dislocation and loss. Such losses are inherent within what it is to live and we are faced with great challenges as therapists today. The philosophy of Hegel, as reconstituted through aspects of Butler's work, continues to offer the possibility of fuller subjects, through the tacit understanding of all that is fractured, untold and out there within.

References

Agel, J. (Ed.). (1971) *The Radical Therapist*. New York: Ballantine Books.

Angelou, M. (1984) *I Know Why the Caged Bird Sings*. London: Virago.

Bach, G. & Hall, B. (Eds) (2013) *Conversations with Grace Paley*. Jackson, MS: University Press of Mississippi.

Beard, M. (2017) *Women and Power: A Manifesto*. London: Profile Books.

Butler, J. (2005) *Giving an Account of Oneself*. New York: Fordham University Press.

Butler, J. (2012) *Subjects of Desire: Hegelian Reflections in Twentieth-Century France*. New York: Columbia University Press.

Crowe, J. (2004) 'Is an Existentialist Ethics Possible?' *Philosophy Now*. Retrieved 12 August 2019, from https://philosophynow.org/issues/47/Is_an_Existentialist_Ethics_Possible, r

de Beauvoir, S. (1949/2011) *The Second Sex*, trans C. Borde & S. Malovany-Chevallier. New York: Vintage Books.

Fisher, M. (2009) *Capitalist Realism: Is There No Alternative?* Winchester: Zero Books.

Gilligan, C. (1982) *In a Different Voice: Psychological Theory and Women's Development*. Cambridge, MA: Harvard University Press.

Gines, K.T. (2018) 'At the Intersections: Existentialism, Critical Philosophies of Race, and Feminism' in Taylor, P.C., Martín Alcoff, L. & Anderson, L. (Eds) *The Routledge Companion to the Philosophy of Race*. New York: Routledge.

Gordon, L.G. (Ed.) (1997) *Existence is Black: an Anthology of Black Existential Philosophy*. New York and London: Routledge.

Greenslade, R. (2018) 'Existential Psychotherapy and the Therapeutics of Activism'. *European Journal of Psychotherapy & Counselling*. Vol: 20.2.

Hanisch, C. (1970) 'The Personal is Political' in *Notes from the Second Year: Women's Liberation*. New York: Radical Feminist, pp. 76–78.

Hegel, G.W.F. (1807/1977) *Phenomenology of Spirit*, trans. A.V. Miller. Oxford, MA: Oxford University Press.

Hillman, J. & Ventura, M. (1992) *We've Had a Hundred Years of Psychotherapy – And the World's Getting Worse*. New York: HarperCollins.

Rashed, M.A. (2019) *Madness and the Demand for Recognition: a Philosophical Enquiry into Identity and Mental Health Activism*. Oxford: Oxford University Press.

11 Subversion therapy and the imperialism of everyday life

Andrew Seed

Introduction

Consider the common phrase, "glass half full or glass half empty". Either way, we define ourselves as a container that needs to be filled rather than the substance itself, the richness of the milk that fills the glass. In religious services we take in a body or attempt to transcend the body; in our capitalist societies we try and fill ourselves with material things. In all cases we miss the immediacy of our flesh. This chapter explores a return of the flesh.

Marcel Proust explores how an external objective assessment can shut down an innate expansion of self. The diplomat M. de Norpois shuts down the narrator's freedom through his objective assessments and expertise:

> What he had done was inform me of the microscopic insignificance of myself when judged by an outside expert, who was not only objective, but also highly intelligent and well disposed to me. I felt deflated and dumbfounded; and just as my mind, like a fluid whose only dimensions are those of the container into which it is poured, had once expanded so as to fill the vast vessel of my genius, so now it shrank and fitted exactly into the exiguous confines of the mediocrity to which M. de Norpois had suddenly consigned it.
>
> (Proust, 2003, p. 49)

In this chapter I explore how our mind can be constrained by a person or system, how our mind itself can be industrialised so it becomes a container that needs filling rather than the substance that fills it, and how a therapy which I call *subversion therapy* can unseat these systems and create space for the return of the flesh – the flesh is the finite limit that un-limits. This therapy aims to create a space where new paths of desire can be spontaneously forged – paths of desire potentially relevant to the individual client and relevant to the times we are in.

In psychotherapy we adopt a certain frame. Can we adopt any frame, without taking on assumptions? We cast a gaze and this act of looking becomes our analytical tool. What lies hidden within this political act? It is my intention in this chapter to deconstruct some of the notions that we, as psychotherapists, take for granted.

Therapy as part of a wider movement against oppression

Subversion therapy is inseparable from a wider movement, a forceful call to arms in a war against increasing industrialisation of desire in society, therapeutic models and mental health services. There is need for a fight, a hegemonic struggle, against the oppression of the ruling economic services and psychologies, the most modern manifestation of human oppression. A need to assert our refusal of being reduced to commodities.

Ever since humans started to draw images on cave walls we have been embedded in a virtual world. The universalisation of capitalist ideologies and their embeddedness within the Western individualistic affective makeup is a more recent phenomenon and something we have very little conscious awareness of. I wake up in the morning in my pokey London flat, I eat *Special K* to keep my heart healthy, I smoke a roll-up and reach for my phone, read the news and see if I have any messages; I haven't so I feel upset and empty. I leave my house, walk to the tube, go to work in the job I hate that holds no relevance to my human potential for 8 hours, or more. I check my phone every minute or two, I make ten cups of tea – a desperate movement towards freedom within a highly constrictive environment. I return home, go for a run to curtail my increasing grossness, watch television, and immerse myself into social media. Watch some online porn, have a quick wank to relax, phone Lucile, and then go to sleep. I repeat.

We are flesh, from the beginning of our lives we reach out into the world, as the world reaches out into us. Our family constructions are intimately interpenetrated by social constructions which form our being from the time of conception. Freud (2017) described an infant as originally polymorphously perverse; our erotic self is free to express itself in many forms. As we mature we move from polymorphous perversity to zones of eroticism. Deleuze and Guattari (2004) describe this as territorialisation, meaning both our bodies and our psyches are circumscribed by the relationship with our environment. Our perceptions of inner and outer territories are determined by individual choices and social norms. This perspective potentially widens the scope of Freudian thought from the familial to the social and situates psychoanalysis in its rightful place as a historical and social movement rather than a universal doctrine or representation of the mind.

The territorialisation is both physical and psychic, the aches and pains of our bodies due to muscle rigidity are corollary to the habits we get into, be they feelings of depression, meaninglessness, or wellbeing. In the UK, an increasingly ordered society, territorialisation is becoming less and less an active mediation between our being and our surroundings and more of an abstract system received from the outside – an alienation of self. This is experienced as emptiness, lack of meaning, or boredom. Women and men become passive, abstract. Living life but not feeling an ownership of life, not feeling the potency of flesh or having an active impact on and in the world.

Debord (2005) links this to the universal movement of capitalist forces, which can separate the individual and their pathways of desire which are encoded in the automatic somatic functioning of our body: "The objects [capitalism] glorifies to the behaviour it regulates, stems from the basic nature of a production system that shuns reality. The commodity form reduces everything to quantitative equivalence" (p. 19).

Desire as commodity

We become the empty shell that forever needs filling rather than the substance itself. Objects and individuals are defined by their quantitative value or what I call container value. This objectifies the individual, sucking them dry of individual traits and converting them into a quantitative number, a cog in the corporate march. The imperialism of everyday life is widespread: normalisation, chains, mediocrity, and the office. Industrialisation spreads its tentacles into all areas of society: our clothes, our buildings, our time, our sex life, and our relationships. Life becomes transaction and exchange.

When we are confined by container value, the multiple pathways of desire converge into a singular point, the transcendental industrialised ego we call "I". Our tactile intimacy with the world feels further and further out of reach. This leads the individual to an ever greater position of lack and abstract need, "glorifying the latest commodities; and in this it is serving a real need, in the sense that increasingly extensive campaigns are necessary to convince people to buy increasingly unnecessary commodities" (Debord, 2005, p. 23). Since Debord wrote *Society of the Spectacle*, even desire itself has become a commodity, which could be the final stage in the total alienation of self. This week I spent an average of 5 hours a day swiping right on the latest dating app, I pay £60 to desperately increase my chances of getting a match and finding love and connection – within the confines of the modern herd, my desire isn't considered safe but is carefully moulded and farmed by the executives in Silicon Valley. Yet I feel lonely, broken and empty, continuously seeking life outside of my actual self. I sit at home in the evening and cannot bear the silence. Online dating is constructed around a fetishised image of desire, each face that appears on the screen of my phone I judge by its abstract quantitative value and the only chance of going beyond the appearance is to objectify myself and become an image. I go to the gym, take pictures of myself meditating on the beach, come up with funny and not too strange statements that will attract daters. As the image forever increases its dominance, the visual field overpowers and diminishes the pathways of our desire that hold a tactile and fulfilling smell or touch.

If humans are not given opportunities to actively forge paths which define their own existence, a vast cavernous space is left undefined and empty. The empty shell is then filled by secondary means such as excessive amounts of alcohol, tobacco, exercise, sex, porn, sugar, protein, boredom, property, travel, or work. For others it can mean despair, excessive anxiety, or fascism. What they all have in common is the craving for external meaning as a result of inner feelings of emptiness. We become obsessed with the act of seeing, counting, rating. We are kept at a distance from our individual fulfilment, always lacking and wanting more production: a Don Juanism devoid of substance. Without paths of desire that form a

craftsmanship, an intimate contact with the world and others, we fall into a perpetual movement of forever hoping for something outside of ourselves to fill the
lack and complete ourselves in an imagined future. If only I can get that promotion, I will be respected, liked, and become fulfilled.

This system ensures power remains with the few who possess the wealth
in a capitalist system. As people become less sure of themselves and more
dependent on the standardised consumerist order, the external system, however absurd, becomes the singular way to feel a sense of contact and recognition – a collective movement towards an empty object. No one knows what the
ultimate goal is but they know their recognition requires a linear and progressive movement up the rungs of the ladder. All across Europe and in the UK we
are seeing the rise of the far right, the empty gap without a cohesive movement
for change leaves an open goal for the far right to quickly fill the space with
populist narratives.

Inner surveillance

> Fragmented individuals are completely cut off from the overall operation of
> the productive forces. To this end the specialised science of domination is
> broken down into further specialities such as sociology, applied psychology,
> cybernetics, and semiology, which oversee the self-regulation of every phase
> of the process.
>
> (Debord, 2005, p. 22)

To measure happiness is to begin with an abstract linear scale and attempt to
reach the upsurge of existence from this objective point – an absurdity. Numerical
orders that link one with the other operate on a system of sameness. The act of
counting pushes the concept of happiness to an illusory level of universality and
strips it of subjective tactile quality. In this process a false ground is created and
the psyche is circumscribed by an order of obedience. Happiness is not a-political
or un-gendered; it is impossible to detach the abstract concept of happiness from
the social order. Just like Proust's M. de Norpois effect on the narrator our being-
in-the-world is narrowed down when categorised and objectified.

Individuals who align themselves to the linear scale of happiness consciously
or unconsciously align themselves to obey the current social order. For example,
one of the categories of "success" in CBT and on CORE monitoring forms is a
return to work, where happiness = work. Happiness comes at the price of submission, the intangible upsurge of existence is categorised, neutralized, and magically transformed into an abstract quantitative value. The person's experience has
already been stripped of its original expression; the part left over then becomes an
aggression against self or in a dialectical reversal a power over others.

One of the purposes of the scale is for the service to share data with their
commissioners in order to prove their service is more effective than other services.
It is also to judge the therapist on how much or little they have arrested people
into happiness. Therapy is *always* a political and social action. If society sees a

movement towards happiness as a virtue, this comes with a backlog of embedded meanings. If as therapists we do not question this backlog, we are swearing a silent allegiance to this system, accepting a false ground and an alienated image.

Foucault (2012) famously envisioned, after Jeremy Bentham, the panopticon, a total form of surveillance that is continuously watching us from every angle. In our progression at work, our dating apps, and our behavioural sciences we are constantly objectifying, comparing, and monitoring ourselves to fit the "right image" or be "good". As the UK police introduce facial recognition there is a real and increasing risk that, if we don't take action, the panopticon will take total control of outer and inner reality. This system of fear, guilt, and diffused anxiety is what subversion therapy aims to overthrow by offering alternative channels of desire that challenge this system at its roots. Debord writes: "In societies dominated by modern conditions of production, life is presented as an immense accumulation of spectacles. Everything that was directly lived has receded into a representation" (2005, p. 2).

I have shown how life can shrink into *container value* or, as Debord puts it, into a *spectacle*. Representational systems dominate life with pre-packaged forms. Life is lived second-hand in the alienation of the signs, symbols, and images that are delivered to us from the outside rather than imminent upsurge of human expression in a direct and tactile relationship with one's socio-politic-familial existence – a process of alienation Marx described as the reification of consciousness. Following Marx, Adorno and Benjamin (1999, p. 321) write: "[A]ll reification is a forgetting: objects become purely thing-like the moment they are retained for us without the continued presence of their other aspects: when something of them has been forgotten".

This forgetfulness is also the body's forgetfulness in losing the ability to touch, suspended at ocular distance from the object of desire.

Extinction Rebellion: an example of subversion in action

I walk along Waterloo Bridge as usual, arm in arm with Lucile, the cars whiz by, I look at my watch. I am late for work. I need to rush past Southbank and skip over Parliament Square and into the office. The buildings, the shops, the bridge, the cars, the time keeping, the clothes I'm wearing pass by me just like every day, they sit silently in the everyday of my existence, my desire channelled down particular paths.

The next day will be business as usual, I brace myself for another day at the office but as we follow our usual path we find the bridge is blocked by *Extinction Rebellion* and replaced by a garden; a large van becomes a stage, a policeman tries out the skate ramp. In a spontaneous moment of change, Lucile and I decide not to go to work. This decision marks a refusal, the blocking of a bridge disjuncts the outer and the inner. This disjunction causes a fault line in *container value* and holds the potential to forge new paths of desire. This active movement of re-imagining the function of the bridge is an act of remembrance which invites the return of the flesh.

Lucile and I stay a while, eat some dahl, and listen to the music. Lucile reads one of her poems, I feel socially awkward, we chat to some hippies, smoke some skunk, go down for a pint at the *BFI*, go down for another couple, and then decide to get arrested, we spend the night in a cell, Lucile in Queen's Park, I go to Lewisham, I eat a sweet and sour chicken in my cell, read some trashy novel. At opposite ends of London, locked between four concrete walls I feel more intimately connected to Lucile than ever. Dominance restrains; resistance creates. A shared spirit brings us together, an urgency to take ownership of the paths of desire which have been handed over, in alienation, to the economic systems. The following week Lucile and I walk down the bridge arm in arm and feel joy in a newfound vivacity and self-determination, a moment of respite from an increasingly passive world.

The protest coheres with the dynamics of freedom central to *subversion therapy*. What makes *Extinction Rebellion* potent is the sustained commitment to civil disobedience which aims to attack structural oppression itself. Lucile and I first refuse the empty shell, business as usual and demand our freedom. We revolt against the consciousness that has destroyed the natural world and multiple flows of desire. This refusal is a negative action that causes a disjunction, shifting us from a passive to an active position. The next moment in the dynamic is a positive movement, holding a tension that forges new paths of desire, which have substance. There are two conditions for the subversion to successfully materialise itself: a physical gesture and a psychical becoming. Bazzano in conversation with Nietzsche (Bazzano, 2019) calls this *active nihilism*. Active nihilism doesn't just refuse business as usual but renews itself by forging new paths of desire.

What does this look like in therapy?

I will briefly give two examples of how *subversion therapy* works in action; the examples are composites of personal material, real life client material, and fictional characters. This is in keeping with the mind's innate process of spontaneous and organic appropriation of personal, collective, and cultural.

Julia is a young artist who suffered abuse from a family friend in childhood and then a number of abusive relationships with men. After a period of holding and stabilisation in line with Rothschild's (2017) work on containership, we build trust and Julia begins to talk about how the horrors of sexual abuse affected her. As an empathic connection builds between us, Julia is able to discover how her affective paths had been manipulated and distorted causing a self-blame and a high level of anxiety. The therapy moved towards actively challenging how the patriarchal order had caused conditions of her disenfranchisement. Over a period of a year, a gradual subversion of the distorted and traumatised paths of desire create space for more fulfilling paths of desire, which hold an active and forceful life force. Oppression holds within itself the seed of its own undoing and in the therapy we take advantage of this dual force by harnessing a counter-oppressive force which challenges her distorted image and introduce contact gradually alongside empowerment and trust. In subversion therapy the therapist doesn't hold the power, the therapist's potency lies in orientating the encounter towards the objective power of subversion where passive alienation becomes active transformation.

Flyvbjerg and Sampson (2001, p. 102) paraphrase Foucault:

> The problem is not of trying to dissolve [relations of power] in the utopia of a perfectly transparent communication, but to give … the rules of law, the techniques of management, and also the ethics … which would allow these games of power to be played with a minimum of domination.

The therapist does not attempt to dissolve power dynamics; instead the therapist plays, in creative tension with the contextual, social, and historical resistance that can produce domination, disempowerment or when sublimated active creation of self.

James suffers a constant feeling of guilt. He has always felt pushed forward by a wave of existence that is not his own. He feels he can't take up space, struggles to pleasure his partner because he feels he himself is not worthy of pleasure. After being bullied as a child, he is left feeling confused about his identity; he fears he will become an abuser and has shut down his active affective intimacy with the world. In therapy we seek to reinvigorate the affects that have been shut down, opening up new channels of desire without guilt. This involves forms of political activism which avoid abuse but celebrate the active masculinity James felt he had to disregard. When aggression is embraced in subversion, potentially dangerous energies can be transformed into connective channels.

Ideal therapist and obedience

In my therapy training much focuses on the Word: as long as we can say the right words therapeutic change will happen. The words transmute potent theory into representational reality, a passive reality that excludes spontaneity or play. Throughout my training I quickly learned that independent thought was considered a threat to the totality of the ideologies sold in the course, that mirrors the oppression we see in the family and in wider society. In order to ensure my free passage, I had to squash my need to create and swallow their theory of mind, like a *foie gras* duck. This becomes problematic if therapists act from a learned position and convert image into a false ground. At its worst and most extreme, therapy becomes fascism.

In order to be faithful to the client's subversions I must avoid positioning myself as an ideal object, a kind of alternative super-ego which secretly evokes a representation of life rather than life itself. This is an idea that has already been critiqued in psychoanalysis; it was once considered that the success of therapy is to internalise the analyst's so-called higher level of ego functioning (Strachey, 1934). Despite these critiques, these ideas seem to have returned with a vengeance in modern therapies, particularly CBT, where the client's success is based on a successful identification (or submission) to the rules of the game. This is as a money-saving exercise in keeping with CBT's conception in a liberal democratic philosophy which leans on over-formulaic rules, an ideology that believes itself to be the total solution and converges towards sameness and ideological moderation.

During Extinction Rebellion, my therapist colleagues were fearful of taking action in fear of being arrested and not being able to get a job, of being judged by the professional body's protocol – this is perhaps more than a fear but a concrete reality. There is an underlying expectation of a therapist to become an ethereal and ideal object, who always says the right thing. The professional bodies, rather than supporting their members, publicly shame and come after them with endless policies, rules, and guidelines. This trickles down to trainings and individual therapists. It pushes therapists away from subversion and tends towards neoliberal allegiance to a long worn-out and boring Western enlightenment illusion.

De-reification of the spectre

Guéroult (1984, p. 52) describes Descartes' Cogito as the "self-enclosed within itself." When Freud discarded his free association and adopted forms of intrapsychic representation, he created a totality of being that circumscribes the psyche and excludes the flesh, a system based on the self-enclosed within itself. It denies the representational model at its foundations and seeks to prove its truth by finding these very foundations outside of itself in the client's mind. The first movement of *subversion therapy* is a disjunction, which fractures this self-enclosed totality; an unseating of the transcendental "I" from his throne.

Davis (2005) describes one alternative non-representational system, Jacques Derrida's hauntology:

> We can interrogate our relation to the dead, examine the elusive identities of the living, and explore the boundaries between the thought and the unthought … the spectre's ethical injunction … in not reducing it prematurely to an object of knowledge … phantoms lie about the past whilst spectres gesture towards a still unformulated future.
>
> (p. 377)

For Derrida, the spectre's secret is a productive opening and creating of meaning rather than a determinate content to be uncovered. Derrida invites the spectre back into a dialectic of recognition without need for a sedimentary materialism, this creates a space for alienated energies to once again become active potentialities. In the therapeutic act of remembrance, the client invites the return of the spectre in forms of active engagement. This active engagement is the return of the flesh.

Contrary to the positions held by the main religions, the flesh is in no way profane, quite the opposite, the flesh is our embodiment, our possibility of connection, intimacy and morality. If we don't speak or act through flesh we become merely avatars, echoes of self. To choose anything other than the presence of flesh is to bind oneself in lack, an external representation. This bondage is inherently laced with guilt, shame, and a secret disgust of self. In directly transposing the structure from monotheistic Western religions, capitalism carried forward a kind of disgust for the physical intimate self.

Therapist as theatrical producer: fleshing out the void

The *subversion therapist*, like a combatant in a guerrilla army, aims to mobilise psychic and physical energy intrinsically meaningful to the individual towards a project that can inject and receive tactile recognition from the socio-political-familial sphere. The therapist explores the many roles and possibilities that create and destroy the self, moment by moment, without leaning on a fixed representation. The hang ups of subjective and objective fall away.

In *The Theatre and its Double*, Artaud (1958) offers much to learn about how the performative can playfully redefine and reintegrate tactility into our language and culture:

> Language created for the senses must from the outset be concerned with satisfying them. This does not prevent it from developing later its full intellectual effect on all possible levels and in every direction. But it permits the substitution, for the poetry of language, of a poetry in space which will be resolved in precisely the domain which does not belong strictly to words … this poetry which can be fully effective only if it is concrete, only if it produces something objectively from the fact of its active presence on the stage; only if a sound … has its equivalent in a gesture and, instead of serving as a decoration, an accompaniment of a thought, instead causes its movement, directs it, destroys it, or changes it completely.
>
> (pp. 38–39)

If it is to maintain its relevance in the modern landscape, psychotherapy must step out of the scientific or clinical into the theatrical, an exploration which creates difference at every turn, every dispute, a non-representational space which allows for spontaneous acts and creative flows which in their impermanence don't decay into sedimentary unifications or idealisms. Over time this subverts vacuous, traumatised or fascist forces, transforming life into an embodied and immediate experience.

Therapeutic change in *subversion therapy* is not a movement from A to B, such as a 5 on the happiness scale to a 7 or 8; it is rather a radical counter-oppression. This is a unique, ever-changing and active process that continually formulates, destroys, and then reformulates the very constitution of self, world, and existence in a gesture of spontaneous craft.

References

Adorno, T. W., & Benjamin, W. (1999). *The Complete Correspondence, 1928–1940*. Cambridge, MA: Harvard University Press.

Artaud, A. (1958). *The Theater and Its Double* (M. C. Richards, Trans.). New York: Grove Press.

Bazzano, M. (2019). *Nietzsche and Psychotherapy*. Abingdon, OX: Routledge.

Davis, C. (2005). Hauntology, spectres and phantoms. *French Studies, 59*(3), 373–379.

Debord, G. (2005). *The Society of the Spectacle* (K. Knabb, Trans.). London: Rebel Press.

Deleuze, G., & Guattari, F. I. (2004). *Anti-Oedipus* (R. Hurley, Trans.). London: Bloomsbury.

Flyvbjerg, B., & Sampson, S. (2001). *Making Social Science Matter: Why Social Inquiry Fails and How it Can Succeed Again*. Cambridge, UK: Cambridge University Press.

Foucault, M. (2012). *Discipline and Punish: The Birth of the Prison*. New York: Knopf Doubleday Publishing Group.

Freud, S. (2017). *Three Essays on the Theory of Sexuality: The 1905 Edition* (U. Kistner, Trans.). New York: Verso Books.

Guéroult, M. (1984). *Descartes' Philosophy Interpreted According to the Order of Reasons: The soul and God*. Minneapolis, MN: University of Minnesota Press.

Proust, M. (2003). *In Search of Lost Time: In the Shadow of Young Girls in Flower* (J. Grieve, Trans.). London: Penguin Books.

Rothschild, B. (2017). *The Body Remembers Volume 2: Revolutionizing Trauma Treatment*. New York: W. W. Norton.

Strachey, J. (1934). The nature of the therapeutic action of psycho-analysis. *The International Journal of Psycho-Analysis, 15*, 127.

12 Hack therapy

A radical existential practice

Greg Madison

Introduction

A 'hack' typically refers to any method or shortcut that increases productivity or efficiency. It is originally a computing term, but now used more generally in activist cultures to refer to novel developments in any area of human activity. 'To hack' something is to apply an unconventional innovation. This requires an openness to see the issue freshly and to challenge any traditional assumptions that cloud creativity.

I'm suggesting we need a 'therapy hack', a *practice* consistent with the spirit of the counter-culture critiques of therapy. 'Radical' without a shift *from content to process* will not be radical enough. This chapter attempts to extrapolate from the singular voice, from the 'individual' to general professional upheaval, in turn undermining political ideologies that now control the psy-professions, trainings, and increasingly the ethics of practice itself. One continuous line. A counter-tradition that is practice and process-based, grounded in the flavour of living sentience.

If you experience the guiding potential of this living sentience, you will prefer it to the imposition of *any* pre-set concepts. Personal biography, professional cultures, society, all impose pre-existing constraints on how we *should* be, how a woman, man, lecturer, trainee, supervisor, critical counter-cultural therapist *should* feel, think, and act. But there is a 'freeing process' (Gendlin, 1986, p. 272) that can arise organismically 'and go counter to the socially imposed forms' (ibid).

Unfortunately, psy-professions seem to get taken over by those most willing to collaborate with the contemporary power structures. And when decent people get into positions of power they either leave quickly or they wither into rationalising voices for various forms of collusion obscured by words like 'professional', 'responsible', 'best practice', 'scientific'… While those who resist are tagged as 'irresponsible', 'ideological', 'dangerous', 'unprofessional', 'unaccountable'…

But *the body* does not respond irresponsibly nor does it resist with chaos and disorder. The body has its perspective, an implying of its own order. We have never followed this through, upscaled it, to its full potential. A profession of psychotherapy and societal organising, informed by embodied process, is the hack we need. We *should* not be trapped between the ideology of the status quo on one hand and some other radical ideology, radically different in content and yet just as conservative in its process of imposition and indoctrination. Social change does not come only at the level of competing social ideologies.

> The body is not chaos with merely imposed form. Neither is it all-wise so that we would not need to think. Both are needed to see and change unconscious oppressive forms. That is one reason we cannot be sure that this process will overthrow every unconscious oppressive form, or arrangement of life. All we can say—but it is a lot—is that this kind of process reveals a more intricate order which can exceed and reorder existing forms. Imposed form is not the only kind of order.
>
> (Gendlin, 1986, p. 274)

Psychotherapy is meant to be, and must be, *emancipatory* for the client, otherwise it ceases to be 'therapeutic'. If therapy is in the service of the person, then in a culture where the person's freedom has seized up, leaving only a puppet of institutionalism and consumerism, *therapy is subversive*. By inviting complexity and uniqueness, therapy contributes to the 'grittiness' of society, not its smooth running. Therapy is not about helping people adapt. If therapy works, the client should exit with more problems, not fewer. But different problems; problems of the shared world. The client will hopefully feel more rebellious, less isolated, less ashamed of their 'secrets', and feel more energy to address the world together with others. The 'successful' client realises that much of what posed as individual psychopathy was familial, systemic, cultural, environmental, political. Not because they were taught to see it, not by replacing society's oppressive acculturation with the therapist's more enlightened one, but because the freeing of their own living process revealed this insight. However, if any of this is to happen, the therapist must straddle the edge of respectability, question consensus, and cultivate rebellion within the profession at every level.

Existential process

I claim the minority view that existential psychotherapy is defined by its process, not its content. I am not an existential therapist because I have read (and largely forgotten) existential philosophy. Person-centred therapists, humanistic counsellors, relational psychoanalysts, gestalt coaches, French waiters, they all read existential philosophy but that does not make them existential therapists. I am 'existential' because of the experiential process that I prioritise and therefore the *existential use* of theories and concepts.

Focusing (Gendlin, 1982) is one simple practice for staying with this experiential process as it unfolds phenomenologically in living bodies. It is not a technique tied to a meta-psychological doctrine, or a set of theoretical beliefs you must adopt. It already belongs to you. You do not need to pay someone for it or gain a degree to use it. Rather than just reading existentialism, Focusing is one way of living what the philosophy *points to* and where it *came from*, standing with the philosophers rather than in the audience while they pontificate on stage.

Years ago while living on Dublin Bay, I found a bird tangled in weighted fishing tackle on the shore; tied so that it couldn't move. I cut the line attached to its breast, thinking it would recover and fly, but it just looked at me stunned, kicked its leg at an odd angle, and huddled into itself. It was still there, on the beach, when I went into town three hours later – with its head turned around and its beak pressed into its feathers.

Does that evoke a feeling in you? If so, that feeling (what Gendlin terms a 'felt sense') is probably more than emotion, not easily described, but felt in the middle of your body somewhere. If you give that feeling your whole attention, phenomenologically – just describing it, holding at bay all your assumptions, not deciding beforehand which aspects from the feeling are important – then you might begin to feel the body come alive and to notice that more information arises with the shift in feeling that accompanies each new insight. The body is telling you its/ your story in response to that allegory. The embodied story that unfolds is fluid and always *unfinished*, undercutting what was a moment ago established by itself. Nothing is taken as conclusive, because the body is always moving beyond the just-established identity, structure, assumption. In its unsettledness, process is taken as more radical than any content, a perpetual revolution of the human soul.

Would you rather give that up to have only an explanation or a theory of why you responded at all (if you did)? Instead just check any concept to see whether it resonates in your body. If you are given a conceptual explanation, you can still protect what is freshly arising in you from being wiped out by that supposed explanation. This is what I would call 'the existential use of theory'; it prioritises existence.

What is the existential use of theory?

The existential use of theory uses concepts differently. They are not imposed as units of interpretation over top of feelings. Concepts retain a fluid and modest claim as 'pointers' that refer directly to felt experience. It is a *pointing practice* when concepts (definitions, terms, labels) become metaphors. This frees us from being pinned down by supposed 'facts'. We can use diverse understandings without aligning ourselves to any one (or more) interpretation … The *meaning* of the concept is in the body, not the dictionary. To think existentially is to notice how the use of the term right now is experientially much more complex than its general meaning. Experiences are not defined by concepts. Concepts are defined by how they resonate in the body, anchored to more felt detail than any concept alone could convey.

We do not want to replace the client with theory. The precision of our thought requires constant checking with the feeling process. Abstraction and generalisation leave the client unmoved, literally. We want language use that feels exact, and 'feels exact' means that which brings movement in the body.

In summary:

> concepts are the "epiphenomena", pointers whose sole meaning consists of the experiential texture at which they point. This method, of course, requires concepts. It is a use of concepts, but a different use than the chain which moves: concept–implication–concept–implication–concept. It is a chain which moves: experiential step–concept–experiential step–concept.
>
> (Gendlin, 1966, pp. 207–208)

How often is existential therapy even 'existential', let alone radical?

I have supervised many existential therapists over the years and there is most often a gap between the practice and the philosophy. The philosophy, if embodied in the therapist, has implications for practice. Yet existential therapists seem often to default to either a person-centred attitude, a slightly persecutory psychoanalytic stance, or occasionally a form of philosophical counselling that sets up the therapist as an expert on how philosophy informs life.

If existential practice is based upon philosophy, it often falls into a conceptual/cognitive approach, an attempt to identify the 'existential issues' (as if there could be any other kind) of meaning, freedom, aloneness, mortality, responsibility, and relatedness … Often I have taught an experiential phenomenological approach to experienced or trainee existential therapists. They are familiar with *philosophies of embodiment* while remaining mostly unaware of their own bodies. Sometimes they even have complicated reasons why paying attention to bodily experience is not possible, *without even trying it*. The body has become a doctrine rather than a locus of being. I try to point out that the intellectual discussion about the body leaves the body behind. Is this phenomenological? Or existential? Is the adoption of any doctrine consistent with an exploration of existence itself?

As therapists we are probably not satisfied when clients just 'intellectualise', restricting themselves to self-analysis, interpreting their actions without any direct feeling. So why *as thinkers* would we accept our own thought being restricted to just the cognitive and intellectual level without the presence of bodily feeling?

From my point of view it matters little what we are *imposing*; attachment theory, neuro-trauma research, Jungian archetypes, self-psychology, existential philosophy, humanistic psychology, relational psychoanalysis, radical ideas from a counter-tradition, Focusing. … If these approaches are imposed conceptually, rather than offered experientially, we are no longer practicing existentially. Even phenomenologically-derived theory is still theory, building blocks, but not the grounded flow of living.

We never know where to start. The therapist searches for the thread; the client picks the wrong spot; it's always somewhere else, more distant, more opaque, more personally shameful and thus more universal. Theory does not know this thread. Philosophy points us in another direction. But the body picks it up and if we have faith we follow in steps below the tight knots of logic and the gross generalisations of theory. A thin but determined course, guiding our way.

Existentialism is not one consistent philosophy and this generates many misunderstandings. One misunderstanding is that it celebrates a kind of individualism. If it does, 'individual' must be first redefined not as internal subject but as *person-world interaction*. I am not an entity inhabiting a head that rides around a body. Phenomenology reveals to us how we exist in the midst of our life situations, immersed all the way through, while continually generating a felt responsiveness to all that permeates us. 'What we actually experience eliminates the old barrier between the objective (geometrically conceived atoms and physical forces outside) and the subjective (entities or forces inside)' (Gendlin, 1966, p. 232). What implications does this have for human relating?

Existential relating

I am already a response to you who has already changed in response to me, but the me as I am created in relation to you. How can I know myself when I am no pure set self but rather a wave on the 'seaful' world?

> When you communicate to me, existentialism implies, you do not rearrange some old entities within me; you affect me in ways in which I have never been alive before. What you stir in me are not entities that sit waiting in me like marbles or rocks or pictures or pathways. I do not first have a given machinery-like nature and am then affected by what happens. ... It is not the case that you act, and then I perceive your act, and then I react to your act out of my own constitution. Rather, as soon as you act, I am already this being affected by you.
>
> (Gendlin, 1966, p. 237)

When we turn our attention inside, we do not find an entity waiting to shake hands. We find a flow of experiencing. It is palpable, before any interpretation. It is the feeling organism processing each moment of 'outside' existing directly 'inside' as our unique worlding. We do not have a defined essence in there. We are not a set menu. The more unknown to myself I am willing to be, the more open I am. We are verbs, moving through the progression of the living world, acting, being affected, inside-outside-in.

It is this concrete ongoing experiencing between persons that we phenomenologically explore in existential therapy. That living automatically gives rise to symbols that are more exact than any formulation. What I am saying here is that it is an attempt to translate existential philosophy into phenomenological practice, to find an existential therapy that is not philosophical imposition or just a re-hash of humanistic or psychoanalytic practices. From here, evidence-based practice means looking to see what impact each intervention, every moment, is having in the ongoing flow with this particular client. It does not mean what 'in general' might work for most people.

"Being-in-the-world" is concrete. It isn't something general; it is always your existence, or mine, or his. "It is my here," says Heidegger. He explains: it isn't this or that mood, but the very possibility of mood or quality of feeling. Feelings are our ways of being affected in the world, more exactly, the very possibility of being affected. What we are is feeling—an "openness to being affected" (Heidegger). Similarly, Sartre points out that our feelings are "possibilities," possible actions in the world. We interrogate what seems like ourselves, down under there (the "absent-present"), but these possibilities are really the stuff of the body. We feel our possibilities before we shape them and verbalize them.

(Gendlin, 1966, p. 238)

All this means that there is no mere professional relationship between a client and a therapist. There is no neutral stance that is in fact 'neutral': Neutrality is a gross imposition on the client (and the therapist). As humans we live mixed into each other and mixed with the world as it floods in and we respond with and from the world already in us. As therapists there is no point in putting on an act. We do not need to belittle our own being in order to be available to the client. Before the client perceives us there is already the fundamental interaction alive between us, making us who we are with each other, making the perceiver *before they perceive*. Perception is the secondary act, not the starting place. We are not primarily an eye-brain-speech system. The therapist's whole being, as it is currently constituted, is already personally implicated before eyes meet and we squirm, too late, to hide all our frailties from the client.

Prioritising existential 'unknowing'

We might say that the world is built out of layers of sediment piled up over generations, each generation mistaking the previous layer for the ground of the world itself. The world is not just *an* experience; it is *experience itself*. The natural scientific attitude is one way of *conceiving* of nature but it is often mistakenly accepted that this is the way nature *is*. Let's remember that underneath the exaggerated certainty, all scientific claims are just that – claims – and as such they warrant perpetual investigation. What then do we actually know? Perhaps very little. And what are the absolute limits of our knowledge? Who knows!

In Oslo many years ago Gion Condrau spoke to us in a cosy lounge warmed by an open fire, snow falling outside. He repeated Heidegger's question: 'Why are we not more open to Being?' This question resounded like a gong, having a huge impact on me for the rest of the afternoon and evening. Being responds to its own question. It is through the body that the existential and the phenomenological actually meet. Nowhere else. No, not on the page.

Existential philosophy depicts us as homeless, thrown into a world that cannot meet the claims of the human spirit. 'Our natural and social environment oppresses us with its foreignness, its unsuitability as a home for all that is specifically human about us as individuals' (Gray, 1951, p. 114). This sensitivity to the human condition feels like we are cut adrift without an omnipotent anchor to manage the undercurrents of everyday life. The only 'anchor' is the ever-shifting experiential process. This is a home of flow, not substance.

We are homeless not because we have been exiled *from* home, but rather because we have been exiled *by* home from the flow of the self. The coziness of the tranquillised 'substantial' distances us from the self that calls to be known as the elusive and ungraspable. We shrink from a world that rests on nothing. It has no basis other than its living migration into the next vast intricacy. There is no full stop, no bottom, no certainty, and no knowing authority that convinces the body. We are the edge of evolution nudged into the expanding darkness by a distracted universe.

Is this life worth living? How could we know? We are taught that our goals are achievable but not to question what the purpose of achieving them would be, given the whole context of a human life. We don't know if human existence is worthwhile and we don't know how we can ever answer that. Yet, we live, without fixed substance, continually re-created out of detritus and trust.

Even well-articulated objections to scientism, arguments against 'evidence-based' dictates, all these progressive critiques too can ape an objectifying and all too conceptual level of discourse that alienates even in its attempt to challenge alienation (like this chapter). It can buttress another concept of 'it' rather than the less grandiose and more radical 'is-ing'…

Shall we ever tame the unknown? Every *genuine* investigation yields more results than any theory can hold, more data than we can fit into our interpretations. Life is like that – it always returns more than we asked for, and this *more* keeps us looking, forever trying to colonise the mysterious beyond.

How can we remain vigilant to subtle collusion with concepts that foreclose our investigations into being? We always claim to know more than we actually do, and always with entreaties to accept this hubris, this jump into reasonableness. These claims to know have become our 'common sense'.

Accumulated past experience *convinces us* to assume probability as fact. The frequency of something happening is not an argument it will happen tomorrow. We do not 'know' the sun will rise tomorrow just because it presumably always has. Tomorrow has never happened. It has never, ever occurred before. It could create itself according to 'laws' of the likes we have never known. And what seems impossible today may be feasible tomorrow. What seems ridiculous today may tomorrow again be a useful working assumption. We are waking up to the realisation that what has worked until now, and assuming tomorrow will be the same as today, has brought us to the brink of catastrophe. Usually any reminder that these are assumptions rather than laws leads to appeals to 'be reasonable!', 'we can take it for granted!' However, these 'laws' have now been revealed as deadly assumptions for our species and our planet. We can no longer pretend to know what we know not.

In addition, our ordinary language use, that science assumes has a relationship to fact, developed as a tool for species survival. 'The only world man can possibly know, is determined by the knowing capacities man has developed for his survival' (Tennessen, 1973, p. 411). If the survival bias within our language constrains what we can know, this inherited emphasis on biological survival will continue to strait-jacket our attempts to think clearly about the world we're born into. It is no surprise that 'valid', 'true', 'real' are labels which have historically become attached to those ideas which mediate life-promoting actions. In mental health, what counts as 'evidence', 'valid', and 'effective' usually equates to what is 'positive and optimistic', 'adaptive', 'hopeful and curative'. We have been confusing truth and happiness; knowing and surviving. This 'happiness bias' does not answer what is so desirable about survival and it usually skims over the top of the deeper bodily resonances we have regarding our existential givens. Using Focusing to 'teach' existential insight suggests that bodily experience could undercut our usual survival-biased everydayness to allow contemplation of human existence more consciously (Kuiken and Madison, 1987).

The assumed priorities of happiness and wellbeing can feel flat and claustrophobic to some of us. The truth that resonates, even in its more unpalatable forms, feels more expansive and life-affirming (Madison, 2014). We should not lean unthinkingly into a chintzy cheeriness that attempts to spin each moment into a positive aphorism. Let's abandon conclusions and avoid trying to 'cure' disquiet just so we can feather our nests as 'health' professionals.

The body bodies-forth according to *its* truth. Life energy is released if we are open to encountering a truthful symbol for what *is*, even when the content looks hopeless. The body is not convinced by wishful thinking.

> The body knows that many of its longings have been defeated and unfulfilled, that it will die; perhaps that each body is a pawn in the survival of the species (of course the body knows its limitations pre-conceptually, not like the suppositions I list here).
>
> (Madison, 2014, p. 117)

Our response to the current environmental emergency is a poignant example of continuing to develop civilisation along a path that once supported human survival but now threatens extinction, therefore demonstrating that this blind preoccupation with whatever has up till now enhanced the continuance of the species, may actually be the shortest route to species extinction. Why has it proven so difficult for us to hear and accept this environmental message and change our behaviour? Can we be sure that in other important ways we are not just perpetuating a happy-go-lucky 'cognitive dinosaur doomed to extinction if it does not show a degree of flexibility that would permit, if necessary, a total abandonment of all the characteristics that have secured its survival *so far?*' (Tennessen, 1973, p. 412, italics in original).

The probabilities of social science are based upon 'reasonable reason' and the scientific community itself is highly susceptible to conformity pressures, competition for funding and tenure, and what counts as success in academia. How many researchers are motivated by personal security and therefore not open to questioning versions of inquiry that are inconsistent with building a reputation? Does the current insistence on 'evidence-based' psychotherapy treatments enhance our understanding of what a person is, what is therapeutic about 'meeting', or is it more about the needs of an academic-industrial complex, personal and institutional security, and the promotion of certain life philosophies over others?

Inconclusive thoughts

> I had hopes for my rough edges. I wanted to use them as a can opener, to cut myself a hole in the world surface, and exit through it. Would I be ground, instead, to a nub? Would they send me home, an ornament to my breed, in a jewellery bag.
>
> (Dillard, 1987, p. 243)

I gave up a tenured university position when I realised that academic psychotherapy was losing its soul. It felt like a marketplace. Students, now consumers. Lecturers, both serfs and hawkers. I ran from a university setting that seemed increasingly beholden to micro-managerialism, fear-based scrutiny, competition (between universities and colleagues), and technocracy. I ran rather than fight. But I feel some fight returning.

We need to retrieve our psy-professions back from the aspects of ourselves that would have us compromise and collaborate with established power. I do not blame myself for running any more than I judge those who have stayed. We are all insecure and fading. And what I am offering here in this chapter is so insubstantial that it cannot be sold – why buy something that you already *are*?

For me, 'radical' existentialism, the implicit experiential kind, offers me some courage to value life as given, without synthetic spiritual niceness or hyped marketplace psychology. This spacious unknowing includes moments of optimism, moments that feel wonderful but make no obvious difference. It is the lack of any concrete source of redemption that redeems me most deeply. We do not only need to learn how to die, we also need to learn to be born, one step at a time. We spend our lives trying to midwife the aspects of self still stuck nascent, waiting to see the light. But how compatible is this with being a therapist today?

Becoming an existential psychotherapist *could* be defined as the ongoing project of becoming ourselves. The project is forever unfinished. It would be the opposite of learning to repress much of ourselves in order to fit into established expectations of a 'registered' professional. I have students who remind me that I have the privilege to say certain things because I have been around a long time, been a lecturer, have a doctorate, all the silly hierarchical things that give me some freedom to be truthful and troublesome. But surely that is not ok, that I have to achieve a minimum rung on the hierarchy before I can speak my truth and not be punished somehow (be told to teach differently, not get referrals or teaching invitations, censured, lose my license, lose my job) ...

If a person is developing towards wanting to be a therapist, he or she soon discovers that the profession insists on a step backwards, into constraints that make you less than who you are now. It is a profession that insists that you become smaller in order to promote yourself as being more 'psychologically developed'. Your body will register this dissonance as cramp and tension. It knows more than any policy-maker, politician, or bureaucrat about what constitutes the unknowing stance that welcomes personal meaning and shared fulfillment back into our work as therapists. We need to talk about how to discover our unique unknowing and prioritise that openness over manualised technique within our therapy trainings.

Psychology and the 'mental health' industry have colluded with the marketing of certainty. We sat with the powerful, stuffing ourselves. But now if we have anything positive to offer the world, it is as humble facilitators working with ordinary people to help them re-discover their own embodied subversive voice and the creative acts that come from there. It would indeed be a 'therapy hack' to develop a movement from the intricate wisdom of the oppressed and silenced within each of us…

The following quote is a rallying cry from our colleagues in psychoanalysis, usually seen as more conservative by those of us claiming to be existential. Do we dare join them, with much less to stand on, and offer our consulting rooms as the front line between 'authenticity' and 'das man'.…?

> To you, the reader, I say contemplate what it would take to step outside of repressive institutions in your daily life. To the psychoanalyst reader, contemplate leaving your institute and forging new ways. … If you're already an institute member, contemplate publicly announcing your departure, and offer supervision outside the institute.
>
> (Brouillette, 2017)

You first.

References

Brouillette, R. (2017). As turning point: Psychoanalysis can no longer be silent on political issues and remain competent. In *The Psychoanalytic Activist*. Online Newsletter. Section IX. Psychoanalysts for Social Responsibility Division of Psychoanalysis, APA: Accessed 25 March 2017.

Dillard, A. (1987). *An American Childhood*. New York: Harper and Row.

Gendlin, E. T. (1966). Existentialism and experiential psychotherapy. In C. Moustakas (Ed.), *Existential child therapy*, pp. 206–246. New York: Basic Books.

Gendlin, E. T. (1982). *Focusing*. New York: Bantam.

Gendlin, E. T. (1986). Process ethics and the political question. In A-T. Tymieniecka (Ed.), *Analecta Husserliana. Vol. XX. The moral sense in the communal significance of life*, pp. 265–275. Boston: Reidel. From www.focusing.org/gendlin/docs/gol_2108.html

Gray, G. J. (1951). The idea of death in existentialism. *Journal of Philosophy*, 48 (5): 113–127.

Kuiken, D. and Madison, G. (1987). The effects of death contemplation on meaning and purpose in life. *Omega. Journal of Death and Dying*, 18: 99–108.

Madison, G. (2014). Exhilarating pessimism. Focusing-Oriented existential therapy. In G. Madison (Ed.), *Theory and Practice of Focusing-Oriented Psychotherapy. Beyond the Talking Cure*, pp.113–127. London: Jessica Kingsley Publ.

Tennessen, H. (1973). Knowledge versus survival. *Inquiry. The Interdisciplinary Journal of Philosophy and the Social Sciences*, 16: 407–414.

13 A person on the edge of inner and outer realities

A therapist's reflections

Yana Gololob

Foreword

When I was offered to take part in this project I felt honoured and confused at the same time. The feeling of confusion was due to the fact that I am neither a writer nor a 'proper' existential therapist. What can I contribute? What experience of my own can be useful to colleagues? The answer came unexpectedly: I can share my experience and reflection and just be myself, a person-centred therapist who lives and works in the dramatic, constantly changing situation of my country. What follows is going to be a patchwork made of different facts, impressions, conclusions and reflections. It is definitely an attempt to look at the whole picture of the Ukrainian way in therapeutic tradition.

Psychotherapy in Ukraine: myth or reality?

Psychotherapy, as it is commonly understood, emerged in our country almost at the same time as the state of Ukraine was formed, at the dawn of the 1990s. It took us almost twenty years to develop therapy in Ukraine, to make this notion acceptable as well as understandable. Therapy in general and the person-centred approach in particular face many challenges in Ukraine at present. And this short survey is an attempt to look at these challenges.

Prerequisites for the development of psychotherapy in Ukraine

Ukraine as a former Soviet republic was also a carrier of soviet totalitarian culture and ideology. It means that all the significant relationships were built on the principles of full control of the state over all spheres of social life. Human rights were reduced to their minimum and due to the characteristics of totalitarianism (Friedrich & Brzezinski, 1965) terror was legalized.

What chances for development could psychotherapy have under such conditions? Being a science closely related to the development of social consciousness psychotherapy at that time was limited and hidden under the cover of medical psychiatry. It had a biomedical background and a very narrow domain: mainly hypno-suggestive, directive approaches evaluated by the state, with ideology looming large due to the active presence of the communist party engaged in "social therapy" (Kisarchuk, 2008, p. 13).

According to Bondarenko (1996) one of the serious prerequisites for the development of psychotherapy in Ukraine was the work of Lev Vygotsky (1992) in the area for scientific search of practical mastery of psychological problems. It gained its further development in the area of correctional pedagogy.

Nevertheless the word 'psychotherapy' itself aroused our fear and awe and was directly associated with the methods of psychiatry of the Soviet totalitarian regime. And even these days, when I sometimes recommend my clients to get a psychiatrist consultation, I am faced with their fear.

Some existential context of our identity – historicity

If I were to ask anyone how long the state of Ukraine has existed and when it was founded, I would get an answer that, relying on Wikipedia, would say something about Ukraine gaining its independence from the Soviet Union in 1991 in the aftermath of its dissolution at the end of the Cold War. On 24 August 1991 Verkhovna Rada of the Ukrainian SSR proclaimed the independence of Ukraine confirmed by a national referendum on 1 December 1991. It was the beginning of our new history but not the beginning of Ukrainian history as it is. Because Ukrainian statehood and identity is rooted in the times of the powerful state of Kyivska Rus (approx. 10th century A.D.). During the Middle Ages up to the thirteenth century the area of our country was a key centre of East Slavic culture.

Since the thirteenth century until 1939 the territory of modern Ukraine was periodically contested, divided and ruled during different periods of time by a variety of other states, including Polish-Lithuanian Commonwealth, Ottoman Khanate, the Crimean Khanate, Transylvania, the principality of Moldavia; Russian Empire, Austro-Hungary and Bulgaria; USSR and Poland. And after that in the late 1940s the territory of Ukraine merged fully as the Ukrainian Soviet Socialist Republic, part of Russia-dominated Soviet Union. Following that, we can conclude that Ukraine during that time could be considered a *colony* with all the characteristics of a colony, as spelled out by Etkind (2016):

- Political domination.
- Economic exploitation.
- Cultural distance.

Ukrainian identity is a very complicated thing caused by its long and divided history, at the beginnings of which is the disintegration of Kyivska Rus (Lysiak-Rudnytsky, 1994). Despite all the difficulties, this identity was preserved through the years up to the time of the formation of Ukrainian statehood. It became possible at early times due to the influence of Ukrainian Christianity on ordinary people, the will of the Ukrainian ethnic group to independence and thanks to the role of the Ukrainian elite in society. Small in number, the Ukrainian intelligentsia in the nineteenth century was engaged with Johann Gottfried Herder's ideas, set itself the goal of awakening national consciousness through education and the development of the Ukrainian literary language (Tyskyi, 2011).

It is an opinion among different people whose Ukrainian ancestral roots go back in time that there is nothing more important than the Enlightenment and that people who consider themselves to be Ukrainian should be a part of the Enlightenment (Filz, 2015). Being a so called 'non-state people', Ukrainians succeeded in transforming themselves into a modern nation under exceptionally unfavourable circumstances (Hrytsak, 2000). Thus several generations of political and especially cultural figures took part in the process of joining forces in the effort to create a Ukrainian identity. A similar task and endeavour took place for psychotherapy.

Such historical context constitutes in a very real sense a difficult heritage for all of us. Personal and national identity, as well as self-perception, is conditioned by all the tragedies. Some of them were experienced and lamented. And some of them not, such as the *Holodomor*.

Trans-generational trauma

Holodomor is the genocide of Ukrainian people, a man-made terror famine in the territory of Soviet Ukraine in 1932–1933. It was enacted by the Soviet Government with the aim of subjugating the Ukrainian people and minimizing all attempts to resist the regime and curtail the fight for independence. This artificial famine was caused by the threat the central government felt from Ukrainian peasants who always maintained a sense of national identity and autonomy that contradicted the ideology of the State. Inhuman laws were issued, according to which people were denied the right to go to the cities, all crops were taken away from them and food supplies were stopped. According to the official site of the Holodomor Victims Memorial, more than twenty-two million people were sent to life imprisonment within the territory covered by the Holodomor. In order to realize the scale of the tragedy it's important to notice that the year 1933 was the year when the greatest number of people died on the Ukrainian territory during its history. And scientists cautiously estimate the loss of Ukrainian population during the whole period of famine as ten million victims. But the official policy declared it to be a famine due to bad harvest years, which was false. And according to the government's policy people were forbidden to admit it out loud. Thus in the Soviet Union, the theme of the famine was taboo.

Modern Ukrainian historian Oleksandr Zinchenko (2018), following previous research of the impact of Holodomor on modern society conducted by Horbunova and Klymchuk (2018), suggests that catastrophes like this cause traumas – unacknowledged trauma passed from generation to generation and inherited through behavioural stereotypes as coping and survival mechanisms. He believes that the evidence of this is still the increase in mortality where Holodomor once took place, and the opposite picture as the decrease in birth rates in other territories. First, the ban on acknowledging and talking about the experience, and then the traumatic forgetting of the events that caused the trauma meant the lack of reflection, and hence the lack of analysis of the consequences of the Holodomor. And hence the limitation of the number of children in families, pessimism, limitation of life prospects, distrust of the authorities and conformism are merely some of the particular features of the average person. To heal the traumas of the past remains not even a question of security, but a matter of existence for Ukraine. Otherwise there's a constant threat of disappearing from history (Zinchenko, 2018).

It is worth noting that now that we have better access to information and we can become the founders of a new tradition – to honour the memory of the victims of this famine – not everybody sees the need to do so. And the most paradoxical thing here is that the most unwilling are among those whose ancestors lived within the territory of the terror-famine and suffered this tragedy at close quarters. According to Roman Kechur, one of the leading Ukrainian psychotherapists, this is due to the collective amnesia that is the biggest defense in the situation, when it is forbidden to mourn while the government kills millions of peasants and acts as if nothing is happening, and furthermore, forces those who have lost loved ones to behave the same way. Unwelcome grief will inevitably turn to disappointment, hopelessness, fear and unmotivated aggression. Kechur writes:

> All of these experiences become symptoms of mental dissociation, a condition that occurs when the strength of the trauma experienced far exceeds the ability of the individual to process it. At the same time, the memory of the event itself is pushed out of consciousness; but although the trauma does not seem to be "remembered", any events that resemble a catastrophe, even remotely, cause inappropriately strong feelings of "fear, anxiety, anger or guilt". And all those so-called unreasonable experiences generate existential anxiety and unexplained distrust of all and everything.
>
> (Kechur, 2018)

I agree with those who believe that we therapists are those who can facilitate recovery from this trauma; we do come across individuals whose despair bears the psychic burden of memories associated with emotions of traumatic experience which exist separately. This despair in its turn increases our connection to that trauma as a sort of 'counter-weight', and despite the fact that we have almost 30 years of Independence. Is it enough for our society to declare freedom and independence when there are still people who don't understand why we put the candle in the window at the end of every November at Holodomor Memorial Day?

Euromaidan driven by emotions and new values

The other significant fragment in our history that played and still plays a crucial role in forming modern Ukrainian identity is *Euromaidan*, the Revolution of

Dignity. It was one of the greatest processes which lasted for three months with at least two–three million participants representing different regions, professions and cultural backgrounds not only in Kyiv and Lviv but also in many other places. It was a movement driven by emotions: people came out to the Square of Independence in Kyiv; some settled down in tents, others, no less active, joined them after work, at night and on weekends.

Ukrainian scientists Ivan Gomza and Nadiia Koval researching the role of emotions and types of moral shocks that drove people to the streets to fight for their rights and values describe the atmosphere of *Euromaidan*:

> [Euromaidan] was profoundly imbued with and driven by emotions: people inspiringly sang the national anthem on Independence Square, ferociously stormed the presidential residence with a bulldozer, resolutely occupied governmental building, triumphantly knocked over Lenin's monuments and hurriedly sought sanctuary in a medieval cathedral after merciless acts of police brutality. We are interested in exploring what role emotions played in mobilizing thousands of people to the streets and in keeping them there for months.
>
> (Gomza & Koval, 2015, p. 39)

In their research, Gomza and Koval came to the conclusion that emotions were an important component of collective identity constructions that helped to sustain protests. They also suggested that it was successful overlapping of two different moral shocks that facilitated rapid mobilization of people. One of them was provoked by the refusal of the government to sign the Association Agreement and the second, more instinctive, was caused by police brutality. They interviewed the direct participants and found that "people rarely experienced spontaneous negative emotions towards the regime; rather, those previously existing beliefs, attitudes, and loyalties were amplified by one or both moral shocks" (Gomza & Koval, 2015, p. 58).

For us, the Maidan has become the point of no return, the turning point of values that united the active majority in the vector of the formation of a new civil society. It was the moment of birth for many debates about values, but it was also the moment of great fear, anxiety and uncertainty. Values usually have their historical and contextual aspects. They are forming slowly from the historical frame but at the same time, given that they are mainly shaped during adolescence and depend on context, they are still vulnerable to change (Hrytsak, 2015). According to SOCIS (Center for Social and Marketing Research) in 2015 values of survival in Ukraine are so much higher than values of self-expression: in relation to the 81.4% against 18.6%.

My colleague Olha Hlushko, Assistant Professor at Dnipro National University, conducted a study that revealed that only these 18.6% of the Ukrainian population, who profess the values of self-expression, are potentially interested in therapy (Hlushko & Bayer, 2019).

Volunteer movement and the role of psychotherapy

According to Olszański, before 2013 only 10% of the population of Ukraine was involved in volunteer work. It focused mostly on charitable activities and environmental issues. But the situation changed during *Euromaidan* and after the war outbreak. It appeared that the state itself was not ready to support people and the aid "came from a quickly-formed volunteer movement made up of hundreds, if not thousands of small groups and centres, created in part on the basis of the previous support structures from the Maidan" (Olszański, 2016).

Thus, in response to the emerging need in December 2013, a volunteer organization 'Psychological Service of Maidan' was formed. The organization includes psychologists, psychotherapists, psychiatrists, doctors and social workers.

The volunteers, being direct participants of the events, provided psychological assistance to all those who needed it: participants of the protest events, injured, those who lost loved ones during these events.

Later on, to the list of those who received assistance were added other categories of suffering people, including internally displaced persons (IDPs) from Crimea and the east, victims of torture, families of deceased fighters, wounded fighters, families of servicemen, and residents of towns who survived the hostilities. Since spring 2014, this service has been transformed into the still acting NGO 'Ukrainian Society of Overcoming the Consequences of Traumatic Events'.

As it's already been mentioned, all the volunteers were witnesses and even direct participants of the whole process at Maidan and later. And we had such a phenomenon when traumatized people helped others who were no less traumatized. According to the psychotherapist and volunteer Halyna Dychkovska (2019, personal communication):

> We are now in constant retraumatization: one injury is superimposed on the other, on the next one. There is a post-traumatic symptomatology in society, from one side, and from the other side - a situation that is traumatizing, is not over. Every day disappointing news come from the forefront: soldiers are dying. It's every day a new tragedy and injury. On one side, if we take it on a national scale, it is a small figure: accidents or domestic injuries cause more deaths. But on the other hand, for all who are in the environment of Ukraine, it is an absolute and special injury. As it shows that the struggle does not stop, this Moloch is not destroyed, and everyone is in danger. Moloch's jaw can open even wider tomorrow, and things can get even worse. And it is difficult: society still needs to "redeem" old traumas, and new and new ones are imposed on them.

New development for psychotherapy

The history of modern therapy is closely intertwined with the modern history of our country. Our up-to-day situation is that we have enormous inflation and the highest level of migration throughout our history. Our people get re-traumatized. Now more than ever before the therapy the urgent task is to rebuild the sense-forming foundations that have been violated. What can we offer in this case? How can therapy be available to people who are merely surviving?

As mentioned at the start of this chapter, psychotherapy in Ukraine in its modern and generally accepted form appeared at the dawn of the 1990s. Both at the beginning and now the biggest public organization within which it is the Ukrainian Umbrella Association of Psychotherapists (UUAP) with the biggest Person-centred community as one of the sections. The ways in which the Person-centred Approach (PCA) is implemented in Ukraine are as follows:

- For those who seek self-expression the person-centred therapists can offer their service mainly in their private practice. Since in Ukraine there is no law on psychotherapy, we don't have sickness funds for it. People pay their own money and obtain necessary help.
- Some of the therapists work for different educational or medical institutions where they also disseminate the ideas of PCA.

Therapy is now in great demand and constantly developing. But this is not enough in the country that comprises such areas as the annexed territory which experiences economic crisis, and a war that has been going on for more than five years. The war gave a huge impetus to the development of therapy, first of all, due to the fact that we had a colossal clash of positivistic and existential reality. It's been an event that not only shocked us but also re-traumatized and realizing it is crucial. If we take a look at the whole patchwork, we see that its biggest patch tells us important things about trauma. And now when our society has two main languages and is still divided in different sections, with people who miss the USSR and want it back, with Russia-oriented people and Ukrainian patriots, psychotherapy can offer a different language. I personally think that trauma can act as a link for all of us. Presenting both in therapist's and client's experience, it can give us the oppor-tunity to find what unites, multiplies and enables us to grow. It acts like a kind of water truce, during which everyone needs the same. Citing Roman Kechur again:

> It is important to realize the tragedy - and not only the Holodomor - to under-stand all its horror and to accept the irretrievable past. Only after experiencing grief we can go forward so that the future has not been forever yesterday's.
>
> (Kechur, 2018)

It could be argued with Stolorow (2017) that trauma is always contextual. For many of us this context was fragmented and partially deleted. In the process of therapy, a person often faces the question 'Who am I?' When he or she doesn't know the answer it's easier to live in the past or dream of a better future.

It's ironic that we grew up in classical literature, with a developed psychic apparatus, but we do not have a good knowledge of working with our experiences.

A psychotherapist is always interested primarily in the individual, his/her quality of life, his/her specifics. A therapist's understanding is a creative act that occurs in the process of being with a client. And psychotherapy in this way is the release of creative potential. Only for this purpose is it important to be able to trust yourself and your soul.

The frame of therapy, especially that of person-centred therapy, allows a person to immerse in experiencing the pain of loss, to allow the process of transformation to happen even when he or she has no access to their own personal history. And accidentally, but not necessarily, he or she could experience his or her traumatic experience as a healing motive force that gives birth to new meanings. Thus, for many of us, the Maidan re-traumatization became an impetus to the destruction of infantilism born by the Soviet system, to the formation of a new common history for the whole nation, to the new experience of change and self-agency in them.

Afterword

The war in our country as the greatest evil that exists, as a new reality in which people are dying, and the social changes that follow it happened suddenly, as something that the mind can neither accept nor change. For most of us, this is the greatest despair, a disturbance of order, to paraphrase Hegel.

Positivistic principles now come into conflict with objective reality, when external circumstances, rather than internal factors that are subject to 'conscious control', determine the emergence of negative feelings. The ability to recognize and complain about the negative aspects that we have forgotten is the ability to face reality and accept it as it is. This is more consistent with our nature and authenticity. A deliberate shift towards positive thinking leaves no room for unconditional acceptance. Positive self-confidence reduces to zero critical social, political and economic problems, as ignoring the context.

The person at the edge of external and internal reality faces a question of the meaning of his or her existence. This meaning is sharpened and these meaningful landmarks are often actualized in therapy. And helping each individual to realize him or herself and his or her personal history in the social context means effectively to write a history of a whole people.

The development of society should be built on shared victories and achievements. But in this case one cannot ignore the need to live and realize the trauma of the past and the present. Especially now.

References

Bondarenko, O. F. (1996) *Psykholohichna dopomoha osobystosti (Psychological Assistance for the Person)*. Kharkiv: Folio.

Etkind, A. (2016) Vnutrenniaia kolonizatsia. Kriticheskaia teoriia parasiticheskogo gosudarstva (Internal Colonization. Critical Theory of the Parasitic State). *Vestnik*

Evropy (Messenger of Europe Journal), 46. Access mode: https://magazines.gorky.media/vestnik/2016/46/vnutrennyaya-kolonizacziya-kriticheskaya-teoriya-parazitischeskogo-gosudarstva.html [in Russian]

Filz, O. (2015) Truskavetskyi psykhoterapevtychnyi proekt, yak dosvid prosvity: istorychna eksplikatsiia (Truskavets Psychotherapeutic Project as an Enlightenment Experience: Historical Exploration). *Naukovo-populiarne vydannia Truskavetskyi psykhoterapevtychnyi proekt (Popular science publication Truskavets Psychotherapy Project).* Lviv. Pp. 4–16.

Friedrich, C. J. & Brzezinski, Zb. (1965) *Totalitarian dictatorship and autocracy.* Cambridge, MA: Harvard University Press.

Gomza, I. & Koval, N. (2015) The Winter of Our Discontent: Emotions and Contentious Politics in Ukraine during Euromaidan. *Kyiv-Mohyla Law and Politics Journal, 1.* Pp. 39–62.

Hlushko, O. & Bayer, O. (2019) Tsinnisnyi portrait ukraiintsia, potentsiyno zatsikavlenoho u psykhoterapii (Value Portrait of a Ukrainian, Potentially Interested in Psychotherapy). *Psykholohiia i suspilstvo.* No. 1–2. Pp. 130–138.

Horbunova, V. & Klymchuk, V. (2018) Iakymy ie psykholohichni naslidky Holodomoru v povsiakdennomu zhytti ukraiintsiv (What are the Psychological Consequences of the Holodomor in the Daily Life of Ukrainians). Ukrainian pravda. Access mode: https://life.pravda.com.ua/health/2018/11/24/225607/

Hrytsak, Ya. (2000) *Narysy z istorii Ukraiiny: formuvannia ukraiinskoi modernoi natsii (Sketches on the History of Ukraine: Formation of the Modern Ukrainian Nation). Second edition.* Kyiv: Heneza.

Hrytsak, Ya. (2015) Tsinnosti ukraiintsiv: pro et contra reform v Ukraiini (Values of Ukrainians: pro et contra reforms in Ukraine). Zbruc. Access mode: http://zbruc.eu/node/37721

Kechur, R. (2018) Nesterpna povynnist rytualu (The unbearable duty of the ritual). Zbruc. Access mode: https://zbruc.eu/node/84860, retrieved 12 August 2019.

Kisarchuk, Z. G. (2008) Istoryko-kulturni peredumovy stanovlennia psykhoterapii yak naukovoi dyctsypliny (Historical-cultural Prerequisites of Development of Psychotherapy as a Scientific Discipline). Aktualni problemy psykholohii (Current Psychology Issues) Vol.3: Konsultatyvna psykholohia i psykhoterapiia (Counselling Psychology and Psychotherapy). Zb. naukovykh prats Instytutu psykholohii imeni G. S. Kostyuka NAPN Ukrainy (Collection of scientific papers of the Institute of Psychology named after G. Kostyuk of NAPS of Ukraine) / Edit.: S.D. Maksymenko, Z.G. Kisarchuk. Nizhyn: Milanik. Issue 5. Pp. 5–19.

Lysiak-Rudnytsky, I. (1994) *Istorychni esse (Historical Essays). Vol. 1.* Kyiv: Osnovy.

Olszański, T. (2016) Aftermath of the Maidan. Ukrainian society two years after the revolution. Access mode: www.osw.waw.pl/sites/default/files/commentary_199.pdf, retrieved 5 June 2019.

Stolorow, R. (2017) *Trauma and Human Existence: Autobiographical, Psychoanalytic, and Philosophical Reflections.* London: Routledge.

Tyskyi, M. H. (2011) Etapy stanovlennia ukrainskoii natsionalnoii identychnosti (Stages of Ukrainian National Identity). *Naukovyi visnyk Volynskoho natsionalnoho universytety imeni Lesi Ukrainky (Scientific Bulletin of the Volyn National University named after Lesya Ukrainka), 21.* Pp. 111–114.

Vygotsky, L. (1992) *Educational Psychology.* Baco Raton, FL: St. Lucie Press.

Zinchenko, O. (2018) My vsi travmovani. Zdolaty travmy Holodomoru, chy znyknuty? (We're All Traumatized. Overcome the Trauma of the Holodomor, or Disappear?). Istorychna pravda. Access mode: www.istpravda.com.ua/columns/2018/11/24/153313/

Websites

Holodomor Victims Memorial. http://memorialholodomor.org.ua/eng/holodomor/
   history/
Centre for Social and Marketing Research
http://socis.kiev.ua/ua/

14 The bi-rooted migrant

An existential journey

Nancy Hakim Dowek

Introduction

> It is … a great source of virtue for the practiced mind to learn … first to change about in visible and transitory things, so that afterwards it may be possible to leave them behind altogether. The man who finds his homeland sweet is still a tender beginner; he to whom every soil is as his native one is already strong; but he is perfect to whom the entire world is as a foreign land. The tender soul has fixed his love on one spot in the world; the strong man has extended his love to all places; the perfect man has extinguished his.
>
> (Hugh of St Victor, in Auerbach et al., 2014, p. 264)

This chapter is a companion piece to a research project; it reflects on the lived experience of *bi-rooted* individuals – both my own and the experience of those I have interviewed and conversed with. The term '*bi-rooted*' is my own conceptualisation of the experience of living with multiple homes; the tension between having multiple 'versions' of one's self and yet experiencing them through that 'same' self. It opens a new perspective on one's world and engenders a sense of being in co-habitation.

Due to the seismic shift that takes place when relocating, most recognisable points of reference that mirror self-image dematerialise (Akhtar, 1999; Grinberg & Grinberg, 1989). Whether this state of affairs creates a mourning period or a sense of liberation or both, it will result in eroding self-assumptions surrounding self-identity. This clearing of the 'décor' that used to be part of the self initially forms a void and initiates a new search for the self in the new context. The *bi-rooted* individual will be confronted regularly with a simultaneous and flexible set of references which will contribute to the sense of being in constant flux; thus creating that unique position which sometimes includes both sets of references, or their being interchangeable (Hakim Dowek, 2019).

Being in relativity

The *bi-rooted* individual's experience of living is filtered through multiple points of reference, in multiple dimensions: cultural, personal, social, physical, emotional and spiritual. It relates to a sense that there is no absolute, and to a notion of relative belonging, seeing home as a relative concept that can exist in plurality, to the experience and ability to live in multiple languages and comparing the sense of self in each language.

There is an ambivalence linked to both countries one inhabits, and with a continuous shift in perspective from the familiar to the new – to the familiar that has become foreign, and to the new that has become familiar. This creates a sense of two realities superimposed upon each other, when the vividness of the images become soft or sharp depending on the geographical and emotional context alike, combined with a blurred sense of past, present and future.

Holding two realities simultaneously is radically different to creating a blend of both. For the *bi-rooted* migrant being 'in relativity' means really being in one place while holding the knowledge that a different, intimately known reality is happening in a different place. For those inhabiting this ambiguous position the outcome is a psychological climate that at best feels more like mental and emotional elasticity developed throughout the years. Nevertheless, this mental space is not an easy one to inhabit. It requires the ability to redefine oneself in uncharted territory outside the safe harbour of one's original self-definition. It evolves from a one-sided perspective and creates complex multiple definitions of self and identity, hence being in the realm of constant relativity.

A relative stance entails an implicit sense of fluidity and a continuous degree of change in relation to different reference points necessitating juggling simultaneous multiple perspectives; hence each perspective is experienced as relative and not as an absolute reference. It implies that there is always an alternative narrative to 'what is' in the present, and in the material reality in which one is anchored. This produces a standpoint from which we not only conclude that a universal objective truth exists only in abstraction, but also that psychological concepts such as theories about emotions, sense of self, belonging, home and identity are comprehended according to interchangeable contexts. This exemplifies philosophical and phenomenological concepts of existential thinkers, such as Sartre's (1966) fluidity of self and Merleau-Ponty's (2002) concept of embodied subjectivity.

Home and *belonging* are often linked together, and although they have different definitions, are often perceived as closely related to each other. To the *bi-rooted* migrant, belonging is experienced as a broad concept, rather than 'all or nothing'. This indicates a dynamic sense of belonging resulting in an inclusive rather than an exclusive state. This dynamic state of being requires emotional flexibility, as it includes elements of alienation as well as moments of belonging to either one or both countries simultaneously. Absolute belonging may provide a sense of grounding and may create a sense of being part of something bigger and meaningful – part of a complex system of attachment resembling the one found in a family. However, using belonging as a fixed concept is often used as a vehicle for the individual to cling to, fostering an elevated higher meaning and sense of purpose abnegating personal responsibilities and decisions. Conversely, when we live outside the realm of fixed belonging, we need to find the sense of purpose from within and therefore take responsibility for our choices.

Home is also a term with different meanings; from home as a geographical place having social and cultural significance, to feeling at home with oneself and with the spiritual environment we inhabit. For the *bi-rooted* individual, home is more than one place and each place has the quality of shifting from one meaning to another according to the context in which the individual is experiencing it. It carries different nuances relating to the cultural, social and personal context which contribute to the creation of a dynamic sense of home and the ability to support continuing personal transformation, or potential for transformation.

This challenges the cosy, customary notion of home as a means to escape confrontation with the existential realities of aloneness, self-purpose, meaning and death. It makes higher demands on the individual and his/her sense of self which requires confronting rather than avoiding existential issues.

Home can be perceived as a temporal connection of past and present; a space in which we constantly create ourselves by restructuring and redefining these connections (Merleau-Ponty, 1968). Our creative tendencies combined with these connections allow us to preserve some defining characteristics (material and spiritual) of our identity, of our perceptions and our need to belong, intertwining these into a unique personal fabric of being and becoming.

This is reinforced by the experience of living with multiple languages. The role of language in expressing, presenting and internally processing our emotions contributes to a state of relativity. Language partly shapes our self-perception; living with multiple languages therefore entails a constant movement back and forth between different versions of ourselves, both consciously and unconsciously, contributing to an interchangeable definition of self.

De Beauvoir's (2003) ontological polarity and duality – both crucial to human existence in their quest for freedom – resonates well with 'being in relativity'. This is understood as a dimension potentially providing a spring board for personal development. The inherent ambiguity of this condition contains various aspects and levels of complexity, including mental, moral and emotional components. Holding both these realities implies a diversity of values and life choices, resulting in potentially clashing life styles.

An eccentric perspective

This multiplicity of reference frames relates to the relational stance for the ethical cosmopolitan/foreigner (Papastephanou, 2016, 2013). Such a perspective involves opening oneself to others and presupposes adopting the position in which the self is relational, rather than the central point of reference. The process of laying down new roots might be demanding and necessitates a relativist attitude that reduces the distance separating the migrant from others. It may require distancing oneself from a basic notion of identity – not its denial – and a more profound reflection on the meaning of identity.

In fact, acquiring an 'eccentric perspective' (Peters & Papastephanou, 2013), in which different interests and aspects don't orbit around a single centre, offers new vistas for the individual with multiple roots and multiple facets of identity. This reflects the complexity and intrinsic fragility of the individual's present attachment and creates a polycentric alternative (Peters & Papastephanou, ibid). This results in the creation of a construct that is not fixed; it pivots from eccentric to concentric and is in perpetual movement. This movement allows us to reduce the distance we maintain towards ourselves and the environment, rather than just altering the personal, emotional and cultural filters through which we comprehend self and other. With the 'eccentric perspective' there is a propensity for both freedom and responsibility which clearly reflects a principle developed and discussed in the traditional existential literature.

Living in the realm of relativity uncovers a diverse multi-layered experience of self and results in raising a new awareness of multiple versions of oneself. It is the very essence of the transformative aspect of this experience, since what has been seen and interiorised cannot be unseen. The existential crisis that accompanies the relocation process to a foreign country engenders anxiety that potentially entails the awakening of self- consciousness. It complements Kierkegaard's (1980) argument that existential anxiety appears with the development of self-consciousness and that anxiety is linked to a higher level of self-awareness. For Kierkegaard, ignoring possibilities and freedom leads to a sterile life, resulting in stagnation and robbing the individual of the hope for a better future. Anxiety is an integral part of the experience of freedom; life becomes worth living through being anxious in the right way.

Being a *bi-rooted* migrant is one out of many possible scenarios that engender an existential crisis and creates the void that ignites a process of self-searching. It expands awareness for the possibility of freedom, i.e. the freedom that results from understanding innumerable ways of being: a door could open onto a different potential, a different unknown. All of which contributes to the higher sense of anxiety, as one is simultaneously attracted by this freedom yet deterred by the strains and responsibilities it imposes. One of the research participants described this stage of her experience as a meltdown of everything she held certain and stable about herself. However, from that difficult space she emerged with a new (freer and truer) sense of self.

Opening oneself to 'being in relativity' is another way of saying one adopts uncertainty as a way of being in the world.

Fragility – an intrinsic sense of vulnerability

Constantly living and moving between two homes, geographically and emotionally, while sometimes settling in the 'non-home' space, creates a sense of fragility which is always present to differing degrees; an underlying thread of instability and uncertainty that translates into feeling exposed and burdened with a sense of personal vulnerability which is at time challenging and difficult to tolerate. Uncertainty is an ontological trait of human lives and precariousness might be our fate in being human and part of the existential given, which becomes vividly exposed in the *bi-rooted* individual's experience.

At first, there may be a conflicting need to preserve one's original sense of self by not fitting in and a paradoxical yearning to slip into a new persona that will fit in comfortably. This is experienced as an ongoing effort that results in a sense of loss of self and authenticity, leaving one feeling exposed and vulnerable. Vulnerability, in this case, is expressed as a feeling of rawness and bareness that results from the collapse of old structures that have not yet been replaced. Time passes, and during the process of creating a life in the new place of residence some changes are noticed which are no longer experienced as inauthentic. The shift happens imperceptibly, when the participants become more involved and engaged in their new lives. It becomes a more balanced experience which includes both positive and negative aspects, and yet it remains tinted with a residual sense of fragility.

This sense is reinforced by the lack of a built-in support network and the absence of close family when the migrant arrives in a foreign country. Research participants expressed this lack of a support network as a significant contributor to the sense of precariousness that fed into the fragility described as part of the experience of being a *bi-rooted* migrant. The absence of a safety net was experienced in times of crisis, whether in the country of residence or the country of origin, when none of the digital technologies that are accessible and normally useful replace a physical presence. This emphasises the presence of a rift between the lives in both places. Additionally, the fact that participants seemingly have the choice of going back home more often, or for longer periods of time, seems to have a double-edged effect of sometimes relieving the pressure but other times of increasing the guilt.

Despite these difficulties, the sense of fragility that was clearly expressed created a chain of reactions leading to a broader experience of self and to a stronger sense of self-reliance; a sense of rising to the occasion and tapping into internal resources that were not obvious to each individual. This sense of self-reliance may be defined as an adaptive attitude following a stressful or traumatic experience. If nurtured and developed, it may lead to the recognition of one's own prejudices and an open attitude towards the needs of others (Rutter, 2006; Seery et al., 2010).

Nietzsche's (1997) three stages of metamorphosis suggests an interesting backdrop for the understanding of this experience. The *camel* is seen as the first step in the quest for spiritual transformation and may illustrate the first stages of the experience. The camel chooses to carry the burden of difficulties, thus inevitably revealing its own vulnerability. By facing its vulnerabilities and difficulties, it moves into the next stage – the *lion*. Here the subject releases him/herself from the immediate allegiance to accepted social values and conveniences; not recognising vulnerabilities will prevent spiritual growth. In the third stage of metamorphosis, the *child*, one opens up in a child-like manner to the wonders of life and one's own creativity, thus developing one's own values.

To my understanding those three stages do not possess a fixed essence. There is no transcendence from one to the other, but a play of intensities. This is why affirmation is not understood as a binary differentiation with negativity but as dynamic movement between the different stages (Lussich, 2016). Our fragility resides in our strength. When touching this vulnerability, we may connect with a different aspect of ourselves, a different aliveness that changes our perception of the world.

Ongoing passive suffering might be meaningless in terms of our life's goals. However, if we could link this experience to our existential faith and commitment, we might draw meaning from it. This resonated very strongly with the participants' stories of being *bi-rooted* and their quest for deeper self-awareness once they accepted their vulnerability in their new lives. This in turn changed their perception and understanding of self in the country of origin.

The particular experience of the *bi-rooted* migrant highlights the urgency of self-rootedness and outlines the scope and nature of its role in one's conduct in the face of challenge. Being emotionally exposed, experiencing pain and struggle would then not be meaningless; suffering would not be just frustrating or difficult if we include these in our life project but can validate our identity.

Being in time

In the lives of the *bi-rooted* individual, lack of clarity with regards to the future arises from many variants and is a constant reminder of the temporary nature of life. The experience of the *bi-rooted* migrant impacts directly on one's ability to picture a clear image of the future. It entails living with a past that is not geographically connected to the present, and where uncertainty creates the potential for (or the projections of) a number of possible futures. It seems as if the links between time and geographical space that are taken for granted by 'mono-rooted' individuals are absent, preventing specific projection onto the future, allowing instead a range of future projections.

The unpredictability of the future is an existential given, and *bi-rooted* migrants have the same basic life choices to exercise as anyone. However, accepting this future of precarious uncertainty creates different shades of meaning for the present than for a person with firmer expectations and safer options.

Kierkegaard makes reference to existential time in his description of the very moment an individual commits himself, which in turn gives his life meaning and shapes his future (Kierkegaard, 2000). From this particular moment, we not only become aware of the present and future but will inevitably hold a new perspective when interpreting the past.

It is our underlying reflection on lived time that relates to our awareness of relational time. Time is experienced as relational in so far as the past is represented in the form of memories, some of which may be very vivid regardless of the objective time elapsed, while others are forgotten or vaguely remembered. The relation to memories may have a strong impact on one's way of being in the world. But how is the relational past impacted by the lack of a clear projection into the future?

The three-dimensional structure of time itself (past, present and future) is the horizon upon which the self is able to become aware of itself. It serves as one of the scaffoldings upon which the self is wrapped and contained. Indeed, the whole of our being is so connected to time that without it we may not have the foundation for understanding our own being. Accordingly, our perception of time is constantly changing as the result of the self naturally developing awareness to these three dimensions and their interconnections. As a result of our emotional responses towards the past, we develop certain perceptions, expectations and hopes for the future. Simultaneously, the past is processed and re-interpreted as perceived from our stand point in the present; we look back at the past and we recreate changing narratives based on our relationships to the actual examined experiences in the present. In this context, the present is an opportunity to relate to lived reality while holding both past and future as dynamic concepts.

A novel view of this temporality emerges from the *bi-rooted* individual's experience. The past that is held internally and is represented in the self is not represented concretely due to a geographical separation, but resides instead in the realm of the self-interpretation of recollections and memories separated from the present. Viewing the past as part of our formative experiences while acknowledging that it is no longer part of the present plays an important role in the *bi-rooted* migrant's psyche. The future is depicted as an embryonic vision of possibilities and potentials but is experienced as uncertain and unknown because of all the possibilities available to the individual. This reflects my own experience and was reinforced by the research participants' experiences. They were not necessarily over-anxious about this nebulous future, and in most cases displayed a strong commitment for a multi-layered and rich present that included multiple versions and interpretation of the past and of future infinite choices. Being aware of time in this way means we become capable of being fully present in a situation; it proposes living in temporality and taking ownership of being in time.

Roots as a metaphor – vertical and horizontal roots

Roots and reference to roots – their different experiences and their meaning emerged strongly as an integral part of the *bi-rooted* migrant's experience. The visual descriptions used by the participants in my research were very personal; from the use of the metaphor of roots itself to the different trees representing an individual's rooting process. However, the original roots are described as strong and intrinsic to the participant's sense of self, regardless of how integrated they feel in their present life. The new roots were not described as organically woven, but rather as the result of active work and investment. They were not described as defining the individual but instead as dynamic, ever-changing and evolving in different directions. The meaning assigned to these roots differed for each participant; for some they are associated with a sense of freedom and for others as a sense of detachment and even alienation. The combination of both new and old roots is essential to the description of this phenomenon, and the existence of this alternate root system is acknowledged throughout.

The land and climate of a particular region are thought to transmit certain characteristics to its inhabitants, whose temperament, language and cultural production are heavily influenced by the topographical, meteorological and botanical features of the place. This belief may stem from a concept used in agriculture describing the relationship between flavour and place. Does the same hold true for humans? A new way of approaching roots, rootedness and rootlessness implies that certainties are hard to come by. How much of our identity relies on our roots and how can we redefine them? How negotiable is our sense of self? How much of our roots determine our actions?

It seems that roots as metaphor are an inescapable aspect of personal, psychological, political and philosophical themes that keep emerging in a vast array of matters relating to human existence (Wampole, 2016). Roots include identity and politics, nationality and multiculturalism, memory and tradition in immigrants' cultures, local and universal in the time of globalisation.

If I were to summarise some of the conceptions of roots held by the *bi-rooted* migrant, I would say the following. The first set of roots is vertical and deeply imbedded in the emotional realm of the subject. These are roots that develop organically from growing up in a place where some of the processes of being rooted are conscious and others unconscious. They are described as grounding, but also absolute, and therefore have a built-in restrictive dimension and by so doing they define the individual. They give strength, but within this depth and stability resides their weakness. This resonates with the exploration of roots as metaphor found in Guillevic's (1973), book *Racines* (in Wampole, 2016). Guillevic wrote an entire poetry book which is an extended poem on the theme of roots. The energy that Guillevic's poem expresses is the sense of a botanical embodiment of an underground vital force, a delving will that inserts itself consciously into the earth. It is an active process of reconnection. According to him, this will bears a resemblance to Heidegger's gloss of the term *Wesen*, which generally means essence, but which Guillevic perceives as *root-unfolding*. This pushing through the soil at a pace almost unnoticed by humans is an action of an organic growth process from childhood. This does not necessarily imply that each individual going through this process will identify with it. On the contrary, s/he may very well rebel against it. But it still constitutes the backdrop for the rebellion and as such plays an important role in shaping one's sense of self. These roots were described by the research participants as being so closely knitted into their sense of self that it was difficult to grasp their extent. However, they were referred to by all as limiting, especially once they felt that they were growing new ones in their country of residence.

The second set of roots is shallow, as it has been acquired during adult life. It has multiple points of entry and multiple connections, and expands constantly in different directions. It does not define the individual but allows him/her the freedom to choose to be flexible and fluid, and this is where its strength and also weakness resides. It allows greater freedom but supplies little grounding. This interpretation is partly and indirectly related to the rhizome (Deleuze & Guattari, 1987). The rhizome is a subterranean stem like a bulb or tuber, so differs from roots (ibid). It opposes traditional 'arboreal' notions of growth. Being a non-linear living organism, it has no beginning or end; it expands, continuously aiming to free itself from the forces that restrict it.

The experience of being *bi-rooted* creates a new concept of root in which rigid differentiation between both sets of roots seems to give way to a more inclusive construct in which both sets inhabit and contribute to the experience of self. Rather than a concentric concept with a central anchor around which the self occurs, it is experienced as an open and dynamic interconnected construct continually becoming and reflecting the self, while simultaneously shaping it.

Exploring the lived experience of bi-rooted individuals raised many existential issues. It highlights the tension between finitude and choices and to our capacity to infuse meaning into our experiences when we are ready to make existential choices. Perhaps it is time to celebrate multicultural differences and conflicts within the self; complexity, difficulties and unfairness are equally important alongside wonder and grace. None of these could emerge in exclusivity and from a one-dimensional way of being.

References

Akhtar, S. (1999). *Immigration and Identity: Turmoil, Treatment, and Transformation*. New York: Rowman & Littlefield.

Auerbach, E., Porter J., & Newman J. (2014). *Time, History, and Literature: Selected Essays of Erich Auerbach*. Princeton, NJ: Princeton University Press.

de Beauvoir, S. (2003). *Pour une morale de l'ambiguïté: suivi de Pyrrhus et Cinéas*. France: Gallimard.

Deleuze, G., & Guattari, F. (1987). *A Thousand Plateaus*. Minneapolis, MN: University of Minneapolis Press.

Grinberg, L., & Grinberg, R. (1989). *Psychoanalytical Perspectives on Migration and Exile*. New Haven, London: Yale University.

Hakim Dowek, N. (2019). The Existential Journey of the *Bi-Rooted* Migrant. Self and Society 47 (1) pp.45–49.

Kierkegaard, S. (1980). *The Concept of Anxiety: A Simple Psychologically Orienting Deliberation on the Dogmatic Issue of Hereditary Sin*. Princeton, NJ: Princeton University Press.

Kierkegaard, S. (2000). *Either/Or, a Fragment of Life II*. In Hong, H.V. & Hong, E.H. (eds). *The Essential Kierkegaard*. Princeton, NJ: Princeton University Press.

Lussich, D.M. (2016). Vulnerability as strength in Nietzsche's Thus Spoke Zarathustra. An Anthology of philosophical studies, vol. 10. www.academia.edu/

Merleau-Ponty, M. (1968). *The Visible and the Invisible*. Evanston, IL: North Western University Press.

Merleau-Ponty, M. (2002). *Phenomenology of Perception*. London: Routledge.

Nietzsche, F. (1997). *Thus Spoke Zarathustra*. London: Wordsworth edition.

Papastephanou, M. (2013). Being and Becoming Cosmopolitan: Higher Education and the Cosmopolitan Self. International Journal of Higher Education 2 (2) p. 184.

Papastephanou, M. (2016). *Cosmopolitanism: Educational, Philosophical and Historical Perspectives*. Switzerland: Springer International Publishing.

Peters, M.A., & Papastephanou, M. (2013). Cosmopolitanism, Emancipation and Educational Philosophy (Cyprus in Crisis): A Conversation with Marianna Papastephanou. Geopolitics, History and International Relations 2 pp.124–144.

Rutter, M. (2006). Implications of Resilience Concepts for Scientific Understanding. Annuals of the New York Academy of Sciences 1094 pp.1–12. https://doi.org/10.1196/annals.1376.002

Sartre, J.-P. (1966). *Being and Nothingness: An Essay on Phenomenological Ontology*. New York: Washington Square Press.

Seery, M.D., Holman, E.A., & Silver, R. (2010). Whatever Does Not Kill Us: Cumulative Lifetime Adversity, Vulnerability, and Resilience. Journal of Personality and Social Psychology 99 (6) pp.1025–1041.

Wampole, C. (2016). *Rootedness: The Ramifications of a Metaphor*. Chicago, IL: The University of Chicago Press.

15 The poetry of the world

A tribute to the phenomenology of Merleau-Ponty

Manu Bazzano

Redefining humanism

Maurice Merleau-Ponty (1908–1961) was a humanist who redefined humanism. At first the subtlety of his stance may feel challenging to contemporary readers because of the facile polarizations of our unsubtle times: believers vs. non-believers, materialists vs. spiritualists, cognitive-behaviourists vs. 'trans-personalists' and so-forth. Straddled between the clunky, fundamentalist materialism *à la* A.C. Grayling and the literalist spiritual evolutionism *à la* Ken Wilber, undecided between the uniformly second-hand metaphysics on offer, it is bewildering to come across a philosophy which praises ambiguity, embodiment, and historicity, never settling for ready-made accounts of reality.

Merleau-Ponty is and is not a materialist: he does not resort to the notion of a spiritual substance to describe experience; at the same time, it is not possible for him to understand humans solely via chemistry and physics.

He is an unusual humanist: he had little time for the Enlightenment notion of a human subjectivity independent of physical, social, and historical contingency; a left-wing Catholic who abandoned the faith because of the Church's shameful complicity with Hitler, he went on to embrace (and effectively restore, in the wake of Bergson and Lukács) humanist Marxism. He was an unusual atheist: his groundbreaking notion of the *body-subject* relies on Christ's *incarnation*, on the idea of God becoming flesh. He was an *agnostic* in the true, now lost, meanings of the word, i.e.: a) one who cultivates not-knowing rather than subscribing to a materialist or spiritualist belief system; b) a non-Gnostic, one who is outside the Gnostic perception of the world as an alien, 'fallen', hostile place. Merleau-Ponty's agnosticism was primarily dictated by humility – less sanctimonious piety than profound grasp of our limitations as necessarily embodied beings.

A profound humanistic message runs through his writings, a paean to human resourcefulness and ingenuity, his investigation scrutinizing painting, literature, film, psychology, and philosophy. His humanism being existential, it never allowed him to minimize the spiritual import of human subjectivity in favour of either the neutrality of language or of a flight into the dialogical, both fashionable moves in contemporary discourse. Language is not like a prison, he would say, into which we are locked, nor is it a guide we ought to follow blindly. And the encounter between self and other implies *risk* rather than reliance on a dialogical matrix or on a set of taken-for-granted dialogical axioms. An ingenious interpreter of the early Hegel of the *Phenomenology of Spirit*, Merleau-Ponty was a *historicist* and could not easily stoop to the notion of timeless, universal structures of thought or to the neutered neutrality of Heidegger's *Dasein*. By the same token he could not settle with Husserl's 'transcendental ego' and provoked his Cartesian readers out of their complacency by asserting: "There is no inner man" (Merleau-Ponty, 1945/ 1989, p. xi); "Internal experience is meaningless" (in Madison, 1981, p. 276); and "The inner life is an illusion" (ibid).

The generation of post-structuralists that came after him, busy demolishing humanism for being too centred on the self and on 'consciousness', chose to ignore his work. Yet his shrewd critique of the subject/object distinction heralded the very 'decentring of the subject' which was to be a key feature in post-structuralism and deconstruction.

Humanism is redefined in Merleau-Ponty as an authoritative reminder of our human (embodied, subjective) situation. Crucially for our time, his brand of humanism neither over-spiritualizes subjectivity and the 'inner life' nor lapses into conceiving them materialistically as an object among other objects.

Beyond the mind/body dualism

In his first book, *The Structure of Behaviour* (1942/1983), Merleau-Ponty investigates the relation of consciousness and nature and presents a critique of 'scientific' psychology challenging the dualistic opposition between the 'mental' and the 'physiological'. Dominant modes of scientific psychology, such as classical materialism (which sees 'mind' as another object in the world, equated with the brain) and behaviourism (which identifies the 'mental' with the external behaviour making thoughts and feelings manifest) rely too heavily on mechanistic conceptions and fail to see that 'behaviour' implies structure, intention, and form. He widens the argument in *Phenomenology of Perception* (1945/1989), a rich and comprehensive work presenting a critical appraisal of empiricism and what he calls 'intellectualism' (the idealist view). His argument here is a version of the same motif rising time and again in his writings: an attempt at navigating a poised middle ground away from one-dimensional polarities.

He chastises empiricism for failing to honour the perceiving subject, for viewing it as an object triggered and impacted by other objects in ways that are too readily explained away by natural science, and for failing to answer for the puzzling connectedness of experience. Before deciding that this is a vague argument and irrelevant to our times, we need to remember that what he calls 'empiricism' is alive and well today in neuroscience, CBT, and the bio-medical model.

He offers an equally fierce critique of the 'idealist' view, originating in Descartes and Kant (and prominent in Husserl's early writings) which sees the mind as giving unity and structure to experience and mistakenly associates perception with thought *about* perception. This view is also influential in our culture today: many believe that thoughts organize experience or even that mind to a certain extent *creates* reality.

What both views have in common is a devaluation of experience; they both fail to see that experience contains its own intelligent form. Once we acknowledge this, we are ready to *describe* perception as we experience it, rather than relying on conjectures. For Merleau-Ponty, a phenomenological description of perceptual experience is "that vital communication with the world which makes it present as a familiar setting of our life" (1945/1989, pp. 52–53). The world becomes the place we inhabit rather than something apart from us, and the way we inhabit it is by being embodied, by being a *body-subject*. We are not pure reason or pure consciousness; we will never be able to absorb and receive the whole of reality. Inhabiting the world as a body means realizing the sheer impossibility of a view from nowhere. It means giving up the notion of objectivity *and* transcendence. The world is unfathomable, our experience ambiguous, forever resisting a completely rational or non-rational explanation of it. Of course, the brain is crucial in allowing us to relate to the world and combine the activities of our sense organs, but this does not mean that consciousness is indistinguishable from the brain, or that I am my brain.

I am not a mental substance or a 'mind' but instead a *body-subject*. Crucially for our cognitively-saturated times of hypertrophied consciousness and 'mindfulness', Merleau-Ponty cautions us that consciousness cannot occupy all of its operations. Consciousness is limited. Descartes' *cogito* (I think) is too narrow; it limits our identity to the conscious mind, separate from 'matter' – a new *cogito* is needed, one that is able to include our interrelated physical embeddedness with a world we *inhabit* rather than *represent*.

Merleau-Ponty's unique version of phenomenology

Alongside Marx, Nietzsche, and Freud (all of whom in Merleau-Ponty's view variously anticipated phenomenology via their hermeneutics of rigorous inquiry), the two thinkers who most influenced Merleau-Ponty were the *younger* Hegel and the *later* Husserl. As with all the great French existentialists who studied left-wing Hegelianism in Paris with Alexandre Kojève and Jean Hyppolite in the 1930s, from the young Hegel Merleau-Ponty learned the importance of history and contingency as well as our all-too-human "desire of another human consciousness" (Merleau-Ponty, 1964a, p. 17): the encounter between self and other out of which (through conflict via the well-known 'lordship/bondage', commonly known as the 'master/servant dialectic', but also through love, friendship, and shared endeavour) real subjectivity is born. The fact that Hegel – particularly the early Hegel of the *Phenomenology of Spirit* – so crucial to French existentialism – is absent from all the syllabi of traditional existential therapy may well account for the approach's arguably poor understanding of history and contingency, for the misguided universalism that characterizes dominant psychotherapeutic readings of the human condition, and for bypassing the role of conflict in shaping human interactions.

Intrigued by an article on Husserl's later version of phenomenology in the *Revue international de philosophie* in 1939, Merleau-Ponty was one of the first visitors to the Husserl Archive in Louvain, Belgium. Husserl's earlier explorations relied heavily on Descartes and Kant and on Franz Brentano's idea, borrowed from medieval thought, of *intentionality*. They were directed at finding a method able to study meanings, understood as the intended objects of a *transcendental* subjectivity, or transcendental ego. In his Parisian lectures *Cartesian Meditations* in 1929, Husserl appropriated a method called *epoché* (a Greek word meaning *suspension*, a.k.a. 'bracketing' or phenomenological reduction) but *diverted* its trajectory by bending it — to his own Cartesian/idealistic agenda. It might be useful here to consider briefly the original formulation of *epoché* which goes back to the Greek philosopher Pyrrho of Elis (c. 360–270 BC). According to Diogenes Laertius, Pyrrho developed his own philosophy after encountering some 'naked wise men' (*gymnosophists*) in India when accompanying Alexander the Great on his expedition. The 'naked wise men' were none other than the philosophers of Nāgārjuna's *Madhyamaka* school of Buddhism (Kuzminski, 2008). For Pyrrho – and much later for Sextus Empiricus (c. 160–210 AD), who systematized his thought and founded Pyrrhonism, *epoché* entails suspending all non-evident claims and embracing immediate experience, i.e. those 'mere' phenomena, as reality itself, *trusting the senses* rather than (in line with religious/Platonist injunctions) suspecting them.

What Husserl advocates in his early version of *epoché* is the very opposite: first, to regard phenomena as the intentional objects of consciousness; then, to move from instances to essences; third, to see essences as necessary rather than contingent. He patiently builds the edifice of a transcendental phenomenology in the attempt to give philosophy the status of rigorous science, a project not entirely dissimilar from the logical positivism of the Vienna Circle.

Merleau-Ponty was highly critical of this position, which he saw as Cartesian through and through, as effectively brushing aside the phenomenal world so as to ascend to an imaginary pure consciousness, a realm of essences and transcendental subjectivity. There is no such thing, Merleau-Ponty says with Simone de Beauvoir: so-called 'inner experience' is not transcendental but *situated*. The entire aim and direction of *epoché* must be changed to its original meaning: to have another look at the world, to unfasten our customary links with it and rediscover a sense of perplexity and wonder. Husserl's notion of essences, freed from a customary Platonic reading, can be useful as the fisherman's net draws up from the depths of the sea shuddering fish and sea-weed.

Most of this was already present in Husserl's later work, partly prompted by his disappointment in seeing phenomenology hijacked by Heidegger. The very direction of *epoché* changes: earlier on he had stressed the need to bracket the 'natural attitude' (i.e. the taken-for-granted view, engendered by science, of a separate solid world of matter 'out there') in the hope of accessing a 'transcendental ego' who would be aware of 'essences'. Now he criticizes Descartes for having equated a separate self with 'soul' and created an artificial division between mind and matter. What we need to suspend are our explanations of experience; the self is no longer seen as separated but as part of the world. In tune with this latter view,

Merleau-Ponty will go on to say that the task of phenomenology is *to put essences back into existence.*

Reclaiming phenomenology from idealist philosophy

One of the first to use the term 'phenomenology' was the German scientist and mathematician Lambert (1728–1777). In a letter to Lambert of 1770, Kant had written of phenomenology as a necessary 'propadeutic' to metaphysics. The study of phenomena of 'that which appears' was for Kant subservient to the existence of *noumena* or pure concepts. One and a half century later Heidegger was to replicate this move: for Heidegger phenomenology is not an independent method of investigation but mere *prelude* to a theory of 'Being'. *Phenomenon* is in his view that which shows itself and phenomenology what makes manifest that which shows itself. Heidegger's pervasive, if befuddling, influence on contemporary existential/phenomenological psychotherapy blinds most practitioners to the fact that he was in my view neither an existentialist nor a phenomenologist but an idealist philosopher within the mainstream German tradition. In Merleau-Ponty we won't find any grandiose attempt to create a 'theory of being', an idle task more suitable, according to Adorno (2002), to closet theologians such as Heidegger.

Compared to Heidegger's, Merleau-Ponty's stance is modest but also far more effective: the task of phenomenology is to clarify our experience in relation to inescapably physical, social, and historical dimensions, finding natural support to our quest from psychology, neurology, psychiatry, and other methods of inquiry all disdained by Heidegger as inferior or, to use his jargon, 'ontic'.

The lived body

Everyone recognizes that perception is related to the body, but the predominant view oscillates between a *passive* view of perception as mere recording of an 'external' action or as an *active* projection of the intellect. In both cases we take for granted a separation between mind and matter, subject and object. But for Merleau-Ponty we *are a body-mind intimately connected to the world*. We are a *lived body*, i.e. not an object that can be objectively observed alongside other objects or a subjective 'interiority'. We are not a Cogito but a *knowing body*. Yet the experience of being in the world is ambiguous because bodily inhabiting the world blurs the customary divisions between subject and object. The body is not an object, Merleau-Ponty says, and because of that my awareness of it is not a thought. How can I know this phenomenal body? There is only one way: we know it by living it, by being an embodied presence in the world. Our being in the world is circular: we experience the body both 'internally' and 'externally', as when I touch an object with my right hand, and my left hand touches my right hand; in that moment I am both *sensing* and being *sensed*.

This process is continuous and circular. This circularity does not produce identity but instead an opening and the possibility of a meaningful life, or, as he writes in a stunning passage in *The Visible and the Invisible* (Merleau-Ponty, 1969), a subject without personal identity who loses track of itself in the perceived spectacle, an anonymous self buried in the world, one that has not yet traced its path. We need to lose ourselves in the world and find a voice, Merleau-Ponty says quoting a poem by Paul Valéry in the very same book: "this solemn Voice/ Which knows itself when it sounds/To be no longer the voice of anyone/As much as the voice of the waves and the forests" (cited in Merleau-Ponty, 1969, p. 155). As it turns out, there *is* room for transcendence in a philosophy which had started along rigorously scientific lines. But *transcendence* is not passage into a spiritual realm but instead the *transmutation of biology into an embodied world of meaning*, into a world both *invented* and *natural*. Before we think this is too abstract, he gives as an example *the kiss*, both a natural gesture as well as a culturally created usage of the body. As humans, we are not a 'natural species' but instead a 'historical idea'. We are not animals endowed with a soul but an integral part of existence, which in itself is a process of the meaningless taking on meaning, for instance in the ongoing movement from the biological to the sexual to the cultural domains – the very process of transcendence.

Inner life and the flesh

The self (or subjectivity) is a central problem in western philosophy and psychology, with the Greeks setting the scene for philosophical investigation way back via the Delphic instruction *know thyself!* However, their notion of self was different from ours and their response was not introspection as we understand it today. The notion of a self endowed with 'interiority' is a modern idea whose foundations were set by Augustine who famously said *Noli foras ire, in te redi, in interiore homine habitat veritas* (Do not wish to go outside, stay inside, truth dwells in the inner man (Madison, 1990, p. 29). The purpose of the Augustinian injunction was not investigation but repentance. Kierkegaard took this injunction to dangerous heights and the early Husserl made it central to his own inquiry. Where Augustine and Kierkegaard in their introspection discovered absolute otherness, a.k.a. God, the early Husserl corroborated Descartes' error of conceiving a self-existing mental subjectivity – which is also what the western philosophical tradition did. From time to time I wonder what it would have been like if we had taken our clue from Michel de Montaigne's notion of interiority rather than from Descartes', given the former's sincere amazement in finding out that *Rien d'humain ne m'est étranger* – Nothing human is foreign to me. We still find otherness in Montaigne's subjectivity but this is wiped out in Descartes' and in the western tradition's not-so-splendid mental isolation from the world of 'matter'. From then on, any philosopher worth the name will try to break free from the prison of Cartesian subjectivity in the attempt to find something 'objective', something 'other', something 'real' (ibid). Heidegger tried to circumvent subjectivity by a return to the pre-Socratics. Philosophy and psychology inspired by Eastern thought did away with the idea of the self altogether. A similar tack is taken by much of post-modern thought which disseminates the self into perspectivism. The current most popular way of bypassing the central problem of subjectivity comes from dialogical and relational perspectives.

Merleau-Ponty's uniqueness consists in taking the delicate stance of going beyond solipsism and at the same time taking subjectivity very seriously. He tried, in other words, to go beyond subjectivism and individualism from the inside. Going inside the cave of subjectivity, he found the *Flesh*.

Merleau-Ponty's notion of the flesh has no equal in the entire history of philosophy. It is an attempt to register fully *the presence of the other in the same*: not only the tangible trace of another in our body/mind but also the discovery that I am a stranger to myself; my body is not only sensible to itself, it is outside itself, it is a stranger to itself. Through the notion of the Flesh, the other is woven into the fabric of the self. He writes in *Signs* (Merleau-Ponty, 1964a):

> Before others are or can be subjected to my conditions of possibility and reconstructed in my image, they must already exist as outlines, deviations, and variants (*relief, écarts, variantes*) of a single Vision in which I too participate. For they are not fictions with which I might people my desert ... but my twins or the flesh of my flesh. Certainly I do not live their life; they are definitely absent from me and I from them. But that distance becomes a strange proximity as soon as one comes back home to the perceptible world [the flesh of the sensible] ... No one will see that table which now meets my eye; only I can do that. And yet I know that at the same moment it presses upon every glance in exactly the same way.
>
> (p. 15)

Merleau-Ponty and the Counter-tradition

The history of western philosophy is the history of the Tradition, variously named as rationalism, metaphysics, systematic thought. According to the Tradition, the universe is not a chaos but a cosmos, well structured and intelligible, fully graspable by reason which is part of a presupposed Totality (Madison, 1981; Bazzano, 2013). The Tradition has dominated the West, our whole way of learning and thinking; its motivation is Promethean, a desire to manage the uncertainty of existence and achieve mastery through science and, more recently, technology. Alongside the Tradition, there has always been a Counter-tradition, "a counter-current which attempts to bring [us] back to a more just appreciation of [our] powers and limits" (Madison, 1981, p. 293). Empirical, skeptical, experiential (and phenomenological): these are a few of the attributes linked to the Counter-tradition, alongside an appreciation of (dynamic) becoming and a critique of (static) being. Heraclitus praised flux, impermanence, the river of life and death; Protagoras and Gorgias disputed the ancient cosmologists; Isocrates debated against Plato; Montaigne critiqued the Renaissance's rationalism; Pascal disputed Cartesian rationalism; Kierkegaard attacked Hegelianism; and finally, Nietzsche deconstructed with nerve and wit any metaphysical pretension under the sun (Madison, 1981). Characteristic of the Counter-tradition are humanism, skepticism, and poetic sensibility. The beauty of Merleau-Ponty's philosophy is that it effortlessly belongs to the Counter-tradition without avowed adherence to it. He does not reject science but forswears (*desaveu*) it; he brackets scientism and all theoretical assumption, stating that after all science is a human endeavour and cannot substitute human experience. He reminds me of Pascal who in his *Pensées* famously states that the last step of reason is to recognize that there are so many things beyond its reach and that it is *un*-reasonable not to recognize this simple fact. Merleau-Ponty's phenomenology presents a similarly rational critique of reason. Rationality goes beyond logic; it is forged in the crucible of *dialogue* and encounter. 'Rational' or, for that matter, 'true' is not what is general, universal, or absolute but a tangible experience. As he puts it in his book *Sense and Non-sense* (1964b): "In the end whatever solidity there is in my belief in the absolute is nothing but my experience of agreement with myself and others" (p. 93).

Epoché (the suspension of any scientific, theoretical, or religious preconception and the invitation to cultivate the attitude of a perpetual beginner) was the great gift of the Counter-tradition. Phenomenology was the natural inheritor of the Counter-tradition in the twentieth century, except that within phenomenology there have been attempts to divert its course towards Cartesianism (early Husserl) and irrationalism (Heidegger). What a practice based on the phenomenological method of *epoché* states is that there is no *fundamentum inconcussum*, no solid ground on which we can build our tower of knowledge, our 'science of reality'. Through *epoché* we experience the failure of a total reflection; we experience the ambivalence of knowledge and the opacity of our very being. We also experience what Merleau-Ponty calls the unmotivated upsurge of the world.

Humanism and terror

Unlike Husserl (who was disinterested in politics and for whom science alone could make mankind blessed), Merleau-Ponty was politically engaged. Unlike Heidegger (who supported Nazism) his politics were on the side of justice and of reasonable discourse. Merleau-Ponty translated his view of the situatedness of the human condition with an engagement with active politics and with Marx, whose thought he considered integral to a hermeneutics of suspicion, which in many ways had heralded phenomenology. Even after his subsequent disillusionment and his heated debates with Sartre over the Soviet Union, which the latter had strategically supported, Merleau-Ponty never forgets that western liberalism is founded on slavery and that Stalin had not *invented* violence. In politics, too, he searches a nuanced position away from knee-jerk reactions. In *Humanism and Terror* (Merleau-Ponty, 2000) he points out that the bourgeois anti-Communist refuses to see that violence is universal, while the exalted sympathizer refuses to see that violence is always unbearable, as in the agonizing scream of a single person condemned to death. Writing at the time of the cold war, his targets are the two superpowers. Writing as a western intellectual, he aims at dispossessing western politics from their clear conscience and reminds the reader that our celebrated capitalist democracies are built "on colonial exploitation, wars, propaganda, wage labour, unemployment, the violent suppression of strikes, anti-Semitism, and racism" (Madison, 1981, p. 162). He engages in a fierce polemic with Mauriac who had written of French colonialism as 'benevolent civilization'. Merleau-Ponty finds it scandalous that a Christian should be so incapable of getting outside himself and his 'ideas' and should refuse to see himself even for an instant through the eyes of others. One cannot help wondering what he would have made of contemporary historians like Niall Ferguson who wax lyrical on the great wonders of the British Empire bringing democracy and civilization to all those poor savages in the colonies.

'Chanter le monde'

I conclude my sketchy foray into the thought of a great thinker by reflecting how in his late writings the psychologist and scientist gives way to a poet or even a mystic of Nature, one in search of the voices that reason alone is unable to hear. Others have spoken of the need for a remembrance of nature in the self, for a necessary re-enchantment of the world, following the thorough dis-enchantment of the Enlightenment project. Merleau-Ponty's own phrase for this is *chanter le monde*, to sing the world. Faithful to reason in the name of reason, singing through the body (how else?), "the more honest and purer voice … speak[ing] of the meaning of the earth" (Nietzsche, 1997, p. 29). The human voice echoes and reproduces "mimetic [and] onomatopoetic borrowings from nature" (Kleinberg-Levin, 2008, p. 48) but also articulates through 'singing' or appreciative expression its own distinctive imprint on the world. This response can only be subjective. True, we are 'born into language' and in our voice we gather the voices of nature. Through articulating our response of a mysterious phenomenal world, we sing its praises with our living body.

A version of this chapter first appeared as an article in *Self & Society, Journal of Humanistic Psychology*. It is reprinted here with the kind permission of the editors.

References

Adorno, T. (2002) *The Jargon of Authenticity*. London: Routledge.

Bazzano, M. (2013) On Becoming No One: Phenomenological and Empiricist Contributions to the Person-Centered Approach Person Centered and Experiential Psychotherapies. DOI: 10.1080/14779757.2013.804649.

Kleinberg-Levin, D.M. (2008) *Before the Voice of Reason: Echoes of Responsibility*. Albany, NY: State University of New York.

Kuzminski, A. (2008) *Pyrrhonism: How the Ancient Greeks Reinvented Buddhism*. Lanham, MD: Lexington Books.

Madison, G.B. (1981) *The Phenomenology of Merleau-Ponty*. Athens, OH: Ohio University Press.

Madison, G.B. (1990) Flesh as Otherness in Johnson, G. A. & Smith, M. B. (Eds.), *Ontology and Alterity in Merleau-Ponty*. Evanston, IL: Northwestern University Press.

Merleau-Ponty, M. (1942/1983) *The Structure of Behaviour*. Pittsburgh, PA: Duquesne University Press. First published in 1942.

Merleau-Ponty, M. (1945/1989) *Phenomenology of Perception*. London: Routledge. First published in 1945.

Merleau-Ponty, M. (1964a) *Signs*. Evanston, IL: Northwestern University Press.

Merleau-Ponty, M. (1964b) *Sense and Non-sense*. Evanston, IL: Northwestern University Press.

Merleau-Ponty, M. (1969) *The Visible and the Invisible*. Evanston, IL: Northwestern University Press.

Merleau-Ponty, M. (2000) *Humanism and Terror*, 2nd Edition. London: Transaction Publishers.

Nietzsche, F. (1997) *Thus Spoke Zarathustra*. London: Wordsworth.

Part III
Unreasonable reason

16 Kafka reading Kierkegaard

Always in a process of becoming

Ross Crisp

Introduction

Søren Kierkegaard lauded "the genuine subjective existing thinker" who is "never a teacher, but a learner," and who "is continually striving" (Kierkegaard, 1992, p.85). Instead of claiming to provide authoritative texts, he was a writer who hoped that his readers would contemplate their own subjective experiencing and venture towards a rigorous, authentic self-reflection (Hannay, 1992; Lippitt, 2016; Pattison, 2009; Podmore, 2009). Franz Kafka was one such reader. In several letters and diary/notebook entries, Kafka referred to the challenge of reading Kierkegaard who for Kafka was both "like a friend" (Diary, August 21, 1913; Kafka, 1992a) and "the Tempter himself" (Letter, March 1918; Kafka, 1977).[1]

I will discuss the extent to which Kafka was receptive to the spirit of Kierkegaard's existential-phenomenology. I will explore three aspects of Kafka's reading of Kierkegaard, beginning with *Kafka's comprehension of Kierkegaard's, and his own, ontological condition of anxiety and despair*. I will suggest parallels between existential therapy and the experiencing of Kafka who was, in Kierkegaard's (1992, 2004) terminology, *always in a process of becoming* in which he struggled to achieve a synthesis of opposites: a rational, constricted self determined by necessity/finitude, and an expansive self represented by possibility/infinity.

Second, I will focus on *Kafka's ethical dilemma*. Kierkegaard's insights raised questions for Kafka which prompted him to articulate his own sense of alterity; for example, in response to Kierkegaard's rendering of Abraham's proposed sacrifice of his son Isaac, he re-imagined Abraham's ethical dilemma in ways that mirrored his own concerns regarding the cultural and socio-historical influences that constrained his freedom within the phenomenal world.

Finally, apropos the *counter-tradition* (as defined by Bazzano & Webb, 2016), I will discuss Kafka's fraught, uncertain subjectivity, his distrust of religious-socio-political rationalism, his (and Kierkegaard's) experiencing of temporality contra to a traditional linear conception of time, and his reading of Kierkegaard's Christian perspective that endorses the truth of subjectivity and the passion of faith which enables a person to endure despair.

Kafka's comprehension of Kierkegaard's, and his own, ontological condition of anxiety and despair

Like Kierkegaard, Kafka wrote about his internal struggles with opposing phenomenal and spiritual worlds. Kafka's artistic *inner* self attempted to strive for transcendence towards a spiritual world while his other self was confined to the reality of finite, concrete worldly existence. His preferred option resided in maintaining his existence in *being* a writer that entailed "a higher type of observation" in which "the more independent it becomes, the more obedient to its own laws of motion, the more incalculable, the more joyful, the more ascendant its course" (Diary, January 27, 1922; Kafka, 1992a). However, the "social order" of Kafka's empirical experience continually threatened to devour his writerly, spiritual world.

For Kafka, freedom was a paradox at the heart of his short parables such as *Before the Law* and his novels *The Trial* and *The Castle* (Calasso, 2005; Karl, 1991; Kaufmann, 2015). It entailed an immediate awareness of being unfree:

> *Your will is free* means: it was free when it wanted the desert, it is free since it can choose the path that leads to crossing the desert, it is free since it can choose the pace, *but it is also unfree* since you must go through the desert, unfree since every path in labyrinthine manner touches every foot of the desert's surface.
>
> (Kafka, 1991a, pp.49–50; italics added)

We are free to act because we have the capacity to be self-organizing and guided by intuition and reason. But our freedom is restricted because to act involves interaction with that upon which we act. We are, as Kierkegaard (2004) argued, a "synthesis of possibility and necessity" (p.70) where *possibility* requires imagination to transcend the socially constructed meanings of the phenomenal world, and *necessity* involves restraint and awareness of one's heredity, social and historical circumstances. For Kafka, freedom could never be fully realized within the phenomenal world. It co-existed with his experience of alienation. He wrote of being outcast within family in short stories such as *The Metamorphosis* and *The Judgment*, and in the wider community in which K in *The Castle*, for example, wanders in a labyrinthine social maze, an outcast whose being in the world is precarious:

> … it seemed to K as if they had broken off all contact with him, but as if he were freer than ever and could wait as long as he wanted here in this place where he was generally not allowed … as if nobody could touch him or drive him away, or even speak to him, yet – and this conviction was at least as strong – as if there were nothing more senseless, nothing more desperate, than this freedom, this waiting, this invulnerability.
>
> (Kafka, 1998, p.106)

While this passage has socio-political implications, it also suggests an inner tension "beneath or beyond consciousness" (Karl, 1991, p.701). K experiences something like an implicit, ontic-ontological sense of being and non-being.

Kafka wrote of the ontological anxiety rooted in his existence that involved the inseparability of *being* and *non-being* that necessitated a realization of finitude:

> Living means being in the midst of life, seeing life with the gaze in which I have created it … The decisively characteristic thing about this world is its transience … centuries have no advantage over the present moment … *the fact that new life blossoms among the ruins proves not so much the tenacity of life as that of death.* If I wish to fight against this world, I must fight against … its transience.
>
> (Kafka, 1991a, p.47; italics added)

His awareness of the polarities of the infinite and his own finitude was exemplified by his experiencing as a writer, by his repeated striving for the textual illumination of his existence *and* veering towards death (Corngold, 2004). In a letter to his fiancé, Felice Bauer, he described it thus:

> What will be my fate as a writer is very simple. My talent for portraying my inner life has thrust all other matters into the background; my life has dwindled dreadfully … I waver, continually fly to the summit of the mountain, but then fall back in a moment … it is not death, alas, but the eternal torments of dying.
>
> (August 6, 1914; Kafka, 1999)

Kafka constructed images and metaphors to convey his being-towards-death in his fiction (see Corngold, 2004, pp.81–93) and in his letters, diaries and notebooks. In February 1918, Kafka (1991a) wrote that an end was "an apparent end" registered by the "cruelty of death" that "brings the real sorrow of the end, but not the end" (p.53). For Kafka, "an apparent end" paradoxically co-existed with a "mad strength of faith" that he "*cannot* not-live, after all" (Kafka, 1991a, p.54; original italics) and which echoed Kierkegaard's (2004) concept of ontological despair that is "an aspect of spirit … something a human being cannot be rid of … since the self is indeed the relation to oneself" (p.47) in which "he cannot consume himself … cannot become nothing" (p.49). Likewise, ontological anxiety is not something we can flee from (Kierkegaard, 2014); nor is it something to be cured by psychotherapy.

Like Kierkegaard's (2003) Knight of Faith, Kafka was perhaps reconciled to the pain and distress that arose from an awareness of being constantly vulnerable to the limits of his existence in the phenomenal world. The Knight of Faith represents the "ideal of mental health, the continuing openness of life out of the death throes of dread" (Becker, 1973, p.258). It necessarily entails an experience of *infinite resignation* in which "there is peace and repose and consolation in the pain" (Kierkegaard, 2003, p.74) that precedes the emergence of the *faith* which "begins precisely where thinking leaves off" (Kierkegaard, 2003, p.82). Thus, a person facing their inner conflict and despair intuitively arrives towards an awareness of their authentic self that oftentimes has been denied to oneself (Kierkegaard, 2004). Kafka wrote:

From a certain stage of knowledge [*Erkenntnis*] on, weariness, insufficiency, constriction, self-contempt, must all vanish: namely at that point where I have the strength to recognize as my own nature what previously was something alien to myself that refreshed me, satisfied, liberated, and exalted me ...

Its influence extended further, raising me then to this higher level. It did not cease to be alien, but merely began *also* to be Myself.

(Kafka, 1991a, p.44; original italics)

Kafka was here alluding to a transformation that signified a "mad strength of faith" (Kafka, 1991a, p.54) or what Kierkegaard (2003) referred to as "the strength of the absurd" (p.85). Further, Kafka wrote that his inner conflicts "these so-called illnesses, sad as they may appear, are *matters of faith*, efforts of souls in distress to find moorings in some maternal soil ... Such moorings ... are *pre-existing in [our] nature* and continue to form [our] nature" (Kafka, 1992b, p.173; italics added). Similarly, Kafka (1991a) referred to an immanent *commandment*:

Is it a continual or only an occasional commandment? ... I cannot be sure. I believe, however, it is a continual commandment, but that I hear it only occasionally ... *I don't know whose command it is and what he is aiming at* ... it finds me unprepared, descending upon me as surprisingly as dreams descend upon the sleeper ... it makes me happy or frightens me, both without cause, though admittedly it does the first much more rarely than the second; *it is not communicable, because it is not intelligible, and for the same reason demands to be communicated.*

(Kafka, 1991a, pp. 44–5; italics added)

In Kafka's rendering, the *commandment* is mysterious and illusory. In a manner similar to Kierkegaard (1992, 2003), perhaps Kafka was postulating the existence of a divine Other that could not be easily comprehended nor communicated in the language of practical reason. But, as Walter Benjamin (1992) argued, it is more likely that Kafka's immediate experiencing was conveyed to him by a forgotten mystical tradition lost to the unfathomable world of his ancestors (that I will discuss later). Since *"it is not communicable"* but *"demands to be communicated,"* he relied on the power of his imagination to produce evocative metaphors. They are analogous to the metaphors deployed by modern science to explain phenomena that are physically present but unseen (Arendt, 2006; Benjamin, 1992[BIB-001]). Thus, Kafka wrote metaphorically about himself:

I was in somewhat of the situation of this flower beside me, which is not wholly healthy, and though it lifts its head to the sun ... is full of secret griefs because of the painful processes in its roots and in its sap ... *it has only very vague, painfully vague information on that and cannot at this point bend over, scratch up the soil, and have a look*, but must act like its brothers and hold itself high. Which it does, wearily.

(Letter, June, 1921; Kafka, 1977; italics added)

While Kafka was unable to yield a rational explanation for his inner experiencing, he could act in unison with others in the phenomenal world without communicating his "vague" experiencing. From the perspective of existential therapy, Kafka need not have searched for a rational, scientifically objective explanation or solution-focused strategy. It was better that he experience emotionally and bodily the "secret griefs" and the "painfully vague information." He undertook an honest and *subjective* account of his own experiencing which is what Kierkegaard demanded of himself and recommended to his readers. Kafka expressed his distress by writing parables about himself based on, for example, the story of Abraham's proposed sacrifice of his son that I will discuss further.

Kafka's ethical dilemma

Kierkegaard's insights raised questions for Kafka which prompted him to articulate his own sense of alterity; for example, in response to Kierkegaard's (2003) rendering of Abraham's proposed sacrifice of his son Isaac, he re-imagined Abraham's ethical dilemma in ways that mirrored his own concerns regarding the historical and cultural influences that constrained his freedom within the phenomenal world.

In a letter to a close friend (June 1921; Kafka, 1977), he re-imagined Abraham unable "to perform the sacrifice because he cannot get away from home, he is indispensable, the farm needs him, there is always something that must be attended to, the house isn't finished … he cannot get away." In the same letter, Kafka imagined other Abrahams who face the impossibility of sacrificing sons they do not have; who "are deliberately not finishing their houses"; and who "are hiding their faces." Kafka had a sense of humour – but, these comical versions of Abraham suggest Kafka's own struggle with the guilt of choosing to be the person he wanted to be opposed to the person his father preferred him to be. Kafka's father would not countenance him leaving his job as a senior civil servant to devote himself exclusively to the more "spiritually" meaningful task of writing. His re-imagining of the Abraham story mirrored the self-criticism and despair of his diaries and letters that documented his struggle to be a writer contra to his father who instead valued business acumen, material wealth and the responsibility of marriage and raising a family (Kafka, 1992a, 2011; see also Stach, 2005). His father was, to borrow Stolorow's (2018) description of his own father, an "epistemic tyrant" who rarely acknowledged the truth and validity of his son's experiencing. The power of the father was considerable in European families of the early twentieth century. The father's power, even with adult children, went beyond that of the legal code, and it was especially strong in close-knit Jewish families such as the Kafkas (Stach, 2005).

Contra to the unshakeable faith of Kierkegaard's Abraham, Kafka (1977) imagined another Abraham who initially wants to carry out the sacrifice of his son, but who avoids the sacrifice because he is afraid of looking ridiculous in the eyes of the world, and because he truly believes he is unworthy to be summoned by God to make the sacrifice. He also suspects that the summons is a mistake and one that is designed to punish him. Further, Kafka (1991a) re-imagined another Abraham who attempts but fails to escape the transient phenomenal world by emigrating to eternity. This failure is due to the "weakness of his voice uttering the commands," his "spiritual poverty" and his being someone who "cannot endure the monotony of the world" (p.52). According to Kafka's close friend, Max Brod, Kafka had originally written this passage in the first person; which lends weight to the views of Benjamin (1992) and others (e.g., Darrow, 2005) that Kafka's parables were about himself.

Kafka's re-imagined Abrahams lack *possibility*; they cannot see beyond the *necessity* of their finite circumstances; they are defined by fatalism and determinism (cf., Kierkegaard, 2004, pp.68–72). Moreover, these re-imaginings of Abraham were contiguous with Kafka's despair of belonging to a Jewish middle-class community that wished to remain Jewish but who did not want to acknowledge their Jewishness and ethnic minority status in a hostile socio-political environment (Arendt, 1992; Stach, 2013). Kafka attributed this problem to the uncertainty and ambiguity of patriarchal power and authority:

> Most young Jews who began to write German [as Kafka did] wanted to leave Jewishness behind them, and their fathers approved of this, but vaguely (this vagueness was what was outrageous to them). But with their posterior legs they were still glued to their father's Jewishness and with their waving anterior legs they found no new ground. The ensuing despair became their inspiration.
>
> (Letter June 1921; Kafka, 1977)

Kafka's inspiration was to construct his artistic *writerly being*; he relentlessly strove for the *possibility* of "writing as a state of being" (Corngold, 2004, p.130). But, Kafka's "waving anterior legs found no new ground" and his ontological "despair could not be assuaged by writing" (Letter, June 1921; Kafka, 1977). Nevertheless, Kafka's letters and diaries suggest that he was constantly searching for, and creating, meaning in his life; and that from an existential therapeutic perspective, he was experiencing his anxiety and despair *as his own*. He was arguably attempting to broaden his awareness of self; to engage in self-confrontation and identify ways in which he was constricted in his own self-awareness; to focus upon his own subjectivity and take responsibility for his own experiencing. It was also an act of defiant self-affirmation that I will discuss in relation to the counter-tradition.

The counter-tradition

Kafka's reading of Kierkegaard belongs in the *counter-tradition* "which continues to remind us of our human limitations and of the ungraspable nature of the world" (Bazzano & Webb, 2016, p.2). I will discuss Kafka's fraught, uncertain subjectivity, his distrust of religious-socio-political rationalism, his experiencing of temporality contra to traditional linear time, his reading of Kierkegaard's Christian worldview, and his resolve to endure despair.

Kafka did not trust the rationalism of both secular *and* religious institutions. He was a Jew living in an anti-Semitic milieu; a speaker of a resented minority language (German) in Prague; a senior civil servant who reported on the disenfranchisement of injured workers denied adequate compensation; and who was, to say the least, ambivalent about the institution of family dominated by an insensitive father. Despite his extensive reading of Christian and Jewish literature, there was very little positive religious content in Kafka's diaries and letters (Stach, 2013). Nor did he wholly embrace the theological aspects of Kierkegaard's writings (Kafka, 1991a, pp.52, 54–55, 105; see also Darrow, 2005). Contra to Kierkegaard, he wrote of his own experience of transcendence:

> Granted, the religious relationship wishes to reveal itself, but cannot do so in the world; therefore striving man must oppose this world in order to save the divine element within himself … However the world is, I shall stay with my original nature, which I am not about to change to suit what the world regards as good. The moment this word is pronounced, a *metamorphosis* takes place in the whole of existence … and everything comes to life: the whole of existence becomes *sheer attentiveness*. The angels have work to do and look on curiously … On the other side, dark, uncanny demons … leap up … they say, here there is something for us …
>
> (Letter, March 1918; Kafka, 1977; italics added)

Kafka's statement that "a *metamorphosis* takes place in the whole of existence" suggests that he viewed his experiencing as a "kabbalistic cycle of transgression, punishment, exile, and trials in hope of deliverance and redemption" (Bruce, 2013, p.200). For Kafka, this cycle was a recurring trial in which all things (apropos the metaphors of "angels" and "dark, uncanny demons") are equally possible. The hope of deliverance and redemption is not guaranteed. Further, Kafka's "*sheer attentiveness*" was, to use Benjamin's (1992) argument, a *gestus* (visible gesture) which signified a sudden awareness of an unexplainable hidden truth, perhaps of something forgotten, an "inexhaustible intermediate world … [that] presses toward the light" (p.127).

In his analysis of Kafka's parable *Before the Law* (published both separately and as part of *The Trial*; Kafka, 1984), Schonfeld (2016) argued that Kafka's "ignorance is not an ordinary one; it is an ignorance conscious of itself … [L]ike Socrates, who *knows* that he does not know, Kafka, through his ignorance, possesses a deep, hidden knowledge" (p.110) that is an attribute of a mystical tradition. He cannot gain sufficient access to it since it is a "broken tradition … *experiencing a crisis of transmission*" (p.116; original italics). Nevertheless, as Benjamin (1992) argued, it informed Kafka's experiencing in the phenomenal world:

> Kafka's work is an ellipse with foci that are far apart … determined, on the one hand, by mystical experience (in particular, the experience of tradition) and, on the other, by the experience of the modern big-city dweller … who knows he is at the mercy of a vast machinery of officialdom … directed by

authorities that remain nebulous to the executive organs, let alone to the people they deal with.

(p.139)

The resultant sense of alienation and despair was experienced by Kafka as a temporal crisis. Like Kierkegaard, he challenged the traditional linear view of time. For Kafka, the "broken tradition" of the past was paradoxically obscure, actual and coeval with the present moment and the future. In his "He" parable, Kafka (1991b) wrote:

> he has actually forgotten what he once represented. Probably it is this very forgetting that gives rise to a certain melancholy, uncertainty, unrest, a certain longing for vanished ages, darkening the present. And yet this longing is an important element of man's vital strength.
>
> (p.110)

He needed his strength to survive in the present which was depicted in Kafka's "He" parable as a conflict between the indeterminate past that presses "He" forward and the future which drives him back into the past. Kafka's "He" dreamt of being placed above the field of conflict by being promoted to umpire (or judge); and this dream could only be realized "in an unguarded moment ... [in] a night darker than any night has ever been yet."[2] Similarly, it was almost always night when Kafka was immersed in the "strange, mysterious, perhaps dangerous, perhaps saving comfort that there is in writing ... a seeing of what is really taking place ... a higher type of observation" (Diary, January 27, 1922; Kafka, 1992a). It was from this vantage point that he explicated a severe temporal crisis:

> First: breakdown, impossible to sleep, impossible to stay awake, impossible to endure life ... The clocks are not in unison; the inner one runs crazily on at a devilish or demoniac or in any case inhuman pace, the outer one limps along at its usual speed ... two worlds split apart ... or at least clash in a fearful manner ...
>
> Secondly: this pursuit, originating in the midst of men, carries one in a direction away from them ... 'Pursuit,' indeed is only a metaphor. I can also say, 'assault on the last earthly frontier' ... launched from below, from mankind, and ... I can replace it by the metaphor of an assault from above, aimed at me from above.
>
> All such writing is an assault on the frontiers ... it would require genius of an unimaginable kind to strike root again in the old centuries, or create the centuries anew and not spend itself withal, but only then begin to flower forth.
>
> (Diary, January 16, 1922; Kafka, 1992a)

Two days later, he wrote in his diary of this "terrible moment" that, on reflection, "is not terrible, only your fear of the future makes it so. And also looking back on it in retrospect." He resolved to learn to endure such moments. A week later, he wrote: "Accept your symptoms, don't complain of them; immerse yourself in your suffering" (Diary, January 23, 1922; Kafka, 1992a). He regarded these moments as an integral part of the human condition.

During these crises, and in the process of writing about them, Kafka found himself radically alone, temporarily ensconced in the "last earthly frontier." From Kierkegaard's (2003) perspective, this process could enable Kafka to confront his despair and abandon his familiar socially constructed self. In doing so, he may paradoxically discover his true "infinite" self and thereafter return re-energized to his activities of everyday life in which he discovers himself open to examining the ambiguities of his life. It would require him to continually synthesize the aforementioned polarities of existence (i.e., necessity-possibility, finitude-infinity). Moreover, it could only be actualized by practising one's relation to an absolute *telos* (end, goal), and by being in relationship with the divine Other who, in a thera-peutic sense, conveys forgiveness which a person cannot articulate for his or her self (Podmore, 2009).

Kafka, however, was not convinced. Despite his admiration for Kierkegaard, Kafka (1991a) accused him of being out of touch with the phenomenal world: "he travels across the earth as upon a magic chariot … In this way his humble plea to be followed turns into tyranny, and … arrogance" (pp.55–56). But, Kafka did not wholly repudiate Kierkegaard's position. He drew on Kierkegaard's work to con-template his own subjective experiencing (as Kierkegaard intended).

Likewise many humanistic-existential psychologists (who secularized Kierkegaard's Christian world-view, e.g., May, 1983; Nielsen, 2017; Rogers, 1961), while they argued that it is the *presence* of the Other (e.g., therapist) which enhances a person's awareness of his or her innermost experiencing, they were receptive to Kierkegaard's view that they too continually strive for self-awareness. Kierkegaard (2014, p.67) had mocked the "starched collar psychologists" of his day who were loathe to look inside themselves, lacked humility and ignored the ontological premise that all persons are equals in their common humanity and mutually constituted. Kafka held a similar view.[3]

For Kafka, early twentieth century psychology was problematic. He dismissed the "mirror-writing" of the psychologists of his generation who ignored the "invis-ible" and "spiritual basis of life" (Kafka, 1991a, p.52). Yet, like Kierkegaard, he recognized that the transcendent nature of human existence may only ever be partially accessible to self-awareness and incommunicable to others. Despite the candour and intimacy of his letters, and regular contact with his interlocutors, he perceived the "unknowability" of self and others. He told his lover, Milena Jesenka:

> You can't properly understand … I don't even understand myself … I'm trying to convey something unconveyable, to explain something inexplicable, to tell of something which I have in my bones and which can be experienced only in these bones.
>
> (Kafka, 1992b, pp.160, 175)

Despite his "unknowability" Kafka regularly enacted a fundamental ethical obligation to be responsive to the Other. His voluminous letter writing was itself an experience that arose "from a consciousness focused on itself" which Kafka believed "expressed and generated closeness" with the recipients of his letters (Stach, 2005, pp.153–154). His letters (as well as his diaries, stories and parables) run parallel to the work of existential therapists and their clients who, like Kafka, attempt to create meanings, appraise ambiguities and confront the uncertainty of their existence.

Notes

1 I will quote from Kafka's letters, diaries and notebooks (i.e., Kafka, 1977, 1992a, 1999). Since they have been published in multiple languages and revised editions, page numbers will not be cited. Instead, the dates of quoted extracts will be cited to enable easiest access for those readers who wish to refer to these sources.
2 I am quoting the longer English translation by Hannah Arendt (2006, p.7); cf., Pasley's translation (Kafka, 1991b, p.106) that excluded the words I quoted.
3 Kafka (1991a) wrote: "The indestructible is one: it is each individual human being and, at the same time, it is common to all, hence the incomparably indivisible union that exists between human beings" (p.33).

References

Arendt, H. (1961/2006). *Between past and future*. New York: Penguin. (Originally published 1961)

Arendt, H. (1970/1992). Introduction. In W. Benjamin (Ed.), Illuminations. (pp. 7–58). London: Fontana Books. (Originally published 1970)

Bazzano, M., & Webb, J. (2016). Introduction. In M. Bazzano & J. Webb (Eds.), *Therapy and the counter-tradition: The edge of philosophy*. (pp. 1–5). London: Routledge.

Becker, E. (1973). *The denial of death*. New York: Free Press.

Benjamin, W. (1992). *Illuminations*. (Trans., H. Zohn). London: Fontana Books. (Originally published 1970)

Bruce, I. (2013). Elements of Jewish folklore in *Metamorphosis*. In F. Kafka, *The Metamorphosis* (Trans. and Ed., S. Corngold). (pp. 197–222). New York: Modern Library.

Calasso, R. (2005). *K.* (Trans., G. Brock). New York: Knopf.

Corngold, S. (2004). *Lambent traces: Franz Kafka*. Princeton: Princeton University Press.

Darrow, R.A. (2005). *Kierkegaard, Kafka, and the strength of "the absurd" in Abraham's sacrifice of Isaac*. Ohio: Wright State University. Retrieved September 29, 2018 from http://corescholar.libraries.wright.edu/etd_all

Hannay, A. (1992). Introduction. In S. Kierkegaard, *Either/Or*. (pp. 1–21). London: Penguin.

Kafka, F. (1977). *Letters to friends, family, and editors*. New York: Schocken Books. (Originally published 1959)

Kafka, F. (1984). *The Trial*. (Trans., W. & E. Muir). New York: Schocken Books. (Originally published 1925)

Kafka, F. (1991a). *The blue octavo notebooks*. (Trans., E. Kaiser & E. Wilkins). Cambridge: Exact Change. (Originally published 1954)

Kafka, F. (1991b). *The great wall of China and other short works*. (Trans., M. Pasley). London: Penguin. (Originally published 1973)

Kafka, F. (1992a). *The diaries of Franz Kafka*. (Trans., M. Brod). London: Minerva. (Originally published 1949)

Kafka, F. (1992b). *Letters to Milena*. (Trans., T. & J. Stern). London: Vintage. (Originally published 1953)

Kafka, F. (1998). *The Castle*. (Trans., M. Harman). New York: Schocken Books. (Originally published 1926)

Kafka, F. (1999). *Letters to Felice*. (Trans., J. Stern & E. Duckworth). London: Vintage. (Originally published 1967)

Kafka, F. (2011). *Letter to father*. (Trans., K. Reppin). Prague: Vitalis.

Karl, F. (1991). *Franz Kafka: Representative man*. New York: Fromm.

Kaufmann, W. (2015). *The faith of a heretic*. Princeton: Princeton University Press. (Originally published 1961).

Kierkegaard, S. (1992). *Concluding unscientific postscript to philosophical fragments. Volume 1.* (Trans., H.V. Hong, & E.H. Hong). Princeton: Princeton University Press. (Originally published 1846).

Kierkegaard, S. (2003). *Fear and trembling*. (Trans., A. Hannay). London: Penguin. (Originally published 1843).

Kierkegaard, S. (2004). *The sickness unto death*. (Trans., A. Hannay). London: Penguin. (Originally published 1849).

Kierkegaard, S. (2014). *The concept of anxiety*. (Trans., A. Hannay). New York: Liveright. (Originally published, 1844).

Lippitt, J. (2016). What can therapists learn from Kierkegaard? In M. Bazzano & J. Webb (Eds.), *Therapy and the counter-tradition: The edge of philosophy*. (pp. 23–33). London: Routledge.

May, R. (1983). *The discovery of being*. New York: Norton.

Nielsen, K. (2017). Kierkegaard and the modern search for self. *Theory & Psychology*, *28*, 65–83.

Pattison, G. (2009). Foreword. In S. Kierkegaard, *Works of love*. (pp. vii–xvii). New York: Harper.

Podmore, S.D. (2009). Kierkegaard as physician of the soul: On self-forgiveness and despair. *Journal of Psychology & Theology*, *37*, 174–185.

Rogers, C.R. (1961). *On becoming a person*. London: Constable.

Schonfeld, E. (2016). *Am-ha'aretz*: The law of the singular. Kafka's hidden knowledge. In A. Cools, & V.Liska (Eds.), *Kafka and the universal*. (pp. 107–129). Berlin & Boston: De Gruyter.

Stach, R. (2005). *Kafka: The decisive years*. (Trans., S. Frisch). Orlando: Harcourt.

Stach, R. (2013). *Kafka: The years of insight*. (Trans., S. Frisch). Princeton: Princeton University Press.

Stolorow, R.D. (2018). Phenomenological contextualism and the finitude of knowing. *The Humanistic Psychologist*, *46*, 204–210.

17 Myth as a container for anxiety

Bion, the unconscious, and Daseinsanalysis

Donna Christina Savery

Introduction

Myths originating in oral form have been passed down from antiquity in the forms of drama and poetry and continue to survive in multiple forms today, not least because they contain human truths concerning passionate forces and powerful drives, complex relationships and existential dilemmas. The tradition of using myth as a specific container, while taken up to some extent in psychoanalysis in its engagement with Oedipal and narcissistic characteristics and in Jungian analysis where myth has a particular status, remains largely absent from a methodological and theoretical discourse in existential therapy – with the exception of a seminal work by Rollo May (1991).

This chapter asks what we might learn from psychoanalysis, in particular from the work of Wilfred Bion, on the container and the contained, and from the plethora of myths available that contain aspects of the human condition – both conscious and unconscious. I provide examples showing what an application of myth in practice can add to an existential approach, given the significance of adopting a phenomenological attitude towards experiencing and understanding existence and our place in it. I go on to consider how we might begin to understand and address this omission in a counter-traditional existential approach.

Phenomenology is as important in existential therapy as the Oedipus complex is fundamental to psychoanalysis. In this chapter I am asking at what point these tenets become maxims that pertain more closely to what Britton and Steiner (1994, p. 1070) have termed an 'over-valued idea'. While we have much to learn in existential therapy from the depth of study and clinical application of the Oedipus complex in psychoanalysis, it is also important to recognise when psychoanalysis might lead us down some well-trodden blind alleys if we follow Oedipus alone, without considering other elements and characters within the myth.

Theatre directors and literary critics are more interested in the relationships between the things than the things themselves and the ways in which myths offer not only containment but complex truths which remain open to interpretation, and which are not fixed but fluid. In a paper of 2015, I argued that "Because myth is polysemic and therefore open to such a wide range of meanings, it is a valuable tool for exploring existential issues safely" (Savery, 2015a).

In this sense myths and their characters, their relationships and the dilemmas they face, the motivations and influences of aspects beyond their control mirror not just the everyday life and relationships of those clients with whom we come into contact – but of each and all of our inner worlds, in which both conscious and unconscious dramas are played out, with certain characters appearing centre-stage and others influencing gently from the wings, or with force from above, like the tyrannical gods of the Greek pantheon.

I now go much further in my belief that myths are invaluable in our practice. In the same way that the form of a theatre production, or the boundaries of the therapy room provide the container for the unfolding drama, I would argue that myth itself can have this function in a very particular way in clinical work – whether existential or psychoanalytic, in that it can provide a container for unresolved aspects of being, to pop up to the surface in a way that enables transformation to take place. I will begin by briefly explaining Wilfred Bion's Container-Contained model, in order to contextualise how this process takes place.

The Container and the Contained

Bion used his theory of the Container and the Contained to exemplify the process through which unbearable aspects of the infant's being and experience in the form of anxiety can be taken in by the mother. In this process the baby, unable to speak or understand, discharges aspects of the psyche into the open mother who provides a container for them. The elements discharged by the infant are in forms which Bion calls Beta, in that they are unable to be used for thinking and instead are formed out of raw sensory experience. The mother, as Container, opens herself to the unknown-ness of this and through taking in the baby's anxiety and feeling it herself she is able to soothe the baby, and to begin to find thoughts and words for the infant's experience – transforming raw Beta into what Bion calls alpha-elements, and gradually giving them back to the infant in order that thinking can take place. The result of this is that a more complex mind begins to form which can, as it develops, tolerate increasing anxiety.

Bion uses this seminal model as a way of understanding aspects of the psychoanalytic process. In a famous 1959 paper, *Attacks on Linking*, he wrote the following description:

> When the patient strove to rid himself of fears of death which were felt to be too powerful for his personality to contain, he split off his fears and put them into me, the idea apparently being that if they were allowed to repose there long enough they would undergo modification by my psyche and could then be safely re-introjected.
>
> (Bion, 1959, p. 312)

While the existential approach is perhaps less interested in processes of projection and introjection than the psychoanalytic, the role and study of anxiety remains central to both. In his book *Psychoanalysis and Anxiety, from Knowing to Being*, Chris

Mawson (2019) brings together both approaches through his study of anxiety, in which he traces the concept back to antiquity (in the work of Lucretius), and through the existential philosophers (including Kierkegaard and Heidegger) to its treatment within the practice and discipline of psychoanalysis. Following Heidegger, he focuses upon the nature of ontological anxiety as distinct from ontic fears – those which can be attended to and relieved to some degree through working through. Following Alice Holzhey-Kunz's Daseinsanalytic model in which she describes how a specific worldly fear, such as feeling inadequate or being afraid of flying, is easier to tolerate than ontological anxiety, which has no object, she argues that we naturally try to attach our ontological anxiety on to a more ontic (and therein conscious and rational) fear. She asks:

> What is the advantage of feeling fear instead of anxiety? It is evident that by the transformation of anxiety into fear the ontological character of the experienced threat is denied. Ontological conditions cannot be changed by any effort. Anxiety discloses my fundamental weakness and helplessness as a subject. That is different when I fear ontic (worldly) dangers … that is why fears of inadequacy, as strong as they may be, are easier to bear than anxiety.
> (Holzhey-Kunz, 2008, personal communication)

Mawson (2019, p. 22) goes on to say:

> Phenomenologically, anxiety can be regarded primordially as a mood in the sense intended by Heidegger, rather than in its conventional sense as a 'state of mind'. … The generic 'everyday' of Heidegger, is from a basic attitude in which the awareness and particular anxieties pertaining to the ontological realm – for which we find special words: dread, awe, wonder, the guilt of existing.

Mawson makes the link between Holzhey-Kunz's distinction, and a corresponding construction of Bion's, in which he uses the term 'Nameless Dread' (Bion, 1961p. 96) to differentiate, from more specific fears, a type of anxiety that has no object ready to hand. Bion distinguishes between the domain of what he calls K – that which can be understood in the realm of knowledge – and O, a domain that as Bion described, cannot be known, only be "be-ed with", as he put it (1963, p. 148). Mawson (2019, p. 23) concludes that before making any interpretations we must try as fully as possible to 'be-with' the other in this state, and through this, become informed rather than establish knowledge.

If, in existential therapy, we tend to follow only those aspects which can be observed, and which are, as a result, already conscious, we will be tempted to fore-close on that which may well be available in the forms outlined earlier, presenting as particular fears on the manifest level. Ironically, perhaps, although traditional existential therapeutic approaches have been aware of the ontico-ontological distinction made by Heidegger in *Being and Time* (2010, p. 12), the focus on what is already conscious may have resulted in missing the unconscious communications of ontological anxiety, made manifest in concrete forms that can be more easily observed. The existing existential method may be much improved by adopting the psychoanalytic approach advocated by Bion and the Daseinsanalysis of Holzhey-Kunz, which offer ways to orient oneself to the ontological inclusions to which we are all subject. One major aspect of this which may lurk behind, for example, a manifest fear of heights or of deep water, both of which feel very specific, is the ontological awareness that we are going to die. As therapists, having an awareness of our own feelings of awe, dread, and death anxiety enables a somewhat different discourse and process to emerge when a client brings such concrete fears as those mentioned earlier. Attunement to language and descriptions which induce feelings of vertigo, unsteadiness, and a sense of drowning in a bottomless void all indicate the ontological dimension, and if this is not interpreted or drawn attention to by the therapist it may remain a source of engagement for both client and therapist in its disguised form, rather than a shared state between both, one which can only achieve some relief through the feeling that one is not alone with the facticity of the human condition, the awareness of our mortality and the anxiety that this produces.

In existential therapy the focus is on attunement and a horizontalised approach to listening. Psychoanalysis uses the concept of "evenly-suspended attention" (Freud, 1912, p. 111) as a similar process to horizontalisation. The notion of attunement does not have a direct psychoanalytic equivalent, but it does, however, have an affinity with the projective and introjective aspects of the Container-Contained process as described by Bion earlier. This concept enables some understanding for existential analysis in terms of the process through which the therapist might be able to bear staying more attuned to the feelings and moods of the client, and in particular, to remain open to our clients' anxiety.

As Bion wrote, the mother, when faced with her baby in acute distress, is required to attend to her infant's cry as more than a demand for her presence. The mother, he says: "Should have taken into her, and thus experienced, the fear that the child was dying. It was this fear that the child could not contain" (Bion, 1959, p. 313). He went on to describe this feeling as 'nameless dread' and drew attention to the human capacity to rid ourselves of this nameless dread and fear of death by projecting it into a receptacle or container (Bion, 1963, p. 31). If we remember that the baby is not doing this consciously, it helps to further our understanding of the specific function of myth that I will go on to describe later.

Myth and anxiety

Myths take many forms although their functions are universal and timeless. Each generation and culture uses myth as a way of attempting to understand something of its state. In spite of its function, myth is a relatively new concept and it is interesting to note that while the terms *mythic* and *mythical* were used in the seventeenth century to mean 'fabulous' or 'fabled' stories, the word myth itself was not used until the nineteenth century. Coleridge (1853, p. 266) is one of the first recorded users of the term in English. In 1817 he states: "The philosopher who cannot utter the whole truth without conveying falsehood … is constrained to express himself either mythically or equivocally". He went on to use the term *Mythos* in 1825 to refer to Greek stories, rendered as The Grecian *Mythi*. The first recorded instance of the noun *Myth* (which was sometimes spelt *Mythe*) was not until the 1830s.

This lack of clarity in terms of an established etymology and definition of the term leads to some interesting considerations, not just in terms of what myth is, but of some important but perhaps less conscious aspects of its function. If we consider the notion of *fabulous or fabled stories*, we find ourselves in the realm of fantasy and even fairy tale. Following Bettelheim's detailed analysis of the function of fairy tales, in his book *The Uses of Enchantment* (1976), literary criticism aims at revealing unconscious aspects of fairy tales. The appeal to adults of fairy tales and myths as 'warning' or cautionary tales for children serves at least one obvious function. For children they can provide a way of entertaining and expressing their fears within the safe container of a story, which usually (although not in all cases – The Grimms' Fairy Tales being a case in point (Grimm and Grimm, 2004)) have a happy, and therefore relieving, ending. The child's pleasure in sharing these tales with an adult with whom they can cuddle up, look, and then look away from, pictures of monsters and devils, and entertain ideas of envious stepmothers and evil witches, points to aspects of the child's psyche which can concoct such figures in phantasy and manifest them behind the wardrobe at night, or from the shadows that the curtains make on the wall. Fairy tales contain such figures as the raping and maiming wolf in *Little Red Riding Hood*, and an older less beautiful woman who is driven by destructive envy and covetousness to attack children in *Sleeping Beauty*. The idea that these figures do not exist in reality as fundamental truths and threats is a fable in itself. However, in considering the various meanings of the term myth, something of its ambiguity as both that which bears a truth that exists beyond the real, and that which is a falsehood, are both retained, adding to the difficulty in defining it.

Because myths contain the most dreadful aspects of human nature, including child eating, curse-making, incestuous unions and wars over a woman's beauty, the nature of myth is also difficult to define because it is the product of aspects of the human condition which cannot be borne in their more real and terrifying forms. If we take Coleridge's definition on p. 196, we understand something key to the function of myth in terms of how we might use it in therapy and analysis. It is, as Coleridge posits, the form through which whole truths can be expressed, and yet his use of the word 'constrained' implies something else that is perhaps more akin to his term *equivocal* in that it depicts something true in a form that is somehow shady, dubious, or deliberately ambiguous. We might ask why such phrases as *urban myth* have come to mean that which is untrue, or that we can dismiss something as 'just a myth'. And so, the relationship between truth and untruths are both somehow contained in the ambiguous term myth which seems to hold both.

Myth as a Container

Bion's Container-Contained model allows for those things that cannot be thought about or borne, being discharged or projected as Beta into a container in order that it can be transformed for thinking as alpha elements. As we have seen earlier, this can happen between the infant and the primary caregiver and in the clinical encounter between therapist and client. If we consider that myth contains not only these most dreadful elements mentioned earlier, but also the ontological elements to which we can relate and which we find in the lives of the mortals in myths who suffer and are faced with often unbearable subjection to elements over which they have no control, death and punishment, shaming and guilt. In all the myths, mortals are forced to face the most dreadful existential dilemmas – such as Agamemnon's choice between whether to kill his daughter Iphigenia in order that the ships might sail so his army can rescue his sister-in law from the hands of the Trojans, or to spare her at the cost of displeasing the Goddess Artemis and not having her support to win the war. "Artemis' request of Agamemnon is a curse, in which he is required to place duty before personal gain. It is also one which sets in motion a set of tragic consequences, which once activated cannot be stopped" (Savery, 2018, p. 113).

Existential ennui such as that encountered by Sisyphus as he endlessly pushes his rock up the hill only for it to roll down, requiring him to begin his arduous journey over and over again until eternity, also reminds us of other existential givens including the facticity that we will die, that we come into and leave the world alone, and that we are, as Holzhey-Kunz (2008) reminds us, ontologically guilty and ashamed as well as anxious in the core of our being.

As I have stated earlier, the unbearable nature of ontological anxiety is such that we naturally flee from it. As Kierkegaard tells us:

> Anxiety is freedom's possibility … no Grand Inquisitor such dreadful torments in readiness as anxiety has, and no secret agent knows as cunningly as anxiety to attack his suspect in his weakest moment or to make alluring the trap in which he will be caught, and no discerning judge understands how to interrogate and examine the accused as does anxiety, which never lets the accused escape.
>
> (Kierkegaard, 1844/2014, p. 188)

Myth in psychoanalysis

The Oedipus complex, as it has been mined for meaning by Freud and interpreted in psychoanalysis, has proved an invaluable container for that which cannot be borne consciously – namely the infant's wish for an incestuous union with one's opposite sex parent, and the annihilation of the other parent in order to bring this about. Understanding aspects of the unconscious through the use of such a myth as a container has proven invaluable in enabling patients to understand and accept aspects of their personality such as their sexual possessiveness, destructive envy, and sibling rivalry. The elements which are contained within the myth have a very particular purpose, in that they are conjoined in such a way that they alert us or orient us towards a particular configuration when it appears in the transference or, in phenomenological terms, when we are in the presence of it in an observable form. This allows for the anxiety generated by that which is unthinkable, to be projected into the analyst as container and for the transformation to take place in the analyst, in order that it can be interpreted and gradually taken back in by the patient as conscious thought. As Maria Grazia Turri (2017) describes in her book *Acting, Spectating and the Unconscious*: "Unconscious emotional processing in alpha-function concerns the relationship between unprocessed emotional experiences (beta-elements) and their transformation into elements endowed with meaning and available to consciousness" (Turri, 2017, p. 98).

The aim of such a process is to make conscious that which may be acted out or allowed to continue unnoticed by the patient. In this sense the patient is then put directly in touch with the types of concerns and dilemmas that are fundamental tenets in existential therapy – once patients or clients have become conscious of their role or actions they are both responsible for them, and, like Agamemnon, free to choose but to face the consequences of that choice – it is at this moment that they are, in Sartre's famous maxim, "condemned to freedom" (Sartre, 1943, p. 567).

In the next section I will demonstrate how certain myths or aspects of myths have become over-valued in psychoanalysis. I hypothesise that due to its unique properties and its dramaturgical elements, myth might be available as a very particular type of container for ontological anxiety, and how this may be of some use for existential therapy in terms of ongoing discourse and practice.

Overvalued ideas

The problem with too much knowledge is that it can lead to seeking that which we expect to find, and either "leaping ahead" (Heidegger, 2010, p. 122), or 'reading ahead' before the true state, or being, of the client has shown itself in relation to the therapist, in a new and unfolding drama, in each session. Existential analysis, unlike psychoanalysis, is not a form of therapy that uses diagnosis, however the setting and mental health of the client or patient is always a factor in determining how to work with each individual as an individual – we might therefore intuitively be less challenging with a highly reactive patient who has undergone severe trauma and who may have a diagnosis of PTSD (known or unknown to the therapist), than perhaps a more robust individual or a student training in existential therapy. We are always in relation to others and the being of the other inevitably affects the way we relate to them. Taking Bion's recommendation for "holding back from premature and precocious knowledge" (1970, p. 125), which, following Keats, he calls 'Negative Capability', we are all prone to thinking about and to some degree remembering the client as the same one who came yesterday or last week, or who reminds us of a similar client we have seen before. In this sense we are imposing something upon our experience or applying apperception rather than waiting to see what emerges. If Bion is right, then it calls to question the whole business of taking notes after each session and reading them as a reminder before the client arrives. If we trust that we can be with the client fully, it seems more likely that we will attend to what is and not what we are consciously selecting as a priority.

If we consider that myth is able to orient us towards the being of a particular patient in their relationships with us and others we can see how valuable it is, when 'Oedipal feelings' of anxiety arise at such times as the therapist taking a break, and the phantasies of the client involve the feeling that their usual time with the therapist is being spent with an 'imagined' other. Because of the regularity with which this occurs, it is easy to assume that whenever the client shows anxiety about a forthcoming break, that Oedipus as a character in this myth proves a useful orienting device. Because, however, there are other characters in this myth, the relationship with his therapist (as Jocasta) is not necessarily uppermost in the client's experience at this point. Other factors that appear in the session may suggest something else, which may be linked to that particular myth, or even to another myth that is not as readily called to mind. If the client has lost a loved one, husband, or child, she may well be much more in touch with mortality and unsustainable loss and suffer anxiety resulting from this. In this case the *Myth of Demeter and Persephone* may be a much more resonant container for understanding her fears that the therapist is going to die in the break and that she will be left with a depression that she is unable to resolve on her own. Bion recognised the shortcomings of prioritising certain myths or characters when working with a patient whom he assumed must be narcissistic. After describing a situation in which he assumes the patient is wanting Bion to *"be a mirror of his excellence"* (1992, p. 238), Bion realises:

> But there is more to this story, the myth of Narcissus; there is a God who turns him into a flower. What is the patient saying that corresponds to this? There *must* be something because my myth tells me that these elements are constantly conjoined; or perhaps this is not the right myth…

Frustrated by his experience, and his recognition that he cannot rely solely on the well-developed but perhaps over-valued tranche of work on narcissism in psychoanalysis, he remarks: "I can see objections. It would be argued that no analyst could possibly have such a store of myths available in his psychoanalytic armoury as this procedure would seem to desiderate" (ibid.).

Anxiety and Echoism

In my work on Echoism (Savery, 2015a; 2015b), following the journey of Echo, the lesser known of the two protagonists in Ovid's *Myth of Echo and Narcissus* (2004, III: 340), I have discovered in my work with clients the value of remaining open to all elements of myth and not to jump to well-trodden paths without staying open to the actual feelings and discourse emerging in the session. I rely on prioritising openness to my own feelings as a guide to this, and not reaching conclusions too quickly nor reaching for a particular myth or structure to relieve me of my own anxiety. Instead I allow my own anxiety to alert me to something particular that is happening in this specific relationship.

A number of what Bion might call 'conjoined elements' that oriented me to what I came to call *Echoism* emerged initially through my experience of working with couples and groups. I noticed in some individuals the following patterns of behaving in the presence of others: a propensity to make the other partner the sole subject of the therapy, a difficulty with silence and a need to bring the other in to fill the space, a certain reluctance to address any issues relating to them- selves in the therapy, and, what I later came to understand as anxiety related to existence and living itself (which I came to call *life anxiety* [Savery, 2018]) – this presented as a difficulty in accepting freedom and responsibility for any part of the dynamics either in the session or in relationships with others. In fact, one of the most startling observations was the way in which these particular individuals rarely, if ever, initiated anything in the session or in the group but always looked to the other or to the therapist to take the lead. These elements may have gone largely unnoticed if these individuals had not been in relationship dynamics with others who somehow 'made-up for' or complemented these ways of being in such a way that they somehow formed a complex between themselves that made every- thing appear perfectly balanced, in spite of some of the disturbing issues they brought to the sessions or group.

It was my background in literature and my knowledge of myth that alerted me to the complex dynamic lived out by both Echo and Narcissus in Ovid's arche- typal version of the myth. On further investigation I discovered that the early research and psychoanalytic study into narcissism was based upon this version in the 1890s when Näcke and Ellis were the first to coin the term '*Narcissismus*' – a condition of self-love which has been written about ubiquitously in psycho- analysis in the period since its inception. While narcissism as a subject has left no apparent stone unturned, I noticed that these individuals whom I encountered as reluctant to take space were largely absent in the psychoanalytic literatures. In reality they were either in relationships with, or seemed to seek out others, who we have come to recognise as more 'narcissistic' in that they not only resembled the character of Narcissus from the myth but they operated destructively and used envy as their primary motivation to exercise power over others. The psycho- analytic literatures of the post-Kleinian analysts have a body of work on narcis- sism so definitive that when we meet it in the therapy room we cannot mistake it – or so I thought!

Because of Bion's discoveries concerning the Container-Contained relation- ship, the notion of projective identification has been strongly related to narcis- sism, and the ways in which narcissists operate projection in a very different way to others. Rather than using projection of unbearable anxiety into the container (mother, analyst, therapist) in order for communication and alpha function to take place, the narcissist projects themselves into the container as a bid to take it over and colonise it. Work with this particular patient group leads to the therapist feeling overpowered, ridiculed, on egg shells, and having a sense that no matter what you say or do your words are simply bouncing off the shell of the narcissist while they penetrate you with their feelings. This leaves the therapist at the end of sessions feeling vulnerable and manipulated, often confused and unclear as to what just happened. As Bion (1961, p. 148) described in his work with groups, when describing narcissistic projection:

> Now the experience of counter-transference appears to me to have quite a distinct quality that should enable the analyst to differentiate the occasion when he is the object of a projective identification from the occasion when he is not. The analyst feels he is being manipulated so as to be playing a part, no matter how difficult to recognise, in somebody else's phantasy.
>
> (Bion, 1961, p. 148)

Bion concludes that shaking oneself out of the numbing feeling of reality is requisite for the analyst. In working with the more Echo-like individuals who I began to see alone and without the presence of the more narcissistic partner, I found a very different experience in myself both during and at the end of sessions to the one described above – I can only describe this as exhausted, drained, and as if I needed to perform and do so much more in the sessions. This alerted me to noticing in myself a very different way of being than my usual attitude as a therapist and I recognised in myself some of the more narcissistic traits I had noticed in the narcissistic partners of some of these individuals. It felt as if the life was being somehow sucked or introjected out of me in order to keep the therapy and (I wondered, rather omnipotently) the client, alive. It was this experience that led me to research Echoism as a subject in its own right as distinct from narcissism, in spite of Herbert Rosenfeld, a very famous analyst having described similar experiences and concluding that the patient who he describes as parasitic relies entirely upon the analyst: "… often making him responsible for this entire life. He often behaves in an extremely passive, silent and sluggish manner, demanding everything and giving nothing in return" (Rosenfeld, 1970, p. 9).

As well as comparing such patients to a stone (a description Ovid makes in relation to Echo and not Narcissus) Rosenfeld concludes:

> I often have the impression that patients like the one whom I described, who experience themselves as dead, and are often experienced by the analyst as so inactive that they might as well be dead, use their analysts aliveness as a means of survival.
>
> (ibid, p. 9)

Rosenfeld continued to regard these patients (whom I would regard as echoistic) as suffering from a narcissistic condition. He made no distinction between them and in this sense mistook their identity by following an over-valued psychoanalytic interpretation of the myth.

Conclusion

I would argue that Rosenfeld's mistake was due to a number of factors that should be taken into account and which familiarity with the existential approach may well have oriented him towards. The first is that Rosenfeld, rather than listening to his own countertransference and recognising that he was somehow being pulled or introjected into a core narcissistic configuration in himself, was perhaps unable to be in touch with his own anxiety concerning his mortality, and was as a result projecting this into his patient, rather than opening himself to act as a container for the patient's 'life anxiety'. The other is that Rosenfeld prioritised one character of the myth, Narcissus, and was therefore unable to see the relational aspects of the myth and the characters within these. As Bion recognised, it is of course impossible to be *au fait* with all the myths, but, as this chapter demonstrates, it is equally hazardous to follow just one myth or one character's journey within the myth in order to determine something of the client with whom we are having a therapeutic relationship.

My work on echoism has enabled me to understand the value of myth and to find ways to help me to develop more tolerance to ontological anxiety and to stay open to very nuanced experiences of being with clients in order that I can take responsibility for the ways in which I relate to them. Psychoanalysis and the extensive body of research that has been carried out in relation to the Oedipus complex and studies on narcissism has much to offer a revised approach to existential therapy. This chapter has endeavoured to show, however, that we must take up our existential freedoms in using the myths in the spirit of curiosity and with an emphasis on staying open to the ontological dimension.

While the psychoanalytic and the existential are based on quite different approaches to understanding, they also have much to offer one another in terms of going forwards in a direction already paved to some extent by the Daseinsanalysis of Holzhey-Kunz. While the use of myth is arguably not essential in both disciplines, it strikes me that because myth acts in a very particular way as a container for the projections of these very anxiety-provoking aspects of the human condition, it is essential that we include it in our thinking and in our therapy as an orienting vessel, in order to avoid Bazzano's fateful prediction: "It seems to me that without myth, poetry and symbolism, existential therapy risks being in the grip of rationalism and 'hypertrophy of consciousness' (Bazzano, 2018, personal communication).

References

Bettelheim, B. (1976). *The Uses of Enchantment: The Meaning and Importance of Fairy Tales*. 1991 edition. London: Penguin Psychology.

Bion, W. R. (1959). Attacks on linking. *International Journal of Psycho-Analysis*, 40: 308–15.

Bion, W. R. (1961). *Experiences in Groups and Other Papers*. London: Karnac Books.

Bion, W. R. (1963). *Elements of Psycho-Analysis*. London: Karnac Books.

Bion, W. R. (1970). *Attention and Interpretation: A Scientific Approach to Insight in Psychoanalysis and Groups*. London: Karnac Books.

Bion, W. R. (1992). *Cogitations* (ed. F. Bion). New extended edition, 1994. London: Karnac Books.

Britton, R., & Steiner, J. (1994). Interpretation: Selected fact or overvalued idea? *International Journal of Psycho-Analysis*, 75: 1069–78.

Coleridge, S. T. (1853). *The Works of Samuel Taylor Coleridge: Prose and Verse*. Philadelphia, PA: Chrissy and Markley.

Freud, S. (1912). Recommendations to Physicians Practising Psycho-Analysis. *The Standard Edition of the Complete Psychological Works of Sigmund Freud*, Volume XII (1911–1913).

Grimm, J., & Grimm, K. (2004). *Complete Fairy Tales*. London: Routledge.

Heidegger, M. (2010 [1927]). *Being and Time* (tr. J. Stambaugh; rev. D. J. Schmidt). Albany, NY: State University of New York Press.

Holzhey-Kunz, A. (2008). Anxiety. *Lecture II of series* (unpublished).

Kierkegaard, S. (1844/2014). *The Concept of Anxiety* [*Begrebet Angest*] (ed. and tr. A. Hannay). New York: Liveright.

Mawson, C. (2019). *Psychoanalysis and Anxiety, from Knowing to Being*. London: Routledge.

May, R. (1991). *The Cry for Myth*. London: Souvenir Press.

Ovid. (2004). Metamorphoses (tr. D. Raeburn). A New verse translation. London: Penguin Books.

Rosenfeld, H. R. (1970). *On Projective Identification*. Bulletin of the British Psychoanalytical Society.

Sartre, J. P. (1943). *Being and Nothingness* (tr. Hazel E. Barnes). 2003 Routledge Classics Edition.

Savery, D. C. (2015a). *Echoism and the Container*, Hermeneutic Circular, Society of Existential Analysis, London. April 2015.

Savery, D. C. (2015b). Echoism: Is there a place for Echoism in Existential Analysis, *Journal of Existential Analysis* 26(2), (243–255). July 2015. Paper presented at Society for Existential Analysis Annual Conference. 22 November, 2014.

Savery, D. C. (2018). *Echoism: The Silenced Response to Narcissism*. London: Routledge.

Turri, M. G. (2017). *Acting, Spectating, and the Unconscious: A Psychoanalytic Perspective on the Unconscious Processes of Identification in the Theatre*. London: Routledge.

18 Talking cure and curing talk

Therapy, theory and the already dead

Jeff Harrison

Talking about is talking with

Language itself, *whatever* it is saying – given its structure and the relationships between its constituent parts – presents a fairly static picture of how things are. This is the case, paradoxically, even though it is an inherently unstable system. In addition, discursive writing like this tends to make general arguments from general propositions. These are cultural phenomena – habits even – that can be as misleading as they are at times useful. Generally, in a chapter like this, a position is taken and – through language-based argument – is defended. That might suggest that we live (and even that the best way of living is) via consistent positions that can be generalised and expressed with words.

Yet if the value of such systematic argument is doubted, it is almost impossible to argue that systematically without falling into the fallacy of self-exception. What is the alternative then? It is, perhaps, to be more strategic, more oblique, more 'deconstructed' in approach. Yet proponents of deconstruction face similar challenges. It is hard to say what deconstruction is when the 'what it is' is precisely what is being questioned.

Having raised these caveats, there are some broad standpoints for this chapter – even though they raise significant issues. No singular position is uncritically proposed and defended. Ontological metaphysics is refuted. This does not mean 'anything goes' in a relativistic free-for-all; but it does mean that nothing is metaphysically guaranteed. Buddhism and western deconstruction (used in a broad sense but still best typified by Jacques Derrida) both reject ontological foundationalism in a radical decentring; though Buddhism extends this to selfhood whereas deconstruction – with its textual idealism – does not and cannot. Embodiment, too, as a way of being and a focus of experience, is held to move us away from static concepts and an unimpeachable, sovereign rationality. The final premise is that the self (including introspective subjectivity) may be regarded as a text-analogue (certainly as soon as we start putting it into words).

Existentialism is a useful pivot between some of these philosophies and traditions. It also offers us no secure metaphysical foundations. It focuses on the human 'condition' rather than the centripetal essence of the human being; but this results in a potentially unsettling challenge in the individual to create a life (rather than to find something pre-given) and fill a void, rather than in an opportunity to delight, as a Buddhist might, in the centrifugal emptiness of self-nature. There may be nowhere to stand; we may be falling, but there is also nowhere to land.

So, with particular reference to psychotherapy, how can we stop ourselves from seeing each new client as a (stable) composite of previous ones; and prevent our own way of being with them from being a mere amalgamation of all the techniques and applications of theory we have ever known? Does what most of us do most of the time amount to a distortion, a sort of 'humanistic' human recycling, aided and abetted by the modern culture of measurement (which is itself often, more accurately, a form of forcing people into preconceived categories)? In person-centred terms, how can we (counsellor and client) be present in our organismic being rather than securely lost in stagnant (self-) concept? How can we as therapists disencumber ourselves from frameworks, and work with, and from, immediate process rather than from theoretical or technical content? These are perennial questions. Even raising them may risk entrenching the problem rather than solving it.

We are back in part to the difficulties that language itself raises. Man is the language-using animal – *zoon logon echon*. Certainly, the prosaic language of theory and the therapeutic model is singularly unsuited to reflect the emergent, contingent, 'poetic' realities of life. Therapies where client and practitioner use language are often designated 'talking cures'; but it is often a certain kind of talk that really needs treatment.

One of the reasons that existentialism places such an accent on personal meaning and the phenomenological-perspectival – our embeddedness within the world – is the non-coincidence of immediate pre-verbal experience (if such a thing even exists) with second-order reflection. There is no transparent 'truth' within (or without) – certainly not one that can survive verbalisation. Language obfuscates, interprets, translates, transforms.

In any 'talking therapy', we can, perhaps should, look at *whether* and *how* our world is created, received and processed via language. That *can* lead to new insights and meaning, deeper 'processing', and may indeed thereby lead to new ways of being. An object, anything we can identify (including a 'self' or an experience) is contextual and perspectival – intentional, to use the language of phenomenology. We take 'angles' on things. But language itself has inbuilt inclinations. Even in writing like this, there is a constant battle with the innate tendencies of textual expression to generalise, reify and dualise.

The absolute and independent object (*in se et per se*) is a nonsensical "illusion of rationalist thought" – there are only "focal figures" against horizons. An open horizon means that the "substantiality" of the object "slips away" (Merleau-Ponty, 1962, p.70). Phenomena arise, abide, depart. What Derrida would call 'presence' "is possible only when in our thinking we forget what we had originally learned in our perceptual experience of the world" (Dillon, 1991, p.123). Such reification (of, say, a percept into a conceptual object) "congeals the whole of existence, as a crystal placed in a solution suddenly crystallizes it" (Merleau-Ponty, 1962, p.71). What we gain in crude clarity we more than lose in texture, subtlety and nuance. In such a way we often lose the individual person in theories of the human.

Nevertheless, language *is* our main symbol-system. We rely on it. We need it for expression, communication and mediation. We develop ideas with it; ideas emerge from it. We use it to classify and clarify experience. To a debatable degree, the world comes to us through it. We *find* ourselves in language as much as put ourselves there. Speech is an eventive and creative process. In dialogue it is co-creative. We might say that it is natal: meaning is born anew, not simply brought forth from a mysterious, pre-existent, inner elsewhere. Merleau-Ponty differentiates between *le dit*, the common coin of social exchange, and *le dire*, the newly minted, emergent language of a specific encounter (Merleau-Ponty, 1962, Part I, Chapter 6). Relation to other is how we are. Words seem to isolate entities; but phenomena are really facets of relational and matrical interconnectedness.

The word-curse and beyond

There is no pure, prelapsarian escape route from the problems of language or self as text-analogue. We can only try to use the insight and words we do have to rescue us from both the unthinking *and* the distorted and excessive thinking that sometimes have us in their thrall.

We can search for metaphors as alternatives to the idea of discrete beings or a unitary Being. Deleuze and Guattari offer the free-wheeling 'rhizome' as evocative of multiplicity, connection, immanence and heterogeneity; the rhizome that "never allows itself to be overcoded" (Deleuze and Guattari, 2004, p.9) or subject to grand narratives and meta-comment. "A rhizome has no beginning or end; it is always in the middle, between things, interbeing, *intermezzo*" (Deleuze and Guattari, 2004, p.27).

Merleau-Ponty, as a phenomenologist of chiasmic, embodied consciousness, wrote: "No philosophy can be ignorant of finitude, under pain of failing to understand itself as philosophy" (Merleau-Ponty, 1962, p.38). As we approach one (philosophical) horizon, another unfolds. The infinite exceeds the grids we throw over it. The world is "an open and indefinite multiplicity of relationships, which are of reciprocal implication" (Merleau-Ponty, 1962, p.71). For Merleau-Ponty the human being is 'possessed' by language; and Derrida, too, riffs on the ontology/hauntology homophone (Derrida, 1994). Man is *in* a world of language as much as he is in a world of perception.

Don Cupitt offers an intriguing bifurcation. He sees Jacques Lacan as the representative of a 'theology of culture' which is bound to a symbolic order; and Gilles Deleuze as the representative of a more libertarian 'theology of desire' (Cupitt, 1987, p.9). The body is then: "the primal surface, a living paper on which the signs move. On the body-surface desire and culture meet, as the body's feeling-expression is converted by culture into the common world of signs" (Cupitt, 1987, p.11). All must be understood immanently, in the manifest world as expressive articulation (of words or movement).

'Scaling' of organismic process is inscribed socially, often as a restraint or suppression of life-energy. (One might think again, in this connection, of the measurements used in evidence-based therapy practice.) In general, then, the theology of culture is reactive, defensive and orthodox compared to the progressive, licentious theology of desire. In the theology of culture, metaphor itself is a safety valve for the desire that threatens to get out of hand – it is repressive and substitutionary, allowing culture to circumscribe and reabsorb whatever is produced. Perhaps the 'poetic' and 'rhizomatic' (as, respectively, a term prioritising the figurative, and an example of such a term) are subject to the same fate: meant to liberate, but reclaimed as less obvious constraints. There is always the danger of such recursive frames, meta-argument, infinite regress. Perhaps *that* is the only way in textual discourse to retain the infinite.

All these dichotomies – whether linguistic, perspectival or epistemological – are, then, attempts to stop the fluidity and spontaneity of existence and experience being arrested and reduced to static *a priori* frameworks. The danger, again, is that they themselves merely invert a duality and succumb to the iatrogenic fate of being cast as new dogma. *Pharmakon* can after all be poison as well as medicine.

Most of the most important words in any language have no consensual meaning. Think: 'love', 'God', 'self', etc. Language use can also leave the 'dyer's hand': one has to put something (an isolated phenomenon or a static concept) there to say that it is *not* there. There is a primacy of affirmation. It is easy to reify whether or not one wishes to; and it is often a short step between reifying and deifying. There are pitfalls everywhere – most of them invisible to the uncritical, and most of them normalised. This is Nietzsche's *god of grammar* (Nietzsche, 2008).

There *are* models that reject stable and essentialist metaphysics – whether that metaphysics is explicitly stated or not. (The near-pervasive verb 'to be' carries with it much of the history of western thought. It is itself a perennial, if unavoidable, footnote to Plato.) Psychoanalysis might be said to attempt "to render the poetry of the human in the language of science" (Phillips, 2002, p.9). Adam Phillips is, in fact, happy to see psychoanalysis as a type of poetics (one of many) rather than a "supreme fiction" (by which he seems to mean a metanarrative) (Phillips, 2002, p.30). The 'poetic' – the text, the human – is empty of reducible or demarcated meaning and, therefore, cannot be fully emptied of meaning. It is inexhaustible and, in any totalised sense, 'unreadable' – it gives infinitely and yet also keeps back. This raises the question as to whether therapists should ever even seek to 'commune' fully with their clients.

With our highly developed reflective capacity, we tend to seek meaning even though many of us may feel fairly opaque to ourselves. Certainly many clients in therapy cannot find a compelling story about how they came to be in their present state. Existential therapy – drawing on a wide, though ill-defined, philosophical school – arguably has a richer and more diverse theoretical basis (meta-stories to frame/explain our individual stories) than any model since psychoanalysis. This is a mixed blessing. It offers variety, subtlety and nuance; but, like therapy *per se*, it, too, risks congealing into unwieldy dogma or self-serving factionalism. Perhaps that simply means, again, that no philosophy, even one paradoxically founded on an anti-foundational stance, can ever really be equal to the emergent quality of life. It can maybe highlight and defend that quality, but never fully map it. It may help us understand where we have been but not necessarily where we need to go.

Vincent Descombes describes Derrida's encounter with metaphysics as:

> a very close contest against a formidable Master, whom we might think certain to win at a game with rules which he himself has fixed. Derrida opts to play a double game (in the sense that a 'double agent' serves two sides), feigning obedience to the tyrannical system of rules while simultaneously laying traps for it in the form of problems which it is at a loss to settle.
>
> (Descombes, 1980, p.139)

Therapists can do something similar. We can listen to, and accept, the client's story and – even in the least directive model/relationship – can reflect its inconsistencies, tensions and strategies of avoidance: can, in fact, facilitate its dissolution as the client comes to understand that it, and the forged identity it underpins and is underpinned by, are no longer helpful. Complete de-conditioning may be beyond most of us; so the client may need another narrative, another partially conceptualised sense of self and possibility on which to string the pearls (and pains) of existence; but hopefully she will find a less restrictive one, one with more 'play' in it.

Unreasonable reason

Mark Edmundson (1995, pp.77–78) claims that over time God has been displaced into reason. The subtext is that, while reason was supposed to free us from superstition, it has taken its place rather than uprooted it. But as long as we are moved by some combination of unconscious process (phenomenological or psychodynamic), bodily intelligence, aspiration and value, and imagination and emotion, 'meaning' must mean more than mere rational sense. Reason is often assumed to be a faculty that all humans share and that we can appeal to in each other. On that basis and in that sense it is synonymous with the *logos* of logocentrism that – in philosophical guise – makes universal truth-claims and is subtly and stubbornly self-justifying. Reason may have 'regenerated' and moved from soul to psyche to head-locked *cogito*, but it brings with it an assumed transparency: the *s'attendre parler* of autoaffection, the *topos noetos* of the punctual self. And with it comes the idea of man as a kind of *homo duplex*, condemned to live a second-rate, second-order existence until he ascends to embrace his own and the world's transcendent essence and truth. It is inherently circular: this truth knows itself as and by itself. For some that is the highest wisdom; for others, mere tautology and fearful evasion.

As a philosopher rather than a spiritual teacher, Derrida cannot (or will not) deconstruct the privileged pole of rational enquiry – however much he unsettles it (Loy, 1998). So he attempts to locate a "non-site, or a non-philosophical site, from which to question philosophy" (Critchley, 1992, p.29). Like the neurotic who, by his very effort at avoidance, constantly ends up back in the place he is trying to leave behind, or the Buddhist who is attached to the idea of non-attachment, Derrida forever risks either falling into the linguistic/philosophical framework (the foundational metaphysics of presence) he is trying to escape, or merely playing word games. Seeking to deconstruct something on its own terms always risks, at some level, affirming them. This danger sometimes even survives Derrida's avowed strategy which is to reveal how texts deconstruct *themselves*. In short, undermining risks underlining.

The existential and post-structuralist responses to these kinds of challenges have been to valorise instantiation over any notional eternal absolute (that which is innately cognized and so need only be re-cognized). The emphasis has been on disruption and irruption whereby the text is scarcely (certainly not totally) commensurable with the intention of the 'writer' (insofar as *that* can be assessed) let alone the receptivity of the 'reader', the latter seen not as a membrane for pure transmission (which would demand a pure correspondence theory of language) but as an order of involvement in a process of co-creation – an active reading. Self can be maintained as a text-analogue – and in that sense people often cannot write themselves with any secure authorial authority or read themselves (or each other) with any guaranteed clarity. Language is inevitably under pressure.

But the question remains: can we ever escape it? Clearly, we need language even to ask it.

Language – when it seems to offer substantial entities and stable relationships and, even more so, when it is held to be the transparent window onto meta-physical presence – offers us a spurious security. The prototypical focus of our uncertainty/insecurity is death. For David Loy, death-denial and fear of death are *the* primary realities for existentialists. In therapy, too, fear of death can be seen as a 'metanarrative' of fear, as the source beam of insecurity that is then dispersed, through the prism of individual history and selfhood, into other fears, phobias and neuroses. Death is, after all, the ultimate in loss of control and loss of self.

As Loy argues: "the Buddhist critique of ego-self suggests that life-versus-death is not a game that the ego plays but that game whose play is the ego" (Loy, 2003, p.21). The ego is *constituted* both by its fear of death and its oppositional stance to emergent experience, to life and living:

> The ego cannot absolve its own *lack* because the ego is the other side of that *lack*. *In terms of life and death*, the ego is that which believes itself to be alive and fears death; hence the ego, although only a mental construction, will face its imminent disappearance with horror
>
> (Loy, 2003, p.57)

The ego creates pain even as it is itself a response to pain. Fundamentally insub-stantial, it is nevertheless near-pervasive. Buddhism is about not adding unneces-sary suffering to the inevitable pain of existence. We may come to know this; but the ego can neither witness nor enjoy its own demise. Just as (for Martin Heidegger) 'conscience' calls us out of insipid existence into a more authentic being-towards-death (Heidegger, 1978), so the *dukkha* – the suffering or affliction – that causes and is caused by the accretions of ego-self can prompt us to begin the work (or surrender) that reveals its delusory nature. Those following the former, existential approach – Heidegger's – may, though, be seduced into trying to give up an unwanted freedom.

Loy continues:

> It is an ineluctable trace of nothingness in my fictitious (because not really self-existing) sense-of-self that is experienced as a sense-of-*lack*; in reaction, the sense-of-self becomes preoccupied with trying to make itself self-existing, in one or another symbolic fashion.
>
> (Loy, 2003, p.91)

We want ego as the 'doer behind the deed' – the controller or author of selfhood – so that we become the first cause in causal chains. That is another illusory reassurance that language can seem to offer. We even seek to be self-caused in quasi-divine *aseity*. We try to get a grip of ourselves in a painful but unproductive contortion with the result that our energies may be deadlocked into depression and fakery or diverted into the frictions of anxiety and internal conflict.

Cogito, ego and self are used interchangeably here – to mean the rational 'centre' of subjectivity that assumes itself to be substantial and transparent to itself. We try to consolidate and bolster it. The *cogito* assumes itself autonomous and self-grounded. It is actually predicated on such an ontological circularity and *petitio principii*. (It has this in common with the foundationalism of logocentrism – the tautology discussed earlier.) What we often end up doing is simply accentuating the sense of deficiency, though perhaps burying it more deeply.

Existential-humanistic therapies often focus on the here-and-now of the relationship. Otto Rank made a similar recommendation within the psychodynamic tradition – and he, too, made a direct link to death-aversion:

> Rank's emphasis on the *here and now* was experienced by his patients as an invitation to aliveness, a chance to glimpse what had been relinquished in a superstitious neurotic bargain with death. ("If I don't fully live, I can avoid suffering. I will limit myself before death can limit me.")
>
> (Wadlington, 2012, p.389)

This resonates with the comment of Paul Tillich (1967, p.71): "Neurosis is the way of avoiding non-being by avoiding being." Such death-contracts can themselves be fatal. The 'beginner's mind' (Suzuki, 2009) avoids such avoidance: in the beginner's way of being, living is endlessly natal, not a mere 'repeat to fade'.

With an absence of self-co-incidence, most of our clamour for substance, solidity and reified agency is, then, security-driven. Once the ego has arisen, the greatest threat for it is *not to be*; and so it bolsters itself as object-image (Fromm, Suzuki and De Martino, 1993, p.146) and then we live diminished lives as distorted self-concepts, made from inadequate words. When we are relieved of such misconceptions, we can see the notional ego-self for what it is: "a project of deception, a masking of discontinuity and disintegration … a construction based on language, a cultural point of view on human life, expressing a desire for unity in the face of dissolution and death" (Watson, 2002, p.124). This is the crux of Buddhist thought: the ego is the image of self, creator of the image of self and maintainer of defences against threats to that image.

Cognitive therapies talk of core beliefs. The core belief that Buddhism challenges – though not merely conceptually – is that one *has* a core. But this raises the question – and it is a question that many techniques of Buddhist practice are designed to raise: *who* practices to come to such an insight? There is clearly a strategic circularity here but it is one that catalyses dissolution and deconstruction (and leads to clarity) rather than one that is metaphysically self-justifying and seeking to justify the 'self'. As seen, existentialism also refutes independent self-nature (certainly with any kind of quasi-Platonic underpinning) but often inflects the resultant 'liberation' as potentially fearsome – for example, in Søren Kierkegaard's depiction of anxiety as the 'dizziness of freedom' (Kierkegaard, 1980, p.61).

The words that are left

Derrida alights on *différance*, perhaps the key term in his *oeuvre*, which can itself be (provisionally) defined as the non-punctuality or non-coincidence of the present (with itself), seeing reality, rather, as disseminated into the "porous borders of the ego, of the author, and of his work" (Habermas, 1992, p.209). The self as text-analogue is equally decentralised. In terms of language this amounts to: "the postponement of settled signification, that keeping in flickering motion which adjourns the illusion, the sterile fixity of definition" (Steiner, 1989, p.122).

It would be easy to argue that the poetic (and rhizomatic), too, seek to avoid the "sterile fixity of definition". That does not, in any way, militate against precision or specificity – quite the opposite in fact.

As glossed by Nichterlein and Morss (2016, p.163), Deleuze himself makes a similar point from a specifically therapeutic perspective:

> The challenge for the clinician, then, is not to read the becomings of those accessing the clinic according to pre-established regimes of signs, but to engage in paradoxical ways with such regimes of signs so as to help those approaching the clinic to transcend those regimes, and become originals.

We saw that Deleuze proposed the rhizomatic as a kind of root-metaphor for the decentred, emergent and non-unitary. With its soteriological and radically transformative aims, Buddhism has to go further, though it can nevertheless retain the botanical image. In R. De Martino's analysis, the ego becomes the *koan* (the puzzle or paradox used in certain traditions of Buddhism to break down, break open and break through the rational, conceptual mind) when it becomes the "root-contradiction" (Katz, 1983, p.186), by which he seems to mean when it is realised as both agent and object of dualism. Because this is realised by itself and *as* itself, it enacts the predicament as well as merely grasps it conceptually. The very term that De Martino uses – "root-circumscription" (Katz, 1983, p.187) – again underlines the parallel natures of ego-self and language. Ego at breakthrough is no longer defined against anything else, but realises its lack of definition (and existence) against itself. It turns on itself as the ultimate pole of privilege, the fulcrum of any bivalent logic, in the ultimate step that Derrida, for example, could not take because it cannot be taken *in* language. Circumscription collapses; and axial, linear expression (and causation and hierarchy) must dissolve, or devolve into infinite matricality.

That line of reasoning-beyond-reason is why Bradford Keeney can write:

> words are always to be mistrusted. They are the play of tricksters and can be both helpful and a hindrance. They are helpful, even a medicine, when they are used to pry us free from the knots that interfere with our being moved by life rather than fixed ideas. Our words are true for the moment that brought them forth; then they must be released to the wind and blown away. We return, as we should over and over again, to the stage of action – spontaneously performed words unscripted by narrative.
>
> (Keeney, 2009, p.289)

Words can be barrier and bridge. Healthy life is improvised, extemporised. As Dōgen knew, better than Heidegger: being *is* time, rather than in time.

Critchley (1992, p.28) stresses "an openness towards the other." This can have an intrapersonal aspect (an openness to the other within); and can also be applied to the idea of self-actualisation in humanistic therapy. There is a *process* of actualisation rather than a stable, pre-given 'person' manifesting it: "To be what one is, is to enter fully into being a process" (Rogers, 1961, p.176). The 'person' is a convenient designation, "a fluid process, not a fixed static entity, a flowing river of change, not a block of solid material; a continually changing constellation of potentialities, not a fixed quantity of traits" (Rogers, 1961, p.122). The 'self' in Buddhism is, similarly, a comparable ever-changing configuration of *skandhas*.

We still have to be very careful, as therapists, and as humans, that "in seeking to think the other, its otherness is [not] reduced or appropriated to our understanding" (Critchley, 1992, p.29). We also have to be careful that, in attempting to grasp and control our own being, we do not similarly reduce ourselves. Therapy, though, like Buddhism, *can* sit with idiosyncratic, even non-verbal experience without philosophy's need to systematise and generalise.

For Richard Rorty, philosophy's illusory 'presence' involves a static mirror-language; and so "non-coercive conversation is the verbal form that breaks up philosophical mirror-gazing" (Edmundson, 1995, p.91). We may not be able to 'reflect' reality with our words. Perhaps we also need the humility to concede that, in therapy, our attempt to empathically reflect our client's experience may be gestural rather than a sure sign of a holy interpersonal communion. Accurately symbolising experience (our own or someone else's) may even be doomed to failure, our verbal reach exceeding our grasp. Rupture and repair (of language and word-wound/thing-murder) perhaps have to exist in language and in therapy. *Trying* to communicate/connect and acknowledging when we cannot *is* perhaps itself adequate connection. If the intention is there, we can be 'good enough' therapists.

While language may never be equal to the experience, a good listener with good intention can hear enough and engage enough. That may be all there is. The desire to share and connect then becomes something more akin to a speech act; and even faltering, imperfect attempts at expression can still give the reassurance that distress is not entirely unspeakable. It can be somewhat symbolised, if not definitively captured. Language can 'work' in spite of its failings:

> Language, to be true, must voice the paradoxical nature, the antinature, of the mirror. It must articulate its own ineluctable failure to copy out the original of reality. The truth of language is precisely its in-turning, its negative employment in bearing witness to this failure, and thus, though inarticulable in language, the demonstration of the very limits of language in its confrontation with the mirror of reality. The usefulness of the raft (*yana*) of speech is fully disclosed only when the other shore has been reached, and, paradoxically, the raft shows forth its uselessness.
>
> (Laycock, 1994, p.121)

In a chapter of that name, the literary critic Cleanth Brooks (1956, p.176) lamented the 'heresy of paraphrase': reducing literary complexity to the crudely literal. In a similar vein, every model of therapy can readily become a Procrustes' bed for experience: proscribing, prescribing and translating emergent phenomena into a foundational framework. Language is a world, an infinity of worlds, not a closed system. It is open-ended. Therapy may offer a place of containment. Language *can* contain; but it also creates and hints at meaning. It is always too much and too little. There is "polysemic and horizontal indeterminacy" (Dillon, 1991, p.130); there has to be in the way we express and describe ourselves unless we wish to bureaucratise ourselves to death. We need as many anticoagulants as we can find. We have to steer a way between the verbal and the non-verbal; between reductive and distorting language and language that is porous and permissive.

We have seen Derrida's "double game"; Deleuze's "paradoxical ways"; and Laycock's "antinature". We have seen Keeney's Janus-faced language that can liberate or entrap. We have seen psychoanalysis reframed as a kind of poetics. These are all strategies of resuscitation – catalysts, medicines, approaches and manoeuvres that seek to reconnect us with the vitality of emergent experience without each becoming another philosophical or psychological 'tar baby'. In several of its early texts, Buddhism uses the idea of a raft (Thera, 1972, p.29): when one has reached the farther shore, the raft used to get there may be discarded. This resonates with Ludwig Wittgenstein's famous image of the philosophical ladder

(Wittgenstein, 2007, 6.54). Insight cannot be gained *merely* from discursive propositions (though they may be useful markers); and it certainly does not remain *merely* in that form in the mind of the awakened. Self-cancelling terms (and the double meaning is a telling one) – *différance* for Derrida and *sunyata* in Buddhism – are also tactical terms, happy to yield to erasure (or, to maintain the textual analogy, obliteration) once their role has been discharged.

We may note, in the idea of the raft, that we take it from the near shore to the far. If one is called by the other, however (and however designated), one might equally imagine it as a raft sent from the far.

Buddhism, post-structuralism and existentialism all reject "the notion that man's essence is to be a knower of essences" (Rorty, 1979, p.367). Many therapists would also be uncomfortable with such a static picture. For in such a picture, where is the room for change? But whether we change by the ignorant freedom of the talking mind (Murray, 2003) or some other route remains ever open to question.

References

Brooks, C. (1956) *The Well Wrought Urn*. New York: Mariner Books.
Critchley, S. (1992) *The Ethics of Deconstruction*. Oxford: Blackwell.
Cupitt, D. (1987) *The Long-Legged Fly*. London: SCM Press.
Deleuze, G. and Guattari, F. (2004) *A Thousand Plateaus*. London: Continuum.
Derrida, J. (1994) *Spectres of Marx*. London: Routledge.
Descombes, V. (1980) *Modern French Philosophy*. Cambridge: CUP.
Dillon, M. C. (1991) *Merleau-Ponty's Ontology*. Evanston, IL: Northwestern UP.
Edmundson, M. (1995) *Literature Against Philosophy – Plato to Derrida*. Cambridge: CUP.
Fromm, E., Suzuki, D. T., and De Martino, R. (1993) *Zen Buddhism and Psychoanalysis*. London: Condor.
Habermas, J. (1992) *Postmetaphysical Thinking*. Cambridge, UK: Polity Press.
Heidegger, M. (1978) *Being and Time*. Hoboken: Wiley-Blackwell.
Katz, N. (1983) *Buddhist and Western Psychology*. Boulder: Prajna Press.
Keeney, B. (2009) *The Creative Therapist*. New York: Routledge.
Kierkegaard, S. (1980) *The Concept of Anxiety*. Princeton, NJ: Princeton University Press.
Laycock, S. (1994) *Mind as Mirror and the Mirroring of Mind*. New York: SUNY Press.
Loy, D. (1988) *Nonduality*. New York: Humanity Books.
Loy, D. (2003) Lack *and Transcendence: the Problem of Death and Life in Psychotherapy, Existentialism, and Buddhism*. New York: Prometheus Books.
Merleau-Ponty, M. (1962) *The Phenomenology of Perception*. London: Routledge.
Murray, L. (2003) *New Collected Poems*. Manchester: Carcanet.
Nichterlein, M. and Morss, J. L. (2016) *Deleuze and Psychology*. London: Routledge.
Nietzsche, F. (2008) *Twilight of the Idols*. Oxford: OUP.
Phillips, A. (2002) *Promises, Promises*. London: Faber.
Rogers, C. (1961) *On Becoming a Person*. Boston: Houghton Mifflin.
Rorty, R. (1979) *Philosophy and the Mirror of Nature*. Princeton, NJ: Princeton University Press.
Steiner, G. (1989) *Real Presences*. London: Faber and Faber.
Suzuki, S. (2009) *Zen Mind, Beginner's Mind*. New York: Weatherhill Inc.
Thera, N. (1972) *The Heart of Buddhist Meditation*. London: Rider.

Tillich, P. (1967) *The Courage to Be*. London: Collins.
Wadlington, W. (2012) The Art of Living in Otto Rank's Will Therapy, *The American Journal of Psychoanalysis*, 72 (4).
Watson, G. (2002) *The Resonance of Emptiness*. London: RoutledgeCurzon.
Wittgenstein, L. (2007) *Tractatus Logico-Philosophicus*. New York: Cosimo Classics.

19 Existence, self, and meaning

A stranger in search of home

Micah Sadigh

Death

Leo Tolstoy spent days planning a final act, to end his life. Surrounded by wealth, fame, and luxury, he had come face-to-face with the realization that his life was devoid of meaning, that death, obliteration of all he was, awaited his arrival at the end of the corridor of life, with no chance of escape. Nothing comforted him. His obsessions, his mental trickery, attending the Sunday mass, the philosophers who used to inspire him—all had left him with naught. A naked self remained. He finally concluded that the path that could free him from such apprehension had to do with living for the sake of others, not for himself.

With all of his belongings taken away, his body shaved, and a series of numbers tattooed on his forearm, Viktor Frankl discovers the meaning of freedom in the dark and horrific days and nights of the death camps in Auschwitz. Imprisoned, denuded of all that externally defined him, he discovers that he can imagine the beautiful face of his wife, speak with her, commune with her, and love her. The poetry and creativity that flows through his thoughts and heart have touched thousands, if not millions; ideas conceived in captivity, ideas that emerged from the freedom of a soul so inclined to find meaning in his suffering and to live even the last minutes of his existence, clinging to the values that he held sacred, those values that defined him.

While marching to a worksite, Frankl shares the following vivid, haunting, and unforgettable words:

> as we stumbled on for miles, slipping on icy spots, supporting each other dragging one another up and onward, nothing was said. ... Occasionally I looked at the sky, where the stars were fading and the pink light of the morning was beginning to spread behind a dark bank of clouds. But my mind clung to my wife's image, imagining it with an uncanny acuteness. I heard her voice answering me. ... A thought transfixed me: for the first time in my life I saw the truth as it is set into song by so many poets, proclaimed as the final wisdom by so many thinkers. The truth—that love is the ultimate and the highest goal to which man can aspire.
>
> (Frankl, 1984, pp. 48–49)

It was experiences such as these that brought him to the inexorable conclusion that "everything can be taken from a man but one thing: the last of the human freedoms—to choose one's attitude in any given set of circumstances, to choose one's own way" (Frankl, 1984, p. 75). "Self-transcendence" was Frankl's central approach to finding meaning in life. To live, we need to live for something or someone.

What is hidden inside of us? Or are we empty shells? In his descent into his inner self, Augustine, the first discoverer of the inner self, finds an opening through a hellish ground, with fierce beast-like forces that he had to subdue. Further along, he finds a path to his God (Augustine, 1997). This same journey is told in a more dramatic way in Dante's *Divine Comedy* (1995)—a descent into hell, a place of purification, an ascent to paradise. The same inner world that centuries later came to be known as the psychoanalytic unconscious—nothing mystical, but physical and physiological with base impulses and drives, with armors and defenses to keep the beast away. But what else is there in such an inner world?

Freedom

In *On the Dignity of Man*, written by the Renaissance philosopher Pico della Mirandola, we read the following as Adam, the first human, is told about the vision of and the mission for his life, which reveals that human existence is very different than that of other animals. The ideas and principles captured in these words resemble, to a large degree, that which is central to the existential philosophy; most notably, Jean-Paul Sartre's assertion that "existence precedes essence" (Sartre, 2007, p. 55).

> We have given to thee, Adam, no fixed seat, no form of thy very own, no gift peculiarly thine, that thou mayest feel as thine own, have as thine own. … In conformity with thy free judgement, in whose hands I have placed thee, thou art confined by no bounds. … Neither heavenly nor earthly … thou mayest sculpt thyself into whatever shape thou dost prefer. Thou canst grow downward into the lower natures which are brutes. Thou canst again grow upward from thy soul's reason into the higher natures which are divine.
>
> (Pico della Mirandola, 1998, pp.4–5)

From this vantage point, our existence is not a curse, but an opportunity; not a set of rules, but choices; not a punishment—an invitation.

At every moment there is a possibility for us to transcend our predicaments, make them opportunities for growth, compassion, and hope for justice. While at the same exact moment, there exists the possibility for deteriorating to savagery, brutality, baseness. Freud was convinced that this is exactly what would happen to us if our basic needs were withdrawn. We would become beast-like, no matter what our social status suggested. Frankl in the rummages of the concentration camp indeed saw the opposite when the choice to help others prevailed in the midst of extreme hunger. Oftentimes, a "higher being" emerged rather than a brute.

Nietzsche offers a more organic rendition of our nature-less nature. There are many pieces within each of us: wood, clay, and hammer, and a sleeping architect, who, when awakened, can turn the raw material into art.

> In man *creature* and *creator* are united: in man there is material, fragment, excess, clay, dirt, nonsense, chaos; but in man there is also creator, form giver, hammer hardness, spectator divinity, and seventh day: do you understand this contrast? And that your pity is for the 'creature in man,' for what must be formed, broken, forged, torn, burnt, made incandescent, and purified—that which necessarily must and should suffer?
>
> (Nietzsche, 1989, p. 154)

Choices, passion, meaning—created or discovered, creativity, an indomitable belief in possibilities—we create ourselves from moment to moment, and only through the choices we make, though they can never define us as we are always becoming. We are always becoming through commitments we make to ourselves and to others.

You are a he, a she, neurotransmitters in action, of a birthplace you did not choose, of a name that was assigned to you, of a culture you did not select, of a sex which was based on probability—an accident—and, perhaps, in time, a diagnosis that has categorized you, separated you from the rest because now you are one of "them". With all that said, can I truly know who you are? Do those labels affixed upon you help me know you? But then, I can say, "what are you?" and suddenly all of those ludicrous words move to the periphery, for your answer reveals, "I am becoming…" And as you are becoming, so am I. The descriptives fade, a journey begins as we move toward becoming. On this journey, however brief or long, I discover that there is an "I" because there is a "you". I don't need to know who you are, for we are together; we are becoming something more or something less than what we were. We walk together, seek together, fall together, rise together, and if for a brief moment the elaborate descriptive cages, those labels, eclipse you as my companion, I fall into ignorance; for as Martin Buber would have put it, you are no longer a "You", but an "It" (Buber, 1996). Our journey ends; detached, we move away; a distance—real and palpable—forms in-between us.

Human existence is tragic! In its midst, we have the potential, the possibility of creating ourselves, while death awaits us no matter how fast we run; we are always running toward it. We know the ending but there is so much that can be done between here and there. We can distract ourselves in some clever ways, perhaps by means of obsessions and compulsions so powerful that by the end of each day, exhausted, we have little to say about the day and how we lived it; we simply survived it. At the same time, we can be just as tired not because of our elaborate life-evading maneuvers, but because we wrestled with life, danced with life, in tension and conflict, "like a bow on a string" (Heraclitus, 2001, p. 37), we made music with life, rolled the rock up the hill, our rock, not as a prisoner—no, as a "form giver", defying the gods, seeing the other side of tragedy: the comedy, the mystery, groundless as it may be.

Some run aimlessly; destiny awaits, nonetheless. Kierkegaard (1987) captures the encounter: "Are you aware that there comes a midnight hour when everyone must unmask; do you believe that one can sneak away just before midnight in order to avoid it?" (p. 160) In the same passage, he goes on to say:

> I have seen people in life who have deceived others for such a long time that eventually they are unable to show their true nature. I have seen people who have played hide-and-seek so long that at last in a kind of lunacy they force their secret thoughts on others just as loathsomely as they proudly had concealed them from them earlier.
>
> (Kierkegaard, 1987, ibid)

The highly clever demon

She was in her late 30s when I met her. She was referred to me for the treatment of refractory "tension-related headaches". She was an affluent woman, with an affluent husband, affluent friends. The headaches came and went and they could become quite severe at times, with no rhyme or reason. All the diagnostic tests, some even painful, had failed to reveal any possible explanations for the crippling symptoms. "Sometimes, I cannot leave the house for days", she intimated with a smile, "on those days I can't attend any functions no matter how important they might be". She then stared at me and spoke softly, arrogantly, "My headaches are real. Just want you to know that I have fired many doctors because their techniques and treatments didn't work". During the next six sessions, I showed little interest in her headaches, unless she wanted to talk about them, as I was more interested in how she lived on those days that she was pain free. "I shop a lot. I need the appropriate clothing for all the functions I have to attend". To her, shopping was more of a chore than a fun pastime.

From week to week, I started noticing that there was something about her attire, although always sophisticated, that looked unique, different, unusual—at times too perfect. Some days, she wore a large straw hat, so large that she had a hard time sitting comfortably on the recliner in my office. Another day, she wore a thin, long silky scarf—beautiful but unusual, especially in the middle of summer.

During the early sessions, she would give a perfunctory, quick report about her headaches. Neither of us seemed interested in the headaches. Then one day, toward the end of the session, with an almost exhausted tone of voice, she shared the following, as though she had no control over what she was saying, "This is going to sound insane. Not sure what you are going to think of me after I tell you. There is this thing I have to do every day."

I am familiar with such moments. They happen from time-to-time and I am often warned that I am going to think negatively about the person after he or she shares something "crazy or insane". The mask falls off briefly. A confession is made.

"There is a tall column of women's magazines, arranged for different seasons, right outside the master bathroom. My husband doesn't understand why they are there. We used to fight about it. He gave up. I need them there."

She paused for a while. She was staring at the wall, avoiding eye contact with me, when she described,

> Every morning, after I walk out of the shower, naked, I enter the bedroom, grab one of the magazines and throw it on the bed. I look at the page where the magazine has opened. On that day, I have to dress the way the model is dressed in that picture. If the magazine opens on a page where there is a picture of a perfume, I have to wear that perfume. I can repeat this for up to 10 times and if I don't have a matching attire in style, I cannot leave the house on that day; I am punished, I am grounded. The next day if I am successful in finding the right outfit, I drive around looking for what I didn't have in my closet the previous day. It's kind of a demon. It controls me.

She said this with an almost helpless voice and with a touch of southern accent that was new to me.

She was silent for a while, as though in a trance; then looked at me with a smirk. The mask was back on. "Well, doctor? You think you can fix me?" All I could think at that moment was, "how ingenious". This was perhaps one of the most creative, elaborate rituals I had ever heard. The hour was up.

A week later, she walked into my office escorted by the receptionist. I stood up to greet her. I couldn't help but notice the combination of colors in her attire. She was a picture out of a magazine that had become animated and was now standing in front of me. She always shook my hand with a firm grip. For the first time, however, I noticed that during the handshake she was inspecting her bracelets, making sure they were properly displayed. She sat in her chair as she landed her large purse on the floor. "Well, doctor," she spoke with authority, "you had a week to think about what I told you. Well? You think you can fix me?"

I had indeed thought about what she had shared with me. Her "demon" was very real and powerful, though it had also saved her.

"I am sorry, I cannot help you. You are not broken to be fixed. I would not change a thing", I spoke gently and, I hope, genuinely.

> What you do day-after-day, is the only thing that gives your life a sense of mission and purpose. You spend your days responding to an obsession that has come to define you, compulsions that structure your days, while containing all sorts of anxieties. I can just imagine how exhausting they must be. Yet without them, your life has very little direction.

She was staring at me with a look of disbelief at first but then she began to nod in agreement. There was a long pause.

"At least you are honest." She grabbed a tissue, blew her nose. Uncannily, her face changed.

"You are telling me my life has no meaning?" she spoke angrily.

"What do you think?"

She stood up, grabbed her purse, turned and stared at the door for several minutes with her back toward me, as though she did not want me to see her face. She was crying. She opened the door and left the office.

A little while later, I went to the reception desk and asked if she had scheduled an appointment for the following week. She had, indeed. I left several messages on her answering machine, to which she did not reply.

A week later, she walked into my office, closed the door and sat in the chair. "Do you like me this way?" she pointed to her outfit. She was wearing a pair of sweat pants, a sweat shirt, and a pair of sneakers. In a way, we had our first meeting.

In the following year this remarkably creative woman, who had devised a most elaborate way of avoiding life, had channeled her creativity into something that was inspiring. Her relaxed voice was warm and sometimes a little funny with a southern drawl. "A simple girl from down south gets lucky," one day she told me, "marries a surgeon, ends up living in hell, becomes a picture in a magazine".

She never fired me. We stumbled together often. There was nothing simple about her, yet she was so resilient. She was a being with tenacity; resourceful, talented, who no longer needed "arrogance" to cover up her "fear of being discovered".

We are the architects of our lives, Alfred Adler (1927) once suggested, who was, in a sense, reminding us that we are responsible for our lives and not life's vicissitudes. And we are at our best, Adler would have suggested, when we cannot help but help others.

Her life, her wealth, her creativity became opportunities to address deeply troubling problems in her community. She loved wearing sneakers. On those days that the "demon" returned, she had fun, and always added something that didn't match. The demon never went away. She was never "fixed" or cured.

Anxiety

Death is the ultimate unknown; and if anxiety is the fear of the unknown, then death must be considered as the mother of all anxieties. A person suffering from panic attacks describes the experience as, "I felt like I was dying". A person who suffers from social anxiety recalls her experience at a social event: "Everybody was looking at me. Their stares were like daggers, stabbing me to death. I wanted to run but couldn't move". Another who is haunted by persistent nightmares fearfully shares: "I had that same dream again. Something was following me. It was going to kill me". However, without death it is difficult to chart one's actions, one's life. If we are conscious of the fact that this hour ends, that this day ends, then we have some choices to make before such endings arrive. If I know for certain that this is the last day of my life, the last time I see a loved one, the last time I stand in front of a classroom to give a final lecture, perhaps that knowing will affect the way I talk, the way I embrace, the way I teach. From this vantage point, the inevitable ending is the opportunity to live those moments as passionately as possible—death suddenly becomes a friend, a teacher, a powerful source of stimulation when fears and pretentions fade and lose their usefulness. The birth of this hour, the death of this hour. The true magic is what happens in-between, when tragedy is transmogrified into possibility, into opportunity, into creativity. Death becomes a signpost, a reminder, a companion. No one needs to grow and evolve, make difficult decisions, such as making a sacrifice, or creating something if this life were simply an act to be repeated again. Then anxiety, in all of its forms—and when properly understood—can offer us energy for giving birth to creativity; not someday down the road, today. What happens in this life matters most, and not what comes next. This is home. "Thus, a person is born only once, and there is no probability of a repetition. Transmigration of souls fails to appreciate the meaning of birth" (Kierkegaard, 1987, p. 40). Birth is the undeniable confirmation of death's presence, and the anxiety it generates can consume us or propel us toward acts of creativity.

The obscurity of life makes us wish for magical interventions, like children hoping for some benevolent fairy to bring the perfect present. At times we may even make a Faustian bargain, selling our soul (freedom, choices, creativity) for some temporary thrill or comfort. But there is always a price tag. Kierkegaard shares his recollection of the tale of *Morad the Hunchback*, in which "A man comes into possession of a ring that provides everything he wishes but always with a 'but' attached—for example, when he wishes for security he finds himself in prison etc" (Kierkegaard, 1987, p. 368). Life must be lived.

We create ourselves by the choices we make. Therefore, the act of self-creating is impeded when another makes those choices for us. Whether the choice is right or wrong is not as important as the fact that a choice was made; the shaping of personality was initiated. An existential "thief" is the one who deprives us from creating ourselves, whether it is a well-meaning guide, a learned sage, a sentence out of a book, a message from the beyond—*if you meet Buddha on the road, kill him*. No one can deny the importance of wise messages, but the one who acts upon them, and is fully responsible for the actions that ensue, is the individual.

The Absurd follows us throughout life and defies any rational explanation. The writer's Muse sings to her, so lucidly, flowingly. She begins to write but the pencil breaks; she runs out of paper, her device suffers a catastrophic collapse. A man works hard, awaits the future when he will find some respite from his grueling job in retirement, with plans to spend his weekends fishing, even ice fishing, and travelling the country in his carpeted camper equipped with a satellite television.

> Finally I have time to live, doc! Finally! Don't have to get up at the crack of dawn. I am going to drain Social Security. I am going to have fun. Look for my postcards! One will be from Nashville.

He dies a few days after he retires.

"I felt like a racehorse in a world without racetracks," Sylvia Plath captures so hauntingly, "or a champion college footballer suddenly confronted by Wall Street and a business suit, his days of glory shrunk to a little gold on his mantle with a date engraved on it like the date on a tombstone" (Plath, 2005, p. 77). The shadow of the Absurd looms over us. The gods must be crazy or they are simply cruel to find enjoyment in human suffering. Perhaps if we would submit to their will and whims, humble ourselves and return broken in need of their forgiveness, then the exile will come to an end. Like little sheep we will be tended to, fed, and smacked on the behind every once in a while for disobeying them and trying to find our own way. But perhaps there is something so noble and profound about humanity that even the gods pause and reflect. Human, troubled—at times a mess—yet with possibilities.

Sisyphus is punished for the whole of eternity and his punishment is the cruelest and only entertaining to the creators who are devoid of any compassion or empathy. He has to roll a rock up a hill, day-after-day, and when the rock reaches the top of the hill, it rolls back on its own weight, when he must repeat the act time and again. Meanwhile, fierce creatures watch him and if he were to stop, torment him so that he will return to the task at hand.

In Camus' depiction of the story, when the gods return to see how their ingenious form of eternal punishment is tormenting their subject, they are confounded. They find Sisyphus rolling the rock with a smile on his face, with his once tormentors now cheering him on—for this is his rock, and no one rolls it the way he does in all the underworld. The triumphant Sisyphus lives on, the gods remain silent (Camus, 2018).

Sisyphus stares at us in the mirror every morning as we prepare to roll the rock that shapes our days. Some roll it almost in a trance, though painfully; some numb themselves—and there are many options—with a plan to end it all, one of these days; while some live consciously, triumphantly, even passionately, as they create in their own way and live each day.

Medicalizing human existence: the wrong invention

Freud was a physician. His job was to address his patients' symptoms. He attributed his successes to making the unconscious conscious, but he did much more. The most detailed description of his analytic work comes to us from a long-term patient, codename "the Wolf-Man", who describes Freud as a brilliant, caring human with some interesting ideas. But what he remembered most was his humanity (Obholzer, 1982). No matter how convincing our formulation of certain behaviors—unconscious or environmental determinants—what matters most is to establish that we respond to life and its circumstances; there is a free agency who is in charge, whether overtly, as in our actions; or covertly as with our attitude. As Frankl puts it, "Suffering is an ineradicable part of life, even as fate and death. Without suffering and death human life cannot be complete" (Frankl, 1984, p. 76). How we respond to suffering is our choice. In our suffering, it is not a cure we seek, but a communion, a togetherness, a shared moment devoid of judgment with utter engagement, even helplessly. Not a therapist in the medical sense, but a companion, a sojourner in a human sense.

It is common to hear the wise admonition that life happens in the "here and now", and magically, people somehow know what one is talking about. Where is here? Is it a place? This place? And when is now, which so quickly became then? Doesn't now carry a piece of the past and an anticipation for a possible future? Why don't we find comfort in the "there and then"? Human consciousness cannot help but project itself into a possible future. If life can be captured in *being-in-the-world* then that denotes one thing: participation—at times passively, remotely, reluctantly, reactively—at times actively, engagingly, resolutely. And what makes the difference between the two? Creating a self through choices and accepting the sole authorship of such choices, and the repercussions of such responsibility, may demand on the way to becoming human. The existential companion, as opposed to a "therapist", like a midwife, remains close and participates in the birth of such a self, in its many incarnations, through choices made.

To understand ourselves we need to be understood by another, Hora suggests, before going on to say:

> To be understood by another he needs to understand the other. When two people understand each other completely, they experience communion. Communion is that union which makes differentiation possible. Man becomes an individual through union with the other. By losing himself in the other he finds himself as the One. For man is wholly similar and wholly different at the same time—just as two mosaic pictures may contain similar stone fragments but be entirely different in their overall design.
>
> (Hora, 1960, p. 496)

In everyday life, uninvited thoughts enter abruptly, demanding our attention, pulling us in every which way in the midst of admiring a beautiful song, a beautiful face, a comforting touch—they cheat us with impunity. There are those moments when, free from such thoughts, we do not know who we are, where we are, and what we are about. "…my mind slipped from the noose of the thought and swung, like a bird, in the center of empty air" (Plath, 2005, p. 216). Such interruptions can be analyzed and reframed, but in the end we must choose to hold onto them or let them go. No simple tricks, a choice must be made.

The suffocating truth

"I began having asthma attacks about a year ago", he spoke with a commanding voice.

> While the allergy tests didn't offer much, it was clear to all the docs that I was allergic to something. I moved out of my office where I used to get the attacks. Now I am in a new office. There is an air purifier in my consultation room and one in the waiting room. I take my shots and carry my inhalers with me and still suffer from shortness of breath.

A friend had shared one of my papers with a psychotherapist. We met for a brief meeting to discuss his symptoms. It was simply a conversation, during which he expressed frustration about how his life was being controlled by the occasional shortness of breath, which had turned him into a cautious, superstitious man. Several of the attacks took place on a Tuesday. Therefore, on Tuesdays he did not see any of his clients. Mobile phones with antennas were not allowed in the house; kids could not use any kind of crayons upstairs, only in the basement; the dog had to go, and on and on. None of them had stopped the unpredictable attacks—most of which occurred when he was doing therapy.

We agreed to meet a few more times. I believe, incidentally, that psychotherapists make the worst patients. "Perhaps you should tell me to reframe that thought", he advised me from time-to-time. My response: "Perhaps we should listen to what that particular thought is telling us." "It is irrational, doc!" he yelled at me.

"Aren't we all irrational at times?"

He once confronted me with the notion that because I had a doctorate and he did not, that didn't make me smarter. I asked him to stop calling me "doc" and simply call me by my first name.

"Thanks, I hate authority", he said, "you are all the same."

It is also a lot easier to blame the authority. He later agreed. When others simply make choices for us, we can also blame them for those choices. Layer by layer the wall between us was becoming more porous. He cried when he talked about how he used to play football with his children, but now he could not afford being outside the house for long, and definitely not rolling on the lawn. His pains and losses were palpable to me. He wanted to come back for another session, at which time he brought in his two kids and wife.

In a subsequent session, he revealed more of his world to me. His patients frustrated him, but he needed them to stay with him. "I have to sit there and listen to them at 80 bucks a pop per hour! I deserve more." The patients were sent to him from a religious community. He was at the mercy of the pastor. He couldn't say no to the referrals and had to prove that he was a good source of referral. The sessions began and ended by his reading passages from the scriptures. One day when he was describing a session with a difficult patient, he spoke out,

> …and I don't even believe in that stuff (the scriptures), but I have to repeat them, comfort the goofball who ain't gonna change. Then I've to say a prayer at the end of the session. I feel like a liar and I am charging them for the session.

We live in a world which we have to survive. Masks and plays, tricks and lies, some obvious and some not, are tools at our disposal. But deep down we know what clever punishments we devise to pay for our inauthenticity. We need no jury or judge; they gather and meet frequently in the corner of our mind. We know how to punish ourselves, through sickness and pain, addictions and afflictions. The most sophisticated interpretation cannot break the spell, only we can—and most effectively in the presence of a companion who does not pretend to know the shape of the spell, but does not run away from it either. In the end, the subjective world of the patient "must speak its own language" (Sadigh, 2017, p. 369), where any hope for redemption lies hidden.

Life

Human existence is tragic; yet in its midst we see nobility, dignity, resourcefulness, creativity—all of which demand conscious, volitional, authentic choices to be made. The comic nature of life has to do with its mystery and the fact that it goes on with or without us. The tragic dimension of life cannot be simply meditated or medicated away. It cannot be analyzed away, reframed and reconstructed; its strengths cannot be reinforced and its weaknesses punished; its anxieties cannot be merely extinguished, wished away or wiped away—it can only be lived by participating in life; by creating a self and using it to make commitments to others in acts of self-transcendence. Such a process of self-creation does not take place in a vacuum but in a relationship, where mystery, healing, and creativity are lived.

References

Adler, A. (1927). *Understanding Human Nature*. New York: Garden City Publishing.

Augustine. (1997). *Confessions*. New York: New City Press.

Buber, M. (1996). *I and Thou*. New York: Simon & Schuster.

Camus, A. (2018). *The Myth of Sisyphus and Other Essays*. New York: Vintage.

Dante, A. (1995). *The Divine Comedy*. New York: Everyman's Library.

Frankl, V. E. (1984). *Man's Search for Meaning*. New York: Simone & Schuster.

Heraclitus. (2001). *Fragments*. New York: Penguin.

Hora, T. (1960). The Process of Existential Psychotherapy. *Psychiatric Quarterly, 34(3)*, 495–504.

Kierkegaard, S. (1987). *Either/Or (Part II)*. Princeton, NJ: Princeton University Press.

Nietzsche, F. (1989). *Beyond Good and Evil*. New York: Vintage.

Obholzer, K. (1982). *The Wolf-Man: Sixty Years Later*. New York: Continuum.

Pico della Mirandola, G. (1998). *On the Dignity of Man*. Indianapolis, IN: Hackett Publishing.

Plath, S. (2005). *The Bell Jar*. New York: Harper Perennial.

Sadigh, M. (2017). The Nightmare of Becoming Human: Metaphors and reflections for individuals in search of authentic self. *Existential Analysis, 28(2)*, 362–373.

Sartre, J. P. (2007). *Existentialism is Humanism*. New Haven, CT: Yale University Press.

20 Meaning and meaninglessness of the self

Noam Israeli

Introduction

The positivist approach in psychotherapy evokes notions of constancy and structure in psychic life through the construct of the self. Psyche emerges in this sense as what can be predicted and evaluated. Existential philosophy aimed, in my view, to refute this notion of self as a referential term. Richard Cohen (2015) argues that existential psychotherapy did make an admirable attempt at providing an alternative to psychological and psychoanalytical concepts by offering alternative – philosophical – notions that are potentially more attuned with lived experience. Despite this, it has remained loyal to the positivist idea of selfhood, and bound to a sense of selfhood that is in dire need of modification. For Cohen, Emmanuel Levinas's philosophy provides a better alternative to the positivist paradigm than the one offered by existential psychotherapy. Agreeing with Cohen's critique of existential psychotherapy, but only partially with his solution, this chapter suggests a slightly different approach. The point at which existential psychotherapy went astray in providing an alternative to positivism in psychotherapy was through its rupture with the term "meaning". Unlike Cohen, who turns to Levinas as a prospective solution for psychotherapy, this chapter is an attempt to reflect R.D. Laing's reliance on Sartre's ideas of consciousness that also comprises a critique of psychoanalysis as a possible anchor to rely on.

Jean-Paul Sartre wrote to Laing and David Cooper:

> Like you, I believe that one cannot understand psychological disturbances from the outside, on the basis of a positivistic determinism, or to reconstruct them with a combination of concepts that remain outside the illness as lived and experienced. I also believe that one cannot study, let alone cure, a neurosis without a fundamental respect for the person of the patient, without a constant effort to grasp the basic situation and relieve it, without an attempt to rediscover the response of the person to that situation - and like you, I think, I regard mental illness as the 'way out' that the free organism, in its total unity, invests in order to be able to live through an intolerable situation.
>
> (Sartre, 1964, p.1)

Sartre expresses his appreciation of his two colleagues, as they share his commitment to phenomenology. This approach understands psychic occurrences as phenomena, rather than facts that will later be decoded within a theoretical matrix (a view that has also been expressed in his critique of psychoanalysis and psychiatry). Sartre, who viewed himself as a phenomenologist within the contours of Husserl's phenomenological tradition, objects to the notion of a split *ego* with one of its parts being unconscious. As he writes:

> For most philosophers, the Ego is an 'inhabitant' of consciousness. Some of them state that it is formally present at the heart of *Erlebnis*, as an empty principle of unification. Others—psychologists, for the most part—claim they can discover its material presence, as a center of desires and acts, in every moment of our psychical life. I should like to show here that the Ego is neither formally nor materially in consciousness: it is outside, in the world; it is a being in the world, like the Ego of another.
>
> (Sartre, 2004, p.1)

The notion that selfhood inherently contains the dialectic of the structural tension between awareness and the world is therefore refuted by Sartre, as he strives to depict consciousness as a relation with(in) the world, rather than an entity. This argument weaves a poignant thread throughout *Being and Nothingness*, as the existence of consciousness, as such, carries the tenuous relation between its facticity and transcendence, hence it is never a fixed entity. Facticity is unified with the transcendental that governs consciousness and envelopes nothingness at its heart. Sartre avers for no fixed psychic structure as a path for understanding consciousness: not biological, nor psychological. Phenomenology cannot surrender itself to *a priori* theoretical tenets as psychology and psychoanalysis. Human existence is selfless consciousness that is only aware of being aware of itself.

This was a central theme for Laing, when he sought to establish a new psychotherapeutic approach that would substitute traditional ones. Laing, like Sartre, claims that psychotherapy – particularly psychoanalysis – takes a structural approach when referring to consciousness, with a close affinity to the natural sciences, and is thus antithetical to phenomenology. This is evident in psychoanalysis' hermeneutics as suspicious of the symptom's authenticity, which always symbolizes other psychic aspects or facts (never a phenomenon), and suspicious of the patient's ability to make sensible rationalization of it. Hence, psychoanalysis offers a theoretical context for unraveling suffering, through the patient's realization as achieved through the filtering of the psychical experiences or material via the theoretical context. The therapist functions as the decrypting mechanism of the unconscious.

In other words, the understanding of the unconscious aspects of selfhood is done via an interpretation achieved by the theoretical compartmentalization of psychic content that the patient/client is unaware of, before and during psychotherapy. Selfhood (striving towards its functional holism) is central in such hermeneutics as an entity that exists immanently and dialectically with the world.

Following Cohen's criticism of existential psychotherapy (namely, not fully disengaging from the notion of selfhood), I will begin with an exploration of how existential psychotherapy has historically failed in creating an alternative hermeneutic for psychotherapy, because it inherently relies on selfhood, continually moving away from phenomenology towards positivistic hermeneutics. Finally, I will consider how a contemporary existential psychotherapy needs to offer a practice that attempts to *suspend the self*, thus allying itself more closely to phenomenology rather than existentialism.

The selfless consciousness

Phenomenology aspires to an appreciation of the unfolding of the world by capturing the appearance of the phenomena in an unmediated fashion. The relation between consciousness and the world itself is a unified twofold, a non-dialectical one. The initial basic movement of consciousness is intentionality towards an appearance of world, an unfolding; as the world reveals itself to consciousness. Consciousness, when capturing the world, already captures itself as in the world and part of the unfolding of the world. Intentionality, as the initial movement towards the world, occurs with consciousness already thrown into the world.

Philosophers who followed Husserl's phenomenology do not refer to a self or an ego as a distinct phenomenon with contours. Rather, consciousness is described as part of the world. The human conscious phenomenon is a *relation to*, not a distinct feature *from*, the world. Rather, it has a unified and circular relation with the world. For example, Heidegger describes the human phenomenon as *Dasein – being there*, inferring that phenomenology of being involves already being thrown and immersed in the world. Levinas asserts that human consciousness is able to capture the world, but this does not involve the formation of certain features, but is instead an ability.

Likewise, Sartre's concern lies in the phenomenology of consciousness with the world and within itself, always tied to appearance of itself and the world, given that "all consciousness, as Husserl has shown us, is consciousness of something. This means that there is no consciousness which is not positing of a transcendent object, or if you prefer that consciousness has no 'content'" (Sartre, 1962, p.11).

In *Being and Nothingness*, Sartre provides a lengthy phenomenological account of such possibility stating that the first being that we meet in our ontological enquiry is the being of appearance (Sartre, 1962). Consciousness is the ability to relate to appearance, but this does not infer any formative properties that characterize it, which would always be accurate and repetitive.

Furthermore, consciousness is consciousness of being conscious, as such it seems unreasonable for Sartre that unconsciousness can be part of consciousness or for it to be separate from the world. As inference and a flow, consciousness carries no properties other than the ability of being conscious.

Sartre holds a principled reservation about the structural depiction of consciousness, and a quick glance at his *Sketch for a Theory of the Emotions* (Sartre, 1962) may exemplify this argument. He argues that the causal explanations of emotions are part of *psychologism* which involves an error of assumption. The error consists of considering the human being as defined by desires, which leads to the illusion of psychic life as a substance. Sartre considers emotions as responses to the world, and his exploration begins with a critique of psychology and its approach to emotions as matter or fact. While acknowledging the importance psychology ascribes to our understanding of the human being, he states:

> The psychologist tries to make use of only two well defined types of experi-ence: that which is given to us by spatio-temporal experience of organized bodies and the intuitive knowledge of ourselves, which we call reflective experience. We must not then count upon the facts to organize themselves into a synthetic whole, which would deliver its meaning by itself.
>
> (Sartre, 1962, pp.14–15)

Psychology limits the ability to capture the phenomenality of emotional experiences, as it relates emotions and emotional events as facts with an almost closed structure. Sartre's claim is that phenomenology holds a clear advantage in understanding emotions:

> Thus there will be, for instance, a phenomenology of emotions which after 'putting the world in brackets' will study emotion as a purely transcendental phenomenon, not addressing itself to particular emotions but seeking to attain and elucidate the transcendent essence of emotion as an organized type of consciousness.
>
> (Sartre, 1962, p.23)

Emotions are part of intentionality towards the world and a phenomenological investigation into the manifestation of existential aspects of being-in-the-world. Such an argument contrasts psychological and psychoanalytical theories that, broadly speaking, view emotions as part of the self and its development.

According to the latter approach, psychological enquiry (psychotherapy being its application) aims to unravel the intricate psychic links and facts of the emotional matrix and some will be deemed by the patient or the therapist as self-defeating or dysfunctional and therefore pathological. Sartre's argument is that *emotions are not fixed entities but in flux* and exist *only in relation to the world*. As such, there is no presumption or inference with the appearance of a certain emotion.

The appearance of consciousness does not infer a certain *I*, a fixed structure. Consciousness and awareness of its facticity is always in relation to its transcend-ence that points to nothingness. The negation that is at the heart of consciousness is the premise for its evolvement and continual digression from itself as manifest-ation and embodiment of its freedom. Selfhood, like emotions, becomes viable in a non-psychological positivistic sense; the possibility of understanding human ontology lies in the descriptive, rather than the hermeneutic.

Following Sartre, Laing writes that existential phenomenological therapy:

> is not so much about an attempt to describe particular objects of his experience as to set all particular objects of his experience within the context of his whole being-in-the-world. … Although retaining the terms schizoid and schizophrenic for the sane and the psychotic positions respectively, I shall of course, be using these terms in their usual clinical psychiatric frame of reference but phenomenological and existentially.
>
> (Laing, 1960, p.2)

Laing's use of psychological terms with the intention of turning them into phenomenological ones is an attempt to create a holistic view of the patient's being-in-the-world. Following this existential scope, subjectivity is understood as an open relation to the world with no contours or tenets, and the psychological terms are descriptive (if to be used at all), hinting at a metaphysical structure. Laing's phenomenological psychotherapy largely avoids any attempt to assert a certain aim or metaphysical structure of assumed theoretical tenets. Indeed, one cannot avoid noticing that Laing struggles to fully disengage from the traditional psychological terminology. For example, Laing's use and development of the term *ontological insecurity* (Laing, 1960) resonates with John Bowlby's attachment theory – despite his attempts to refute such terminology (Laing & Esterson, 1960). This signifies the beginning of existential psychotherapy's struggle with positioning itself between phenomenology and psychology; between the idea of selfhood and selflessness; between philosophy and positivism.

Gradually, the schools of existential therapy have attempted to promote phenomenology within clinical practice, and have fostered terminology that is psychotherapeutic and includes philosophical terms. As we have seen, Cohen's criticism is that such adaptation causes the existential therapies *to regress to a positivist sense of selfhood*. If Laing's struggle was to follow Sartre and disengage from positivism in favor of phenomenology, existential therapy has ironically come full circle, back towards positivism and psychological hermeneutics. Steering away from clinical hermeneutics and moving towards phenomenology proves to be difficult within a therapeutic setting. The question is whether the shift from positivism has perhaps not occurred in the way Cohen argues, which is where our exploration takes us next.

Rupture with meaning as a return to selfhood

Meaning in psychotherapy, as developed by Viktor Frankl (1970) and contextualized by Yalom (1980), has since become ubiquitous in existential psychotherapy. Frankl's *Logotherapy* explicates the responsibility of the person to respond to his circumstances. Such responsibility always involves the will to determine meaning: "Logotherapy does not spare the patient a confrontation with the specific meaning which he has to carry out and which we have to help him find" (Frankl, 1967, p.22).

Humans are inherently free and carry a will for meaning, striving to live a meaningful life, especially when facing suffering. For Frankl (1967): "If man were really driven to meaning, he would embark on meaning fulfillment solely for the sake of getting rid of the drive, in order to restore homeostasis within himself" (p.22).

Meaning is a structural attribution and is central to wellbeing. Frankl claims that a phenomenological description of one's circumstances paves the path towards unraveling the meaning of life; that it signifies what one gives to the world, receives or takes from it, and the stand taken with regards to finite circumstances.

The poignant search for a cause, a reason, a motivation, an ideal is central for humans. Meaning holds guiding attributions for an *existent*'s orientation in finding a path through her *existence*. The meaning is personal and unique and the individual has an obligation to unravel it. There is an implicit assumption that life is meaningful and that each person's life has a meaning that needs to be discovered. The premise of this assumption is somewhat incongruous with phenomenology and existentialism. When consciousness captures appearance, it is not immediately inferred that there is an inherent meaning for being-in-the-world. Existentialism that endorses freedom has accepted the possibility of meaninglessness as much as meaningfulness. It also remains unclear how to decipher meaning from phenomenological descriptions. When facts are assigned meaning, the person has provided these facts with a formative sense of subjective conceptuality and termed them as meaningful, but such an act remains relative and temporal (Israeli, 2018).

The unraveling of meaning, as Frankl describes it, materializes as the unconscious. The therapist's aim is to help the suffering patient to discover it – and not to create it – as one of the main characteristics of selfhood that leads to wellbeing. For Frankl, meaning, as depicted in Logotherapy, replaces Sigmund Freud's reality principle. Yet adapting and bringing a different term into psychotherapy does not alter the hermeneutics, whereby meaning is presented as a formative aspect of the person, the self. Frankl's style of writing and presentation resonates with psychological theory, with descriptive characteristics of being human. Meaning is a central aspect in the wellbeing and formation of the person. The meaning of one's life is self-indicative; as such it needs a certain self whose meaning it would be. Phenomenology used in Logotherapy is an uncovering tool for an already existing, yet hidden or unknown, aspect of selfhood.

In his description of meaning in existential psychotherapy, Yalom (1980) acknowledges the difficulty in discussing meaning within the confines of existential philosophy, which describes the world as contingent, thus creating a difficulty in considering human life in absolutes. Any cosmic meaning linked to a belief in a higher form, or meaning without a God figure, is subject to a choice that person is making. For Yalom, Albert Camus was aware of the tension between nihilism and ethics, and so was Sartre, who advocated the meaninglessness of life, although both acknowledge the need for some sense and both strive towards an ethical life. However, it is difficult to infer that they point to the meaning of life as the root of a possible ethics. Yalom goes on to consider various possible aspects of meaning: self-actualization whereby selfhood becomes meaningful by dedication to a certain set of actions a person performs in his/her life; dedication to a cause whereby a person considers it to provide a meaningful sense; creativity in the sense of living life to maximize enjoyment in and astonishment at the world.

The motivating rationale that guides meaning is rationality, as the premise for excreting meaning from any aspect or life event relies on the idea that there is a logical relation in the sequence of events. It represents an opposition to banality or meaninglessness in the beauty of life, trauma, suffering and tragedy. It evokes comfort that suffering is not in vain, existence is not benign, but rather has a sense that can be meaningful and transformative. Meaning functions as a guiding idea in existential psychotherapy and provides a potentially flexible approach in the psychotherapeutic process. Meaning is almost an ethical proposition to guide life.

Existential psychotherapy has embraced Logotherapy's meaning, and it has become central to clinicians working in this paradigm. The appeal of the term is that it provides an organization within the ontological phenomenological descriptions of patients/clients. Life events, facts, persons, etc., create chaos as the ontological description of the patient unfolds. Meaning functions as a decoder of the phenomenological descriptions; it provides them with an orientation as to the importance the patient ascribes them according to how influential they are in their being.

There is a parallel concern that meaning, as presented by Frankl and Yalom, seems at first glance descriptive more than prescriptive; philosophical more than psychological; humanistic more than positivistic. However, a closer glance reveals that it operates in existential psychology as a structural theoretical assumption for the understanding of consciousness. The manner in which meaning is used and presented appears to be a replacement of psychological terms. The meaning is an unfolding not in a transcendental sense but as an essential aspect to be discovered in therapy.

The urge for meaning in existential psychotherapy and the uncovering of the repressed from the unconsciousness in psychoanalysis is equal. Patients and humans in general seek an eschatological and vital element for their wellbeing and self-understanding, one that has yet to be discovered. The circumstances and symptoms function as signifiers for this unraveling.

Meaning, it seems, is similar in its hermeneutic to unconsciousness, hence its usage shifts existential psychotherapy into positivism. In other words, the depictions of meaning express essentialism; pointing at selfhood that affirms its meaning of life, contrasting phenomenology whereby consciousness is a relation without essentialism.

If I acknowledge my own experience as a meaning for myself, I position my viewing externally to myself, by looking at myself as an essence. My being is construed as formative and structural. Into this formation, I can ascribe a certain sense as meaningful. Reflection that ascribes meaning for myself, as such, always involves a relation to some formation of selfhood that is beyond cognition. Reflective awareness that deems an aspect as the meaning in my life or meaning of my life involves viewing myself as a self, as meaning that is non-temporal; it refers to a certain essence that has been a formation. Meaning reverts to the self, as there is no possibility of finding meaning of something in a meaningful sense without it being a formative certainty that can be recognized. Meaning must refer to some consciousness that ascribes it to itself, and for this consciousness to grasp its meaning, it needs to be a thing in the world.

The problem of meaning as self-ascribed realization, from an existential position, is that for this relation to exist the person subjected herself to a fixity, similarly to matter. If meaning is flowing and non-temporal than it is different to the way it has been depicted by Frankl and Yalom.

One of Sartre's critiques of psychoanalysis focuses on his objection of ascribing structural properties to consciousness, which furthers it from its freedom. A form of positionality that has fixed preconceived tenets negates the possibility of consciousness digressing from itself, abolishing its transcendence. Meaning refuses the idea of negation as it always seeks to look at what *is*.

The introduction of meaning into the equation reverts the exploration to selfhood, in the way this term is normally understood in existential philosophy and psychotherapy. By substantiating meaning itself, we bolster selfhood.

Possible prospects

Existential psychotherapy attempts to provide a different terminology to describe psychic life as it appears, using different terms from traditional psychology. It uses terms such as hopelessness, boredom, angst, anxiety, meaning, purpose, responsibility and so on. The intention is to be more elaborate of the experience of being alive than the traditional psychological terms evoke. It seems that their use in existential psychotherapy has opened a dialogue closer to the experience of psychotherapy. However (as it is the case with the notion of meaning), existential psychotherapy has not been able to provide an alternative paradigm to psychotherapy as attempted and hoped for by Laing. How can such psychotherapy be realized? This section considers three possible suggestions: *phenomenology*, *hospitality* and *divergence*.

Phenomenology – To continue Laing's effort towards a phenomenological approach and to create a paradigm that has closer affinity with phenomenology, there should be a consideration not only of the terms used and the attitude of the therapist, but the phenomenological position. As phenomenology in psychotherapy is not merely a technical term, but one that infers openness, that does not pursue any terminology or possibility.

This is a dialogue of a '*yet*', psychotherapy that has little hermeneutic in the mind of the therapist – philosophically or psychologically. The feature of being-in-the-world of the patient does not suggest any certain intentionality or concepts by the therapist, other than guiding exploration and highlighting notions without any focus. The unfolding of the patient's ontology of becoming will drive the process to some realization. The unknowing, in its most fundamental sense as any appearance, is crucial. The phenomenological quest as such is open and evolving towards the process of appearance, while the therapist withholds his dilemmas, without offering an interpretation – but acting as a containing reflector.

Hospitality – Such phenomenology resonates with Levinas's hospitality, whereby the turn towards the other is such that it welcomes the other with an attempt to see beyond the face. This hospitality asks the welcome party to see beyond the face towards the possibility of the transcendence that the other embodies. Such an opening neither asks nor gives anything other than hospitality to the other. Other than the relation that aims to be open (aiming towards ethics before ontology), there is no anticipation or demand. The acceptance is asymmetrical as the welcoming party as such is always responsible. Levinas admits that it is confusing for

> … ethical relation to lead transcendence to its term, this is because the essential of ethics is in its transcendent intention, and because not every transcendent intention has the Noesis - Noema structure. Already of itself ethics is 'optics'. It is not limited to preparing the theoretical exercise of thought, which would monopolize transcendence. The traditional opposition between theory and practice will disappear before the metaphysical transcendence by which ethics is the royal road. … This apparent confusion is deliberate and constitutes one of the theses of this book.
>
> (Levinas, 1979, p. 29)

Hospitality is inevitable as the other is such that it does not evoke my self-awareness, but my obligation: despite being a monad, our duty for the guest constitutes our very humanity. The welcoming is part of an openness that language denies, let alone theory. It is not a joining of two subjects, but a turn of one towards the other. Both options lean towards a selfless and meaningless (as *a priori*) and a relation of consciousness with itself and towards the world.

Divergence – The previously mentioned solutions may insinuate a third possibility that questions the compatibility of philosophy and psychotherapy. As existential psychotherapy has not fully disengaged from both the positivist as well as the psychoanalytic paradigms attempting to formulate an open phenomenological dialogue. However, such dialogue may prove to be incompatible for psychotherapeutic work within medical health systems that respond to life threatening situations, as phenomenological dialogue may not be able or could not respond to such circumstances.

Phenomenological dialogue – that is closer to philosophy – has explorative intentionality, while psychotherapy has a determined intentionality in relation to the resoluteness of the patients' suffering and symptoms.

Laing struggled to disengage from positivistic psychology and phenomenology with difficulty that has led to a limited success – as we have seen – in the evolvement of existential psychotherapy. Possibly, the psychotherapeutic process cannot function without the notion of selfhood. Psychotherapy has a specific intention from its onset: to relieve the patient's suffering, thus to contextualize her suffering in a responsive paradigm for such context. Bearing this in mind, it is difficult to assume that therapists can be satisfied with purely phenomenological descriptions of dangerous mental states.

This leads to a possible new relation between philosophy and psychotherapy – *divergence*. Philosophy can offer important insights and reflections that are informative and important to psychotherapy but functions as an informative perception. Psychotherapy's complex relation to philosophy illustrates the possible contours of theory and practice. The contextual framework of psychotherapy may still need the hermeneutics of suspicion of the symptom and some structural tenets to operate. The boundaries of the relation reiterate the role of structural paradigms as important, and the use of philosophy as a radiant perception, rather than a psychotherapeutic tool.

References

Cohen, R. A. 2015, Preface. in Krycka, K., Kunz, G., and Sayre, G. G. (eds), *Psychotherapy for the Other* Duquesne University Press, USA.

Frankl, V. 1970, *Man's Search for Meaning* Pelican Books, UK.

Frankl, V.1967, *Existentialism and Psychotherapy* Pelican Books, UK.

Israeli, N. 2018, The Face of The Other – Levinasian Perspective on Nudity and Danger. In *The Journal of Existential Analysis*, 29.2 July 2018: UK.

Laing, R. D. 1960, *The Divided Self*. Penguin, UK.

Laing, R. D. & Esterson A, 1960, *Madness and the Family*. Penguin, UK.

Levinas, E. 1979, *Totality and Infinity*, trans. Lingis, Alphonso. Martinus Nijhoff Publication and Duquesne University Press, UK.

Sartre, J. P. 1962, *Sketch for a Theory of the Emotions*, trans. Mariet, P. Methuen & Co. UK.

Sartre, J. P. 1964, Forward. *Reason and Violence* by Laing, R. D. and Cooper, D. G. Vintage, UK.

Sartre, J. P. 2004, *The Transcendence of the Ego*, trans. Brown, Andrew. Routledge, UK.

Yalom, E. 1980, *Existential Psychotherapy*. Basic Books, USA.

21 Existentialism or a philosophy of existence?

Shestov and existential therapy

Mo Mandić

In memory of my brother-in-law, Ljubiša Denić (1964–2019)

Introduction

The term 'existentialism' was only introduced into mainstream philosophy in the earlier half of the 20th century, becoming popularized as a movement first in France through the contributions of certain key thinkers. A commonly overlooked fact, however, is that this popularization was preceded by a fertile and lively period of debate and disagreement between philosophers and thinkers who were similarly preoccupied with the central questions of human existence. Given this oversight, the focus of this chapter is two-fold: to bring out the contribution of the most important of these earlier 'philosophers of existence', namely, Lev Shestov, in order to reclaim his place as a key thinker addressing such questions related to existence; and also to show that, as existential therapists, existentialism, or existentialist thought, potentially limits our reflections and understandings on such questions when contrasted with any philosophy of existence.

Mélissa Fox-Muraton (2017) has similarly identified a distinction that can be made between such philosophies of existence, inspired by Søren Kierkegaard and forged in France in the 1930s, and the existentialist philosophy that had developed through such well-established figures as Jean-Paul Sartre, Simone de Beauvoir and Maurice Merleau-Ponty in the 1940s. It is this earlier phase of existential philosophy that really set the ground for what came later, not only in opening a space for such an approach, but for espousing a certain attitude that later transformed itself into existential*ist* philosophy, or existentialism. As Fox-Muraton says, these earlier Paris-based philosophers of existence – Jean Wahl, Rachel Bespaloff, Lev Shestov and Benjamin Fondane – were highly critical of existentialism, since it transformed their own attempts to address the complexities and irreducibilities of human existence into a system, or '-ism', but also: '[o]n the philosophical grounds that that it failed to properly take into account the notion of subjectivity, reducing it to a mere subjectivism. In so doing, existentialism … moves away from Kierkegaard's more rigorous philosophical constructions of subjectivity. (Fox-Muraton, 2017, p.7).

This difference between subjectivity and subjectivism, as a distinction, can be discerned as we familiarize ourselves more with Shestov's approach to thinking about existence.

Whilst it is true that Jaspers, Heidegger, Sartre and others also drew significantly on the work of Kierkegaard, their philosophical approaches differed substantially from the course taken by the philosophers of existence. Further, it should also be noted that Shestov, Fondane and Bespaloff all devoted some degree of attention to the German philosophers of the time, submitting compelling critiques of both Jaspers' philosophy as well as Heidegger's earlier work, *Being and Time* (1927/1962). But, as is now abundantly clear, existentialism took hold and proliferated more widely than was the case with their philosophies of existence. As Baugh notes,

> [t]he diversity of existential thought in the 1930s has been largely eclipsed by the phenomenal success of the humanist phenomenological existentialism of Jean-Paul Sartre, Simone de Beauvoir, and Maurice Merleau-Ponty after 1945, for whom "the three H's" – Heidegger, Husserl, and Hegel – became the touchstone.
>
> (Baugh, 2016, p. xviii)

What has therefore become a marginalized fact is that 1930s Paris was rife with a richer array of approaches taken by individual thinkers than could be captured or subsumed under any broader, unified, umbrella term. Each of these positions was, therefore, absorbed in lively critique and dispute in the course of assessing each other's perspectives. Such debate inevitably centred around, amongst other things, the particular nature of the language introduced, not least its terms, distinctions, characterizations and expressions, to describe aspects of existence. Whilst, in some cases, debate and disagreement led to outright dismissal and rejection of others' philosophical perspectives, in Shestov we see a genuinely respectful, careful and balanced engagement throughout.

Context

In order to provide an introduction to the relevance and significance of Shestov's work, I set out some historical and contextual background that earlier thinkers developed with regard to human existence.

Existential thought can properly be traced back to the nineteenth century, or even prior to this, with the writings of Blaise Pascal, though the articulation of the very tensions of human existence might be originally attributed to the influential work of St. Augustine. It is only in the 19th century, however, that a more emphatic focus on the meaning of human existence itself was mainly, though not solely, brought to the fore with the writings of Kierkegaard, Nietzsche and Dostoevsky.

All three thinkers were primarily concerned with the question, and place, of God in our cultural epoch, which can be considered as the starting point of their respective philosophies, and certainly acknowledged as the beginnings of existential philosophy itself. In the case of both Kierkegaard and Dostoevsky, Christianity was in need of rescue if human beings were to survive the loss of ultimate meanings in their lives. They proposed to do this by returning, in their own ways, to the original or initial experience of trying to understand Christ's radically new existential ideas. This return, for both, meant that Christianity could only be saved by understanding it through an existential lens; in other words, its Platonic, metaphysical, theological and even theoretical aspects needed to be abandoned, in order to return to the experience of involved, engaged, embodied, subjective and concrete living activity. For Kierkegaard, this was brought into even sharper relief by his reaction to the dizzyingly abstract philosophy of Hegel, and for Dostoevsky, in his strong opposition to the Westernization of his own world of Russian culture, through the increasing encroachment and prevalence of the Enlightenment and scientism. However, for Nietzsche, the idea of a supreme being, God, that had once been a source of ultimate meaning for us in our Western tradition, had now turned out to be 'our longest lie' (Nietzsche, 1887/1989, p. 152). Here, he was at pains to dismantle our need for any metaphysics, or a dependence on an other-worldly dimension, as the basis for understanding and thereby grounding ourselves in meaning.

Since 'God was dead', to be read as the idea of God and religion no longer playing a pivotal role in our lives as it did in pre-Modern times, this now leaves us bereft of the moral absolutes that have previously been handed down to us by God, and that we can turn to in order to guide our actions and reassure us that we have lived a good life. In the absence of moral absolutes, and given our continuing need for certainty, to what, or where, can we turn? Or, turning this around, if there is no certainty that can be delivered up to us, does this mean that everything now becomes arbitrary? This is the key question that preoccupies both the philosophers of existence and the existentialists, even though they pursue distinctively different ways of thinking.

Among the various thinkers that engaged with these earlier writers, the philosopher Albert Camus seemed to be very closely attuned to the tension that was at the core of the felt experience, which he called the *Absurd*. For him, this is captured in the very divorce between, on the one hand, our desires, wishes and searches for meaning, or things making sense to us, and on the other, the world's intrinsic silence and indifference – its non-rationality – to such desires and yearnings for meaning and sense. His characterization of the Absurd, to put it differently, *is both* the Heideggerian hyphenation that simply *is* a unity, *and* its rent from any ability to truly dwell in the world. The Absurd does not *itself* lie either just on the side of the human being, *or* alternatively on the side of the world. Rather, it is the paradoxical scission or incommensurability of something already pre-given as a unitary, interwoven phenomenon.

Camus chides both previous writers on existence and also his existentialist contemporaries for failing to face up to the Absurd, and resorting to forms of avoidance or escape, by invoking meanings of one sort or another to assuage and protect themselves from this deeply unsettling experience. In other words, they draw on some kind of reconciliation that comes either from the human being, or from the world, to resolve this painful tension. Amongst those whom he identifies as being guilty of this escape and resolution is Lev Shestov. However, this way of engaging with Shestov suggests that Camus is both appreciative of Shestov's ideas, but also dismissive of his conclusions. Camus, in fact, inadvertently reveals that he misreads and misrepresents him by accusing Shestov of enacting Camus' 'leap' (Camus, 1942/1988, p. 36) to an inauthentic place of safety beyond the Absurd, even though Shestov was *himself* an early exponent of the idea of the absurd in existence. In order to grasp more comprehensively the real value of his ideas, I now turn to Shestov himself.

Lev Shestov

Lev Shestov (1866–1938) has been generally considered as an existential and religious philosopher, both in his native Russia, as well as Europe. In this, he might be deemed to be no different to his contemporaries in pursuing fundamentally important questions on human existence, though an immediately obvious difference that we initially encounter on first reading him is his particularly unique way of setting out his thinking and questioning throughout his texts. This was, in no small part, down to the way in which he entered into dialogue with other thinkers. In the course of doing so, he pursued a deconstruction of others' work that, according to one commentator, Hillel Zeitlin, was even more radical in nature than Nietzsche himself (Finkenthal, 2010, p.125). But his own work also took on another scope and dimension, that of also challenging the whole of the Western philosophical tradition as an overarching paradigm; incidentally, this aspect of Shestov overlaps, to some degree, with the philosophical project that we encounter in Emmanuel Levinas, and also in Heidegger, though for entirely different reasons.

(a) Philosophical style

Rather than following the traditional path of formulating a philosophical system of his own, Shestov engaged with the writings of Kierkegaard, Nietzsche and Dostoevsky – as well as Heidegger and others – in order to critique their philosophy. This, at the same time, invariably pushed his own stance in an even more radically creative direction than those philosophers had pursued. Shestov claimed, in Nietzschean fashion, that we philosophize from the very perspective that we happen to embrace in our lives – that is, live *out*, and *from* – rather than from a more neutral position that attempts to pursue a rational or logical path of enquiry. In this sense, Shestov advocated a certain awareness and acceptance of our human condition that affords us a 'way in' to philosophical activity, and one that is markedly different to those of past philosophers, such as Spinoza, Kant and Hegel. This is quite distinctively exemplified in his own writing style, which is very much alive, existentially, we might say, to the issues that he is addressing.

Shestov was mindful of his and our relation to the texts that we read, and not succumbing to treating them as a source of information, or even as being authoritative on a subject-matter. Rather, he implored us to take a position on what we read, such that our thinking took shape and became the unique experience that manifested the stance that we took on any given ideas. As well as this, his own writing style reflected the fact that he was not afraid to show to the reader the movement in his thought, which also disclosed elements of contradiction, confusion or uncertainty in the very content of his thinking and writing.

Shestov engaged with the writings of such established thinkers as Kierkegaard, Nietzsche and Dostoevsky not so much as to demand from them some direct insights on how we should live – as he claimed that Jaspers was inclined to do (Shestov, 1964/1982) – but to take a more critical attitude towards them, whilst at the same time being in a respectful dialogue with them. In fact, according to Finkenthal (2010), it was those *negative* aspects of their ways of existing, as discerned from their writings, that could open up the challenges for us to think, for ourselves, about the question of how to live our own lives. We had been all too clearly made aware of the sufferings that all three writers had undergone over the course of their own lives, and it is this that allows us to embark on questions that matter to us personally. As such, then, Shestov was advocating a philosophy based on the affects, not on reason. In order to convey something of Shestov's way of engaging and reading other thinkers, and, I suggest, ones who matter to us as existential therapists, I will address his reflections on Nietzsche, Kierkegaard and Husserl.

Shestov on Nietzsche

Boris Groys (2012) describes Shestov's approach as one of:

> transposing [real and personal experiences] out of the linguistic realm [i.e. in his simple, ordinary use of language] into the realm of life...a theoretical, philosophical or scientific position is investigated not in terms of its 'objective' validity, but rather of its origin in 'life'.
>
> (p.38)

We see Shestov applying this concern, too, when he considers Nietzsche's particularly striking writing and thinking style. He avoids the use of general and abstract principles, since to do so is a way of symbolically rescuing oneself from unsuccessful situations where one has experienced failures or defeats. Rather, he writes in a very personal and affirmative way, free of objective statements that effectively serve to save, protect or hide him from such situations, in some way. But Shestov takes Nietzsche's approach and radicalizes it further, by turning it towards Nietzsche *himself*. He argues, with admirable courage and contentiousness, that, as Groys puts it,

> the 'life' that Nietzsche speaks of is a no less abstract concept than 'reason', 'science', 'freedom', and so on. ... When Nietzsche praises victorious life, preaches *amor fati* and identifies himself with forces of nature that are bound to destroy him, he simply seeks to divert himself and others from the fact that

he himself is sick, poor, weak and unhappy. The actual personal problem of Nietzsche – namely, the sickness that was steadily killing him – brings out in Nietzsche the same resentment that he denounces in all others, and forces him to adopt the pose of someone speaking in the name of life, which is a similar pose to that which people customarily speak in the name of reason, morality or science.

(Groys, 2012, pp.38–39)

Shestov claims that Nietzsche generalizes his personal situation, and inadvertently presents objective truth to his readers. This makes him no different to those very philosophers whom he criticizes for their strategy of searching for universal truth. Nietzsche has elevated his own life circumstances, and situation, from which he has generated such ideas as *amor fati*, self-overcoming, and the will to power, to one of being relevant and applicable to others' lives generally. Surely, Shestov challenges, we each live *different* life circumstances and situations: not all of us are in a similar situation of sickness to Nietzsche, for example. To paraphrase Nietzsche somewhat, his reply to this might well be, 'This is my way, you have yours'. Even so, Shestov seems to have identified a certain tension in Nietzsche's position.

Shestov on Kierkegaard

Shestov takes Kierkegaard to task for the way in which his own philosophy neglects to recognize that 'a personal, physically determined situation is not a concrete case of the universal condition' (Shestov, 1964/1982, p.40). Human experiences as despair, anxiety and love, for example, succumb to becoming generalized and abstract concepts, whilst, in the same breath, are assumed to remain within the realm of subjectivity.

Kierkegaard's own existential concerns revolve around his relationship with his fiancée, Regine Olsen, and it is from the *personal* nature of choosing not to eventually marry her that his philosophy emanates. Shestov identifies a form of sickness in Kierkegaard, without which he would not have attempted to articulate his philosophy. Such a philosophy was precisely his attempt at a *cure*. As with Nietzsche, Kierkegaard's inability to find a cure that would rescue him from philosophy itself was a sign of his lack of courage to follow through, confront and risk challenging himself to the possibility of overcoming his sickness. Shestov argues that, instead of staying at the level of the personal, Kierkegaard universalizes his sickness and presents it as a problem of existence.

In view of this, it is helpful to consider Shestov's own thoughts on possibility and impossibility. As Groys explains (2012), the difference between the two is a philosophical difference that is laid down by reason. Reason, as understood in traditional approaches to philosophy, dictates the conversion of contingency into necessity. Shestov's reflections on this are influenced by Dostoevsky, whose famous narrator, the underground man, says that: 'when confronted with an impossibility [most people] immediately capitulate. Impossibility is a stone wall. Now what do

I mean by stone wall? Well, the laws of nature, the conclusions of natural science and mathematics" (1864/2009, p.12).

As Dostoevsky goes on to say, our ability to reason and use logic is undoubtedly a valuable human faculty, but it does not capture what is fundamentally human about us. For Shestov, as for Dostoevsky, reason and logic ignore the fact that human existence is something other than laws, rules and limits: it is freedom, defiance of conformity, transcendence. And freedom clearly matters so much to us that we are even prepared to endure suffering in order to safeguard it. Shestov, however, pursues this further, identifying a certain paradox, namely, of contingency somehow becoming transformed into necessity by the work of reason. Perhaps in the case of Kierkegaard, at least, he lived out of a necessity that drove him, which, in a sense, drove *out* possibility. The problem is that, according to Shestov, had Kierkegaard remained in uncertainty and possibility, he would not have capitulated before the stone wall of philosophy that he developed.

Shestov on Husserl's phenomenology

Since, for most, if not all, existential therapists, phenomenology centrally informs and shapes therapeutic enquiry during sessions with clients, Shestov's own remarks surely bear some relevance on this approach. Both Shestov and his colleagues maintained a very close relationship with Husserl, the founder of phenomenology, even though Shestov was sharply critical of Husserl's project and claims. Shestov's essay, *Memento Mori* (Shestov, 1923/1968), subjects Husserl's philosophy to extensive evaluation, whilst a later work (Shestov, 1964/1982) reveals his great admiration and respect for Husserl. Shestov targets Husserl's work through two publications: *Philosophy as a Rigorous Science* (1900–1/2002) and his *Logical Investigations* (1900–1/2001). Whilst he offers a range of critical comments, Shestov mainly objects to, as Valevičius says, 'the rational substructure upon which phenomenology is built', adding: '[Shestov] does not believe that philosophy is, or should be, a science' (1993, p.100).

Shestov is wholly opposed to Husserl's motivation to get to the essence of a phenomenon, since it already anticipates something necessary. This endeavour grounds itself in reason and the rational, and is an enterprise that is concerned with knowledge. But for Shestov, this is far removed from life itself, since life has a much richer horizon: it vastly outstrips logic and logic's two-dimensional framework, whether this be typically expressed in terms of, for example, right or wrong, accurate or inaccurate, good or bad, or true or false. Shestov therefore mounts a concerted attack on Husserl's very characterization of philosophy as being based upon the 'sovereignty of reason' (Shestov, 1923/1968, p.338). However, as is the case in all of his writings, Shestov's style here, again, is engaging, exploratory, open and absorbing, rather than stodgy, safe and sterile. We are taken sympathetically through Husserl's thinking, with Shestov's approval and agreement in places, and then invited to consider where possible contradictions and paradoxes arise in Husserl's very own stance.

(b) *Some general remarks on Shestov's approach*

Overall, Shestov was worried that philosophy had taken a wrong and empty path, even if it was nevertheless immersed in grappling with some important questions. For him, an existential philosophy was centrally based on human despair, not on reason, logic and an attempt at standing back from life in order to subject it to further contemplation. In addition, as he assumed was true for Jaspers, he felt that philosophy was in pursuit of some kind of eternal truth, which, for him, was an untenable endeavour.

Shestov was opposed to a systematic approach to thinking and philosophy that had been dominant up to his own time. But, as with all his critiques, Shestov was more concerned to point out that, whilst we are free to adhere to a way of presenting ideas that systemically fall into place, we should also be sensitive to the fact that this is not ultimately going to prove very rewarding as a fruitful path, from a concrete point of view. In keeping with his own non-systematic approach, his writing also exemplified a way of avoiding a sense of completion and finality to his thinking.

Shestov also attended to the way in which philosophy ignored its own assumptions, and did not subject them to further scrutiny. It was also susceptible to making erroneous assumptions. This overall way of undertaking philosophical activity was not helped by its rigidity and resistance to internal challenge and criticism. This was not so much a case of there being something wrong about assumption-making, but only that we assume a sense of the 'eternal' that insidiously enters our experience, such that we exclude other possibilities that readily come to us through the imagination and our creative, alternative ways of thinking. That is, given the way that we have become so accustomed to grasp things in the ways that we do, we take it that this will always be the case. As Shestov says, again referring to possibility and impossibility:

> In our minds ... the conviction is firmly rooted that it is impossible to pass certain limits, and painful to try: a conviction founded on experience ... the most lasting and varied experience cannot lead to any binding and universal conclusion.
>
> (Shestov, 1920, p.143)

There is, then, a resulting inclination to lose the tentative character of our reflection on existence, and to move towards a more general or universal metaphysical picture. In doing so, we experience something calming and settling. This is not to say that we should rule out our reliance on such 'lasting experience', and on making judgements and generalizations as a result, but only that we acknowledge to ourselves that they do not ultimately hold over the course of time. They are more like fallible and provisional guides, in other words.

Shestov was also interested in pursuing a *metasophia*, that is, a new philosophy that went beyond established forms of philosophy. In this, he leads a way for existential therapists to consider their own relation to texts that are taken to be central to their approach in understanding human existence. Too much importance and emphasis has been devoted to approaching enquiry by unveiling a structure to phenomena, as is clearly the case in early Heidegger's *Being and Time* (1927/1962), for example. The same can also be said for Merleau-Ponty's *Phenomenology of Perception* (1945/2012), and Sartre's *Being and Nothingness* (1943/1958). However much these thinkers might consider their project to involve an existential undertaking, this seems to be considerably compromised by the rational and structural framework that they rely on in order to do so. In contrast, Shestov mounts a radical challenge in and through his actual writing, as the reader encounters a true embodiment of uncertainty, self-contradiction and an openness and trust in the power of revelation (rather than a sole reliance on rational inferences and logical or dialectically progressive thinking).

Shestov was never afraid of returning to themes and ideas that he had previously already addressed. In fact, as I attempt to flesh out his many thoughts here, I too find myself falling into a certain repetition in re-introducing those same ideas that I have already covered. This, I think, shows the generally interconnected nature of his thinking, but it also discloses something of the more interpretative, rather than logically linear, character of his thought. In this instance, however, we see him returning time and again to philosophy's dependence on necessity. As he puts it, '[w]hatever field of philosophical thought we approach, we always run up against this blind, deaf and dumb Necessity. And we are convinced that philosophy begins only where the kingdom of strict Necessity discloses itself' (Shestov, 1938/2016, p.81). He goes on to say that 'philosophy … was, is, and wishes to be, a looking backward' (1938/2016, p.82). That is, it is preoccupied with that which is set, constant and enduring, or eternal, much like Plato's metaphysical Forms.

By way of bringing together here what has already been said previously, it is not only necessity, but reason and logic, too, that are inadequate ways and means of grasping, and being in sync with, the temporal, dynamic flow of life itself. But it is not only philosophy that is drawn to necessity and logic: *we* ourselves are drawn to them, through philosophy, and it is *we* who then impose them on our lives, particularly as we adopt a 'philosophic world-conception' (Shestov, 1920, p.112) in our attempts to reckon with life. In fact, when it comes to living, for Shestov, even 'our moral deductions are arbitrary' (Shestov, 1920, p.112).

Shestov makes much of the endless possibilities of the imagination and creativity, which are central to our being, rather than living, again, according to any philosophically rational and logical framework. This, once again, ties us to his comments on the constraining nature of necessity and logic. Shestov (1920) illustrates this using the story of the pike (p.142), but this can be similarly depicted in the example of the fly trapped in a glass jar covered over with a transparent glass lid. Each time it attempts to fly out of the covered jar, it bumps up and into the solid resistance of the lid. The fly repeats this manoeuvre countless times. After numerous attempts to fly out of the jar, the glass lid is removed, but the fly continues to reach the very top of the now *open* jar, only to stop, and then make its descent to the bottom, following its by now accustomed pattern of behaviour. Shestov's message is for us to reflect on this, rather than offer any definitively settled answers. The tendency of philosophy, he thinks, has been to offer up ideas which then become fixed, and potentially ossified in character: we assume a fixed and rigid limit, or *partition*, beyond which we cannot go. His concern is to get us to reflect on the real possibility that this has been self-imposed, and that we can go beyond, or transcend, what we take to be a truth, or given. In other words, we experience 'limit' and boundary in the very attempt to explore the nature of things as they present themselves to us, but we neglect to consider that this limit might not, or might no longer, exist, or even be valid. Here we come to a central tenet in Shestov's work: in his very own words, and as the title of one of his books has it, *all things are possible*: in fact, for him, even the impossible is possible.

Final remarks

How does Shestov's thinking inform our approach to existential therapy itself?

Perhaps a striking aspect of his approach is to *question everything*, even thinking itself. In the process, he 'existentialises' his own philosophical process, laying bare his uncertainty and honesty in a way that is radical, open and courageous. He is not afraid of being repetitive or self-contradictory at times, and showing that he is actively engaged in a process of working out his thoughts as he goes along. That is, nothing is settled, whether we take that to mean being settled once and for all, or even *once* so, in the moment or instant. This serves as a better reminder for us as therapists that, if we are truly following an existential path, Shestov is a more compelling example of the philosophical approach that we need to adopt than that presented to us by the existentialists. Even Heidegger's considerable influence over existential therapy is in need of urgent re-appraisal, given the incisive comments and criticisms made towards his philosophy, not only by Shestov, but also by his colleagues, Benjamin Fondane and Rachel Bespaloff. Even though this very idea might be uncomfortable for some Heideggerians, it is surely appropriate to remind them, if they take themselves to be existen*tial* therapists, that 'all things are possible'.

References

Baugh, B. (2016). Introduction. In *Existential Mondays: Philosophical Essays by Benjamin Fondane*. Trans. and ed. B. Baugh. New York: New York Review of Books.

Camus, A. (1942/1988). *The Myth of Sisyphus*. Trans. J. O'Brien. London: Penguin.

Dostoevsky, F.M. (1864/2009). *Notes from* Underground. Trans. R. Wilks. London: Penguin.

Finkenthal, M. (2010). *Lev Shestov: Existential Philosopher and Religious Thinker*. New York: Peter Lang.

Fox-Muraton, M. (2017). Philosophy of Existence in France in the 1930s. In A. Grøn, R. Rosfort, K. B. Søderquist (eds.) *Kierkegaard's Existential Approach*. Kierkegaard Studies. Berlin: De Gruyter.

Groys, B. (2012). *Introduction to Antiphilosophy*. Trans. D. Fernbach. London: Verso.

Heidegger, M. (1927/1962). *Being and Time*. Trans. J. Robinson & E. Robinson. Oxford: Blackwell.

Husserl, E. (1900–1/2001). *Logical Investigations.* Trans. J.N. Findlay. Edited and revised D. Moran. London: Routledge.

Husserl, E. (1910–11/2002). Philosophy as a Rigorous Science. In *The New Yearbook for Phenomenology Phenomenological Philosophy*, 2: 249–95. Trans. M. Brainard.

Merleau-Ponty, M. (1945/2012). *Phenomenology of Perception.* Trans. D. Landes. London: Routledge.

Nietzsche, F. (1887/1989). *On the Genealogy of Morals.* Trans. W. Kaufmann. New York: Vintage Books.

Sartre, J.P. (1943/1958). *Being and Nothingness: An Essay on Phenomenological Ontology.* Trans. H. Barnes. London: Methuen & Co. Ltd.

Shestov, L. (1920). *All Things Are Possible.* Trans. S.S. Koteliansky. London: Martin Secker.

Shestov, L. (1923/1968). *Potestas Clavium.* Trans. B. Martin. Chicago: Ohio University Press.

Shestov, L. (1938/2016). *Athens and Jerusalem.* Second Edition. Trans. B. Martin. Ed. R. Fotiade. Chicago: Ohio University Press.

Shestov, L. (1964/1982). *Speculation and Revelation.* Trans. B. Martin. Chicago: Ohio University Press.

Valevičius, A. (1993). *Lev Shestov and His Times: Encounters with Brandes, Tolstoy, Dostoevsky, Chekhov, Ibsen, Nietzsche and Husserl.* New York: Peter Lang.

22 Questioning existential psychotherapy from some critical existential-analytic moments

Del Loewenthal

Introduction

Is existential psychotherapy too caught up with modernism? Is it possible nowadays to consider experience, meaning of life, let alone despair, without being caught up in a modernist framework? Readings of Sartre's *I am my choices* are too often taken as a standard bearer of being subject to nothing and nobody, resulting putting oneself rather than other first, privileging autonomy over heteronomy (Levinas 1991). Indeed even the title of this book *Re-visioning Existential Psychotherapy* can (with great respect to the editor) be seen to be yet another of modernism's imprisonments. Though this problem would appear to have been around before Sartre. As Wild points out: 'Totalitarian thinking accepts vision rather than language as its model. It aims to gain an all-inclusive, panoramic view of all things, including the other, in a neutral impersonal light, like the Hegelian Geist (Spirit) or the Heideggerian Being' (1991, p.15).

So are existentialists far too caught up with modernism's theoretical foundations, individualism, pseudo-science and the language of medicine for our clients' good? This chapter considers what we might need to do to readdress such fundamental concerns.

Post-existentialism (Loewenthal 2011a, 2017), which I am more recently referring to as 'Critical Existential-Analytic Psychotherapy' (www.safpac.co.uk) is an attempt to offer a space where we might still be able to think about how alienated we are through valuing existential notions such as experience and meaning, whilst questioning other aspects such as existentialism's inferred narcissism and the place it has come to take up with regard to such aspects as psychoanalysis and the political. The post-existential would also include the post-phenomenological (Cayne and Loewenthal 2011) where, for example, Merleau-Ponty's notion of being open to what emerges in the in-between (Merleau-Ponty 1962), as well as his notion of embodiment, would be given primacy over Husserlian notions of intentionality. As a result, questions such as those of mystery, an unknown and an unconscious, and the non-intentional can be re-examined. A third element to be explored is the extent to which we might consider more recent ideas – for example, those of de Saussure, Levinas, Derrida, Foucault, Lacan and Wittgenstein (see for example Loewenthal and Snell 2003) – without becoming too caught up in them.

It is hoped that by having a possible space to explore what some would now call our 'wellbeing', theoretically through post-existentialism, and methodologically through post-phenomenology, that this can provide a loose base, without concerns of any further generalisation, for a greater possibility of accepting, rather than escaping, who we are (Loewenthal 2011c, pp.1–2).

What's wrong with existentialism?

I am interested in phenomenology and existentialism for, as David Cooper has written, 'existentialism is worth revisiting at intervals for the help it may offer with themes of contemporary interest' (1990, p.vii). But what happened to phenomenology with the advent of postmodernism and what are the potential implications of this for existential psychotherapy and counselling (and psychotherapy and counselling more generally) in the twenty-first century? Are we now in a neoliberal world where '...we are all – like it or not – post-modern existentialists, searching for connections and meanings, trying to find our way' (Margulies 1999, in Frie and Orange 2009, p.120)? My book *Existential Psychotherapy and Counselling after Postmodernism* (Loewenthal 2017) is a further exploration of these questions.

To say something of where I think I might be coming from: like so many young people of the 1960s, I was influenced by the existential-analytic psychiatrist R. D. Laing (1960, 1969, 1972, 1990), and particularly his book *The Politics of Experience and The Bird of Paradise* (1967). For example: 'the really decisive moments in psychotherapy, as every patient or therapist who has experienced them knows, are unpredictable, unique, unforgettable, always unrepeatable and often indescribable' (Laing 1967, p.34).

In 1980, after having been involved in counselling more humanistically at South West London College/The University of Surrey's Human Potential Research Project/Quaesitor as well as the Henderson Hospital's Therapeutic Community, I was then personally introduced to existentialism by Emmy van Deurzen. I subsequently started my training at the Philadelphia Association in London, which Laing and others had established (and where Laing was in the process of being booted out!). It was here that I developed my interest in continental philosophy.

This chapter is less about existential psychotherapists, such as Binswanger, Boss, Frankl, van Deurzen, Spinelli, and more about revisiting some implications for existential/phenomenological therapy stemming from those such as Edmund Husserl, Martin Heidegger, Merleau-Ponty and Levinas in the light of postmodernism. Thus whilst my students over the years have found Yalom's (1980) givens of death, freedom, isolation and meaninglessness an initial useful introduction and then 'progressed' to Rollo May's (1961) six characteristics of the existing person, I frequently attempt to avoid (though as you will see not completely successfully!) such enumerations as struggling with original texts (though not exclusively) is a more 'pukka', if not essential, aspect of existentialism. In this way, this approach can be seen as one evolution of R. D. Laing's approach to existentialism, including the influence of psychoanalysis, though this is preceded by giving a primacy to the existential relationship.

Post-existentialism is for those who privilege such notions as 'meaning and experience in ways of becoming in the world with others that can be astonishing and changing' (Heaton 1990, p.2). In some ways this can be seen as an attempt to revisit for example Kierkegaard's 'becoming', Heidegger's 'in the world with others' and Laing's 'experience'. However,

> A part of existentialism's popular appeal may have been that it provided a way to think through the issues of choice and individual responsibility. But as a theory of the self, existentialism remained within Cartesianism. Its psychology tended to portray the individual as a rational, conscious actor who could understand the basis for his or her action. It remained firmly rooted in a philosophy of individual autonomy and rational choice.
>
> (Sarup 1993, pp.5–6)

The inherent ego-centric narcissism of existentialism is criticised through postmodernism, with the hope of freeing up both existentialism and ourselves. This is regarded as a vitally important opportunity before we are submerged in neoliberalism's hypermodernity (Attali 2013). The problem seems to be that a circle gets closed, which destroys the initial vibrancy and potentiality. An example of this is given by Sarup (1993):

> A few years later, during the May '68 uprising, it was felt by many students and workers that a liberated politics could only emerge from liberated interpersonal relationships, and there was an explosion of interest in Lacanian psychoanalysis – a movement which seemed to reconcile existentialism and Marxism.
>
> (p.5)

But where is Marxism in existentialism, main-stream Lacanian or any other form of psychotherapy, psychoanalysis and counselling today?

Furthermore, founding authors of existentialism, as with Rogers and Freud in humanistic psychology and psychoanalysis (who, importantly, are not dismissed in post-existentialism), have been simplified and are perhaps sometimes in danger of being sanitised. Thus existential talking therapies have been popularised through the schemas of those such as May and Yalom in the USA and Spinelli and van Deurzen in the UK. However, post-existentialism is more about the implications for our practice of being influenced by existential thinkers, whilst in keeping with these philosophers minimising working with the client through a specific existential schema. As mentioned, it might be seen as a development of R. D. Laing's more existential-analytic approach.

Existentialism thus is of less help 'with themes of contemporary interest' as it has become increasingly stuck in a 1950s/60s modernism where everything returns to the subject who is not subject to language, an unconscious, writing, the political, etc. It is as if existentialism allows for expressions of good and evil, albeit in a world which itself is influenced by the ideology of an apparent positive psychology.

I consider being invited to write this chapter as requesting me to write a story revisiting some of the previous stories I have told. In thinking about this, I do of course privilege certain notions, but hopefully this cannot be reduced to a simple schema, particularly given my criticism earlier, which could be more than just an envious attack on others' greater popularity! I have become clearer (Loewenthal 2011a) that the psychological therapies are better seen as cultural practices (Wittgenstein 1998; Heaton 2013). Freud and others first discovered practices, which they then tried to develop theories for and they and we continued to attempt to legitimise these theories using changing notions of research, which can also be seen as cultural practices.

Some underlying post-existential assumptions

However, I will try and note and then elaborate what I think are my assumptions underlying post-existentialism, which are:

- to start with practice;
- that existential ideas (and other theories) have implications rather than applications for practice;
- to wonder whether existential concerns need not be just narcissistic or ego-centric – we are all subject to language, etc., and it is better to give a primacy to heteronomy over autonomy;
- it is important in listening to be open to what comes to mind and be able to wonder how much it's one's own associations;
- to be able to stay with not knowing;
- that research is another changing cultural practice and does not necessarily have much to do with being thoughtful;
- that so long as one doesn't start with them, some psychoanalytic notions and practices can be helpful; and
- that the political/ideological is everywhere. (Rather than at very best tacking it on somewhere, it may be more appropriate to start with questioning where we are coming from politically as psychotherapists and counsellors – though we may not realise it!)

In starting with practice some implications of phenomenology may be helpful – but whose? Phenomenology was intertwined with existentialism by Heidegger, through Husserl. Levinas brought this to France influencing not only those such as Merleau-Ponty, Simone de Beauvoir and Sartre, but also a further generation including Lyotard and Derrida. There are, however, two other strands in post-existentialism, which may be less in evidence in other more recent texts on existential psychotherapy and counselling. The first is the presence of psycho-analysis. Thus the term 'existential-analytic' will be considered, beyond implying an analysis through existentialism and to include implications of some psycho-analytic notions. There is the caveat that existential must come before analytic – 'being in the world with others' must precede any psychoanalytic or other technical frame-up. However, at least early Freud can usefully be read phenomenologically. Freud, after all, did, as with Husserl, attend Brentano's lectures on descriptive psychology. Furthermore, in my own practice and in supervising others, I have often considered it helpful when the client has explored founding relationships discovering they have repressed what was too difficult to acknowledge, in what might for them have been traumatic situations. There is the question of how far should one consider here psychoanalytic concepts? In general, as with any theory, I attempt to minimise using such technical language and reification. However, this doesn't mean that an idea, of, for example, Jacques Lacan, can't helpfully come to mind when working with somebody; but, to completely adopt a Lacanian or any other school of therapy is a totalising move which potentially may greatly increase as will be argued, doing violence to the client or patient. I think it is also noteworthy that probably the most important phenomenological influence in the talking therapies is through the humanistic tradition of Carl Rogers, who was influenced by Kierkegaard amongst others. (Indeed, as a way of helping my students over the last thirty and more years start with practice, I have introduced them initially to Rogers, whilst subsequently as with all other theories, then been critical of each theory.)

The other important development for me is the place of the political in existentialism. Previously, as for those early Lacanian students, and existentialists such as Sartre, the political was very much part of practice (indeed, Sartre was also very knowledgeable about psychoanalysis in arguing against it). It would appear that our current era of late capitalism (now more frequently termed 'neo-liberalism') has been very successful in removing radicalism in general, including from existentialism. Yet, as Hannah Arendt (1958) pointed out, it's how we are in the world with others that is so vitally important. Our alienation is now such that it seems we can't even see the potential for self-interest in the common good.

I have been very influenced by Levinas, who was very influenced by Heidegger but was also critical of him, arguing that the ethical must precede the ontological – our responsibility to put the other first before ourselves. So whilst I suggested previously that existentialism should come before any psychoanalysis, if 'being' of 'being in the world with others' is given a primacy, it too quickly becomes 'my being'. More recently, I have been interested in how one might operationalise this, not just in terms of our responsibility for the client's responsibility but our responsibility socially, economically and ideologically for others' responsibilities in these spheres. (I was at these times tempted to return to calling all this 'existentialism'.) In so doing, I had hoped there would be a greater chance the term existentialism could continue to astonish and change (Heaton 1990) rather than being imprisoned and contorted by modernism.

Critical existential-analytic (post-existential) psychotherapy after postmodernism

It would appear that we are now in an era beyond postmodernism, which some would call 'hyper-modern' (Attali 2013; Charles and Lipovetsky 2006). Here, there is an even deeper faith than in modernism in our ability to understand, control and manipulate every aspect of human experience. Such thinking will return us to ego-centrism, whereas through post-existentialism I am attempting to create a space where after postmodern ideas we can lessen our desire to understand, control and manipulate ours and others' experiences, but instead be open to potential existential registers that would otherwise be muted if not strangled.

As I presented (Loewenthal 2011b), from such a new existential/post-existential perspective, we might ask questions such as the following about all psychological therapies:

- Is psychotherapy first and foremost a practice?
- Are theories more attempts to explain practice?
- Do changes in this practice have more to do with changes in our culture that lead us to be more interested in different theories?
- Is research another cultural practice which changes to legitimise the changing dominant culture?
- What place has psychoanalysis in all this?
- Is post-existentialism just attempting to replace one theory with another or is it as my colleague Richard House has kindly said (in Loewenthal 2011a), 'a reformulation of existentialist ideas within therapeutic practice which prepares the ground for the critical deconstruction of these very same foundations'?
- To what extent has our attachment to a particular theory to do with inadequacies in our own foundations and to what extent does any change threaten our very foundations?
- Or, are all these different psychotherapeutic notions really to keep the psychotherapist occupied while something else therapeutically useful can happen?

However, I am taking the opportunity of writing this chapter to re-examine these questions from a critical existential-analytic (post-existential) psychotherapy and counselling moment, as shown in see Table 22.1.

Theoretical foundations

To what extent, if any, can counselling and psychotherapy be said to have theoretical foundations? There is an argument that those such as Freud and Melanie Klein were following a tradition that discovered practices that appeared to be efficient and subsequently attempted to create theories to explain it. We might therefore see the various different schools of existential counselling and psychotherapy more as cultural practices and the various theories, if not to be dogma, may have implications but not, as they are not foundational, applications. This means we

Table 22.1   Some possible Yes and Nos of existentialism and post-existentialism

	Existentialism	*Post-existentialism*
Theoretical foundations	Y?	N?
Psychology	Y?	N?
Research	Y?	N?
Have goals	Y?	N?
Follow a method	Y?	N?
External evaluation criteria	Y?	N?
Diagnosis & Treatment	Y?	N?
Clients know what they need	Y?	N?
Primacy given to autonomy	Y?	N?
Wellbeing and a therapeutic ethos	Y?	N?

cannot, when in seeing a client, start by applying a theory though one may come to mind. Here, phenomenology, when considered as what emerges between therapist and client, may be helpful.

Psychology

Unless as a therapist one's practice is either behavioural or cognitive behavioural, the current discipline of psychology (particularly as taught in predominantly Anglo-Saxon countries) is of little use for counsellors or psychotherapists. Whilst psychology's founding fathers had ideas which could be helpful to today's practitioners, they are not currently prevalent. Thus, for example, whilst Wilhelm Wundt (1904/1874) stressed the importance of marrying the empirical with the historical and cultural, this was not taken up particularly by the Anglo-Saxon world.

Research

The nature of therapeutic knowledge itself is more tacit than explicit, dependent also more on timing and judgement rather than rationality. The danger is that we are too often being sold a corrupt science (Loewenthal 2020; Dalal 2018). Furthermore, even when science is not corrupt, Plato suggested we always needed to be reminded through his definition of *therapeia* that whilst science and technology are important, they are secondary to the resources of the human soul (Cushman 2001). Hence, it is argued that existential and other more intersubjective modalities of psychotherapy and counselling have their own approach to research involving a process of clinical supervision and sometimes presenting cases. Having written and edited several books on psychotherapeutic research and being the past Founding Chair of one of the first national psychotherapy research committees, I came to the conclusion that my own therapeutic practice has not been influenced by current notions of empirical research. The research projects students carry out may be of benefit to the individual student but are increasingly of far less benefit to anyone else.

Have goals

There seems to be an increasing interest in establishing goals, not just for behavioural therapy, but this is not always possible in the psychological therapies. If one breaks one's wrist it can be clear to both patient and physician as to the goal of having full use of one's wrist back. However, if one breaks one's heart how clear is the patient's desire? Unlike the physician, it is not for the counsellor or psychotherapist to say what the client's desire should be. The danger is that unhelpful goals are established at the start of therapy in order that research can be carried out in the vain attempt to show the results as empirically validated.

Follow a method

There is an argument that if we want truth we cannot use a method (Gadamer 2013). It is, however, expensive to train counsellors and psychotherapists so that they can usefully stay with not knowing, including not knowing what to say. *It is far easier and less expensive to train technicians.* Again, here we can turn to the Greeks, for example, with Aristotle's notion of practice wisdom which was not a set of rules but considered an art of living wisely with others. However, there are more recent concerns from elsewhere about therapy trainings' blind adherence to a particular method and theory 'thinking relationally, psychoanalysts are beginning to contemplate its very nature as a discourse, its status as a "theory"' (Aron and Harris 2005 in Loewenthal 2014).

External evaluation criteria

The argument here is that evaluation criteria *emerge from the therapy itself* in a similar way that our legal system, again evolved from the Greeks, looks to determine the criteria as to whether someone is guilty or innocent, not from external criteria but emerging from each presenting situation itself. The same should be true of therapy. It is the natural; it is what comes out of itself. The imposition of external criteria can too often be too violent. Do we really need external criteria?

Diagnosis and treatment

There is not adequate knowledge available that would allow for diagnosis and treatment. Even if we were to assume that such categorisations as the DSM could be helpful, there is no body of therapeutic knowledge that can be specifically employed to treat the diagnosis. Doesn't the same hold true for different counselling and psychotherapy schools' own attempts at diagnosis?

Clients know what they need

This also links to not having goals. The danger is that we are in an era of customer rather than human relations; often our clients do not know what they need and it can be that what they think they need is more part of the problem than the solution. This is not to say that the therapist knows what the client needs but rather that it is possible for it to emerge.

Primacy given to autonomy

Whilst some clients may need to develop their autonomy, therapists, including existential therapists, may focus on this to the detriment of heteronomy. The argument is that we have a responsibility for our clients' responsibility to others and the communities they are part of. The danger is that we will promote individualism (and get too caught up in unifying notions of self) at the expense of others and our society in general.

Well being and a therapeutic ethos

To what extent can therapists help prevent future unhappiness and to what extent is this possibility severely limited if they are too caught up in the dominant discourse? It has been attributed to Ricoeur (1970) that we should be in a position to interpret the concealed political interests not only by those in the family and subculture but more generally by morals imposed by others who have no intention of keeping them themselves and by the very nature of different forms of capitalism. Our society appears to increasingly endorse a need for counsellors and psychotherapists so long as they are increasingly regulated. Yet there is a lack of provision, for example for community therapy let alone giving serious attention to developing a preventative therapeutic ethos (House and Loewenthal 2009). What if we were to provide existential counsellors and therapists with an *education* and not just a training? Shouldn't we then have a greater sense of how economic social forces, for example through different taxation and austerity policies, have an effect on emotional distress? Indeed, as Webber (2018, p.202) concludes: 'Attention to this social dimension of existentialism could therefore inform the procedures of psychotherapy as well as illuminating the causes of distress and suggesting ways of overcoming it.'

Whilst there are interconnections regarding the ten explorations in this chapter, the hope is that if just one of them is seen to have some credence this may enhance the thoughtful existential practitioner. (Indeed, don't questions such as these from a post-existential/critical existential-analytic psychotherapy and counselling challenge what is seen as questionable assumptions underlying too much of current counselling and psychotherapy?) Otherwise existential (and other psychological therapists) will be too caught up with theoretical foundations, individualism, pseudo-science and the language of medicine for our clients' good. For to return to the argument against vision (which can lead more to totalitarianism) in favour of language 'where there is always room for the diversity of dialogue, and further growth through the dynamics of question and answer' (Wild 1991, p.16) can't existential psychotherapy be too easily wrongly caught up with the following:

> To be free is the same as to be rational, and to be rational is to give oneself over to the whole system that is developing in world history. Since the essential self is also rational the development of this system will coincide with the interests of the self. All otherness will be absorbed in this total system of harmony and order.
>
> (Wild 1991, p.15)

The danger is existential psychotherapists and their clients can then become totalisers who 'seek power and control [and] are satisfied with themselves and the systems they can organise around themselves as they already are' (Wild 1991, p.17).

How can we instead consider, for example, '... not becoming social by first becoming systematic [but becoming] ... systematically and orderly in our thinking by first freely making a choice for generosity and communication' (Wild 1991, p.14)?

Conclusion

I have argued that one answer is to consider that a therapeutic exploration of existential concerns is not necessarily helped when it is imprisoned in any one theory, let alone a narcissistic ego-centric formulaic ideology at best suited to a time just after World War II. Instead, consideration is given to starting with practice, with some help from phenomenology, if not post-phenomenology. Furthermore, the psychological therapies might be better seen as cultural practices where our concerns about life and death can be helped by considering the implications, but not applications, of various (and not necessarily one of the) existential philosophers and other thinkers. Perhaps thoughtful practice cannot sufficiently occur if there is a specific method, map or particular technique employed. Instead, would it not be better if the existential therapist needs not only to have such capacities as being able to stay open to what emerges in practice; but also, is able not to have a dependency on a particular theory? In contrast to Levinas, whom I am in danger here of relying on too much, it may be important for the therapist to have had their own personal exploration of what has been termed 'the hermeneutics of suspicion' (Ricoeur 1970). Here, critical existential-analytic therapists, in order to be able to explore existential concerns, may also have considered: their own potential sexualities and violence (through Freud et al.); their own ideological ensnarements (through Marx et al.); and their own values and moralities (through Nietzsche et al.). Might then we get nearer to hearing and responding to that which we think we might have, but probably never will have, heard?

References

Arendt, H. (1958) *The Human Condition*. Chicago, IL: Chicago University Press.

Aron, L. and Harris, A. (2005) *Relational Psychoanalysis v.2: Innovation and Expansion*. Hillsdale, NJ: The Analytic Press.

Attali, J. (2013) *Histoire de la Modernité: comment l'humanité pense son avenir*. Paris: Editions Robert Laffont.

Cayne, J. and Loewenthal, D. (2011) Post-Phenomenology and the between as unknown in Loewenthal, D *Post-Existentialism and the Psychological Therapies: Towards a Therapy without Foundations*. London: Karnac.

Charles, S. and Lipovetsky, G. (2006) *Hypermodern Times*. Cambridge: Polity Press.

Cooper, D. E. (1990) *Existentialism: A Reconstruction*. Oxford: Blackwell Publishing.

Cushman, R. (2001) *Therapeia: Plato's Conception of Philosophy* (new ed.). Piscataway, NJ: Transaction.

Dalal, F. (2018) *CBT The Cognitive Behavioural Tsunami*. Hove: Routledge.

Frie, R. and D. Orange (2009) (Eds). *Beyond Postmodernism: New Dimensions in Clinical Theory and Practice*. New York: Routledge.

Gadamer, H-G. (2013) *Truth and Method*. London: Bloomsbury Academic.

Heaton, J. (1990) 'What is Existential Analysis?', *Journal of the Society for Existential Analysis*, 1.

Heaton, J. (2013) *The Talking Cure: Wittgenstein on Language as Bewitchment and Clarity*. Basingstoke: Palgrave Macmillan.

House, R. and Loewenthal, D. (2009) *Childhood, Well-Being and a Therapeutic Ethos*. London: Karnac.

Laing, R. D. (1960) *The Divided Self: An Existential Study in Sanity and Madness*. Harmondsworth: Penguin.

Laing, R. D. (1967) *The Politics of Experience and The Bird of Paradise*. London: Tavistock Publications.

Laing, R. D. (1969) *Self and Others* (2nd edition). London: Routledge.

Laing, R. D. (1972) *Knots*. London: Penguin.

Laing, R. D. (1990) *Sanity, Madness and the Family: Families of Schizophrenic.s* London: Penguin.

Levinas, E. (1991) *Totality and Infinity: An Essay on Exteriority* (Trans. A. Lingis). Dordrecht: Kluwer Academic Publishers.

Loewenthal, D. and Snell, R. (2003) *Post-Modernism for Psychotherapists: A Critical Reader*. Hove and New York: Brunner Routledge.

Loewenthal, D. (2011a) *Post-Existentialism and the Psychological Therapies: Towards a Therapy without Foundations*. London: Karnac.

Loewenthal, D. (2011b) *Psychotherapy without Foundations?* Saturday 29 October, Anna Freud Centre, London.

Loewenthal, D (2011c) 'On the very idea of existentialism' in Loewenthal, D. *Post-Existentialism and the Psychological Therapies: Towards a Therapy without Foundations*. London: Karnac.

Loewenthal, D. (2014) 'Relational ethics: from existentialism to post-existentialism' in Loewenthal, D. and Samuels, A. *Relational Psychotherapy, Psychoanalysis and Counselling*. Hove: Routledge.

Loewenthal, D. (2017) *Existential Psychotherapy and Counselling after Postmodernism: The selected works of Del Loewenthal*. Hove: Routledge World Library of Mental Health.

Loewenthal, D. (2020) 'NICE work if you can get it: Evidence and research in the psychological therapies as cultural, politically influenced practices' in Shamdasani, S. and Loewenthal, D. *Towards Transcultural Histories of Psychotherapies*. Abingdon: Routledge.

Margulies, A. (1999) 'The end of analysis? Or, our postmodern existential situation. A review essay on Ritual and spontaneity in the psychoanalytic process: A dialectical-constructivist view by Irwin Z. Hoffman', *Contemporary Psychoanalysis*, 35, 699–712.

May, R. (1961) *Existential Psychology*. New York: Random House.

Merleau-Ponty, M. (1962) *The Phenomenology of Perception*. London: Routledge.

Ricouer, P. (1970) *Freud and Philosophy: An Essay on Interpretation* (Trans. D. Savage). New Haven, CT: Yale University Press.

Sarup, M. (1993). *An Introductory Guide to Post-Structuralism and Postmodernism*. London.

Webber, J. (2018) *Rethinking Existentialism*. Oxford: Oxford University Press.

Wild, J. (1991) 'Introduction' in Levinas, E. *Totality and Infinity: An Essay on Exteriority* (Trans. A. Lingis). Dordrecht: Kluwer Academic Publishers, pp. 11–20.

Wittgenstein, L. (1998) *Culture and Value* (2nd edition) (Trans. P. Winch) G.H. von Right, in collaboration with Heikki Nyman, revised by Alios Pichler (Eds). Oxford: Blackwell.

Wundt, W. (1904/1874) *Principles of Physiological Psychology* (Trans. E.B. Tichener). London: Allen.

Yalom, I. (1980) *Existential Psychotherapy*. New York: Basic Books.

Part IV
The clinic and the everyday

23 The psychotherapeutic use of psychedelics

Reflections, critique and recommendations

Niklas Serning and Nina Lyon

A new beginning

Psychedelics are newly respectable. Evidence suggests that a variety of ills, from anxiety and depression to addictions and PTSD, respond to them in a way hitherto unseen within psychiatry. The researchers involved have been careful to clean up the reputation of a class of drugs that, despite a wealth of promising evidence for their therapeutic effects in the 1960s and 70s, met with a moral panic that stigmatised them for decades after.

It probably didn't help that the psychedelic community has a historic disposition towards hyperbole: blown minds, quantum leaps and paradigm shifts. Enthusiasts are prone to metaphysical speculation: I dropped a tab of acid and realised that the universe was, in fact, composed of discrete bits of matter, said nobody ever. Instead, the psychonaut meets God, or at least the noetic dissolution of their ego.

Current researchers, in a drive to clean up previous Learyesque associations, are more circumspect, but the claims remain big. There is a growing and convincing body of data to support the use of high-dose psilocybin to treat anxiety and depression. The profound and often psychologically challenging psychedelic experiences of ego loss, or the philosophical reappraisal of pre-existing beliefs and worldviews, are considered key therapeutic features rather than problematic side-effects.

Another interesting facet of the current research output is that the explanatory mechanisms offered by its authors – typically neuroscientists and psychiatrists – are often psychological, even psychotherapeutic, in character. Even as neuroimaging edges towards mapping what we once called the ego (Lebedev et al, 2015), the eliminative materialism some predicted to kill off folk-psychological understanding of the mind (Churchland, 1981) is in scant evidence.

Theories offered for the efficacy of psilocybin in recent studies include the notion of connection: the psychedelic experience imposes a sense of profound hyperconnection to the world at large, as well as encouraging the patient to engage with past experiences that may have previously fed patterns of belief and behaviour that saw them disconnect from other people and their environment (Watts et al, 2017). Some of the change takes place in the domain of beliefs we have, whether about ourselves or the world around us. A study of the impact of lifetime psychedelic use on social and political beliefs showed that the experience of ego-dissolution predicted increases in openness, nature relatedness and liberalism, and a decrease in authoritarianism (Nour et al, 2017).

Perhaps the most notable of the recent psilocybin research publications was the Johns Hopkins study on the effects of high-dose psilocybin for depression and anxiety in cancer patients, in which 80% experienced significant improvements in well-being and life satisfaction (Griffiths et al, 2016). The factor during the psilocybin session day that best predicted improvement was the so-called mystical experience (Griffiths et al, 2016), and a variety of mystical experience scales exist for use in psychedelic research (Griffiths et al, 2016), essentially seeking to describe and quantify the classic high-dose mysticism described in the 'trip reports' shared by the lay psychedelic community (Erowid.org, 2019). The MEQ30 incorporates the subjective perception of mystical experience, positive mood, transcendence of time and space and ineffability – the degree to which participants experience the dissolution of their sense of self, and the ensuing perception of connectedness to a beyond-material world, seems not only to predict but explain their subsequent well-being in otherwise challenging circumstances (Griffiths et al, 2016). The correlation between 'mystical' or 'peak' experience and subsequent subjective well-being is seen across the various research groups and patient populations on both sides of the Atlantic; some research groups use slightly different scales and terminology, but the takeaway is the same. When the self is in distress, temporarily dismantling it seems to be extremely helpful. Given the tendency within conventional psychotherapy and contemporary mental health discourse to focus on the self, there may be much to learn from this.

Therapeutic professionals schooled in predominantly narrative or qualitative approaches to understanding the mind might baulk at the notion that Meaningful Existence (Cohen et al, 1995); Death Acceptance (Reker, 1992); Death Transcendence (VandeCreek, 1999); Purpose in Life (McIntosh, 1999); and Coherence in one's own logically integrated worldview (Reker, 1992) are quantifiable metrics, but it is hard to argue with the stories some of the Johns Hopkins patients, along with those at other therapeutic psilocybin study centres, tell in a series of short videos about their experience, and indeed to remain unmoved by them (Heffter.org, 2019). Psilocybin evidently worked to help them make sense of the ultimate existential concern.

Where does this leave psychotherapy? If high-dose psilocybin can effect such a profound change on patients facing terminal cancer, leaving them with an account of their existence both on earth and beyond that allays their fear and discomfort, one might argue that it spells the end, or the beginning of one – perhaps psilocybin might end up being better at psychotherapy than any therapist ever will. Both Johns Hopkins and Imperial, while 'checking in' with patients to see how they are feeling during intermittent physiological monitoring, are non-directive during psilocybin sessions, encouraging patients to let go and be open to their experiences, even where it becomes psychologically challenging (Griffiths et al,

2016; Carhart-Harris et al, 2016). While discussion takes place before and after the session, the lasting changes seen appear to arise from the experience itself.

However, in response to critiques suggesting that the timescale of beneficial effect in the treatment-resistant depression studies – 6–8 weeks – might entail placebo responses (e.g. Hendrie and Pickles, 2016), the Imperial team acknowledged that the psychological preparation and support provided before, during and after the psilocybin session needed to be considered in future randomised controlled trials (Carhart-Harris et al, 2017). The first RCT commenced in January 2019. Until the results become available, the possibility remains that access to a team of exceptionally able and experienced clinicians may have an impact in its own right. If, as is expected, the evidence for psilocybin's therapeutic effects is convincing, the question of best psychological practice in preparing for, managing and integrating sessions will be of continuing importance (Carhart-Harris et al, 2017).

Furthermore, observers of the unregulated wild west of psychedelic therapy – the underground shamanic-style ceremonies where psilocybin mushrooms, ayahuasca or other psychoactive concoctions are consumed in groups with spiritual and therapeutic intentions – are beginning to query the wisdom of believing that the 'medicine' can safely do all the work (Moran, 2019).

Integration is the term used within the psychedelic community for the processing and sense-making that is sometimes needed after an impactful psychedelic experience. It can be done solo, and often is, but the concern is that the rise in popularity for psychedelic 'solutions' to distress might encourage individuals who are not necessarily equipped to negotiate the impact of a challenging experience, or a profound change in their understanding of the world, to go ahead with it anyway.

The epistemological rethinks that often take place after a psychedelic experience are compatible with many of the tenets of existential psychotherapy. In addition, the metaphysical inclinations of the psychedelic experience, in and out of the clinic, tend to leave people with a profound sense of the phenomenal nature of experience. There is nothing like altering one's mind to understand its mediating power over reality.

As psychedelics become clinically mainstreamed – many in the field predict that within 5–10 years, psilocybin will be legal in a licensed clinical setting – there is the prospect of their psychotherapeutic use broadening beyond end of life anxiety and treatment resistant depression.

Therapists in the existential-phenomenological tradition should be well-equipped for this. While the authors of this chapter are sceptical of labels and best-modality claims, working with the phenomenal experiences of the client, and taking an expansive, open and philosophical view of those experiences, are considered best practice in the current research. There may be opportunity, as changes in the law and appropriate trainings allow, to work within psychedelic-assisted psychotherapy. As the stigma around psychedelic use diminishes, therapists may also see more clients seeking to integrate prior psychedelic experiences. This has certainly been the case in Niklas' recent practice. The Multidisciplinary Association for

Psychedelic Studies hosts a public registry of therapists experienced with integration for this purpose.

While psilocybin, in particular, is one of the safest psychoactive substances available, it remains illegal. It is also by no means certain that clients using psychedelics will always be doing so wisely. The 1960s mantra of 'set and setting' – ensuring that one is in a resilient mindset and a physically and emotionally safe environment before taking psychedelics – is a useful guide. But individuals' judgement can be biased by their sense of distress and urgency, seeking to fix it now, or by social factors: there are, for example, some factions of the lay psychedelic community inclined towards a Panglossian view of psychedelics as panacea in which the answer is always more. This means that therapists need to stay circumspect, on the one hand staying open to their client's phenomenal experience while also being prepared to advise caution when faced with a situation in which the continuation of psychedelic 'self-therapy' might present further risks for that client.

The vast majority of Niklas' clients' use of psychedelics has been beneficial. Some of them microdose on a weekly basis in order not to get stuck in patterns of thought that are unhelpful and instead direct their energies to more helpful patterns; others do yearly ceremonies spring-cleaning their lives. The drugs are an assistance to well led lives, tools rather than crutches for their being in the world. The therapeutic component involves an in-depth exploration of the experience, and subsequent linking of the experience into their lives and surrounding systems. Still, there are pitfalls, and two brief case studies might help illustrate them.

An elusive panacea

Edward had tried everything – from the standard NHS treatments of CBT and counselling, to going further via EMDR and psychodynamic therapies, and ending up in the domains of the psychospiritual and psychedelic. He tried CBT, hypnotherapy, EFT, rebirthing, trauma-focused body psychotherapy, transpersonal therapy. He attended a series of ayahuasca ceremonies which he hoped would bring him breakthrough, and was disappointed to not find the relief that he had been expecting. He nonetheless felt that important unconscious transformations must have taken place, even if he was not yet consciously aware of them. His aim was to cut to the heart of his pain, find that nugget of trauma at the core of him that, once discovered and dealt with, would liberate him and allow him to live a good life. He was shy and timid, with low drive, and believed this to be a result of trauma due to early parental separation. This was how he had always been.

His was a genuinely impressive and moving account of hard work at finding a better way to live. However, I could not escape the feeling that he was looking for a singular trauma to explain his problems. As his account unravelled, I became increasingly convinced that this was mistaken. The nugget he was aiming for, whether it was an insecure core attachment, conditional love or maladaptive core belief, didn't exist. Personality and social systems don't work like that: they are too complex and messy.

Even if all his woes stemmed from his father, why would this knowledge automatically sort his life out? Finally, the plethora of therapies, psychedelic substances and gurus he had worked through indicated that the tools he was deploying did little to help.

Psychedelics can tweak and reset to a degree, but the hardware and patterns that are us are resistant to magic. Their reset is a soft reset, not a formatting of the hard drive. They give us freedom to re-choose, but within the limits of our selves and our world.

Maybe Edward could have changed into an extraverted, jovial and happy man, but after twenty years of trying, I doubted it. Much to his disappointment, I tried to focus on how it would be to be as he was, what options he still had within the scope of his low drive and shyness. Did I give up on Edward? I'd rather say that I gave up on the imaginary Edward and worked with the real Edward that was sitting in my room. He never came back, and I will always hope that I was wrong, and that perhaps for him, there was this one thing that could be found, understood and worked through in order to bring radical change. Failing that, and more likely in my view, I hope that he would learn to accept his situation and being, and learn to choose ways to enjoy life within these confines.

Challenging a challenging experience

Veronica had an exciting, roller coaster life – a nomadic, troubled and joyous journey from partners and places, occupations and identities. Her experience with LSD was difficult, with a vivid experience of being raped by her father, and she contacted me to make sense of her trip. Though her father was stern and often difficult, she had no indication apart from her trip that he had ever been sexually inappropriate with her.

We chose to work with her LSD trip as an analogy: it linked up with how she saw figures of authority, the powers that be, and how they continually beset and defiled nomads like her. Moving further into the trip, there was an understanding of the tension between the conservative and the radical, an ability to resonate with the reasons for people being oppressive, even an appreciation and acceptance for that way of life. The metaphors delivered to us by psychedelics, as with dreams, are seldom simplistic, and we must not take them at face value – but we can learn from them.

It is also notable that Veronica, like many of my psychedelic clients, was far more focused on the here and now than the there and then. The metaphors drew upon imagery from her past personal history as well as mythology and contemporary media, but the message concerned current ways of being in the world. As we began to consider her experience in terms of what it had to say to her, Veronica concluded that she was coming to terms with contemporary authority structures rather than processing childhood trauma.

Appearance and reality

How is it best to respond when a client like Veronica reports a traumatic experience arising during psychedelic use? Writing on trauma arising in ayahuasca ceremonies, psychedelic integration therapist Kerry Moran quotes Gabor Maté in a 2017 Psychedelic Science conference workshop: 'There's no such thing as a bad trip on ayahuasca,' Maté believes. 'People say, "I felt fear, terror, rage, confusion such as I never felt before." "Yes, you have," I say. "You just don't recall it"' (Moran, 2019).

This is, at least on the surface – we do not have a full transcript of the workshop in question – a strong statement in favour of taking psychedelically-evoked experiences to be real. Moran goes on to discuss how trauma from very early childhood might not be consciously accessible but could arise as part of a 'difficult ayahuasca experience.' Maté states elsewhere that 'Ayahuasca can evoke direct but long-suppressed memories of trauma. It can also trigger emotional states and visions of horror that are not direct recollections, but emotional imprints of trauma' (Maté, 2014).

While there is abundant anecdotal evidence from individuals who have successfully used ayahuasca ceremonies to recover from various forms of trauma they have conscious experience of, it seems risky at best to treat a psychedelic experience as reflecting something historically real. Under the influence of psychedelics, individuals have on occasion believed that they can fly, but it doesn't make it sensible to encourage them to follow through on that belief. There may be a grain, or more, of truth in a psychedelic vision, but it might equally be just that: a vision. We tend to treat dreams as metaphors: they sometimes have something useful to tell us, but that does not mean that the substance of the dream correlates to an external reality.

Carhart-Harris et al mention the case of one patient in an early study who:

> reported a vision of his father attempting to physically harm him when he was child, something he claimed not to have been previously conscious of. This patient subsequently felt confused about the authenticity of this putative memory and this was associated with a transient worsening of symptoms.

The Imperial team 'felt it best practice not to make a judgement on the veridicality of this alleged memory but open and compassionate listening was maintained and the patient subsequently improved' (Carhart-Harris et al, 2017).

The cautious approach espoused in clinical psychedelic research is a useful guide for integration with clients who have taken psychedelics outside of a clinical setting. The term 'psychedelic' was coined from the ancient Greek *psyche-deloun*, mind-revealing: we may reveal the contents of our mind, but we should be careful not to confuse its contents with reality. Staying open to the client's experience while maintaining a level of awareness regarding its phenomenal quality is key in allowing them to process it safely.

Wiping our ideas clean puts us in a position of possibility, and with that comes a degree of vulnerability. If psychedelics are to become a feature within psychotherapy, either as legalised psychedelic-assisted psychotherapy or in the form of integration sessions, it is of utmost importance that the therapist offers a space in which the client can reappraise their experiences and ideas free of ideological and metaphysical bias. Any therapeutic modality runs the risk of imposing its theoretical prejudices onto those experiences: if we believe that all negative emotions arise from trauma, we may impose a trauma narrative where it wasn't merited. We should remain self-aware about our own intellectual and ideological biases.

Just as psychotherapeutic modalities have the potential to lapse into dogma, so do some of the stories and norms in some ceremonial circles. Opening one's mind and heart, a common psychedelic ceremony maxim, is generally sound life advice; when we see all of our problems stemming from not doing so adequately, and are encouraged to 'go deeper' into psychedelic rumination on our failure in that domain when the underlying issues might be unrelated, and perhaps even prone to be worsened from ongoing use of psychoactive substances, it ceases to be useful.

Ceremonies can, however, be highly effective and valuable as a form of mutual support. Their reported success is enough that the Imperial research group is currently undertaking a survey in order to better understand their therapeutic potential. When we take psychedelics in a spiritual space, the experience is informed by the spiritual or religious tenets of that space. Those might work very well for everyone, or they might work for some and not others, but there is often a shared story of the world that shapes the experience itself and subsequent processing of it. Love and light is pretty benign in the grand scheme of things, but would-be shamans abound. The best shamans hold space, creating a warm and positive atmosphere for people undergoing psychologically challenging experiences. Others might seek to impose their own reality onto others, in good faith or otherwise.

Moving on

Shamans aside, existential phenomenological therapy may turn out to be a very good fit for psychedelic integration. The focus on the subjectively mediated experience of reality is highlighted by psychedelics, and is central to phenomenology. An open and broad take on reality and paradigms of meaning-making within it is core to existential thought. We can leverage the tenets of phenomenological enquiry and existential sensibilities when integrating the psychedelic experience.

As our minds settle after a ceremony or trip, we have a moment of space, a moment of increased freedom to choose how we want to be within the confines of facticity. Helpful aspects of ourselves come in more clear contrast with less helpful ones, love and friendship stand out next to constructs of fear and disconnection, and we have a degree of choice as to where we want to direct our endeavours. The key questions of what we saw, what we learned from it and how we intend to put that into practice can be considered. Our framing of existence can be subtly tweaked, especially when we realise the degree to which our framing of experience substantially determines experience itself. Drawing on extant myth as well as the individual myth created by the trip, and taking myth as metaphor rather than concrete reality, we can help turn philosophical understanding gained in the psychedelic experience into concrete life changes, and lives well led.

References

Carhart-Harris, R. et al. (2016). *Psilocybin with psychological support for treatment-resistant depression: an open-label feasibility study*. The Lancet Psychiatry, Vol. 3, No. 7, pp. 619–627.

Carhart-Harris, R. et al. (2017). *Psilocybin with psychological support for treatment-resistant depression: six-month follow-up*. Psychopharmacology, Vol. 235, No. 2, pp. 399–408.

Churchland, P.M. (1981). *Eliminative materialism and the propositional attitudes*. The Journal of Philosophy, Vol. 78, No. 2., pp. 67–90.

Cohen, S.R. et al. (1995). *The McGill Quality of Life Questionnaire: A measure of quality of life appropriate for people with advanced disease. A preliminary study of validity and acceptability*. Palliative Medicine, Vol. 9, pp. 207–219.

Erowid.org.   (2019).   https://erowid.org/experiences/subs/exp_Mushrooms.shtml# Mystical_Experiences. (Accessed 22 September 2019).

Griffiths, R. et al. (2016). *Psilocybin produces substantial and sustained decreases in depression and anxiety in patients with life-threatening cancer: A randomized double-blind trial*. Journal of Psychopharmacology, Vol. 30, No. 12, pp. 1181–1197.

Heffter.org. (2019). https://heffter.org/media. (Accessed 22 September 2019).

Hendrie, C., Pickles, A. (2016). *Psilocybin: panacea or placebo?*. The Lancet Psychiatry, Vol. 3, No. 9, pp. 805–806.

Lebedev, A.V. et al. (2015). *Finding the self by losing the self: Neural correlates of ego-dissolution under psilocybin*. Human Brain Mapping, Vol. 36, No. 8, pp. 3137–3153.

Maté, G. (2014). 'Postscript—Psychedelics in Unlocking the Unconscious: From Cancer to Addiction'. In: Labate, B.C., Cavnar, C., eds. *The Therapeutic Use of Ayahuasca*. pp. 217–224. Heidelberg: Springer.

McIntosh, D.N. (1999). 'Purpose in Life Test'. In: Hill, P.C., Hood, R.W., eds. *Measures of Religiosity*. pp. 503–508. Birmingham: Religious Education Press.

Moran, K. (2019). *We need to talk about when people feel worse after ayahuasca*. Available at https://kahpi.net/after-ayahuasca-trauma-integration/

Nour, M.M. et al. (2017). *Psychedelics, personality and political perspectives*. Journal of Psychoactive Drugs, Vol. 49, No. 3, pp. 182–191.

Reker, G.T. (1992). *The Life Attitude Profile-Revised (LAP-R)*. Peterborough: Student Psychologists Press.

VandeCreek L. (1999). 'The Death Transcendence Scale'. In: Hill, P.C., Hood, R.W., eds. *Measures of Religiosity*. pp. 442–445. Birmingham: Religious Education Press.

Watts, R. et al. (2017). *Patients' accounts of increased "connectedness" and "acceptance" after psilocybin for treatment-resistant depression*. Journal of Humanistic Psychology, Vol. 57, No. 5, pp. 520–564.

24 Understanding Francisco's schizophrenia

A humanistic phenomenological research method

Juliana Pita and Virgínia Moreira

Introduction

The aim of the present chapter is to discuss Francisco's case by using the *humanistic phenomenological method* to research his lived world (*Lebenswelt*) of schizophrenia. This term was proposed by Tatossian (1979/2006) to indicate the functioning or an existential style that characterizes someone who has been diagnosed with schizophrenia, in addition to the diagnosis itself.

Francisco was a patient at the psychiatric day hospital in the city of Fortaleza, Brazil. It was difficult to approach him because he was always participating in group therapy activities and he was not interested in talking, so we first spoke to his mother, Madalena, and observed him from a distance.

While observing Francisco during the activities at the day hospital we sought to approach him, since "there is not a word, a human gesture, even if distracted or habitual that does not have a meaning" (Merleau-Ponty, 1945/2006b, p. 170). Conversing with his mother we sought to understand what she was experiencing in her relationship with Francisco in order to have a first sense of the lived world of his schizophrenia. The purpose of talking to Madalena was not only to understand how she comprehends her own world, but rather to get to know Francisco at the intersection of their lived worlds.

Understanding the lived world occurs ambiguously, both as a private and singular world, but at the same time as a collective experience of the world: my world is always our world (Tatossian, 1996/2012). Hence, it was important to understand the lived world (*Lebenswelt*) of one who lives with Francisco on a daily basis, in this case his mother Madalena, to be able to reach his schizophrenia.

Methodology

Our phenomenological research deals above all with "the meaning of experience" (Amatuzzi, 1996, p. 5), characterized as the "study of the living or immediate pre-reflective experience, aiming to describe its meaning" (p. 5) and "to understand the person in their totality" (Giorgi, 2012, p. 3).

Among the different models, we chose the critical phenomenological method inspired by Merleau-Ponty's phenomenology of ambiguity (Moreira, 2004, 2009), believing that this phenomenological approach provides the description and an understanding of the meaning of Francisco's schizophrenic experience in his lived world (*Lebenswelt*), through the way he relates to his family and to other people who accompany him, "since we are this bond of relationships" (Merleau-Ponty, 1945/ 2006b, p. 18).

As it is not possible to offer help to a disturbed person through any theory, we understand that this is also not possible in psychopathology research, which seeks to understand the lived experience. Thus, this phenomenological case study was based on the following research instruments: 1) clinical encounters with the research participants: Francisco and Madalena; 2) descriptive reports of the clinical encounters; 3) observations of Francisco during the day hospital visits over the course of six months.

The clinical encounter is understood as a meeting that occurs in the intertwining of the lived world (*Lebenswelt*) of participants, as an interlacing between two people (researcher and Francisco, researcher and Madalena), who, when they meet, will always partake in their intersubjective experiences. It is an experience of clinical facilitation that allows the lived experiences in the relationship to emerge.

Because it is an experience that occurs while meeting the other, time is required for trust and cooperation to build. Thus, in this research we use the facilitating stances proposed by Carl Rogers seeking to establish facilitating relational conditions to describe the schizophrenic experiences of Francisco. The facilitating attitudes of the psychotherapist proposed by Rogers within psychological practice, which aim to assist in the process of growth and client change, were used for research purposes based on the humanistic phenomenological clinical method developed in psychotherapy (Moreira, 2009).

Congruence is understood as the integration between the experience of the self and the expression of experience. In the phenomenological humanistic perspective, this attitude was put into practice by the researcher during the clinical encounters.

Congruence contributed to the building of a relationship in which the researcher and the patient diagnosed with schizophrenia and a family member could trust the researcher's company during each clinical encounter and feel safe to express freely what he was feeling.

The second facilitating stance used in the research was unconditional positive regard, i.e. welcoming, accepting and unconditionally considering one's own as well as the other's experience: "basic trust – a belief that this other person is somehow worthy of trust" (Rogers, 1974/1977, p. 149). Consideration is an important attitude in clinical encounters because we seek to understand the lived world (*Lebenswelt*) of the person with schizophrenia, and not just the pathology. This was the approach used by the researcher during the clinical encounters with Francisco and Madalena.

The third facilitating attitude was empathic understanding and it refers to understanding the other person. This attitude was of fundamental importance as the researcher needed to avoid any immediate evaluation of Francisco's or Madalena's thoughts to prioritize understanding, having to "abandon one's own self in order to enter the clients' world to help them" (Fontgalland and Moreira, 2012, p. 8).

In clinical encounters, the humanistic phenomenological researcher needs to be sensitive to the feelings and personal reactions that participants experience at any given moment when they are together. They need to pay attention in order to understand the experiences being described by the participant and to establish comprehensive communication.

The second stage of the methodology, the descriptive report, is intrinsically connected to clinical encounters as two sides of the same coin. The descriptive report is the stage of the research tool in which the researcher reports what has happened and describes how the clinical encounters occurred during field research.

The reports of the clinical encounters consisted of the researcher's written reports of the experience after each clinical encounter with participants. They were written in the first and third person singular and aimed to describe the experience of each clinical encounter as accurately as possible, including possible feelings and observations about the development of the relationship through the phenomenological and facilitating attitude of the researcher. The reports included the observations at the day hospital, which helped the researcher perceive how the participants moved and expressed themselves with their body, their relationship with the world, space and time, and the mutual exchange relationship among the researchers, participants and the surrounding world.

Results and discussion

Four clinical encounters were held with Francisco and two with his mother, including the observations on how he acted and placed himself in the group activities at the hospital during the weekly visits over the course of one semester. Francisco looks serious, does not smile, wears glasses and always wears a black shirt with a rock band's logo on it, jeans shorts and flip flops. He rarely talks, and when he is not participating in group activities, he sits far away from his other colleagues, picks up his notebook and pen and writes something down.

The clinical encounters with both Francisco and Madalena were always based on the phenomenological attitude of the researcher of abandoning *a priori* notions and possible prejudices towards Francisco, including the notion of schizophrenia or even how the family relates to a relative who has been diagnosed with schizophrenia. Our goal is to understand the lived worlds (*Lebenswelten*) of participants. As Merleau-Ponty writes:

> He must abandon these two views, he must eschew the one as well as the other, since taken literally they are incompatible, he must appeal beyond them to himself who is their titular and therefore must know what motivates them from within; he must lose them as a state of fact in order to reconstruct

them as his own possibilities, in order to learn from himself what they really
mean in truth, what delivers him over to both perception and to phantasms
in a word, he must reflect.

(1964/2009, p. 38)

When Madalena describes the relationship with her family, she seems to be
affected by the life story of her son, who is both part of her flesh and, by affecting
her, also, as it were, *impregnates* her. Merleau-Ponty (1964/2009) emphasizes that
the concept of flesh allows the radicalization of the phenomenology of ambiguity by showing that whenever we approach an object to touch it, we sense
a lack and presence at the same time, and that we never touch the object as
it is. Addressing ambiguity through the visible and the invisible, Merleau-Ponty
(1964/2009) defines the invisible as being found behind the visible, as an emptiness existing in the visible and the possibility of manifestation of the visible.
Although the researcher is not in the presence of Francisco, she meets him every
time she meets Madalena.

Understanding the lived worlds (*Lebenswelten*) of Francisco and Madalena

Francisco was born with a cleft lip and underwent annual reconstructive sur-
geries until he reached adolescence. Francisco's childhood and adolescence were
normal and Madalena began to identify the symptoms of the disease when he
was eighteen years old. At another time in our meetings, Madalena recalled that
Francisco already isolated himself in his room at the age of seven, but she does not
describe the isolation in further details.

The mother's experiences are constantly connected to those of her son.
According to her, her family members must also express themselves and live in
accordance with Francisco's experiences. By living and feeling the world and by
being congruent while listening to Madalena's accounts, the researcher became
restless: Does this family only turn to Francisco? What about the other family
members? How does daily coexistence with the schizophrenia of Francisco occur?
The intertwining of the lived world (*Lebenswelt*) of Madalena brings us closer to
the phenomenological point of view of Merleau-Ponty (1945/2006b) concerning
habit, that is, "knowledge in hand, that only surrenders to the corporal effort
and that cannot be translated by objective designation" (p. 199). The mother's
habitual way of living, directed at providing her son's well-being, is felt in the clinical encounters with the researcher, as she expresses the need to help Francisco feel
better. Her daily life always converges to Francisco.

At the age of nineteen, Francisco began breaking objects at home and
Madalena found that her son was not well and became concerned. A few days
later, Francisco had convulsions in the morning; she claims that her son had
freaked out, breaking several objects around her, which made her decide to take
him to CAPS (Psychosocial Care Center), a service offered by the public health
network, to begin psychiatric follow-up, but the service had no vacancies at that

time. Madalena cannot recall the exact dates of the events, but she recalls that Francisco was about twenty when he told his mother he was schizophrenic, as he described seeing fireballs and hearing voices, which, for him, were symptoms of the pathology.

Erased expression of the lived world (*Lebenswelt*) in schizophrenia

In 2017, Francisco changed and became more restless, once again breaking objects at home. His room had no furniture or a television, as he had destroyed everything. He would usually apologize short after his outbursts. The experiences of loss of natural evidence (Blankenburg, 1971/1991) in the lived world (*Lebenswelt*) in schizophrenia began to stand out as the guide for Francisco's experiences. He disconnects from others and becomes apathetic with apparent inability to feel, both significant when we focus on the description of his outbursts. These always happen in situations when he cannot relate to others, which indicates his difficulty in the field of intersubjectivity that so characterizes the experience of schizophrenia.

Madalena reports that her son had already threatened to kill her with a knife. At that time, she looked at him and said that they would both die. Francisco then stopped, approached her and apologized.

Madalena does not talk much about her family. She is a hairdresser, has five children, three boys and two girls. She takes her son to the day hospital every day and goes back home alone. She pointed out several times during her meetings with the researcher that she was the only person who knew how to deal with Francisco's suffering. According to his siblings, he should be hospitalized, because they do not understand the situation and fight with him a lot. She has to constantly repeat to the other children that Francisco is not an animal and that he needs support at home. She points out that he tries to include him in the family activities, but the siblings do not understand him, and Francisco constantly needs his mother to mediate relations with them.

Madalena instructs her son to actively participate in the meetings with the researcher, since she believes that these conversations would help him feel better. Using a phenomenological attitude, the researcher bracketed her biases about the kind of help that could be offered. Madalena hoped that after participating in the research, her son would feel at peace and calmer.

During the first clinical encounter with the researcher, Francisco was asked whether his mother had spoken to him about the research. He nodded but remained silent. Observing the lack of verbal expression, the researcher asked him if he wanted to talk at that moment. Francisco agreed by nodding both when he was asked if he felt comfortable talking to the researcher in the room and if he wanted to sit somewhere else in the hospital. One of the lived characteristics of Francisco is the reduction in intensity of his presence in the world, as if he lacked energy. Sass and Parnas (2003) call this aspect a diminished self-affection of the schizophrenic patient.

When Francisco and the researcher sat in a different place, she told him again that she is conducting a research, that she wants to get to know him to understand what it is like to experience schizophrenia and learn from him. Francisco confirms that his mother had told him about this, but that he thought the meetings would be similar to the ones with Juliana (a nursing assistant). He abruptly changes the subject and begins to report his arrival at the hospital, when he was afflicted by an intense crisis and became aggressive with his niece. He does not provide further details and becomes silent. Merleau-Ponty (1942/2006a) points out that:

> [T]here is the body as mass of chemicals components in interaction, the body as dialectic of the living being and its biological milieu, and the body as dia-lectic of social subject and his group; even all our habits are an impalpable body for the ego of each moment.
>
> (p. 325)

This dialectic makes it possible to understand the behavior of the body's action over the soul and "perception must in turn be included in a dialectic of actions and reactions" (Merleau-Ponty, 1942/2006a, p. 252), such as a dia-lectic without synthesis, as constant movement in an unfinished world. My body is my point of view of the world; I am my body in the world and I am the way I perceive my relationship with the world. Madalena perceives her relationship with the world as intersected by the intention to make her son feel better, normal, as she stated, that is, she wants to see him studying and working because he is an intelligent boy. In view of the difficulty to understand Francisco's lived world, since he rarely expresses himself verbally and his body movements are slow and without liveliness, Madalena's lived world is somehow forced on him, impregnates him.

It is as if Francisco did not interact in the world with others, while Madalena, at different times, takes his place by reporting his experience to the researcher, or mediating his relationship with his siblings. Francisco's diminished self-affection (Sass and Parnas, 2003; Hann and Fuchs, 2010) has implications on his relationships with others at different levels, that is, as a diminished "sense of basic self-presence, an implicit sense of existing as a vital and self-possessed subject of consciousness" (Sass and Parnas, 2003, p. 428).

Seeking to bracket this observation about diminished self-affection and by being congruent in the relationship with Francisco, the researcher seeks to empathically understand the lived world. She seeks to experience what is revealed in the rela-tionship. At various moments, the researcher sought to be attentive to her pos-sible feelings and observations during the clinical encounters with Francisco and Madalena, seeking to foster an attitude of empathic understanding in order to understand their experiences. Her facilitating attitude of congruence was also constant in clinical encounters when she sought to use her own feelings and perceptions that emerged in these encounters to facilitate the understanding of the lived experience, to reflect on what emerged in the relationship between her and Francisco and Madalena and the world.

Francisco's aggressiveness with his relatives or the breaking of furniture at home show his apparent difficulty in experiencing a feeling and owning it, in this case anger and aggression. There seems to be a distortion akin to what Binswanger (1956/2002) calls anthropological disproportion. By excluding himself from the interaction with others, Francisco's actions are no longer intentional and focused on something or a situation. This way of inhabiting the world reveals his difficulty in expressing a feeling, and so he often finds himself insensible in the world, something which, in turn, is related to the loss of natural evidence as an intersubjective difficulty in his lived world of schizophrenia.

We emphasize this aspect since the feeling is intentional, directed at something or someone. The feeling resounds in the person who is feeling and is bound to space and time, it has movement and direction (Tatossian, 1979/2006, Bloc and Moreira, 2016). Francisco follows an inverse path: he cannot place himself in relationships; he avoids contact with others. He has difficulty experiencing intentional feeling and cannot connect with others when experiencing anger or aggression. Thus, he is constantly apologizing without realizing that others are hurt. He does not grasp what he is experiencing, experiencing a feeling that is not evident to him.

Francisco's lack of initiative can be understood as a negative symptom of schizophrenia (Blankenburg, 1971/1991; Parnas and Bovet, 1991; Sass, 2003) and it is a way of protecting oneself from contact with the world, which is not evident. The lived world of schizophrenia brings an inability to organize one's experiences and an incapacity to be with others. This is what happens to Francisco, who closes himself in schizophrenic inauthenticity (Tatossian, 1979/2006), a striking characteristic of the loss of natural evidence, loss of self-understanding, returning to oneself in intersubjective relations and being autonomous in these relationships (Blankenburg, 1971/1991).

Being empathic implies understanding others by connecting with a consistent and available presence. Being empathetic with Francisco, seeking to understand his lived world, demands constant congruence and authenticity on the part of the researcher. Deep into this processual relationship of constant exchange and experience, the latter is affected by the silence, lack of answers and the difficulty in connecting with Francisco, but she always seeks to use her clinical experience as a psychotherapist in this relationship to build a bond with him. It is more difficult to apply empathic understanding when dealing with psychotic patients (Sommerbeck, 2003; Stanghellini, 2004; Wolf-Fédida, 2006; Englebert and Valentiny, 2017) and the researcher feels frustrated in her efforts to reach his lived world with him.

Francisco is always alone, has no friends and he avoids contact with other people. He relates little to his brothers and his past experiences reflect prejudice and harassment. According to Francisco, people tried to kill him, poison him and drug him, but he does not name them. He also tells his mother that he once tried to hang himself because he wondered if he was worthy of living because he could not live an ordinary life like other people. Madalena states that these situations never took place and that they are delusions.

Nowadays, Francisco does not have any hallucinations, although he questions whether his wondering thoughts represent reality or not. His thoughts are connected to an "explicit subsumption" (Merleau-Ponty, 1945/2006b, p. 179), that is, he cannot relate thought to a broader situation and needs external confirmation to validate if something happened or not.

Conclusion

This humanistic phenomenological case study shows the ambiguity of the schizophrenic experiences of Francisco and Madalena at their intersection; while at the same time experiencing individual experiences, experiences are shared with others and collectively experienced.

There is no single meaning for the lived world of schizophrenia, not only for those who experience it and for those who interact with the one who experiences it, but also in relation to the fact that when these schizophrenic-world experiences intertwine, a new meaning arises from experience, similar to our understanding of how schizophrenic experiences are lived by Francisco, his mother and family.

These experiences appear in Francisco's relationship with the researcher, highlighting his dissociation with the other: his lived world closes in and alienates him in his delusions and hallucinations. He disconnects from the sharing of experiences with others, with himself, and consequently becomes detached from common sense and the lived habits in daily life.

Merleau-Ponty's phenomenological contribution stands out in our phenomenological humanistic research method that seeks a critical and comprehensive view of these experiences of schizophrenia that are so difficult to share with others. The clinical encounters, during the first stage of the method, required the researcher to have her clinical training with a phenomenological humanist attitude to be with Francisco and Madalena.

The phenomenological attitude of abandoning a set of *a priori* thoughts and biases is the framework of our clinical phenomenology that seeks to understand the lived world, taking into account that, according to Merleau-Ponty, it is this attempt to bracket all prior knowledge of the world that allows us to understand the rooting of the human being in the world, never forgetting that completely bracketing is never achieved. But we understand that phenomenological experience in the clinical and psychopathological context such as schizophrenia lacks the establishment of space of trust and acceptance that makes participants feel at ease to freely express themselves. Clinical encounters take place between two people who affect each other when they are together, and it is important for the researcher to engage in this relationship in an authentic way and express herself in accordance with what she feels with the participants. This was possible from the humanist perspective used in the field research.

In this research concerning the experiences of schizophrenia, we argue for the need to apply the facilitating stances present in Carl Rogers' humanistic psychology: unconditional positive acceptance, empathic congruence and understanding, to facilitate the full expression of the person, and, from a

Merleau-Pontian perspective, taking into consideration one's rootedness in the world. The researcher's humanistic phenomenological stance is paramount in here, and it walks alongside, as it were, Francisco and Madalena in their lived worlds (*Lebenswelten*) at the intersection with the researcher's *Lebenswelt*. In this clinical research method, the researcher is sensitive and available to meeting the other, strives to unconditionally accept all forms of expression of the other, is congruent and understands her lived world, so as to be more able to encourage the other to get in touch with their experiences.

Our humanistic phenomenological stance makes it possible to raise discussions in clinical and psychopathological practice. We are intertwined with the world and we start from a place in which abandoning the natural attitude is never complete. It is not a matter of seeking total detachment as with the classic views of psychiatry and psychopathology. We nevertheless conclude that it is important to open more doors to questioning our clinical actions in psychopathological contexts such as schizophrenia, since we are dealing with people like Francisco who feel and cannot express their feelings, and that is why they often feel devalued and ignored by those around them. Francisco needs to be seen as a person in constant development and change, not only as one who has a pathology, but as a free and autonomous person. Further studies on schizophrenia from a comprehensive humanistic phenomenological perspective may contribute to helping people like Francisco.

References

Amatuzzi, M. M. (1996). Apontamentos acerca da pesquisa fenomenológica. *Estudos de Psicologia*. 13(1). 5–10.

Binswanger, L. (2002). *Trois formes manquées de la présence humaine*: la présomption, la distorcion, le maniérisme. Paris: Collection Phéno. (Originally published in 1956).

Blankenburg, W. (1991). *La perte de l'évidence naturelle*. Paris: Presses Universitaires de France. (Originally published in 1971).

Bloc, L. & Moreira, V. (2016). Introdução. In A. Tatossian; L. Bloc; V. Moreira. *Psicopatologia fenomenológica revisitada*. São Paulo: Escuta.

Englebert, J. & Valentiny, C. (2017). *Schizophrénie, conscience de soi, intersubjetivité*. Louvain-la-Neuve: De Boeck Supérieur.

Fontgalland, R. C. & Moreira, V. (2012). Da empatia à compreensão empática: evolução do conceito no pensamento de Carl Rogers. *Memorandum*, 23, 32–56.

Giorgi, A. (2012). The descriptive phenomenological psychological method. *Journal of Phenomenological Psychology*, 43, 3–12.

Hann, S. de; Fuchs, T. (2010). The ghost in the machine: disembodiment in schizophrenia – two case studies. *Psychopathology*, 43, 327–333.Merleau-Ponty, M. (2006a). *The Structure of Behaviour*. São Paulo: Martins Fontes. (Originally published in 1942).

Merleau-Ponty, M. (2006b). *Phenomenology of Perception*. São Paulo: Martins Fontes. (Originally published in 1945).

Merleau-Ponty, M. (2009). *The Visible and the Invisible*. São Paulo: Perspectiva. (Originally published in 1964).

Moreira, V. (2004). O método fenomenológico de Merleau-Ponty como ferramenta crítica na pesquisa em psicopatologia. *Psicologia: Reflexão e Crítica*, 17(3), 447–456.

Moreira, V. (2009). *Clínica Humanista-Fenomenológica*: estudos em psicoterapia e psicopatologia crítica. São Paulo: Annablume.

Parnas, J. & Bovet, P. (1991). Autism in schizophrenia revisited. *Comprehensive Psychiatry*, 32, 7–21.

Rogers, C. R. (1977). Pode a aprendizagem abranger ideias e sentimentos? (R. Rosenberg, Trad.). In C. R. Rogers & R. Rosenberg. *A pessoa como centro* (pp. 143–161). São Paulo: EPU. (Originally published in 1974).

Sass, L. A. (2003). Negative symptoms, schizophrenia, and the self. *International Journal of Psychology and Psychological Therapy*, 3(2), December, 153–180.

Sass, L. A. & Parnas, J. (2003). Schizophrenia, consciousness, and the self, *Schizophrenia Bulletin*, 29(3).

Sommerbeck, L. (2003). The client-centred therapist in psychiatric contexts. *A therapists guide to the psychiatric landscape and its inhabitants*. Ross on Wye (Inglaterra): PCCS Books.

Stanghellini, G. (2004). Disembodied spirits and deanimated bodies. *The Psychopathology of Common Sense*. Oxford: Oxford University Press.

Tatossian, J. (2006). *Fenomenologia das Psicoses*. São Paulo: Escuta. (Originally published in 1979).

Tatossian, A. (2012). A fenomenologia: uma epistemologia para a psiquiatria?. In A. Tatossian & V. Moreira. *Clínica do Lebenswelt: psicoterapia e psicopatologia fenomenológica* (pp.149–167). São Paulo: Escuta. (Originally published in 1996).

Wolf-Fédida, M. (2006). Troubles neurologiques, états limites et crises confrontés à la psychose. In M. Wolf-Fédida. *Psychothérapie phénoménlogique* (pp.87–108). Paris: MJW Fédition.

25 Dream harder

A phenomenological exploration

Ondine Smulders

Introduction

I notice that I am expecting her to turn, to speak. She sits in profile, staring at the wall, into the distance. I see my intention to listen. Silence still. My mind drifts beyond her to where I glimpse trees, waving faintly in the breeze, reflections of the day's last sunrays on their leaves.

Always a bit of a dreamer, like so many of us, my mind escapes into memories, hopes, desire, fantasies, dreams, bright images, music, stemmed initially from a need before becoming a pleasure. I noticed during my training as a psychotherapist that regularly detaching myself from reality was interfering with my ability to attune myself to the world, and live my life in the presence of others. Based on my own experiences and those described by some of my clients, I want to use this chapter to expand on an essay I wrote as a student in which I investigated my personal experiences of day-dreaming. I believe it may be useful to you, the reader, to gain some insight into the personal experiences of daydreams—an exploration and a layer-by-layer unpacking of the process.

I will reveal how I tried to grasp the contours of the misty lands of daydreams and reveries, a bit like those first rays of sun at dawn when they pierce through the darkness enveloping the land. I will sketch a personal journey hither and thither, illustrating it with my imagery and emotional experiences. I will speculate about the moment of daydreams and the world we flee into. I use the word speculate as it is impossible to exactly remember the experience. It becomes lost before I'm aware that it has occurred. I can only attempt a reconstruction based on our experiences of a lingering smell, a taste, a sound, or a vision. Last, I will try to depict our awakening or return to the world and ourselves. Although I will use some philosophical concepts to frame my experience, considering spatiality and temporality, I will try to steer clear from theory or judgements to remain open to the meaning of the moments. Finally, I will also probe into what it cost me to become more present in the real world, and look at the precious, dreamy bits of myself that were lost. I may live more peacefully attuned to the external world, but suspended alongside there is a fleeting sadness that I am left bereft of my inner day-world.

I invite you to read this chapter through the filters of our experiences as we live them and make meaning of them—my own experiences as I write this, and yours, as you keep reading: 'Meanings are inherent in a particular world view, an individual life and the connections between self, other and world' (Moustakas, 1990, p.32).

She turns, looks straight at me, she is not here yet. Her eyes downcast, black buckled boots, they flutter, one hand grasps a knee, gentle stroking.

I wait … I wonder … what just happened between the trees and her turn? I shift my weight to the right, cross my legs. She resumes …

An absurd quest

To understand the process of day-dreaming, I want to describe the process in as much detail as possible by drawing it out step-by-step and relating the body-thought-emotions in the living present. I worked phenomenologically and heuristically as defined by Moustakas, meaning in an experiential-introspective way (Robinson, 1996), through listening, observing, witnessing, and paying special attention to my lived experience, and over the years to my clients' descriptions of their experiences. It was, and still is, a return to a childlike attitude of amazement that allows for the phenomena to emerge into the awareness of my senses: my vision and hearing, my imagination and my memory. It should have been an easy exercise to portray these daydream experiences. After all, my clients are so familiar with them, so close to them, and yet, it was also like Achilles' heel. How can we create the necessary distance to observe and describe a process while also living it?

My client moves along, ignoring my invitation to describe where she has just spent the last few minutes. Was she where her current words are formed and chosen, her sentences are crafted? Did she meet her censor? Where is all that I wonder?

I listen, no words, no interventions.

Attempting phenomenology while relaxing mentally into a daydream is somewhat absurd: how can we pursue 'the path of reverie' while our 'consciousness relaxes and wanders and consequently *becomes clouded*' (Bachelard, 1992, p.5)? What I saw was different from what I felt, and what I sensed was distinctive from what I heard—each sense brought me something that the others could not, and yet, it was impossible to remain open to all of them at once. Some form of hierarchy seemed present; in my case, the visual tends to dominate. The importance was to move with the flow, and opening and responding to the process as it unfolded (Bollas, 2007). Ihde (2007) has a similar understanding, writing about a perpetual motion of fading and emerging, appearing and disappearing. He calls this the *core-fringe structure* (Ihde, 2007), which shows that as we focus on one aspect of our experience, another feature grows more diffused.

In the mood

What makes us seek escape, what drives us away from ourselves and from the moment? Prior to day-dreaming, we usually find ourselves in a certain mood. Certain moods push us to flee the body and retreat from ourselves into a more pleasurable state. When I am writing, for instance as I am now, I tend to feel harried, exhausted, accompanied by a desire to get it over with fast, a wish to rush the process. Sometimes I am even on the verge of (a deadline) panic. In its shadow grows an overwhelming pressure from and on my body that feels like a slow build-up towards panic: an intensification of the energy in my feet and hands, a gentle pulsing that becomes a tingling, that slowly builds to a throbbing and a growing urge to escape this body. The mood consists of what I can only describe as an anxiety over my deadline accompanied by a diffuse sense of boredom with the process.

A room with a view, a favourite spot, always permitting an escape, awful temptation, freedom just out there, a few steps away. A safety net. This is not helpful. Write, go on, just do it, it is easy. Do not be lazy now. The trees beg me. Typing away in the room, thinking among the trees. They have shot up. The sun struggles to get through these days.

My pre-writing disposition is tinged with anxiety and being bored *with*, but mostly being bored *by*. I am anxious as I have something to create, structure, and write. I am bored by the months of reading. I have had to sift through so many articles and books (way more than the references at the end would suggest), a lot of it uninteresting and of no use to this chapter. I am bored with the highlighting, the note taking, all that goes into my process of writing. Even when I stumble upon an exciting reading or I find a way to make a paragraph flow well, something that should feel satisfying, interesting even, I am still bored. It is not my work that is boring, I am bored. *A squirrel racing through the gutter, prancing along the shoots, the trees. An unwanted memory, the sparrow hawk, the enemy, on the ledge, gorging on a blackbird, the cacophony of birds, sheer terror. Go away; I do not want to think of that. Feathers, everywhere, blood. Disgust, fascination, a* nature-morte *in the urban sprawl. Look at the sky. I feel a sharp pain, my temples. The sky, ash-yellow, a watery colour. Cold spreads through my body, shivers in my feet, my legs. The heating, I must turn the heating on.*

In this mood, the noise in my head gradually grows louder. My 'thought in the form of inner speech' (Ihde, 2007, p.214) seems to wash over my brain like a flood. It is taking me over, crushing me. My inner speech has the spatiality of an auditory space; it is also visionless (Ihde, 2007). It is always brisk, but now it accelerates to an astonishing tempo. I may turn the volume down but it will still be there, talking in the background, enfolding me. It can never be turned off entirely. I am fully cloaked in my thoughts, 'just as auditory space surrounds me and may, in the striking sound of a symphony, fill my being' (Idhe, 2007, p.214). I am present to myself but I also become the 'imaginative inner presence' (Idhe, 2007, p.215) to myself.

The cold. More tremors, restlessness. I need to get up, move. Tension builds in my head, behind my eyes, at the top of my skull. A dull tightness, sharp edges, a black cloud, heavy, pushing on my eyes. My head, thick, weighty, threatening to drop onto my body, forward, left. My eyes pinched, half-closed, the left a bit more, like going to sleep but not.

It is raining harder. I catch whooshing, splashing. I seem to have stopped typing. I am staring at the screen, the sentences no longer sentences, the words no longer words just letters, dots, spaces, the black and the white, the font, the letter size. I notice I am rubbing the hard skin on my thumb.

It becomes increasingly hard to stay with this mood. There is an urge to flee, a need to erase myself from this world and to re-appear in the other. I want to bolt out of my present, my past, and future, momentarily. I am turning away from my being and the task at hand. In his early work *On Escape* (1935/2003), Levinas explored the urge that we feel to escape ourselves. Escaping was for him a search for the fabulous: 'In escape the I flees itself, not in opposition to the infinity of what it is not or of what it will not become, but rather due to the very fact that it is or that it becomes' (Levinas, 2003, p.55).

Racing thoughts dance through my head, I cannot grasp them. Then a tinkle … drops, reflections appear like silver flakes falling from a slate sky. Through my computer glasses the words on screen are clear, the world beyond the screen through the window blurry, the trees, singing birds, playing squirrels and shy foxes.

Dreaming harder

Fleeing into a daydream is an act which we can open ourselves to when the mood catches us. We can prepare ourselves to some extent and hope for its visitation, but we cannot force it into action. The more we will it and yearn for it, the more elusive it becomes. Merleau-Ponty (2012) talks about a voluntary attitude and a delivery of our body that helps us reach the desired state. I realise that my detachment, daydreams, and fantasies generally occur of their own accord, as 'they arise from a source of embodied spontaneity' (Fuchs, 2010, p.242).

I stare out, nothing, energy subsiding, draining to my legs, my toes, out. I hesitate … shall I follow … or stay? It is no struggle, I drop deeper, plunge in head to toe, I am emptying me. I imagine myself diving into the greenery, like in flight, my arms stretched upward, outward. I want to abandon this body, its confines, lose myself to a deep stillness, a pleasure … a freeing of my body, my mind, from all that surrounds me.

Merleau-Ponty's description of willing oneself to sleep is useful when thinking of the process of moving into a daydream. Just like the would-be-sleeper desires for 'the visitation of sleep by imitating the breathing and the posture of the sleeper' (Merleau-Ponty, 2012, p.166), we daydreamers also wish to join that other world. We dull our senses, slow our breathing, and stop paying attention to our surroundings. We go with the flow and let our body and mind flow freely with the stream.

The actual moment of slipping into a daydream always proves elusive.

> [It] arrives at a particular moment, it settles upon this imitation of itself that I offered it, and I succeed in becoming what I pretended to be: that unseeing and nearly unthinking mass, confined to a point in space and no longer in the world.
>
> (Merleau-Ponty, 2012, p.167)

We can never sense at what point exactly we cross the boundary from one world to the other—'a boundary is not that at which something stops but … is that from which something begins its essential unfolding' (Heidegger, 1993, p.356). While we are at times bodily present in our nightly dreams, in our daydreams we are usually not bodily present. We tend to be body-less—'only when my body becomes imperceptible to me, do I achieve contact with the world I seek' (Fuchs, 2010, p.241).

A physical stillness, a dulling of sounds, slowly turning the volume down, thicker eyelids, freezing vision, where sight and thoughts intersect, become one. What I see is where I go, where I am. Moving along on a wave; there is only me in the sky, brushing by the clouds … a gust of wind picking up the leaves and throwing me through the air.

While day-dreaming, we suspend our relation with the world and thus with time; 'details grow dim and all picturesqueness fades' (Bachelard, 1994, p.206). It is an existential as well as temporal-spatial experience where time has no place. We only become aware of the time that has passed when we return to the world with others where we live in time. We do not know until that point how much time has passed, or whether it passed quickly or slowly. The world that is over there, not here where our body is, has a spatial character as well, extending into endlessness (Bachelard, 1994). We may feel at home when we dwell there, as in a supportive and encouraging connection: 'The basic character of dwelling is to spare, to preserve … dwelling itself is always a staying with things' (Heidegger, 1993, pp.150–151).

I have a sense of no longer inhabiting the body, a softening, like borders dissolving. Being outside it, not seeing it, a welcome absence. Not an unsafe feeling, not naked, powerless. I fall into it, I get drawn in, pulled in, into it, I am melted into it.

My dream world is visual, coloured, and spatial. It has sense and auditory aspects. My field of vision is everywhere, unlike the real world where my vision is restricted to what is ahead of me (Ihde, 2007). We shape our daydreams over and over again. It is no effort. It just comes to us. It is a combination of atmosphere, a state of mind, a reflection on our personal lives, and all that exists in our world. In this world, we always find 'what is alike' but usually do not 'encounter the same' as we do in the waking world 'which is determined by the everyday historicity of *Dasein*' (Heidegger, 1993, p.228). I am in my dream world and it is in me. 'We no longer *see* it. It no longer *limits* us, because we are in the very ultimate depth of its repose' (Bachelard, 1994, p.241).

Rekindling awareness

A voice, a sound, a sight, and a smell—an interruption comes into my awareness. Back to the boundaried body. Compress myself back in, re-explore it, travel back into its endings, my hands, fingers, toes, eyes, claiming ownership once again. Moving into the orderliness of this body, in this room, in this chair. Stretching my back, my neck. Relief washes over me, shoulder tension melts away, liquefies, hanging down loosely. The neck strain, accentuating the back of the spine earlier, pulsating gently, quiet now.

While we are daydreaming, we are never completely gone, we can always return. 'The sleeper is never completely enclosed in himself, never fully asleep, and the patient is never absolutely cut off from the inter-subjective world' (Merleau-Ponty, 2012, p.167). In the same way that we use our body to abandon this world and detach, we also re-link ourselves to the world through our body using our sense organs and language (Merleau-Ponty, 2012). The experience of the instance of return is just as elusive as its opposite—the spell is broken abruptly, and we regain 'an awareness of the environment which destroys the experience of mystery' (Langeveld, 1983, p.188). Upon return to the world, we are ready to rekindle our consciousness of this world 'that includes inner and outer life, a world therefore in which both possibilities meet' (Langeveld, 1983, p.14).

Tranquillity. A quiet body, no more pulsing, humming, tingling, just a certain comfort, a harmony. The window is empty, some of its charm spent, the clouds just clouds. A fleeting trace of sorrow, I am here, they are out there.

The beauty of the visions that inhabit my dream world touches me, and I sense their presence in everyday echoes as they accumulate in my real world, which is often a little duller, louder, and smellier.

Finding pleasure in daydreams is 'an escape that fails' (Levinas, 2003, p.62). It can never give what it promises, a total loss of us. Inevitably, we return to ourselves and realise that time has passed. In my particular case, I am now just that little bit closer to this chapter's deadline. It carries with it a greater sense of urgency, more anxiety, and a deepening boredom. It does not take long before I am beset once more with another bout of anxiety and boredom, triggering an urge to escape and detach—an all-too-familiar-cycle that enacts itself—until at last I am ready to write as you can read me writing now.

In practice

What just happened? Where am I? Fidgety, an edgy energy vibrating along my legs, my fingers twitching. The client continues speaking … blank … where is she, I?

My commitment to dig into my own depths again and again, and the hours I have spent listening to clients talking about similar experiences, produced a slow and deliberate shift in my being. It guided me towards a new understanding of the inner experiences of the other and allowed me to gain a deeper appreciation for their uniqueness and the places where we can meet. However, in making the unconscious conscious, I lost and gained. My ability to disappear into the bliss of a daydream has vanished, for now at least. I gained an intention to meet clients with my whole being as well as a greater awareness of others and their inner lives.

Now, when the urge to flee descends upon me—and it still does—I only glimpse it through a crack in the fence—the emergency exit to my reverie has been closed. It fills me with a profound sense of sadness, a heaviness in my chest that weighs me down because I am not going anywhere, I am stuck here. I used to love my escapes, they were so pleasurable. My body was my 'life's hiding place' (Merleau-Ponty, 2012, p.167). I opened the door and I escaped, a bit like having a drug, soporific, on tap. I anticipated that moment of grabbing the handle, pushing it down, opening that door, never hesitating, all to lose myself and join the pleasure of my world beyond. 'A threshold is a sacred thing' (Porphyrus, as cited in Bachelard, 1994, p.238). Levinas echoes my sentiments when he writes how we find 'pleasure in abandonment, a loss of oneself, a getting out of oneself' (1935/2003, p.61).

How present have I been? Did she notice, does she remain caught up in her story? Have I been nodding and smiling in a fake way? Fleetingly, a hint of panic rises into my throat, then the training kicks in, I feel my legs on the seat, my feet on the ground, I straighten my back. Here I go, centre on the client.

These days I feel like when dreams elude the sleeper. The more consciously I try it, the less it occurs. Trees, sun or rain, reflections and colours beg me from outside the window, but I can only admire them; they no longer offer a diving board to immersion into their world. For a long time, this fleeting sadness that I was bereft of my inner dream world, left me feeling empty, like a head without its echoing thoughts, in a blank, filled with absence. In the early days when the extent of the shift dawned upon me, I dreaded the empty house, the bus or tube ride, the silence. Gradually I have become more present, and learned to live in peaceful attunement to others and the external world. I console myself knowing that I have found comfort in the silver linings of my work or, as Jean Giraudoux puts it so much better than me, 'sadness flies on the wings of the morning, and out of the heart of darkness comes the light' (1974, p.65).

In the minutes before meeting a client, I prepare to open myself out and receive the other. I ground myself spatially and temporarily. I notice the time, a few minutes to go; is it passing quickly or slowly? I take a few deep breaths, press my feet on the floor, and settle myself into the chair. I notice the window, the trees, and the sky. I note my mood, my emotions. I clear a space in my mind to meet the client by (momentarily) letting go of personal anxieties and desires. The ritual helps me to drop into my body, inhabit its hollows and extremities, and to meet the client with an open, interested, and accepting attitude. Over the years, I have noticed that my best interventions, those that clients cite back to me (sometimes enthusiastically), are those that were made without much internal deliberation but that occurred to me naturally and in the moment. Once I step away from gifting the client my overwhelming attention in the here and now, a space opens up where clients can think more openly while I can communicate more intuitively (Bollas, 2007). Looking back to those instances, it felt as if my body, mind, and feelings were all working as one, present to me and yet not present at all, rhyming with the client, fused into a most natural state of being. Only when I am open to the client, can I hope to meet him and show that 'all real living is meeting' (Buber, 1958, p.11).

Exploring the nature of my daydreams has taken me closer to the other, and I have developed a greater awareness of their inner experiences. I am now more able to get closer to the other's experiences, their moods, insights, and meanings. When clients talk to me of their reveries and daydreams, I feel a real curiosity and an openness to engage with their world. I believe it is an opportunity for the client to learn more about themselves and for me to understand another aspect of their being and their world, to lay down another piece of their puzzle: 'To know and understand the nature, meanings, and essences of any human experience, one depends on the internal frame of reference of the person who has had, is having, or will have the experience' (Moustakas, 1990, p.24).

Shall I mention her absence, her daydream or am I simply reassuring myself I may have some-thing to add? Talking, she sounds bathed in it still, disconnected from herself, me. Better stay quiet, intervening now would just be filling space…

I have noted that it helps clients to become reflective of their reveries (and other processes) by focussing on description and the body, sensations, and emotions, or as Rollo May would say 'helping the patient to recognise his own existence' (May, 1983, p.152). I tend to use my unpacking process and the manner in which I investigated it in myself as a starting point with clients when considering their particular experience of daydreams. I ask them for descriptions of imagery, sounds, smells, and visions. Clients generally describe quite easily the bodily texture and the spatial-temporal character of their reveries. On the other hand, telling me about the instant of the break or what brings them back to their body is often the hardest part of the work, the most elusive.

I am inclined to explore with clients the emotional state prior to the episode because we usually find ourselves in a particular state that is neither outside or inside. Together we try to figure out what it means to feel a 'need to transcend the limits of finite being' (Levinas, 2003, p.53). I sometimes wonder if unpacking their daydreams helps clients to become more aware and self-reflective of their own creation, or were they all along just waiting for their inner world to be revealed?

We consider the experience itself, but also explore the other layers that belong to it, such as its origins, how the client uses it, and whether this has shifted over time. Over time, a picture may emerge that has existential meaning for the client and they tend to become more aware and self-reflective: 'Conscious awareness can establish and guide new ways of dealing with the world until they have taken on the character of habits and have "become second nature to us"' (Fuchs, 2010, p.241).

Conclusion

Delving so deeply into these experiences, I attempted to daydream, remembered, put pen to paper/finger to key, explored, lost, and regained. The probing and the layer-by-layer unpacking of the experience have helped me to come to a new life-station where I understand the process somewhat better and, as a result, understand myself better. Being able to grasp at a cognitive, emotional, and embodied level what daydreams represent to me has helped me to accept another piece of the puzzle of my being. I sit a bit easier with anxiety and boredom, as it becomes a more familiar facet of myself. The need to escape is still there, beckoning me, but the urge is no longer so pressing. More often than not these days, I follow my call of conscience which addresses me from within, helping me to remain more present in my uncomfortable moods.

References

Bachelard, G. (1992). *The Poetics of Reverie. Childhood, Language and the Cosmos*. Transl. Russel, D. Boston, MA: Beacon Press.
Bachelard, G. (1994). *The Poetics of Space*. Transl. Jolas, M. Boston, MA: Beacon Press.
Bollas, C. (2007). *The Freudian Moment*. London: Karnac.
Buber, M. (1958). *I and Thou*. 2nd ed. London: Continuum.

Fuchs, T. (2010). The Psychopathology of Hyperreflexivity. *The Journal of Speculative Philosophy*, 24, 3, pp239–255.

Giraudoux, J. (1974). *The Madwoman of Chaillot*. Transl. Valency, M. New York: Dramatists Play Service Inc.

Heidegger, M. (1993). 'Building, Dwelling, Thinking' in *Basic Writings*. Transl. Hofstader, A. London: Routledge.

Ihde, D. (2007). *Listening and Voice*. New York: State University of New York Press.

Langeveld, M.J. (1983). The Secret Place in the Life of the Child. *Phenomenology and Pedagogy*, 1, 2, pp181–191. Retrieved from https://ejournals.library.ualberta.ca/index.php/pandp/article/view/14872/11693 on 30 September 2015.

Levinas, E. (1935/2003). *On Escape*. Transl. Bergo, B. Stanford, CA: Stanford University Press.

May, R. (1983). *The Discovery of Being*. New York: W.W. Norton & Company.

Merleau-Ponty, M. (2012). *Phenomenology of Perception*. Transl. Landes, D.A. London and New York: Routledge.

Moustakas, C. (1990). *Heuristic Research. Design, Methodology and Applications*. Berkeley, CA: Sage Publications, Inc.

Robinson, S.M. (1996). Seminar Evaluation 12/16/96. Retrieved from www.academia.edu/12895110/Seminar_Evaluation_Research_Methodology_Phenomenology_Hermeneutics_and_Heuristics on 21 June 2019.

26 'Igor's pet cemetery? Igor is out. Burying cat'

A memoir of living and dying

Deborah A. Lee

A man at work has blood trickling down his face. He walks slowly towards me, past me, eyes staring unseeing.

He and his friend guffaw, because dress-up and play-acting for Halloween are GREAT FUN.

I hear the ambulance but, of course, there has been no accident, and there *was* no accident.

I called 999 only because his breathing was suddenly so frightening. I'd been saying that it was fine to go, darling; but choking is no way to die.

"I'll stay with you on the phone until they're there." We are an emergency, as if we can be saved.

The consultant didn't even sit down; there was nothing he could do, no, nothing. Go home and deal with that, I guess.

A perplexing conversation with a nurse about which days chemotherapy takes place – chemotherapy which won't be any use – and then we're back in the sweltering August heat.

I'm wearing a blue poncho, he a white croquet shirt; there are Bakewell tarts in the bag.

And we do deal with it, one way and another.

"Is there anything for partners?" (Not carers, not yet.) "Leaflets, and you could have a referral to a clinical psychologist." The GP gives a prescription for pills that make your bones break: "I want you to take one tonight."

Some people's timing sucks. A close friend promises to call and never does. I'm so angry that I ask for the car keys to be hidden: "How dare he do this to you?" "Hope it's not too stressful," writes a therapist (a therapist). At the worst time, a couple of people kick the boot in and I retaliate: there's no way back for any of us.

Some people are stars. Four friends will be loved forever.

And we're stars. We do a complex dance of anticipatory grief and absolute disbelief, and we keep going. Our usual calls and responses: "I'm hungry,"

"And I am the representative of the Czech Republic!"

When he's not watching, I prepare the house for living and dying.

And now it's August again.

When the sirens are coming for you, they're deafening.

(When they've been for you, they stay deafening.)

I never saw the ambulance, I ran down and left the door open, ready. Five very young paramedics are in our bedroom, all wanting to help. It's so unlikely, that someone so sharp until yesterday can't see me. "I want to get up", "I want to get up", but he can't.

The leaflets tell you how to bulk up the sauce for the conventional dinners he'd never have eaten even when he was well; while the well-meaning bereavement counsellors' blogs chastise (what they see as) thinking cream buns will keep someone alive.

The man in the cake shop (who doesn't know) jokes that I will be in again tomorrow.

In time, Google searches start to offer 'cachexia'; it's hidden under thick jumpers and trousers. We both strain to pull socks over swollen feet, to strap up weak ankles with wrongly-sized bandages (the pharmacy hasn't got the right ones). It makes your head shrink.

I can't get him what he wants today: morning hot chocolate with extra sugar, (a little bit of) jacket potato (with beans in a separate pot) from the deli for lunch, croquet scores to follow online, cricket on the radio, a chance to tease me for wanting to speak to the Occupational Therapist, for "always having something to say", back and forth to/from the bathroom when he calls, gently steering him back to bed so that he doesn't quite notice what I'm doing, two new hot water bottles arranged just so each time, hair pulled from the bathroom sink, a scoop of ice cream from the sweet shop for afternoon tea.

For a while, afterwards, I do my shopping on Sundays when everywhere but the supermarket is closed; I live on crackers, cheese, and tortilla chips.

Writing instructions for a nurse, I realised the danger of our latest bathroom trips. That last climb up the stairs that could have killed both of us. If you've always been a bit melodramatic, it's easy to forget that you might *not* be able to make that final step.

The commode, expected yesterday, didn't arrive (the OT made a formal complaint). Shitting in a pad isn't for this man, no, never, even if I deal with it as he knows I will. He has his own mind, as they say. He narrowly misses "FUCK" being his last word.

He's going where I can't follow; I'm aware of standing back.

They refuse to take away the paraphernalia of dying two days later. I'm "not a priority" as we didn't have a hospital bed. I have to hang up on a call centre operative, ring back and demand to speak to the manager. I'm asking them how they know the size of my house, what I can store there, if they know what it's like to STILL have the equipment after a death. "WELL DO YOU?"

They didn't bring the commode, the commode that might have helped.

I've eaten nothing, so while the paramedics (try to) work on his blood sugar, I work on mine. Iced coffee/chocolate. Then a quick text with a friend to say that we're in trouble. When you're a 24-hour carer you have to find ways of keeping going, no-one's coming to help (or if they are it's going to be over quickly). While you see death coming, you don't.

It's weeks before I can stand to drink coffee. Cake makes me sick (but I don't lose any carer-weight). In fact, most things make me sick. I learn to stop saying: "I'm not hungry". I catch flu for the first time in years; breaking classes just in time to throw up.

"Gradually his breathing will slow down, and then stop." We're back there.

He breathes in and out – strong, deep breaths – for hours. If he were speaking he'd be saying (as usual): "I'm not going anywhere, I'm going to turn the corner!" In his beautiful (he liked the word 'mellifluous') voice, the one for the small-hours politics phone-ins. While he was "Adam from Northampton", I was always asleep.

The lead paramedic stays, stays for hours. She's sitting there on the landing, on the pine dining chair the nurse hauled up there, the nurse who was going to come twice a week 10pm–7am so I could have a sleep, the person for whom the medicine in the kitchen cupboard was suddenly not "anticipatory". The medicine I carried back from the head-shaking pharmacist, that he brought home the pre-scription for (displeased), leaning heavily against the porch, hoisting his trousers up, out in his car (against my wishes, but he said he wouldn't drive if he really didn't feel capable).

God, he hated that nurse, even the thought of her: "Maybe she can come another night, when I'm feeling better?" He'd been feeling sick, a new symptom, and I'd called for a doctor; she gave a prescription for nausea, asked if I had questions. They hadn't come when I'd rung previously, they'd questioned what I might *want* for this "brutal illness", because there is *nothing*, don't I know that? Palliative care.

A croquet friend rang and I'd said, while holding him up, "Can he call you back later?" Later, I fluffed the line of "I am his partner" with an ominous "was", feeling my cheeks burning with shame that I'd given the game away.

If I had known it was his last night, I wouldn't have left his side. Not for a second. What use is sleep anyway? The pharmacist had advised against caffeine products, but I had them in mind.

I was called at 2am, for a bathroom visit. She wouldn't do it ("If you break your femur, I won't be able to keep you out of hospital".) But I am a soft touch, until it was clear that he couldn't stand.

Someone asked me, later, if I thought she'd given him "too much" when he finally agreed, at 3am, to take diamorphine. How can I say? I know I wish she'd woken me before she gave it to him, so we could have spoken properly before he died, so that my last words to him wouldn't have been the exhausted carer's "Be nice to the nurse or she might not come again".

She won't come again. A nurse comes (not, thank fuck, the one who asked him "So where are you on the journey from diagnosis to death?", the one I escorted out of the house, advising him to be careful with his language; or the one who diagnosed death over the phone, and I only realised *what* she'd diagnosed when the 'end of life' team marched in wearing plastic aprons, and started trying to talk over me). She administers more of that diamorphine, and then there's no more talking.

I show her the photograph of him receiving his PhD, anxious but handsome ("Not too bad, thank you", he would say, basking in his beauty). Wake up, darling, say something witty and wait and see if we'll get the joke, your eyes luminous with play.

"What do you call a man working in a cake shop?" I'd asked people a few weeks ago. Only he knew the answer: "The boss".

A woman had come ("Is Dad upstairs?") to sell us a device that you can press if you've fallen out of bed. I was pleased with the thought of it – in case I had rushed to the shop. She was very earnest and we both leaned in earnestly for: "Do you have any questions?"

"Can I eat it? … It looks like a sweet".

We both laughed in surprise; and as time goes on I notice that *nobody at all* is funny, and my face has taken on a new shape.

The man who was to install the key cupboard to go with the device rang me the evening he died. "We've decided not to go ahead with that", I said. "Right-oh", said the man pleasantly. We. I hear a lot of We. People whose partners I've never met are part of the We who is 'sorry' for me. We are a We, and You Are Not.

I use his graduation photo for my second social media announcement of the day. Someone I quite like later tells me that he and his friends (some of whom I don't like) tried to guess his age from tweets. *How much* of a tragedy is this for him/them? Is this a tragedy that might visit *us*? (Psst, you can die at any age.)

His friend from South Africa wrote later to say he was 'timeless'; yes, he was, but his time came.

He's dead now, at 1.45pm on Monday 12th August 2019, and people are still 'liking' a Tweet from the morning, where I say he's "seriously ill, send positive thoughts". I've used a photo of him from before my time, that I found in the bureau while the paramedics were upstairs. He's at a croquet match he's won; there's the trophy; he's looking laid back, sated, all is well in his world.

It feels bad not to tell them.

But maybe they're right, maybe he's not dead. He loves sleeping, almost as much as he loves television, almost as much as he loves me (ranking the three, choosing between two – regular activities: "What's *on* the television?!") He's still here in the room, tucked up under the duvet, sweep's brushes caressing his cheeks.

He's still here in the room for a couple of hours as the GP on-call doesn't call. I'm clenching my teeth. I don't stop clenching my teeth. I haven't stopped clenching my teeth. I've faced dying and death and have to Keep. Facing. It. I haven't left his side since it *wasn't* anaemia, and I'm not going to now.

When another GP does call, after the surgery is told the delay is unacceptable, he congratulates me on staying, seeing it through, as "you could have left". I don't understand, say we were together 20 years (where would I have gone?). I don't argue; you can't really, with your partner's dead body still in the room, can you?

You can afterwards, of course, but you don't get anywhere, and you look ungrateful, deranged.

And so began life after death, where this relationship, for some, didn't really happen, or didn't mean so much. A disenfranchised love, it has no piece of paper to certify it, not even the shared utility bills/mortgage statements that, apparently, *prove* that you were 'committed', 'exclusive' – 'a couple' even. I get asked who is the executor, told I'm not family, not the next of kin, that I don't hold Power of Attorney (all wrong).

The neighbours are unpleasant, not realising that I am their new neighbour. It's not so long since the newsagent told him: "I don't like to think of you alone there, I know you've got that girl looking after you, but…" "That's my partner." Pre-cancer, we had tended to be at my house. "Have you come to look after him?" "I'm his partner".

The only nice neighbour, after a particularly bad week of shouting/blaring horns at my decorators for parking in a public road, says that maybe they're worried about "whether an ambulance could pass through".… It's a bit early for that one.

It's October, not August, and perhaps I'm no longer recently-bereaved, if I ever was bereaved at all, so perhaps you can now shout at my decorators, the ones it takes all I have to let in. He hated the smell of paint.

No-one ever asked me if I was his wife while he was dying (I had worn a ring for hospital appointments, just in case). On the final night, I was asked my view on resuscitation. The cynic in me says it didn't matter then because I was doing all the work. They say end of life care is free but it's not true. What they mean is that if you need to spend a few days in a hospice (if there is one) when you're almost dead, then you don't pay, or if you need a carer to run in/out a couple of times a day, yes you can have that. A life ending takes longer than that, merits more than that.

The company who deliver pre-packaged frozen desserts (he liked a jam sponge and custard) ring, as they haven't heard from us, and – chuckling – they hope everything's ok. While she chats away, digging herself in deeper, I have time to try out a few ways to tell her. I'm factual and kind, but she's mortified; her day is over.

Mostly it's me who is mortified. Bureaucracy takes me from who I'd begun to think I was, someone who, if she could cope with the "journey from diagnosis to death", could cope with, could do, ANYTHING, to someone Googling how many diazepam it would, you know, take.

The registrar of births and deaths is in a nearby town that he didn't like (I'd never been there). It's a freezing August day; and while fruitlessly trying to find a shop in which to buy a jumper, I nearly ring him to say he's right, it's the pits, there are no actual shops. It's the first days of the relentless, exhausting "Why haven't I rung him?" loop.

The sign-in panel isn't working and the receptionist looks me up and down: "Have you come to register a birth or a death?" I register a single man's death. The registrar is nice. It's pouring with rain so I sit down in the empty reception, but it's clear that now my business is complete I'm not welcome. An ashen-faced couple wait where I once sat; they've definitely come to register a death; what do I look like?

I go through everything with one company, then ring back a couple of days later with a question, only to discover that they didn't record anything, nothing at all, and I have to tell them again that he has died. He has to die again. I complain on social media and an operative chastises me for posting personal data (which I am not). The same day I am trolled – not the worst, but ungenerous, unkind.

After threatening texts that I don't believe, the phone is cut off, because they've updated their records to show my contact details but they're trying to take a payment from his closed account. It's all my fault, apparently, because I didn't register the death *quickly enough*. They talk me through the days between when he died and when I called. "We're sorry for your loss, but you should have…". I must pay a reconnection fee if I want phone/internet again. After a 40-minute wait (twice, I was cut off the first time), and a long conversation, a worker finally realises what I'm saying: I didn't know when the payment date was.

The gas/electricity company insist I can't cancel a policy because *I've* already started paying it, but I haven't, *he* did. They won't believe me (one instance, I suppose, where we *were* seen as a couple) and insist I have to pay now for a full year. "I'M PAYING YOU NOTHING MORE, DO YOU HEAR?" When I ring back and tell her manager that he just died, she's audibly shocked and authorises a £10 apology payment. I've got a few of those and I hate them.

The tax situation is completely sorted through Tell Us Once – a service whereby you can inform a range of government agencies in England & Wales of a death. And then a letter arrives to my address, addressed to him, saying that he (not me) needs to do 'one last' self-assessment, and needs to inform them if his 'circumstances change in future'. If you're not dead in the future? Do a self-assessment for the year that you died? The automated voice asks why I'm ringing: "It's about a death," I say.

"A debt. You're ringing about a debt?"

"A DEATH."

"You're ringing to pay a debt?"

A real person tells me to ignore the letter, it's come out in error. "This would push some people over the edge," I observe mildly, but I can't get an answer to how, why, the letter was even *generated* let alone sent; case closed, bye.

Our solicitor is fabulous.

The bank is nothing but helpful. It has a bereavement service.

"Have you got a bereavement service?"

"A what? Oh, no, we just deal with that here."

"We're sorry for your loss…"

"We're sorry for your loss…"

"We're sorry for your loss…"

Polly want a cracker. "I DON'T CARE if you're sorry for my loss. You don't care. We both know you're just following a script…".

"He can't fill in a form because he's DEAD. Do you want me to go down the churchyard and ask him?" Sometimes I want to shock, because I am now beyond shocked. I have to bite my tongue, choose my battles; anger is physically painful. Once, just once, pushed way too far, I completely lose it; I'm threatened that the recorded call will be "listened to". (Shit.)

The same close friend wasn't there a second time; I'm neither angry nor sad – this isn't about me, and others have taken his place: I make two unexpected close friends in the aftermath. One comes to help me choose a cat, well two cats actually; they're older but with lots of life; the other asks after them (and me) from the Pyramids.

The bureaucracy isn't over; but sequestration is (sort of) and I have to deal with more and more people who are acquaintances.

"Have you got *friends* you can talk to?" (which means they think you might not have; you might be a bit of a loser in more than one way).

"Hope you have friends you can talk to" (which means they don't care if you have or not but at least they've said something 'supportive'. This one is stablemates with: "Hope you're getting some support!").

Someone writes using the phrase "at this time in your life". Her text gets deleted; it's not the only one. FUCK OFF (something I *don't* say).

One person told me, with absolute conviction, that it's my job to tell people what I might need from them. Ah yes, another job for me, let's add that to the list shall we? The non-bereaved don't have to think ahead, the bereaved do. Personally, I'd sooner stick pins in my eyes. It takes me weeks to say that I can't do something, that I just can't, and I can't look the person in the eye that I told that to.

Some people are *never* sorry for my loss, thanks for that; some hear about it weeks or months later and then they're sorry, red-faced and awkward, a bit pitying – so it's never just October, it's also always potentially August.

There are happenings that he would have enjoyed: "so she said ... and I said...! And then they all, one by one, marched past the window carrying boxes and staring..." Things just fade away unexplored. A new landscape, not pleasant to look at.

What I'm finding I enjoy (even more than before) is taking photographs of the local countryside, the area he chose, that I now live in, on my own. I get unexpectedly good at it, and am offered a paid gig!

Anyway, it's Halloween; people are dressing up as the dead, changing their social media profile pictures to grey-faced corpses.

I wonder if they know how your lips freeze and stay frozen when you kiss a dead person goodbye? What it's like when the undertaker asks if this is the *last* time you'll view the body (the second and last, when you've brought a photo where he's very much alive and – by coincidence – wearing the same tie as you chose for him now he's very much dead), because if so he's going to "seal up the coffin". A panic attack on the bus, if you must know. When the doors closed.

There's a class to teach whether I'm traumatised or not.

People are told that #ItsOkNotToBeOk, but that's untrue. Once you've reported a death a few times you know in your bones that your feelings don't matter. Keep going, ride the waves of anxiety, try to look normal.

And if anybody can't keep going, or can't just be better after some tea and a chat, it's 'oh, complicated grief', the preserve of 'mental health services', time to let 'professionals' take over, not our job, nothing we can do, no, nothing.

'Mental health', 'physical health', neither reliably compassionate. Offered clinical psychologists, drugs, and leaflets, I'll always take the leaflets and run. The leaflets speak to me as if I'm thick, but they do tell me how to get a dead person off junk mailing lists.

My personal therapy is self-funded, established, and cognizant of complexity: I don't have to answer to anyone for it.

The class is for first years, who weren't even alive when our eyes met at a university interview …

There are three jobs on offer and I'm pitching for ALL of them. Interview number 13, and if this doesn't work, I am never applying for another job in a university. I've finally realised that my soul is being destroyed by rejection. We're sociologists but no-one's told me we don't live in a meritocracy.

I've done the 'what I can offer to the Department' presentation (whatever you want, for fuck's sake). A man who has been asking very sticky questions sits back sated; Jesus, finally.

And then *he* comes into view, looking for all the world as if he has fallen in love.

(Oh, and the title of this piece? One of his favourite ways to answer the phone. Always funny. You need timing to say it. He had timing. Well, usually.)

Note

Acknowledgements

I would like to thank my first readers – Rose Barbour, Clare Shaw, Jonathan Wyatt, Tess Wyatt, Manu Bazzano, and Gottfried Heuer.

27 Metaphoric affect processing

Reflecting and transcending self as metaphor

Melissa Johnson Carissimo

Introduction

The ubiquitous "How are you?" can pose a challenge under the best of circumstances. In the context of illness, for patients and medical professionals alike, the question may seem unanswerable. Strategic implementation of metaphor, not only as an instrument of description, but of pre-verbal perception, can help us find words. It can embody, bear witness to, and transform feelings that might otherwise go unexpressed. Metaphoric affect processing, the topic of this chapter, is a structured, metaphor-based interview developed and codified in the public hospital settings of oncology and in-patient psychiatric care. The technique allows participants to identify, verbalize, and regulate emotion as poetic metaphor, expanding perspective, empathy, and wellbeing. The technique is illustrated here in vignettes and briefly contextualized in fields including metaphor theory, narrative medicine, and neurolinguistics.

Metaphorically speaking

Metaphor is quick, discreet, and spacious, uniquely suited to witnessing, naming, and containing complexity. In hospital settings, these qualities are invaluable to both patients and medical professionals. When encounters are data-based, hurried, anguished, or all three, the full arc of a person's story can be unwieldy. Patients may find themselves at a loss for words, with medical professionals at a loss for empathic responses to meanings they haven't heard. Nothing less than human connection is at stake. Metaphor, on the other hand, reveals meaning in manageable bits. For the speaker as well as the listener, it carries intuitive, pre-verbal form from mind to body and *vice versa*. In the wilderness of raw experiential data, a truly resonant (often unconventional) metaphor can express the otherwise inexpressible. It expands us beyond ourselves. It is sensory, yet transcends. Metaphor is a process, a neural phenomenon (Lakoff and Johnson, 1980). It is relational and intrinsically empathic because both speaker and listener embody it, and so together gain access to the metaphoric space between them, simultaneously inside and out. As long as we don't reduce it to rubble with the little hammers of our logic, form born of metaphor bestows meaning.

Metaphor-mirroring

The following recounts the development and implementation in public healthcare of a structured, metaphor-based dialogue of my own design, which I have termed *metaphoric affect processing* (MAP). In hospital treatment settings including post-surgical oncology, chemotherapy, hemodialysis, and acute-care psychiatric units, patients and medical staff are using MAP to identify, verbalize, and regulate emotion as metaphor. Participants address feelings and professional burnout through the strategic engagement of metaphor, not only as an instrument of description, but first of sensory perception. For certain individuals, open-ended introspection can trigger negative or counter-productive thinking modes associated with stress, rumination, anxiety, and depression—where rational reflection, by delivering "what we already know," can be counter-productive and self-perpetuating. The MAP interview is designed to mitigate this risk.

More than a thousand metaphor-based interviews in "extreme listening" hospital environments have contributed to the development, codification, and research of MAP, or *metaphor-mirroring*. At the center of the process is a metaphor-based Q&A that lets us answer the ubiquitous—but potentially daunting question, "How are you?" In MAP, the elegance of the answer is not deliberate. For the participant, it's almost effortless, "automatic" poetry. Throughout the process, MAP foregoes self-explanation and inward-directed analysis (the only analytical forays allowed are into a hypothetical dictionary). When metaphor-mirroring sets about problem-solving, it actively guards against interpretation, personal association-making and "why's." MAP comprises five phases: *framing, perception, description, definitional commentary*, and *revision*.

I have conducted most of my interviews at bedside, in cancer, psychiatric, and hemodialysis wards, chair-side in the cases of waiting rooms and chemotherapy armchairs. In these hospital settings, healthcare recipients are almost exclusively referred to as "patients," so I am using that term freely here, too.

When I meet them in their various limbos of illness and its treatment, my patient-poets—disproportionately female—are in positions, if not mind-sets, of compulsory repose. Reclining women. They measure caesura in minutes, hours, days, months, years. For some, time is running out, though this reality, with its emotional and existential implications, will probably not be openly addressed in-hospital. In these life-and-death treatment settings, death often remains the unnamed attending. Physical death, psychic death, grief *before death*, and the fear of losing the self we know, will likely go unspoken, which makes it harder for these reclining women to feel alive. Enter, Metaphor.

Throughout, identifying details, dialogue, and texts have been changed as necessary to protect the privacy of individuals.

A definition

"The essence of metaphor is understanding and experiencing one kind of thing in terms of another" (Lakoff and Johnson, 1980, p. 116). From its Greek and

Latin roots, metaphor is generative, active, transformational: to transfer, to alter, to change. *Meta* gives us "over, across, and between:" a sense of bridging. The Greek *pherein* gives "to carry over," and "to bear," and even to bear children: a sense of offering, continuity, or, in my personal etymology, magic.

Day-hospital, chemotherapy

To find the words to contain the disorder and its attendant worries gives shape to and control over the chaos of illness (Charon, 2001).

Her husband had led me to her, asking if I might help calm her down. Her whole young body was folded in upon itself. She was seated outside one of the treatment rooms, which meant her blood-work had checked out and she could proceed with her chemo today, a small victory for most patients.

The waiting room and chairs along the adjoining halls were full, so we stood as close as we could. Without making eye contact, the young woman began whispering an apology about being afraid of needles. She wore a polka dot scarf to cover the bareness of her scalp and fingered it where her hairline would have been, while her husband half-heartedly reminded her that the blood-drawing had gone just fine, that she'd been brave, that it was all good. I crouched down and reached up to put a hand on her shoulder. Her husband took the opportunity, somewhat sheepishly, to back away. This chemotherapy day-hospital was treating over seventy patients a day, five days a week. He slipped into the current of doctors, patients, family, and pastel-coated nurses moving up and down the long hall and in and out of rooms. He looked almost as undone as she.

A poet and a scribe

Still touching her shoulder, I ventured, "May I ask you something strange?"

She nodded toward her lap.

"What color is this feeling you're feeling, right now?"

Without missing a beat she said, "Gray." This happens often, that the color of a feeling is there, at the ready and available for verbalization as if the visual cues were actual.

"What kind of gray?" I asked.

"Like clouds…"

"Can you tell me about the sound of the feeling? What sound is it?"

"It's loud breathing. Hard," she said. After a rough pause, she glanced up and added, "Labored."

"Going back to the feeling, can you tell me what it's like to the touch? You hold it, put your palms against it…. What does it feel like?"

Here, we were using metaphor as an instrument of pre-verbal affect perception, which almost immediately, with seeming effortlessness, becomes verbal description. I instruct my accidental poets not to create their metaphors, not to try to be clever, but to wait for them, discover them, sense them. To let them emerge.

I asked the young woman a few more questions. I called them "sense-metaphor questions." She was calming visibly, poet to my scribe, as we went on. I wrote down her answers in a column on the clipboard I carried for the purpose, with an old-fashioned sheet of carbon paper tucked between the top and second sheets.

When we had completed my "questionnaire," I asked permission to read her answers back to her—we'd made a poem, I told her. A "metaphor-mirror." Almost imperceptibly, she shrugged, which I took as assent.

"The title," I said, "is 'Waiting for My Chemotherapy.'" I leaned in close enough to conjure a quiet space in the crowded hallway and began to recite.

Waiting for My Chemotherapy

> I am gray,
> gray like clouds.
> I am the loud sound
> of breathing,
> hard, labored breaths.
> To the touch I am dense,
> the smell of something burned,
> a sour taste.
> I envelop all things
> and carry them away.

As I put her words between us, she began to unfold a little. She looked at me frankly now, openly.

"That's how I feel," she said.

"Yes," I said. "They're your words."

She had stopped shivering. I had been with her for just a few minutes.

The safety of definitional commentary

The next step in MAP is *definitional commentary*, which is how we talk about poets' metaphor-mirrors. Definitional commentary pushes back against our natural tendency to wonder "why?" We look together at the poetic text, at single words and phrases, and we start with those that strike us most. Definitional commentary (which doesn't preclude a poet's working alone) steps back from the feeling, moves to the text, and aims for objective witnessing. It is rigorously non-interpretative, non-analytical, non-associative, and non-judgmental—in a word, definitional. This allows for an expansion of perspective and an influx of new information free of limits that can result when we begin to explain. Upon hearing or reading their metaphoric self-reflections, participants/poets often ask, "What does it mean?" My answer is always, emphatically, "I don't know. That's not the point…" ("The drive to explain is an epidemic in modern thought…" (Yalom, 2016)). The goal here is to listen and look closely at words and phrases, noting definitional meanings, resonance and juxtapositions, citing and defining terms as fully and precisely as if we were dictionaries or Wikipedia.

"If we open a dictionary," I asked the young woman, "What might we find in the entry for 'gray?'"

"Black plus white," she said.

"Extremes," I said.

We went back and forth, offering many possible, often conflicting, but never perplexing objective implications of words as they came to us.

Clouds? Vapor, impalpable, high over head.

Hard? Not soft, more like stone—you can't change it. Or to change it you'd have to cut it with a special blade, or crush it.

Breathing—a sign of life, necessary, air in and out, expansion and contraction, again and again, all on its own, oxygenating a system, nourishing and cleansing. *Bad* breath.

Loud—can't ignore it, not silent.

Labored—labor is work; past tense means work has been done, something ventured, something accomplished.

Dense—not easy to see through, or move through, not fluid.

Burned—made hotter and hotter till the original stuff is changed.

Burned—tricked. Cheated. Or betrayed.

Envelop—wrap up, softly surround.

Carry—to bear something forward, its weight or its essence.

Away—not here. To carry away.

The nature of definitional commentary is fundamental to metaphoric affect processing. It keeps us from dropping back into the repetitive, habitual act of expressing what we already know, which old information we are aiming to refresh and expand (and possibly redirect toward practical problem-solving) rather than entrench. Long after this dialogue took place in chemotherapy, I read Rita Charon's depiction of "close reading" in a narrative medicine program with a group of medical interns. She writes:

> We were doing with the literary text something not unlike what [the interns] were doing with the dead human body that had been entrusted to them, respecting the architecture while taking it apart, comprehending that there is a life in its unity that cannot be seen in its parts, yet one must see the parts in order to see the whole.
>
> (Charon, 2017, p. 180)

"Away," the young woman repeated. "Not here."

I thought to myself, her body will do the carrying. Her body will carry her "self" away from "here," where, by all logic, her body must be.

"It's not just the needles," she said.

Ever so gently, we were talking about death.

"Your poem is very powerful," I said.

"I want to read it to my husband."

"Would you read it to me, first?"

Whenever possible, this is part of the process.

The young woman recited her lines with great dignity, not seeming to mind that patients to our left and right were listening attentively. Each metaphor hung in the air between us like an emotional hologram.

By reading her text out loud, the young woman was reasserting her authorship, taking control of her own words and images by speaking them again, this time with broader and deeper awareness.

Revising affect as metaphor

To move us into the final, "revision" phase of the process, after a natural moment of silence, I asked if she could tell me which among her words and phrases were closest to the core of her discomfort.

She thought for a moment, and answered, "carry them away."

"Regarding your title, 'Waiting for My Chemotherapy,' if you move toward a sensation of embracing that *feeling* of carrying away," I asked, "what does the movement, this *action* of 'carrying away' become?"

"It becomes something that can last, like family".

This was the first step in the optional, revision phase of the work, in which the first metaphoric affect representation of present-moment emotion, instead of the emotion itself, is sensorily re-processed toward widened perspective and mood-change. During revision, the participant-poet sense-metaphorically embodies the revised state as he conjures it. He or she actually *feels* different as his affect state begins to reflect his metaphoric perception of it. This effect has been self-reported by our poets, and observed: maybe it's the eye contact, where before there was none, or the smile, or an opening of the chest and dropping of the shoulders, or even tears—of self-recognition, and then a sigh of relief. This is no cure. It is, though, an opportunity to embody—thanks to metaphor—another way of being, even if only for a moment. The revised metaphoric text can serve as a map to this found destination. It provides relief and a moment of clarity perhaps previously unimagined.

The young woman's revision:

Today, Waiting for my Chemotherapy
I am the yellow of light.
Silence,
and softness.
I can last,
like family.

The topsy-turvy metaphor-mixing that happens in a metaphor-mirror is at once deeply felt and deeply nonsensical. Viktor Frankl observed, "The more comprehensive the meaning, the less comprehensible it is." He goes on to say, "Here is the point at which science gives up and wisdom [or poetry] takes over" (Frankl, 1984, p. 136).

I slid her page off the top of my clipboard and handed it to her. With her okay, I kept the carbon copy for myself.

She looked up, smiling faintly.

"Thank you," she said.

Shortly after, she raised her hand when a nurse stepped into the hall and called her name, which made me realize I was hearing it for the first time. All those questions and I hadn't asked her name. Somehow it wasn't a bad thing.

The metaphor-mirror in context

From the beginning, the ease with which metaphor-mirroring accessed meaningful introspection and dialogue was immediate and striking. I began trying to contextualize its effects in various fields.

Many of the concepts illuminating the efficacy of MAP came well after its codification, including premises in the field of *Narrative Medicine* (Charon, 2017), onto which MAP, to my delight, maps, and which perfectly captures the relational spirit and intentions of a metaphor-mirroring project (Spiegal and Spencer, 2017); Carl Rogers' necessary and sufficient conditions (Rogers, 1942); Eugene Gendlin's focusing—many commonalities—and *felt sense*, "One has a felt sense when one can feel more than one understands…" (Gendlin, 1982, p 145); Matthew Lieberman's Symbolic Processing of Affect (SPA) as central to his Disruption (of negative thinking patterns) Theory (Lieberman, 2011), and related to his group's *f*MRI studies showing the neural address in the right ventrolateral pre-frontal cortex shared by the events of SPA and disruption (Lieberman et al, 2007).

Today, as they apply to the resonant triad of self, metaphoric self, and other, I am also finding relevant the work in conceptual metaphor theory (CMT) of George Lakoff and Mark Johnson, and on metaphor and neural theory where:

> [C]omplex metaphors arise from primary metaphors that are directly grounded in the everyday experience that links our sensory-motor experience to the domain of our subjective judgments, thus primary metaphor's independence from language; and that … neurons connected to the source and target neural ensembles … are coactive during [their] conflation.
>
> (Lakoff and Johnson, 1999, p. 254)

In metaphor-mirroring, a participant self-generates metaphor in response to questions that *propose both* source and target domains. He scans his "target"—the landscape of *feelings* he wishes to explore—until a self-generated metaphor-match emerges from the proposed sensory—visual, aural, tactile, spatial, motile—"source" domain. Similarities across fields and among theoretical systems helped me better conceptualize the movement back and forth between MAP's favored modality and the other. When I reached out to a noted professor in the field of metaphor, to describe metaphor-mirroring and raise questions about the potential overlaps above, her prompt email response included the phrase, "You are doing what I always thought should be possible."

Quantifying the benefits of metaphor-based dialogue

The benefits of MAP have been demonstrated in a number of in-hospital research projects, including the few I list here.

Working with acute care psychiatric in-patients, we looked at correlations between alexithymia scores assessed by the TAS-20 (Parker et al, 1993) and metaphoric reflections of affect state as elicited by MAP. We found that even patients scoring high on the scale—indicating deficits in ability to identify and verbalize feelings, and to engage imagination—reported, often with surprise, that they recognized in their metaphor-mirrors accurate expressions of their feelings in the moment.

On the same ward, I adapted Russell and Barrett's original Map of the Circumplex Model of Affect (Barrett & Russell, 1999; 2005), which represents affect in four quadrants as degrees of activation in relation to positive/negative emotional valence. Following metaphor-mirroring sessions, patients consistently indicated increases in the less-activated/positive emotion quadrant (calm, contented, etc.), independent of improvement in the other three quadrants. We saw this as a possible indication that MAP was effectively improving the quality of participants' experience of present-moment emotion-states, regardless of change in the emotion-states themselves.

Most recently, in hemodialysis, nursing staff members successfully addressed symptoms of burnout (Karkar et al, 2015) and the three components of the syndrome—depressive anxiety, depersonalization/lack of empathy, and satisfaction—as defined and measured by Cristina Maslach's Maslach Burnout Index (Maslach et al, 1996).

In-patient, acute care psychiatric service

"Man is oriented toward the world out there, and within this world, he is interested in meanings to fulfill, and in other human beings" (Frankl, 1984, p. 138).

"I, Metaphor…"

Thirteen women, early 20s to late 60s, were seating themselves. They were examples of degrees, on a sweeping scale, of self-care, self-composure, social status, diagnosis, and pharmacological intervention. The important common denominator beyond gender and the fact of their hospitalization was their voluntary participation in this metaphor-mirroring session. They had agreed to follow me into the dayroom because they were curious, or bored, or because they saw others wandering in and so followed. Sometimes I felt like a pied piper. But it didn't matter why they came, just that they wanted to be there.

One shy poet positioned herself on a windowsill outside the circle. She and I had worked together one-on-one earlier that morning. Could she just listen? she'd asked. In my observation, listening can be as helpful as actively participating. The same metacognitive introspection takes place, just in silence. The unusual act itself, of scanning the interior landscape for a sensory-metaphoric match to a feeling, is what nudges us off the neurological groove of a habitual or negative thought-mode, and (I imagine) safely into the right ventrolateral prefrontal cortex.

> Today, we hear:
> I am dark brown.
> I am bright red.
> I'm black like my hair.
> Black like nothing.
> Grey like fog.
> Dark blue, bright blue.
> Grass-green.
> …I don't know …
> Brown, like the hospital-blanket.
> Fuchsia.
> Navy.
> Blue deep sea…

Deep listening and intrinsic empathy

Of course, the quality of the self-reflection-as-poetry is never meant to be judged, but the quality of the *listening* that takes place is, and it is invariably high. The sudden poetry of emotion, the impact of seeing ourselves in the mirror of a metaphor and hearing our feelings—the artistry of them—*recited by another*, is moving to listeners and poets alike. Yet the process doesn't seem to "over-stimulate"— which had been a concern early on in psychiatric wards. Patients who are loud in the hall tend to be quiet here. Patients straining against the effects of medication often find a reserve of concentration. Line by line around a circle, verses emerge. Patience is deep. Patients wait. They nod at each others' images. They crane to see a speaker. They leave with their poems in hand. That one poet's response rarely "contaminates" another's is also noteworthy—my black is not *your* black. The specific sensory quality of an emotion-state is typically clear and precise to the speaker because she is *experiencing* it as she speaks. The listener feels it, too, such that recitation in group work creates a kaleidoscope of feelings-as-senses, sensory notes in symphonic counterpoint that stir us all and underpin the empathy intrinsic to MAP.

The following list are images taken from the metaphor-mirrors we made that morning, each from a different text. The last is from a nurse who paused in the doorway for a moment to see what was going on, which meant he had to answer a few SMQ's himself. Patients may listen without metaphor-mirroring, but anyone else present is urged to participate. The title of each metaphor-mirror was "*I am:*"

> two little birds
> arguing between themselves
> limp and rigid
> like the chord of a violin
> transparent
> the sound of a tsunami advancing
> a mouse running away
> a messy room

And from the curious staff member,

> I'm the screeek of a door's hinge,
> A cat in front of its bowl…

Then he disappeared—off to lunch.

Metaphorically speaking

> [T]he intellectual 'knowing with the head' or 'knowing that' of Propositional meanings … effects emotion only indirectly.… Implicational meanings capture the 'deep structure' of experience…
>
> (Teasdale & Chaskalson, 2011, p.113)

They'd hung umbrellas in the city center (part of a publicity campaign for a convention in town). There were umbrellas everywhere, of every color and arrangement and bold attitude floating improbably high overhead with no people attached. There were phalanxes of them in long, sharp rows, and riots of them in wind-blown bunches strung on wires across the city's *piazza*'s and *vicoli*. There were umbrellas dangling straight up and down, others tilting at each other at wild angles, and others, singletons, framed alone in the dead-ends of medieval cul-de-sacs. There were even casualties up there on those high wires, octagons deformed where nylon had atrophied off its spokes, umbrellas blown inside out in arms-up images of surrender, or battery, or ruin and abandonment. All colorfully suspended.

I imagine a brain with a wedge removed to show the right ventrolateral prefrontal cortex. I imagine all of humanity glimmering there in Lieberman's two yellow spots.

The meaning of it all

Not long ago, I was standing in an endless checkout line at IKEA when a young man, already cashed out, began calling "Excuse me!" from beyond the register while waving in my direction. When I realized he was waving at *me*, he pointed to the young woman beside him. She was grinning, shifting the weight of a big blue bag so she could wave with both hands.

"Remember me?" she called out.

I did. These years later, even without the polka dot scarf.

"I still have the poems!" she waved, beaming for a few seconds more. I kept waving and beaming back till the flow of the milling, exiting crowd carried the young woman and her husband forward, and I returned to shuffling my own stuff forward as well.

References

Barrett, L.F., Russell, J.A. (1999) The structure of current affect: Controversies and emerging consensus. *Current Directions in Psychological Science*, 8 (1), pp. 10–14.

Barrett, L., Russell, J. (2005) Affect states arise from cognitive interpretations of core neural sensations that are the product of two independent neurophysiological systems vs. discreet neural system for every emotion. *Developmental Psychopathology*, pp. 715–734.

Charon, R. (2001) The patient-physician relationship. Narrative Medicine: A model for empathy, reflection, profession and trust. *Journal of the American Medical Association*, 286 (15), pp. 1897–1902.

Charon, R. (2017) A framework for teaching close reading, in Charon, R., Das Gupta, S., Herman, N., Irvine, C., Marcus, E., Colòn, E., Spencer, D., Spiegel, M. (eds.) *The Principles and Practice of Narrative Medicine*. New York: Oxford University Press, p. 180.

Frankl, V.E. (1984) *Man's Search for Meaning*. New York: Simone & Schuster.

Gendlin, E.T. (1982) *Focusing*. New York: Bantam, p. 145.

Karkar, A., Dammang, M., Bouhaha, B. (2015) Stress and burnout among hemodialysis nurses: A single-center, prospective survey study. *Saudi Journal of Kidney Diseases and Transplantation*, 30 (3), pp. 560–754.

Lakoff, G., Johnson, M. (1999) *Philosophy in the Flesh*. New York: Basic Books.

Lakoff, G., Johnson, M. (1980) *Metaphors We Live By*. London: The University of Chicago Press, 2003 edition, pp. 5, 254, 256.

Lieberman, M. (2011) Why symbolic processing of affect can disrupt negative affect: Social cognitive and affective neuroscience investigations, in Todorov, A., Fiske, S., Prentice, D. (eds.) *Social Neuroscience: Toward Understanding the Underpinnings of the Social Mind*. Los Angeles: University of California, pp. 188–209.

Lieberman, M., Eisenberger, N., Crockett, M., Tom, S., Pfeifer, J., May, B. (2007) Putting feelings into words: Affect labeling disrupts amygdala activity in response to affective stimuli. *Psychological Science*, 18 (5).

Maslach, C., Jackson, E., Leiter M. (1996) *Depressive Anxiety Syndrome; Depersonalization; and Reduced Personal Achievement, Masclach Burnout Inventory Manual*. Palo Alto, CA: Consulting Psychologists Press.

Parker, J., Bagby, R.M., Taylor, G. (1993) Factorial validity of the 20-item Toronto Alexithymia Scale. *European Journal of Personality*, 7, pp. 221–232.

Rogers, C. (1942) *Counseling and Psychotherapy: Newer Concepts in Practice.* New York: Houghton Mifflin.

Spiegal, M., Spencer, D. (2017) This is what we do, and these things happen: literature, experience, emotion, and relationality in the classroom, in Charon, R., et al. (eds.) *The Principles and Practice of Narrative Medicine.* New York: Oxford University Press, pp. 37–59.

Teasdale, J., Chaskalson, M. (2011) How does mindfulness transform suffering? *Contemporary Buddhism*, 12, pp. 103–124.

Yalom, I. (2016) *Creatures of a Day, and Other Tales of Psychotherapy.* New York: Basic Books.

28 Researching existential therapy's reference points

Elita Kreislere

Paying attention to existence

What is the *tradition* of existential therapy? Am I a traditionalist or a counter-traditionalist? These questions leave me lost and puzzled as I really don't know. Is there such a thing as tradition in existential therapy? I think it is a valid and serious question as here and there in the world we can witness ambitions to become "The Tradition", or at least to own the right to decide what is and what is not "The Tradition" in existential therapy. And it's a serious question also because there are psychotherapists like Irvin Yalom (1980) who don't consider existential therapy as a distinctive modality but rather a stance of any psychotherapist interested in so called existential "themes".

In the briefest possible way, I can define existential therapy as a *practice of paying attention to existence*. So the essence of existential therapy slips through the net, thrown by the rationally asked question "What is it?" I think that's because all the three components: practice, attention and existence are not objects but processes.

Luckily until now there are no prescribed users' manuals for existential therapeutic work, so usually we come to conclusions about existential therapy by thinking *about* it. But a problem arises here: such method leads to a person's opinion. Recently some of us witnessed and participated in a prolonged collision of such separate opinions via emails. In 2015 and 2016 a few existential therapists from around the world made an attempt to define together existential therapy. In fact Ernesto Spinelli at first invited the existential community to rethink existential therapy, but soon enough it turned into a more goal-oriented discussion. So after a year and a half we got seven pages of diplomatic consensus and hardly anyone was happy with it. Why? Because existence precedes essence (Sartre, 1956) and existence is always oneself's (Heidegger, 1927/1962). When another person rationally defines how you are paying attention to existence in existential therapy, you will never be satisfied with this definition as it will not grasp the deepest layers of process during therapy. I am not mystifying nor trying to make existential therapy into something very ethereal, but simply pointing to the problem: existential philosophers have given us a deep and profound insight into what it means to be a human, but that doesn't mean that we as existential therapists fully reflect and understand how it relates to our being a human-therapist. There is also a lack of adequate language to hold this narrative among professional therapists. I think that the wind of these shortages blows a lot of existential therapists into safer waters with seemingly less anxiety and unpredictability and more users' manuals.

Real life context

Speaking of the connection between psychotherapy and philosophy, Alice Holzhey-Kunz emphasizes that the definition of psychotherapy depends on how one understands human mental suffering: the philosophical understanding of human suffering and psychopathology is prior to the understanding of psychotherapy (Holzhey-Kunz & Fazekas, 2012). Here the next question arises: can the existential therapist's philosophical understanding of human mental suffering be a theoretical knowledge? Or does it rather stem from a deeply personal revelation of what it means to be human and to suffer from own existence? This leads us to a completely different and usually more hidden territories, namely, a therapist's own intimate answers to these complicated questions. So, we can assume that the most important layers of understanding of existential therapy often remain hidden.

The idea of studying the reference points of therapeutic work arose from a simple observation which can be made by every supervisor: there is a great difference between a beginner and an experienced therapist. Despite the popular humorous saying according to which "the method of existential therapy is an absence of method", the seasoned colleague knows, does or feels something differently than a novice. That means something important has happened in the process of becoming an existential therapist and it can be worthwhile to try to find out and conceptualize what this is.

Here are some of the basic ideas which led to the design of this research: keeping the awareness of the *real life context* of the practice of existential therapists; the core of the research must be thoughts, deeds and feelings of real existential practitioners. The aim of the research is to recognize common patterns in unique responses of specific therapists.

The heart of the Birštonas School of existential therapy is the Institute of Humanistic and Existential Psychology (HEPI), founded in 1996 in Birštonas, Lithuania. Around HEPI lives a large community of existential therapists from Latvia, Lithuania, Estonia, Russia, Ukraine, Belarus and other countries of the region. Many of those who have studied at HEPI are united in the East European Association for Existential Therapy, which annually publishes the professional journal *Existentia: psychology and psychotherapy*, and every September in Birštonas hosts a conference "The Existential dimension in counselling and psychotherapy". Now the East European Association for Existential therapy unites more than 300 therapists. Since 2013 the Association has been an organizational member of the European Association of Psychotherapy (EAP). In 2015 HEPI became an official training institution of EAP enabling graduates to receive EAP Certificates. HEPI has several education programmes: existential therapy, group psychotherapy, existential supervision, psychological counselling and Dasein analysis. HEPI was founded and until now is led by Rimantas Kočiūnas – a professor at Vilnius University. Since its foundation, around 700 students have studied there.

Two points are particularly interesting about the studying process in HEPI. Firstly, students come to the tranquil town of Birštonas for two weeks to live and study all in the same house, which intensifies the study process incredibly. The second, but possibly the most important, feature of education in HEPI is that there is a complete absence of "the right way" of practising existential therapy. Everyone has to find their personal path in existential theory and practice as there reigns a marked emphasis with regards to diversity: students, tutors, recommended literature, leaders of therapeutic groups, books, conference guests – all are very different and all have the right to be there and find their own way of being there.

Exploring the reference points of therapeutic work in the Birštonas School of existential therapy

I am going to investigate the reference points of therapeutic work by exploring the embodied existential therapeutic work by therapists from the Birštonas School of existential therapy.

The choice of participants had to meet the following criteria: they had to be fully-trained, practising existential therapists; they had to be trained only in existential therapy; they had to be graduates or tutors of HEPI; they need to have experience practicing existential therapy for at least ten years. All respondents met the criteria: eight out of ten are supervisors of HEPI; eight women, two men; the average age being 50; all of them have academic psychological education; three are also medical doctors; all have extensive psychotherapeutic work experience for more than ten years with different groups of difficult clients. It seemed important to choose participants representing different therapeutic styles and generations from different countries.

Thematic Analysis was chosen as the most appropriate research method – a qualitative method developed for psychology by Braun and Clarke (2006). Ten 60-minute long expert interviews were conducted. The main research question comprised two aspects: "What do you think is helpful in your work as an existential therapist for your client?" The first aspect of the question invites participants to reflect at a high level of conceptualization on their work, while the second focuses on the understanding of their personal experience.

Interviews were recorded, transcribed and then coded. At first, each interview was processed separately, then all the themes found in separate interviews were grouped, then the final themes, revealed in the whole body of data, were formulated (Guest et al, 2012). The study process was like an endless circular movement from the received data to understanding and ideas, then back to the data, then modification of conclusions and their reformulation, discussing with participants and again reformulating themes.

An immense difference of the possible themes was observed during the first stages of the study. Yet all therapists in the interview talked about three topics: their relationship with the clients in the therapeutic process, about therapeutic work and the understanding of the therapeutic process itself. This led to the three main groups of themes or *dimensions*:

(a)   dimension of therapeutic relationship;
(b)   dimension of therapeutic interaction;
(c)   dimension of theoretical understanding of therapy.

The word "dimension" is used to emphasize the wholeness and indivisible character of therapeutic work in existential therapy which cannot be divided into separate parts, but can be contemplated from different points of view. We can also understand "dimensions" as different focuses of attention. Although the participants were not encouraged to theorize about therapy, but rather to disclose their personal experience, some themes pointing towards the theoretical basis of their work were identified.

Three dimensions of therapeutic work in the Birštonas School of existential therapy

In existential therapy the question "How?" matters maybe more than "What?" It is therefore important to characterize the style of a participant's speech. Although all of them are experienced professionals, in every interview there was at least one moment where therapists were concerned and did their best to avoid high-flown phrases, generalities or banal truths. This shows the therapists' subtle self-reflection and reveals their trained skill and ability to be as personal and honest as they can be. Standardized statements like "as Buber wrote" or "people suffer from anxiety" were very rare and were not coded. The quotes of participants have been italicized. In the following the term "therapists" refers to existential therapists of both sexes of the Birštonas School, and the same applies to *"clients"*.

(a) Therapeutic relationship

Three themes clarifying this particular dimension of the therapeutic relationship were discovered. They reveal how a therapist experiences the relationship with a client; the therapist's attitude to the client and the therapist's attitude towards himself. Nearly all participants emphasized the pivotal role of the therapeutic relationship in existential therapy.

The first theme is *A sincere and honest therapist's attitude towards the client as a partner in a vital and real relationship*. The theme of honesty and candour in interviews with therapists manifests in a variety of contexts – the therapist's honesty to the client, to themselves and the therapist's experience of fairness and candour as an outstanding unspoken requirement in training in HEPI. Therapist B states that an honest and sincere therapist's attitude forms the basis for a trusting and open relationship, therefore the client is able to be honest with the therapist and "most importantly, to himself," the client has a chance not to "pretend" in front of the therapist. For therapist K, partnership in therapy is a movement from *"now"* towards what the client really wants. "It is probably some kind of alliance, it's an equal and mutual following this path with the client."

The second theme – *The therapist's accepting attitude as openness to the client and as willingness to meet and respond to everything that will occur in the therapeutic process* – holds one of the most common terms in contemporary discourse, i.e. an "accepting" attitude. Often acceptance is meant as a word which does not need further exploration or understanding. These interviews give us a deeper insight into the connection between "acceptance" and "openness". Acceptance of the client means remaining open to anything that emerges in the therapy process. Therapist D said: "I am ready to meet everything. I mean everything, what can and will occur in the therapy process". Therapist A explains the difference between acceptance of everything emerging in therapy and agreement with everything:

> to be open doesn't mean embracing everything … when the client is furious at me for a long time, I am responding openly, I tell that it's difficult for me, so it doesn't mean I embrace everything, I mainly mean responding openly.

The meaning of "acceptance" in the participants' wording is: "to stay in contact", "respond openly", "embrace", "allowing to be", "allowing to happen". Therapists talked about the inner work, required by such a therapeutic position, mainly about ability to withstand the anxiety of uncertainty: "it takes a lot of effort – to stay there, to not hinder, to not clutter up the space in which there is a fundamental permission for everything to appear".

The third theme is *the therapist's respectfulness towards a client's freedom and responsibility for his own life and his chosen way of being.* Therapists referred to clients as the only experts of their life and this therapeutic stance we can call "an invited guest's position" in the client's world. The client is seen as the only one who owns his existence and gives the therapist permission, an invitation to attend, "to be in his world and to explore it", so they are limited to guest status, and respect the client's lived world's order. Interviews did not show an intention by the therapists to accept a knowing and teacherly position. The client is the only free and responsible master of his own life. Instead therapists tend to pass the responsibility to the client for his chosen way of life.

(b) Therapeutic interaction

The second dimension clarifies the more directly observable side of the therapeutic process, i.e. the work of therapy undertaken by the practitioner. This group of themes is much more versatile than the two others. Still this diversity brings no surprise, as existential therapy does not suggest any particular methods of therapeutic interaction and the results of this study show that the choice of any methods or techniques depends on every unique therapeutic situation.

The most repeated pattern in this dimension was the following: *The therapist's care for the client as an ongoing conscious monitoring and evaluation of the client's mental strength, resources, state of therapeutic relationship and attuning therapist's reactions in accordance with this.* This theme was one of the surprises of the research and reveals a seldom-explored aspect of existential therapy. All participants spoke about ongoing conscious evaluating work they do during the whole therapy process. Therapist C says: "intensity of help must be directly proportional to the readiness and ability of the client to live through suffering or trauma." Therapist J emphasizes caring about the whole situation of the client, including physical condition and special carefulness if the client's condition is clinically serious: "clinical symptoms serve as a sign to me to be even more considerate and careful, that every word I say, must be weighed very carefully and accurately." Therapists also make a clear distinction between "caring about relationship in therapy" and "talking about relationship between therapist and client".

The theme *Phenomenological therapeutic position as ability to constantly reside in uncertainty and continue cooperative exploration of the client's life* clarifies two things: (a) the practical content of the phenomenological position of the therapist; (b) phenomenological research as a method in existential therapeutic work. During interviews, therapists characterized their attunement to explore in words such as: "true interest", "full attention", "openness", "genuine wonder", "true intention to understand", "careful watching". Successful phenomenological exploration of the client's lived world rests on a trusting relationship, but also on the therapist's disposition to cooperation and unprejudiced exploration.

The theme *Therapeutic listening as the therapist's ongoing perception of himself and the client through thoughts, feelings and sensations* unfolds therapeutic listening as a holistic process. In the briefest way it is represented in therapist G's quotation: "the basis for the client's reliance on the therapist can be grounded in the therapist's striving to listen and understand the client with his mind, his feelings and body. Only through the mind not very much can be understood". In the same holistic way therapists constantly listen to themselves during therapy.

The essence of the theme *The creativity and freedom of the therapist in finding the unique way of therapeutic interaction with each client's world* can be grasped in this short quotation by therapist E: "the freedom of the therapist in choosing the appropriate methods of work is limited only by the needs and condition of the client". A therapist's ability to use everything – from what happens in the therapeutic process to their personal weaknesses – for the benefit of therapeutic process, can be considered an important sign that the therapist can freely and creatively choose methods of his therapeutic work. Therapists are not inclined to use ready-made therapeutic techniques.

The theme *Collaborative exploration and acceptance of the client's lived world as a method of transforming the client's assumptions about himself and his life* clarifies the "how" and "what for" the repeatedly mentioned exploration of a client's lived world takes place in therapy. Therapist A, in answering the question about the usefulness of such exploration work, says: "this leads to a greater acceptance, a man can change something only when he sees it and has accepted it, until there is acceptance, no change is possible."

The theme *Limitations of the therapist as an obstacle to the therapeutic process* provides us with an interesting nuanced aspect of existential therapy. Nearly all therapists in interviews mentioned one or another group or kind of clients they have particular struggles to work with and that they always think twice about whether they personally are able to handle what this client brings. Usually psychotherapists of other modalities try to identify whether this particular client is suitable for the therapy they practise. Here we see another attitude, as participants of research show their respect for any client and their right to receive help, but are considerate and critical about their ability to do it themselves in a noble way.

The theme *The therapist's ability to keep a long-term openness to any feelings of the client – the central aspect of the therapeutic emotion work* is self-explanatory. The most precise expression of this theme is found in therapist M's interview: "If there is a very intense feeling, then you must be able to stay open and to respond to the client openly, if needed".

He also specifies that not to be open means: "hide and defend yourself, i.e. close yourself for the client." To accept and respond openly can sometimes mean also "openly not to accept" the feelings of the client and speak openly about it with the client.

The theme *Exploration of the client's psychological resistance as a natural way of his being in the world* emphasizes a significant feature of existential therapy practice. Therapist K puts it in these words:

> If a person in therapy is very withdrawn, my interest will be attracted exactly by his withdrawnness, I will look at how much I can talk with him about how he feels himself in his withdrawnness which I experience while being with him, yes … at first comes the acceptance of him being withdrawn.

So therapists empathically refer to the resistance of the clients as their natural behaviour which has its meaning in the client's life.

The theme *The asymmetry of devoted time and attention to the client and the therapist in the therapeutic process* emphasizes that therapy time is devoted to the client; his needs and his life is the central focus in therapy despite the partnership-like, mutual and collaborative relationship with the therapist.

The next theme is *Setting of therapeutic goals through mutual exploration of the client's needs and his life's difficulties*. Therapist K says: "the goal of therapy must be perceived by me and my client and both of us must understand this goal." Discussion and setting of therapeutic goals is not an act or an action limited in time, but is a prolonged circular process which can be repeated several times during therapy. The therapy goal always arises from the client's needs and his own conscious decision to change something in his life. The client's conscious decision to change nothing is equally respected.

(c) *Theoretical understanding of therapy*

This dimension clarifies the theoretical comprehension of some aspects of existential therapy. Participants were encouraged to speak about their personal experience rather than theorize, but still some patterns were found which clearly relate to the theoretical aspects of existential practice.

The first theme *Fundamental human interrelatedness with others* is an interesting finding of this study and the most frequent pattern in theoretical dimension although none of the therapists specially focused on it. It was instead present in their narrative as something that goes without saying. Therefore, it was not noticed by the researcher for a long time, but when the pattern was discovered it became clear that therapists put this principle as a cornerstone of their work. Therapists do not see clients as isolated subjects or objects on whom they perform therapy, but see human beings as fundamentally interrelated with others: "each therapeutic process is unique with each client", "I never know before what the path with every person will be", "we don't try to change people, but still they are changing", "experiencing something together with another person is healing", "people can change because they are in fact open to the world and to others". Therapists refer to client and therapist as two others who constitute each other.

The theme *Phenomenology of the uniqueness of the client's lived world* clarifies phenomenology as a method of cognition allowing one to explore the client's lived world in its uniqueness. When used as a method of cognition, phenomenology means paying attention to what is directly perceived by the therapist, what constitutes the therapist's direct experience before he attends to his rational assumptions, but as well phenomenology as a method of cognition means focusing on the client's pre-reflective experience. None of the therapists used the word "phenomenology", but they talked about "exploring the life experience of the client as a whole", "to see how the client is present here before all the labels and before all my concepts", "trying to grasp how he sees the world", "the client's unique lived world is an indivisible entity and I can experience, perceive something from it through experiencing my own being with the client". Speaking about exploration of the client's lived world, therapists frequently mentioned the category of time: "the right time"; "everything takes time in therapy"; "simultaneity"; "give time to the client"; "therapists share their life time with the client and vice versa"; "it's important not to hurry"; "not helping too fast".

The last theme *Openness to life experience as healing* clarifies an important theoretical question about healing, health, illness and the nature of human suffering. In interviews therapists talked about health, illnesses and diagnoses and this matched with therapists' phenomenological position towards clients and their life-experience, including their experience of diagnosis. Therapist M says about a diagnosed client: "of course, not the diagnosis itself says something about my client or his illness, but his own life, his own experience". Therapist A says:

> I can see a client as healthy if he can be open to different opposites, joy and sadness, wealth and poverty, company and solitude, but if he runs away or closes completely to one polarity, he won't feel healthy soon.

Interviewees connect mental health and healing with the ability of a person to keep an open, accepting attitude towards everything that is in his life and with the ability to integrate this experience.

Conclusion

This research was started with a good dose of skepticism as there was no idea if any repeating patterns could be found at all. The first impression of richness obtained in in-depth interviews only strengthened this feeling. It was present until three main dimensions were noticed showing that all participants speak about: therapeutic relationship, therapeutic interactions and theoretical understanding of therapy.

Pulling the findings of the research together we can say that the Birštonas School of existential therapy has strong roots in an existential and hermeneutic tradition. Most of the themes show the presence of ideas of such authors as Husserl, Heidegger, Buber, Sartre, Medard Boss and Levinas. The main common methods of therapeutic work in the Birštonas School are phenomenological exploration and hermeneutical understanding of the client's life as being-in-the-world (Spinelli, 2005). In therapists' narratives we can discern ideas close to Gadamer (1975/2013). First of all, that in comprehending some phenomena we always have presuppositions, prejudices from our past. Research shows that existential therapists of the Birštonas School have a different position from practitioners such as Spinelli, who speaks about bracketing or setting aside therapists' biases and assumptions to focus on the immediate experience. Therapists in interviews showed a different strategy: they detect their assumptions and during the whole therapy process evaluate the impact of their presuppositions; they tend to "look after" them, but quite often therapists can introduce them into the therapeutic dialogue as the sign of a therapist's otherness and by doing so pay respect to a client's otherness.

Quite often we hear that existential therapy is not a distinct modality among other psychotherapies, that there is only some kind of existential stance or approach to psychotherapy. Such a position is maintained, for example, by Yalom (1980), but this research challenges such an attitude. Existential therapy practice can be hardly imagined without a deeper understanding of *conditio humana*, without setting the therapist's own questions about human existence, human suffering, without putting his questions in context with existential thinkers. This study shows that to explore the lived-experience of every client, no matter if they are a drug-addict or a murderer, without slipping into a much easier and less anxious knowing, curing, educating or theme-discussing position, arouses a lot of anxiety in the therapist. Energy, vigour and commitment is necessary in ongoing exploration. An existential therapist needs some systematic understanding of why it can be useful to stay in such a humble, sometimes dejected position in front of a client's suffering. She needs to have some answers as to why a therapist's answers are not so important to the client, she needs some knowing as to why she has to stay with un-knowing. If this is not on a therapist's everyday professional agenda, it's problematic to speak about an existential stance in therapy. The results of this research showed that for existential therapists of the Birštonas School of existential therapy these are weighty issues which are alive in their relationship with clients.

The most important precondition for a successful therapy process is a collaborative, trustful and free therapeutic relationship. Through this short formula of success we can discern the ideas of such existential thinkers as Sartre (1956) and Levinas (1969/1991) as these thinkers have brought us to a whole new level of understanding of the role of the Other, who is always already present in our understanding of ourselves. This study emphasizes the importance of a therapeutic relationship where the otherness of therapist and client is not camouflaged, but creates the uniqueness of every therapeutic relationship. Uniqueness becomes reality through a sincere and honest attitude towards the client and therefore it opens up a variety of conscious possibilities for the client to constitute himself in the presence of the therapist in a new way. Therapists in interviews expressed their awareness of the unavoidable change every client brings into their own world. Therefore, this stance has some reverberations with the philosophy of the Other we know from Emmanuel Levinas.

The understanding of healing in the Birštonas School reflects the findings of late existential thinking. Therapists in interviews linked clients' health and healing with openness to their lived world and the ability to integrate their life-experience.

According to the results of research, the central focus in existential therapy process is the client's life as a wholeness in all its manifestations. This forms one of the significant distinctions between existential therapy and other psychotherapies where there are other focuses – mainly intrapsychic processes. The main content of therapeutic work in the Birštonas School is associated with clarifying and unraveling the complex interweaving of possibilities and limitations in the client's existence and his inter-relatedness with others.

In every unique therapeutic situation, therapists of the Birštonas School choose freely their methods of therapeutic interaction, but in general they are not inclined to apply ready-to-use techniques. An important and interesting aspect, formulated as one of the themes, allows us to say that existential therapists do constant assessment work during the whole therapy process and see this work as care for their clients and therapeutic relationship.

The study of the reference points of therapeutic work in the Birštonas School of existential therapy gives us a reason to assert that therapists of this school are more explorative, and neither clinically nor educationally oriented.

This study also allows us to speak about a distinctive Birštonas School of existential therapy among others in a wide spectrum of different existential therapies and gives us a reason to rethink critically the understanding of existential therapy in Europe or worldwide. I hope it can encourage further qualitative in-depth research of "embodied" existential therapy.

References

Braun, V. & Clarke, V. (2006). Using Thematic Analyses in Psychology. *Qualitative Research in Psychology*, 3(2):77–101. Online access: www.academia.edu/3789894/Using_thematic_analysis_in_psychology, accessed 03.05.2015.

Gadamer, H.G. (2013 [1975]). *Truth and Method*. Trans. Weinsheimer, J. & Marshall, G.G. New York: Bloomsbury.

Guest, G., MacQeen, K. & Namey, E. (2012). *Applied Thematic Analysis*. London: Sage.

Heidegger. M. (1927/1962). *Being and Time*. Trans. Macquarrie, J. & Robinson, E. Oxford & Cambridge USA: Blackwell.

Holzhey-Kunz, A. & Fazekas, T. (2012). Daseinsanalysis: A Dialgoue. In Barnett, L. and Madison, G. (eds) *Existential Therapy: Legacy, Vibrancy and Dialgoue*. New York: Routledge.

Levinas, E. (1991 [1969]). *Totality and Infinity: An Essay on Exteriority*. Trans. Lingis, A. Netherlands: Kluwer Academic Publishers.

Sartre, J.P. (1956). Being and Nothingness: An Essay on Phenomenological. In *Ontology*. Trans. Barnes, H. New York: Philosophical Library.

Spinelli, E. (2005). *The Interpreted World. An Introduction to Phenomenological Psychology*. London: Sage.

Yalom, I.D. (1980). *Existential Psychotherapy*. New York: Basic Books.

29 Beautiful losers

Manu Bazzano

For K.

Passion and modesty

Simone de Beauvoir was not in touch with her feelings. In her novels and essays, they feel stunted and are clumsily expressed. But her letters to her Chicago lover Nelson Algren tell a different story. "Paris seems dull, dark, and dead" she writes on 18 May 1947, after their first separation.

> Maybe it is my heart that is dead to Paris. My heart is yet in New York, at the corner of Broadway where we said good bye; it is in my Chicago home, in my own warm loving place against your loving heart … With you pleasure was love, and now pain is love too. We must know every kind of love. We'll know the joy of meeting again.
>
> (de Beauvoir, 1998, p. 18)

Why the gap between letters and published work? She herself put it down to language. It was good to write in English, she told Algren, for then she was not doing literature but speaking directly. It is notoriously hard to write of sexual love but in her letters, unburdened by her public persona, she did it beautifully. She did it *incidentally*. Like death, like the sun, sexual love may not be stared at without falling prey to hubris. Reading William Faulkner's *Wild Palms*, she gasped in awe at the novel's indirect yet real erotic intensity. In *The Mandarins*, her 1954 novel dedicated to Algren, where he puts in an appearance as Lewis Brogan, their love is portrayed with intellectual detachment. Even the scene of their first sexual encounter, tenderly recounted in the letters, is rendered in the novel with a frosty touch of irony. The narrator finds it amusing to meet in the flesh what she sees as a classic American type, the self-made leftist writer. Yet even in this mannered book (where she ends up slighting Algren, to his chagrin, describing him as sulky and withdrawn), she captures one essential trait, seeing him as a man who while making no claims on life is nevertheless animated by great hunger for it. Despite the stilted tones, the novel conveys her love for someone who could be both passionate and modest.

If her letters to Algren are unremittingly beautiful, perhaps that's because she was writing to him, because she couldn't speak to anyone the way she spoke to him

(Rogin, 1998). Until meeting him, the thirty-nine-year-old Simone was a provincial, bourgeois woman who had lived a bookish and sheltered life – convent school as a child, philosophy student at the Sorbonne, then a teacher and a writer who had remarkably succeeded in carving a place for herself in the Existentialist Boy Club of Paris Left Bank. Nelson's story was different: "the son of a semiliterate mechanic who went bankrupt, [attending] a state college, [then] five years drifting around the country looking for work" after graduation (Asher, 2019, p. 225).

Imagining their love, I see pleasure held and suspended, the very endgame of teleology suspended. Call it bracketing if you must. I see a momentary exit from the linear trajectory of being-towards-death punctuated by the obligatory *petite mort* at the end of each love-making; I see a refusal to climb up the Ladder of Success and the related anxiety of 'making it', of building a new tower of Babel, a Stairway to Heaven, a *scala paradisi*. I see them walking arm in arm, each of them in turn skipping a step to harmonize with the other's rhythm; I see her gently mocking him for pulling an umbrella that's too small under the icy drizzle of the Chicago winter night. He marvels at her skin, the beauty of her slender curves, 'the power of a woman's body', he says in a whisper, 'a flower of the mountain', quoting Molly's monologue in James Joyce's *Ulysses*. She liked his wispy whispery shimmering voice and the beautiful lines. But that's just me, daydreaming of Simone daydreaming of having Nelson, feeling tired the next day but good tired. It's just me, daydreaming of Nelson daydreaming of Simone and her beauty; he's tired too but it's a welcome tiredness as a tangible memory of her.

Things became difficult – how could they not? They ached for one another and there was an ocean in between. Their long-distance flame roars in spells of heaving love-making in hotel rooms and getaways. Then it shimmers unsteady under a cold sky, in drawn-out spaces of daydreaming, where a pain builds that no lyrical praise of the spiritual beauty of longing can ever mend.

When things got hard, they fell back on their shelter of choice. Call it secure base, if you must. For her, it meant loyalty to Sartre, her constituency of readers, her increasingly public persona. For him, devotion to his doomed and glorious mission as the Dostoevsky of Division Street, the deprived area of Chicago of Polish and Italian immigrants that gave him inspiration. When Simone spoke in defense of Paris ("I could not live just for happiness and love, I could not give up my writing … in the only place where my writing and work may have a meaning"), Nelson shot back in defense of Chicago: "My job is to write about Chicago and I can only do it here" (Sigal, 1998).

The poet of Perdido Street

> I made myself a voice for those who are counted out.
> (Algren in a letter to Max Geismar, cited in O'Hagan, 2019, p. 6)

As he saw it, Chicago "had only two sides, the wrong and the wronger" (Algren, 1956/1999, p. 33). He lived with (and among) junkies, petty thieves, sex workers, hustler, drifters, dealers and the whole array of the dispossessed and unrepentant inhabiting the city, adding grim beauty and urgency to its streets and alleys. His short stories, collected in *The Neon Wilderness*, and his novels, e.g., *A Walk on the Wild Side*, burned with a different intensity than what fuelled the more rarefied Parisian literature hosted by *Les Temps Modernes* and its New York equivalent *Partisan Review*. Up until the success of his novel *The Man with the Golden Arm*, Algren made a better living as a dealer at the poker table than as a novelist, and could boast of a fairly unique reason for ending up in jail: stealing a typewriter. He wrote agonizingly, realistically, influenced by Emile Zola, Anton Chekhov and Russian realists such as Aleksandr Kuprin (1870–1938). He was the poet of the streets, the poet of losers.

The entwined destinies and random encounters depicted in *A Walk on the Wild Side* are punctuated by a rhythm that is now lyrical, now staccato, both aching and sharp, not unlike the cadence of the twelve-bar blues:

> You've been had, you've been paid for, you've been rented by the minute. Now anything goes no matter how wild so long as it keeps off the Storyville Blues. It was cocaine, it was whiskey – who wouldn't get the blues? It was brawling in the alleys, it was falling on the floor. It was everything to give and not a thing to lose. It was men, it was gin, it was all night long. It was have a ball and spend it all – 'Daddy, buy me one more drink and do just what you want with me.' That was what they called fun on old Perdido Street.
>
> (Algren, 1956/1999, p. 179)

He couldn't stand schlock, stayed well away of happy endings and hated the cheesy film version Hollywood made of his novel *The Man with a Golden Arm*, with Frank Sinatra in the main role. His stance is one of compassion without senti-mentality – more Chekhov than Charles Dickens, for he conspicuously lacked the latter's taste for the moralizing redemption that one fine day (a Sunday?) will make respectable citizens of us all. Among the young sex workers mercilessly and violently exploited and manipulated by their pimps, "the coaltown and the cotton-mill kids took to it easiest of all", because to them hard times meant nothing: "they had never known any other kind" (ibid). They were not frightened of law, jail or sickness. They would deride bespectacled professors, pious men of God and the dapper lawyers too who came along to peep and stare and take a furtive bite of the forbidden crop.

A deranged preacher harangues a congregation of bums on a street corner; they all know he's only a poor lonesome fellow whose wife left. Yet like an existen-tial trainer at an existential training course he has them enthralled with the fear of hellfire just as first-year trainees are spellbound by the high fees and the crawling angst haunting their genteel case studies.

Hungry for reality

De Beauvoir loved New York but was ill at ease there among the intellectuals of *Partisan Review*. In 1947, the year of her journey through the States via train, plain, car and Greyhound bus, the first frosty winds of the Cold War could be felt in both France and the US. At a time of strong polarization, some felt compelled to support the USSR while others chose the US. A third way, what she and her fellow-travellers Sartre, Merleau-Ponty, Camus and others were seeking, was hard to find. The once-radical New York writers opted instead for American 'democracy', sympathizing with the curbing of rights to suspected Communists and with other measures that amounted to the first wave of political witch-hunt and unwavering conformity that was to follow shortly with McCarthyism. They were also snobbishly rejecting the realism of American writers so loved by the Europeans – John Steinbeck, Ernest Hemingway, John Dos Passos, Richard Wright – in favour of authors seen as psychologically more astute and sophisticated: Henry James, Herman Melville, William Faulkner, Henry David Thoreau. De Beauvoir was hungry for American reality – and for American realism. This is how the name of Nelson Algren came up; he was someone the New York intellectuals couldn't stand, alongside the murky, raw riches of his vision. De Beauvoir made sure to seek him out as soon as she got to Chicago.

Friday evening magic

When his phone rang that Friday evening, Nelson was making himself dinner. He didn't recognize the heavily accented voice and hung up. The phone rang three more times. 'Wrong number!' he shouted the second and third time, annoyed, but on the fourth he heard an operator saying 'Please stay on the line, Sir'. Then a woman spoke, saying she was passing through Chicago and would he like to meet. Her accent was French. Uninterested, Algren was about to hang up a fourth time when the woman mentioned his close friend, the black Chicago writer and Paris expatriate Richard Wright, as well as his other friend Mary Guggenheim. He agreed to meet her at *Le Petit Café* in the Palmer House Hotel. He boarded the El, came out at Monroe station and walked east towards the posh hotel. He entered the lobby; there were thick carpets on the floor and an elaborate mosaic of gold, alabaster and green tile on the ceiling. He looked around, found the entrance to Le Petit Cafe and saw a pale and slim woman in a white coat and a green scarf around the neck, her dark hair pulled up on top of her head. She was standing there with a copy of *Partisan Review* in her hand. Nelson hesitated; he stood in a corner watching her for a moment, trying to get a sense of her. Finally he came forward and introduced himself. Her name did not ring any bell; conversation was difficult: his French was the slang from his days in the army; plus, his Chicago twang was incomprehensible to Simone. He talked about the war, and then suggested they go out – not to the jazz clubs, too dull in his view, nor to a burlesque, but somewhere, he said, where you have probably never been to. She eagerly accepted for she was by then thoroughly fed up with the mercantile glimmer of five-star America. They went to a small club.

> They bought drinks and found seats near the back of the room, and then Nelson announced: Everyone here is sinister and dangerous. Beauvoir had developed a taste for his flavor of humor by then, so she shot back, 'I think

you're the only sinister thing around here' The room thrummed with life. A few black musicians played with their backs to the rear wall, and couples moved in time with the beat. … The club was a world all its own, and she was only welcome because Nelson was a regular. "It's beautiful," Beauvoir said. The comment surprised Nelson. "With us," he said, "beautiful and ugly, grotesque and tragic, and also good and evil—each has its place. America doesn't like to think these extremes can mingle".

(Asher, 2019, p. 226)

The night was young, as they say, and on they went to another place that by midnight filled with all sorts of people, many of them so dirty, Beauvoir was to remark later, that she thought their bones too were grey. Nelson introduced her to a woman behind the bar. Turns out she knew everything about French literature and asked Simone about Sartre and André Malraux. De Beauvoir was stunned. The woman runs the bar as well as a shelter, Nelson later explained, and spends her free time reading and getting high, going back and forth between hospital and prison. Then it was high time to go to his place. They made love, Simone later wrote, first because of comfort (she was saddened by the poverty she'd seen), and then because of passion. She wrote:

> He lived in a hovel, without a bathroom or a refrigerator, alongside an alley full of steaming trashcans and flapping newspapers; this poverty seemed refreshing, after the heavy odour of the dollars in the big hotels and the elegant restaurants, which I found hard to take.

(de Beauvoir, 1998, p. 13)

She later told Algren that in defence of existentialism in his public debate with the writer Louis Bromfield, he should say the following: "I know Simone de Beauvoir and when she is in bed with me, she does not look hopeless or nihilist". They talked; she told him of her passionate interest in the situation of women in the world; he told her she should write a book out of the essay she was working on; his encouragement and political insight into racism in the US inspired her to turn the essay into a book, and this was the seed of what was to be published, two years later, as *The Second Sex* (de Beauvoir, 1949/1999).

The meaning of success

It has now been well documented that Algren's life and career was ruined by grim avatars of conformity such as J Edgar Hoover, infamous director of the FBI, and the self-declared paleo-neo-con Norman Podhoretz, who grumbled that for Algren "bums and tramps are better men than the preachers and the politicians". This is the very same Podhoretz now eulogizing Donald Trump's wonderful 'patriotism' (O'Hagan, 2019, p. 6). Algren was guilty of not believing in the American dream and being instead determined to describe the rage and wit, the love and despair that animated the wretched of the earth and those inhabiting the slums and whorehouses and blues dens of Chicago. Ahead of the 1960s, he depicted (and lived first-hand) the drifters' refusal to swear by the claptrap of 'success' and the self-defeating scramble to 'making it'. He did it through a brilliant prose that owns as much to jazz and the blues as to the ever-fermenting slang of the street. With Colin Asher's biography and his books now being reprinted, including the hard-hitting essays collected in *Nonconformity*, he is gaining the praise and attention he deserves – a wonderful, if posthumous, achievement. All the same, it is scary to look at the life of Nelson Algren: it spells out that talent, compassion and refusal to obey the Powers can demolish a person in the same way as mediocrity and compliance can. There was a long FBI file on him: his allegiance with the Communist Party; his contributions to the John Reed Club and other lefty magazines; his encouragement to his novelist friend Richard Wright – all was duly and doggedly documented. His name was on the black list, which meant that publishers dropped him; travel outside the US was denied, an agonizing blow for he could not go to Paris to pursue his love affair with de Beauvoir. The sad irony is he attributed his decline to himself rather than seeing it as the result of political hounding.

It made him go towards internal exile and repudiate his talent in later years through poverty, wretchedness and disenchantment. It made him recant his love for de Beauvoir who (despite her allegiance to Sartre and her pardonable subterfuges and rationalizations) continued to love him and referred to herself in his letters to him as his wife.

In striking counterpoint to Algren's, you could think of hers as a success story. Think again. Her name and quotes (and all too often misquotes and misinterpretations) adorn many a book on existential therapy. The glory of the leading intellectual may amount to their name printed in a university handout and quoted by the trainee anxious to pass a case study, a viva, a dissertation. De Beauvoir's name embellishes quotes by contemporary feminists at a time when virtually all emancipative narratives have been co-opted by neoliberalism with only a handful of privileged women in Hollywood and the media getting their grievances heard. Misogyny and hatred of difference continues to thrive, with mainstream feminism standardized within what Susan Watkins (2018, p. 17) calls "the anti-discrimination machinery". So-called diversity and so-called anti-discrimination brought "a progressive sheen to the company image at no extra cost … With globalization, 'diversity' became a capitalist asset" (ibid, p. 15). For many management consultancies, who may liberally quote de Beauvoir, gender equality means above all smart economics. More to the point, her trenchant case in *Ethics of Ambiguity* for emancipation and responsibility, her appeal to leave behind our metaphysically privileged existence as overgrown children and stop delegating our power, freedom and responsibility to those in authority is all the more poignant at a time when heads of state and heads of government are every-where elected who are themselves the embodiment of immaturity, privilege and conceit. Her appeal has failed and continues to fail because stupidity is perpetu-ally in love with the trappings of power. What makes it still valid, however, is that it is now our turn to enact our own splendid failures.

Despite its proclivity for normative ideals and constructivist or closet-theological socio-political compliance, existential therapy (as I understand it) does provide a set of emancipatory narratives and practices. Its problem is that it is trying too hard to become 'successful'. There are in my view two main reasons as to why we should be wary of emancipatory narratives and practices becoming 'successful': (a) it very often means they are neutered, and made palatable to the status quo, and ultimately 'harmless'; (b) we may forget that there is value in failure, for the latter is closely linked to creativity. A therapeutic practice worth its salt is not geared towards compliance but is keen instead to foster creativity, broadly understood in Nietzsche's (and Otto Rank's) sense, i.e. as *self-creation* (Bazzano, 2019, pp. 127–142).

Relevant insights come from within (some areas of) psychoanalysis, a heterogeneous approach that traditional existential therapy has perhaps too hurriedly dismissed. For Michael Eigen (1996), who in this instance draws on Bion, creativity "fluctuates, flickers and … breaks down" (Voela & Rothschild, 2018, p. 63); it entails the cultivation of an inherent trust in collapse and resurgence. We need to be able to create and fail, and withstand that failure as an essential part of the process. We don't have to know before we create – whether a work of art or our own self; we don't need to know before we act.

For André Green (1999), psychological transformation is *the work of the negative*. Acting and creating ensue in relation to the loss of unity, in this case with the maternal body. (Incidentally, whether or not this unity was imaginary in the first place remains to be seen; much of psychoanalysis – just like existential therapy – has barely considered either Nietzsche or post-structuralism.) But the notion of the negative is nevertheless useful and not entirely alien to existential thinking. It is from absence that a desire arises: to transform this absence through creation, through acting, and acting out. Crucially the urge to create allows us to imagine "a way forward when destruction threatens" (Green, 1999, p. 16).

It is from the above that *creative failure* stems. Creative failure constitutes, uncannily, the best response to capitalism's *creative destruction*, to a capitalist machine that "works by breaking down" (Deleuze & Guattari, (1983, p. 31).

In the more relatively private domain of intimate relationships, creative failure may point at loves that although not lasting, not sanctified or endorsed by either marriage or cohabitation, remind us of love's infinite ways to dance its dance and leave its indelible mark, even if every signature is but a signature on water. Too often we hear in our clients' stories how this love or that marriage 'failed' against a normative dictate of what constitutes real love.

In one of her letters, dated 2 June 1947, Simone wrote: "I cry because I do not cry in your arms" (de Beauvoir, 1998, p. 25). When she was buried, many years later, she still wore the ring Nelson Algren had given her.

References

Algren, N. (1956/1999) *A Walk on the Wild Side*. London: Canongate.
Asher, C. (2019) *Never a Lovely so Real: the Life and Work of Nelson Algren*. New York: Norton.

Bazzano, M. (2019) *Nietzsche and Psychotherapy*. Abingdon: Routledge.

de Beauvoir, S. (1949/1999) *The Second Sex*. London: Vintage.

de Beauvoir, S. (1998) *Beloved Chicago Man*. Edited by Sylvie Le Bon De Beauvoir. London: Gollancz.

Deleuze, G. & Guattari, F. (1983) *Anti-Oedipus: Capitalism and Schizophrenia*. Minneapolis, MN: University of Minneapolis Press.

Eigen, M. (1996) *The Psychotic Core*. New Jersey: NJ: Northvale.

Green, A. (1999) *The Work of the Negative*. London: Free Association Books.

O'Hagan, A. (2019) 'Singing the Back Streets' *The New York Review of Books*, LXVI, 17, pp 4–6.

Rogin, M. (1998) 'More than ever, and forever' *London Review of Books* www.lrb.co.uk/the-paper/v20/n18/michael-rogin/more-than-ever-and-for-ever, retrieved 18 Jan. 20.

Sigal, C. (1998) 'The Torrid Affair Between Nelson Algren and Simone de Beauvoir' *Los Angeles Times*, 18 October www.latimes.com/archives/la-xpm-1998-oct-18-bk-33545-story.html retrieved 18 Jan. 20.

Voela, A. & Rothschild, L. (2018) 'Creative failure: Stiegler, psychoanalysis adn the promise of a life worth living', *New Formations*, 95. London: Lawrence & Wishart, pp. 54–69.

Watkins, S. (2018) 'Which Feminism?' *New Left Review*, 109, pp. 5–80.

Index

For Product Safety Concerns and Information please contact our EU
representative GPSR@taylorandfrancis.com
Taylor & Francis Verlag GmbH, Kaufingerstraße 24, 80331 München, Germany

www.ingramcontent.com/pod-product-compliance
Lightning Source LLC
Chambersburg PA
CBHW050332270326
41926CB00016B/3417